Contents

Preface

This book is an attempt to provide a basic grounding in psychology, presented in such a way as to draw out the relevance of the subject to medicine. Where possible, medical examples are used to illustrate psychological principles and particular attention is given to aspects of medical care, such as the doctor–patient interview and compliance with medical advice. We have tried to present research critically; for example, discussing how a result might be interpreted in more than one way. Our view is that the ability to evaluate 'facts' is as important as the 'facts' themselves. It has been said that medical knowledge has a half-life of about five years. The rate of change in psychology may be similar and we hope the book will provide the reader with some of the skills required to appraise research work in the future. We have attempted to include sufficient source references to enable the reader to pursue aspects of particular interest, either simply for further detail or for research purposes (some medical schools include a small research project as part of their behavioural sciences course).

Ideally, the book would be most usefully read from beginning to end as concepts and methods are introduced and developed as the text progresses. To this end, the book is divided into three sections: psychological processes, human development and doctor–patient communication, the first laying foundations for the second, and both of these adding to an understanding of the third. Inevitably, the boundaries between the sections are to some extent arbitrary and there are also overlaps between chapters. To draw together topics which appear more than once, there is a *subject index* to allow easy cross-reference. Further *suggested readings* are given at the end of each chapter to enable more detailed study of particular areas. We have been selective in the choice of topics, covering those areas which seem, to us, most relevant to the psychological aspects of medical care. There are many areas of psychology which are not covered. There is little discussion of physiological psychology, and many topics which may be of interest to the reader such as anorexia nervosa and dreaming are not mentioned. So that the reader has access to such topics, a short *appendix* on how such information might be obtained from the library is included.

GK MD
January 1986

Part 1

Psychological Processes

1

Making Sense of the Environment

Introduction

The information a scientist can collect about the environment depends on the instruments available. The arrival of the telescope in Europe, for example, meant that the moons of the planet Jupiter became readily discernible, leading to the downfall of the Ptolemaic (earth-centred) view of the solar system. The development of instruments sensitive to small variations in the speed of light made the Michelson–Morley experiment possible, calling the Newtonian view of physics into question and opening the way for Einstein.

Even though ways of collecting and recording data about the world have become increasingly sophisticated, it does not necessarily follow that people agree about what the data mean. The analysis and interpretation of the information provided by even the most advanced scientific equipment depends on how this information is processed. The development of chest X-rays for the detection of lesions associated with active pulmonary tuberculosis provides an example of this. In the 1940s it was hailed as the most important medical advance of the half-century. However, the enthusiasm was soon tempered by the realization that many physicians disagreed about the presence of lesions on the films. In one study,[1] competent radiologists viewed over a thousand films, but there was much disagreement between them, with one doctor finding 56 positive results, another finding 100. The second doctor's cases did not include all of those found by the first. In all, there was disagreement about positive films one time in three. When the same films were shown to the same radiologist on two occasions, he found 59 positives on the first run through, but 78 on the second.

In other words, the way that people process information is not straightforward. This field forms an important field of psychological study and is characterized by many and varied theories. One way of viewing the manner in which we process information is in terms of three interdependent phases.[2] This chapter includes a brief description of the first, or sensory, phase but is largely devoted to the second, or interpretive, phase. Interpretation provides a way in which people can organize and understand incoming information and thus reduce their uncertainty about their environment. The way in which people interpret their world is dependent on, for instance, past experience and the context in which the event occurs. Some aspects of the third phase, memory, are also covered here, others in Chapter 4.

Sensing the environment

The sensory phase has been studied in several ways. One approach has involved the tracing of neural connections between the sensory receptors (visual, auditory, etc.) and the brain. Here, the concern has been with the ways that the anatomy, physiology and biochemistry of receptors (such as the rods and cones in the eye) affect how the environment is encoded and how the messages are passed along pathways to the cortex.

Related to this approach is a concern with patterns of neural firing in the brain. Some of this work has involved the recording of single cells in the cortex, exploring the ways in which lines and angles are coded in the brain. Perhaps the best known workers in this field are Hubel and Weisel, who studied the recordings from micro-electrodes inserted into the visual cortex of cats while showing them horizontal or vertical lines. They found that some neurons fired only when a vertical slit of light was presented in the cats' visual fields, others fired when the line of light was horizontal, and yet others when the line moved[3]. The patterns of firing were found in specific neurons, suggesting that they had a defined and limited function.

Various techniques have been used to investigate how neural pathways develop, generally involving the study of animals reared in controlled environments. Early researchers reared animals in the dark and found irreversible damage to the visual pathways such as atrophy of the retinal ganglion cells. It seems from work of this kind that although the pathways are 'wired-up' from birth, exposure to stimuli is necessary if they are to develop fully. When cats were shown only vertical stripes from birth, they were apparently blind to horizontal stripes: both behavioural and electrophysiological measures of these animals indicated little response to horizontal lines. Using Hubel and Weisel's technique of single cell recording, no neurons could be found that fired to lines oriented at right-angles to the cats' early visual environment.

Conversely, cats which saw only horizontal stripes from birth showed no response to vertical ones.

The effects of brain damage due to injury or disease have also helped in the development of neuropsychology. One of the oldest controversies has concerned the degree of localization of function within the brain. Since there is ample evidence that lesions in different parts of the brain have different effects (e.g. the association between language loss and lesions to the left hemisphere), there appears to be some localization of function.[4] On the other hand, there is certainly no one-to-one relationship between individual functions and particular parts of the brain, so that a simple mapping of areas is an oversimplification. Recently, there has been increased interest in the factors that are associated with recovery from neurological injuries and the development of programmes to assist recovery.[5]

Signal detection theory

Yet another approach to the study of people's senses has become known as signal detection theory. One concern has been with the question of sensory thresholds. The intensity of a stimulus can be said to have reached an observer's threshold when he can detect it 50 per cent of the time, but there is no simple relationship between detection and intensity. A short experiment can be conducted to test this. Place a clock on one side of a quiet room and walk away from it: stop when it can no longer be heard and then walk back to where it can just be noticed. While standing in this position, the ticking will fade in and out. Sometimes it will be necessary to walk closer to the clock in order to hear it and sometimes it will be possible to walk further away. The fading in and out is due to spontaneous neural firing in the central nervous system, which generates 'noise'. Whenever a stimulus is detected, it is seen or heard against this background activity. Sometimes a signal will be heard when none is present, sometimes a signal will not be heard when it is quite loud. This means that there is no simple on–off threshold in the detection of a light or tone, only a probability that a certain intensity will be identified. The clock experiment illustrates that it is not possible to specify a person's experience from knowledge of the event or stimulus alone.

When detecting the presence or absence of a fracture or pulmonary lesion on an X-ray, a similar process seems to occur. In this case the background noise is not spontaneous neural firing so much as the consequences of making a false-negative (where a fracture or lesion is missed) compared to a false-positive (where a lesion is 'seen' where none exists). Although services would be used inefficiently if too many false-positives were identified, the consequences to the health of the patient of a false-negative could be serious. With such priorities, when viewing an X-ray, physicians are much more likely to over-read than to miss a problem.[6]

These approaches to the study of sensation cannot be considered in isolation from higher-level processes such as interpretation and memory. An example of their interdependence can be easily arranged by putting this book down and listening to the sounds being produced around you. The first notable feature will probably be the large number of sounds which you probably didn't hear when you read the above paragraph. You were attending to the reading and ignoring this irrelevant noise. A similar phenomenon can be experienced at a party: in spite of the music and loud voices, it is possible to attend to one conversation out of many. Your attention may be changed if someone calls your name, a particularly meaningful stimulus. A second notable feature of the noises around you is that you will find yourself labelling or interpreting each one. As you listen to each sound, you make sense of it by explaining its source. A series of low-frequency sounds outside the room was translated into someone's footsteps; a high frequency sound outside, a car's brakes. It is difficult to hear the sound alone without making some kind of interpretation about it. The sounds are processed to become integrated into a meaningful environment. It is this feature that characterizes the second phase of information processing, in which the data provided by the sensory systems are given meaning.

Interpreting the environment

It is often difficult to appreciate that the environment is not only sensed but also interpreted. Most of the objects we see are unambiguously one thing or another, and we have no apparent difficulty in making sense of them. However, the ease with which interpretations are made is an indication of the familiarity of most objects we encounter in our daily lives rather than evidence for a simple and direct link between sensation and understanding.

The process of interpretation can be illustrated in several ways; one way is to provide only a proportion of the information which is usually available about some object and ask people to try to make sense of it. Fig. 1a may appear to be a random jumble of fragments with no obvious meaning. It is instructive to try to make sense of the figure. However, when the information shown in Fig. 1b is superimposed on these fragments (for instance by tracing Fig. 1b on a thin piece of paper and moving it up the page until the gaps in Fig. 1a are occluded) their organization becomes apparent.

This process of fitting together apparently unconnected pieces of information to make a meaningful picture is one which is constantly being performed in daily life. For example, an individual might be concerned with piecing together the reactions of other people in order to develop an idea of how he or she is seen by others. The process of diagnosis is another example. Initially, a series of seemingly unconnected complaints may be presented by a patient. These symptoms are explored, additional information is gathered, and past experience consulted. Some kind of overall link which connects the previously unrelated symptoms together is sought. These links are hypotheses which are tested through further questioning and physical examination. In a difficult case — where the link is difficult to find — others' views of the condition might be sought in order to make the interpretation.

In practice, the process of diagnosis is rather more complex than this, since symptoms often do not fit a classical clinical picture. Once a diagnosis has been formed, a doctor may ignore information which would disconfirm this hypothesis. Over time,

Fig. 1. It is difficult to see what (a) represents without the additional information given in (b).

a diagnosis may be changed: one study indicated that about half the diagnoses for patients admitted with abdominal pain were changed during their stay in hospital. Although controversial, there is increasing interest in computer-assisted diagnosis with some research indicating that computers are more accurate than senior clinicians for some conditions.[7] The aim of the following sections is to consider the importance of context, past experience and selective attention during the interpretive process.

Context

In performing a dissection a major source of information is context. The decision that a particular nerve is the one you are looking for is made easier if there is no other structure that appears more similar to the textbook example. Context provides a pattern into which the ambiguous stimulus can be fitted. It does this in part by arousing expectations about what is to follow,

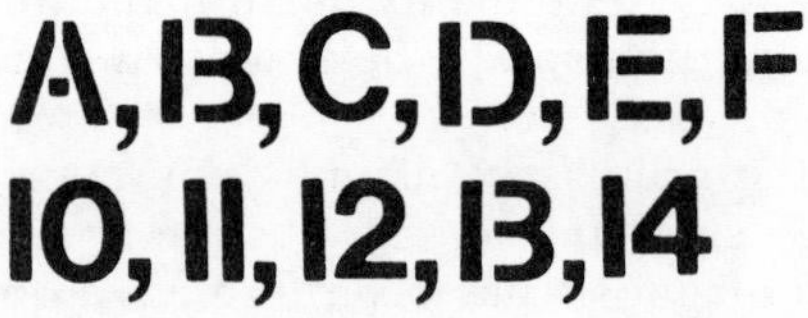

A, B, C, D, E, F
10, 11, 12, 13, 14

Fig. 2. The effect of context on recognition. The same symbol is identified as 'B' or '13' depending on its context.

whether the situation is dissection or, as in Fig. 2, a series of numbers or letters. Most people read the top line as A, B, C, D, E, F and the bottom line as 10, 11, 12, 13, 14, yet B and the 13 are identical. The context in which the symbol is embedded determines how it is 'seen'.

Psychologists often use illusions to explore the importance of context. Illusions are objects or pictures that encourage the viewer to perceive something which is really non-existent. Representational paintings are illusions, in that the artist attempts to portray a three-dimensional space on a two-dimensional plane. The illusion of depth is achieved in several ways, but primarily through the use of perspective (parallel lines that seem to come together and meet at the horizon), size constancy (although the retinal image of an object varies according to its distance, it is not interpreted as changing in size) and interposition (near objects overlap far objects). The ways in which perspective and size interact are shown in Fig. 3. Figure 3a indicates the relative size of three cylinders. But the same two-dimensional drawings take on different meanings when context is added as in Fig. 3b and 3c.

The social context (the halo effect)

Context is not limited to visual features. A way in which it plays a role in the perception of other people has been termed the 'halo effect' — the tendency to generalize from one attribute to a number of others. Physical appearance seems to be a particularly important characteristic. Dion[8] asked people (or 'subjects' as the participants in psychology experiments are usually called) to judge the misbehaviour of young children, some being physically attractive, others less so. The attractive children were judged less harshly than the unattractive children, with more lenient punishments recommended for the same behaviour. It seemed that physical attractiveness modified perceptions of why the children misbehaved. Several other assumptions are also made about attractive people, including the expectations that they will obtain more prestigious occupations and have happier marriages. There is also evidence that this 'beautiful is good' stereotype affects the first impressions of health professionals. Many medical staff were

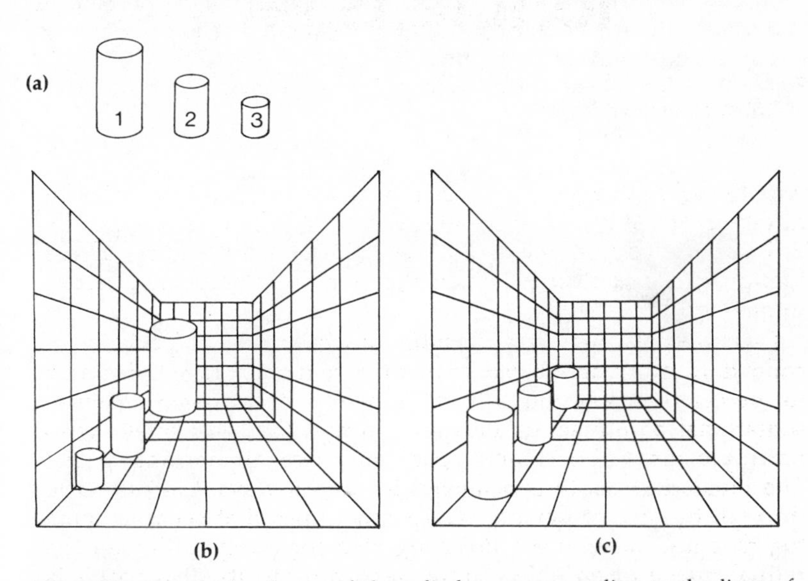

Fig. 3. The perceived volumes of the cylinders vary according to the lines of perspective. (Reproduced from Lindsay, P. H. & Norman, D. A. (1972) *Human Information Processing*, by permission of Academic Press, Inc.)

asked to indicate their impressions of patients shown in a series of photos. In some cases the photos depicted a physically attractive man or woman, in other cases the individual shown was unattractive. On 12 of the 15 scales used, the medical and paramedical staff indicated more positive impressions of the attractive people than the unattractive ones. For example, they were taken to be more responsible, more motivated and more likely to improve. There were no differences between the professionals, doctors being just as likely to make these assumptions as were the paramedical staff.[9]

Generalizations about people on the basis of those they associate with is another example of the halo effect. In one experiment, subjects were shown a silent film of a couple talking. The man was said to be the boyfriend of the woman in the film. In some films, she was made-up to look attractive, in others unattractive. The subjects' task was to rate the man's characteristics on a checklist. On virtually every scale, the woman's appearance had an effect: the man was rated as more friendly, intelligent, energetic and physically attractive, for example, when the woman was attractive. The favourable characteristics of one person were attributed to both members of the couple. The woman's perceived intelligence was also altered by telling the subjects that she was either a waitress or a medical student. This condition had much less effect on the subjects' ratings, although the man was said to be more intelligent, self-confident and talented when the actress was said to be a medical student.[10]

The medical context

When conducting a medical interview, the patient's social class appears to be an important contextual influence in how much information doctors believe their patients want. Pendleton and Bochner[11] videotaped consultations between doctors and their patients and noted that fewer explanations were volunteered for the patients of lower social class than for those of higher social class. This does not seem to be due to the former wanting less information about their difficulties, since they express a desire to know more, not less, than higher social class patients. Despite this, they obtain less of the information they want.[12]

There are other instances where the use of context can have a detrimental effect on patients. Maguire and Granville-Grossman[13] found that 33 per cent of patients suffered from a physical illness in a sample of 200 admissions to a psychiatric unit, yet it had been diagnosed in only half these patients. Conversely, 23 per cent of a sample of inpatients in medical wards were found to have psychiatric disorders, but few cases were recognized by the medical staff.[14] It seems as though each unit provided expectations about patients that made diagnosis of particular complaints less likely.

Another study of psychiatric units illustrates this point in a slightly different way. Rosenhan[15] reported a study in which eight experimenters had themselves committed to various psychiatric hospitals, claiming that they were hearing voices (a symptom often associated with schizophrenia). After admission, these 'pseudo-patients' acted in their usual way and the research question was how long it would take before the staff (who were unaware of the study) realized that there was nothing abnormal about these patients and discharged them. In fact, staff recognized none of the pseudo-patients (although some patients did) and some experimenters had difficulty in obtaining their release. Part of the difficulty here seemed to be that although people in psychiatric hospitals are expected to be unusual in some way, they often act normally, making it difficult for the staff to distinguish between the real and the feigning patients. Given this ambiguity, the safe course of action in this context was to assume that the experimenters were schizophrenic and should not be discharged.

In these studies, the context of a psychiatric unit or a medical ward appears to have led the staff to expect certain conditions but not others, making some interpretations more plausible than others. Context in everyday situations is similarly based on past experience (either directly or through reports by others) and can be modified by future experiences. This second aspect of the interpretive process is considered in the next section.

Experience

Much of the research on the importance of past experience has been concerned with visual phenomena. One line of evidence is cross-cultural: people with very different environments from ours perceive the world in quite different ways. One investigator[16] lived with the Bambuti pygmies, forest dwellers whose vistas extend to 30 metres at most. Once, he took a tribesman onto a broad plain where there was a herd of buffalo some miles away. Because the buffalo looked small, the pygmy thought that they were some kind of insect. He became increasingly puzzled and concerned as they drove closer and the buffalo 'grew'. The pygmy had little experience with large distances and therefore did not, in this situation, use *size constancy* — the tendency for the perceptual system to compensate for changes in retinal size with viewing distance.

Similar observations have been made with adults in Western culture who, having been blind since infancy, have had their sight restored. Gregory[17] describes how one such patient thought that he would be able to lower himself to the ground from his window, which was in fact 30 to 40 feet above the ground. Because he had no past experience with depth cues, he was unable to see that the ground was far below. Conversely, past experience can serve to mislead an observer about objects. Several 'impossible objects' have been designed that confuse the viewer and make an integrated interpretation difficult, such as the 'devil's tuning fork' (Fig. 4).

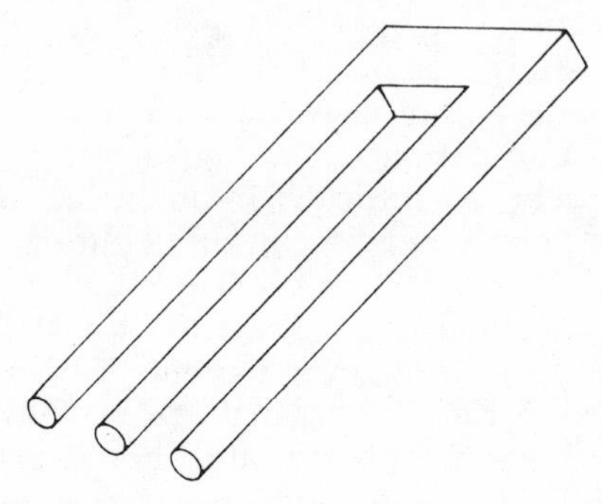

Fig. 4. An 'impossible object'. The depth cues in this picture are conflicting, making it difficult to interpret in an integrated way. People unfamiliar with graphic representation have little difficulty in reproducing this figure from memory. (Reproduced from Kimble, G., Garmezy, M. & Kigler, E. (1974) *General Psychology*, 4th edn., by permission of John Wiley & Sons, Inc.)

A classic example of the role of experience in perception is the young/old woman demonstration.[18] This illustration does not depend on cross-cultural differences and provides an opportunity to perform a simple experiment. Figure 5a can be seen as a young attractive woman or as an old unattractive one, depending on how her features are interpreted. Looking at Figs. 5b and 5c may make these two possibilities clearer. A simple experiment would involve showing Fig. 5b to some subjects and Fig. 5c to others. In a good experiment the subjects in each group, or condition, would be randomly assigned. This could be accomplished by, for instance, placing all their names in a hat and as the names are picked out assigning individuals to one condition or another by flipping a coin. Fig. 5a would then be shown to all subjects. Those who saw Fig. 5b would tend to see the composite drawing as an old woman, while those who saw Figure 5c would tend to see the composite as a young woman.

Mental sets

A particular example of how past experience can affect perception is called mental set — the tendency to use a solution which has

(a)

(b)

(c)

Fig. 5. (a) can be interpreted as a young woman or an old woman, but seeing (b) first predisposes the observer to see the old woman, whereas seeing (c) first encourages the perception of the young woman.

worked well in the past on problems where this solution is not the best one. The jar problem[19] is a good example of this tendency. Table 1 presents six problems, the task being to use jars A, B and C to obtain the amount of water indicated in the right-hand column. After a little thought, a way of obtaining these amounts becomes apparent. Before reading further, it is instructive to perform all the tasks.

All of these problems can be solved in the same way (B–A–2C), but looking at problem 6 again, it is possible to see how a routine has built up which led to a failure to use the simplest solution (A–C).

Table 1. The jar problem. Use the jars to obtain the amount of water indicated in the right-hand column.

Problem	*Jar capacities*			*Amount to be obtained*
	A	*B*	*C*	
1	21	127	3	100
2	14	163	25	99
3	18	43	10	5
4	9	42	6	27
5	20	59	4	31
6	23	49	3	20

The evidence that mental set can be problematic in medical care comes from several descriptive studies. For example, Stimson[20] outlines the experience of one woman who had a history of respiratory problems which frequently required prescribed antibiotics. It seemed to her that the doctor was too willing to diagnose all her problems as connected with the respiratory condition:

> No matter what I have got wrong with me, if I go over to the doctor with a terrific headache that I'm getting — 'Oh, it's all to do with your chest' — anything, no matter, if I'm worried about something

> now, and I want to go to the doctor's, see, perhaps I'm getting these headaches or something and I'm getting a bit concerned about them now, no matter what, I can guarantee when I come out of that doctor's, it's to do with my chest. No matter what I get, you're missing a period and he says — 'It's to do with your chest'. (Ref. 20, p. 102)

Apparently, the physician had solved her problem in one way in the past and this prevented him from entertaining alternative possibilities.

It seems likely that medical training can induce a kind of mental set in doctors, leading them to interpret what a patient says in certain ways. One of the first decisions a physician generally makes is to diagnose a complaint as physical or psychiatric, and most doctors tend to exclude the possibility of physical disorders before considering social or psychological problems. Since medical training is primarily concerned with physical diseases, doctors may be much more aware of physical aetiologies and treatments than social or psychological ones. For example, Maguire and Rutter[21] found that medical students in their final year obtained less social and psychological information while taking case histories than first-year students. It seemed that the senior students asked more questions about and attended more closely to symptoms of physical distress than those of psychological distress. The idea that once people come to view a problem in a certain way they often attend to information selectively is the next step in the process of making interpretations.

Selective attention

In a sense, people can be regarded as scientists who have developed theories in order to interpret the environment. These theories make it possible to organize the vast amount of data which impinge on our senses. However, these theories also encourage us to attend to information selectively (looking for data which will confirm our hypotheses) and to disregard other kinds of information which appear to be irrelevant. Thus, perceptions become biased in certain directions, depending on the assumptions made by the individual. As an example of this, Abercrombie[22] describes how a child with a persistent cough had its throat X-rayed. The radiologist reported that there was nothing in the radiograph to show why the child was coughing. The cough persisted, however, and a second X-ray was taken. This time the shadow of a button was seen in the throat, the button was removed and the child stopped coughing. When the first radiograph was re-examined, the shadow of the button was seen there, too, but the radiologist had explained it away to himself, supposing that the child had been X-rayed with its vest on. The information was there, but not processed in the most useful way.

In a further test of his idea that diagnosis of mental illness is influenced by what staff expect to see, Rosenhan[15] led the staff of a teaching hospital to believe that within the next three months one or more pseudo-patients would attempt to have themselves admitted to the psychiatric unit. Of the 193 patients admitted during this time, 41 were alleged to be pseudo-patients by at least one member of staff, 19 by a psychiatrist and one other staff member. In fact, there were no pseudo-patients: the faulty theory led to incorrect expectations and thus to misperceptions. When Maguire and Rutter[21] found that senior medical students were less aware of the social and psychological distress in their patients than the first-year students, this could be because they attended to this information less closely while concentrating on physical symptoms.

Thus, once an initial interpretation has been made on the basis of context and past experience, there is a strong tendency to follow up on this impression with further questioning while neglecting other information. This process has been studied in diagnostic interviews by looking at the ways in which clinicians conduct their consultations. Barrows and Bennett[23] coached people to simulate neurological disorders and neurologists were then asked to reach a diagnosis through questioning and examination. Findings elicited by the neurologists were often totally absent from their reports and completely forgotten unless they were relevant to one of their hypotheses. Once some possible diagnosis had emerged, the doctors asked questions which were inquiry-oriented; that is, aimed at acquiring specific items of information.

Selective attention can be obvious, as in this general practice consultation:

> Patient: Am I going to be able to go back to work?
> Doctor: Let's not worry about that at the moment, let's consider the treatment. (Ref. 24, p. 60)

or less clear, as in this example:

> Doctor: Good morning. Sit down. What can I do for you today?
> Patient: Well, I think I've got the 'flu, doctor.
> D: Well, there's not much of it about now.
> P: Well, I've got this cold.
> D: Yes, I can see that. Shivering a bit, are you?
> P: Yes.
> D: Mmm. Well, there's not a lot to worry about is there? Now you take this to the chemist and you'll be all right in 3 or 4 days. (Ref. 24, p. 102)

In this case, the patient was the last of a crowded morning surgery.

He had appeared just before the doctor was about to leave on his morning calls and nine of his previous patients had also suffered from 'common colds'. This led him to diagnose a cold and not to give either a physical examination or to ask further questions. Unfortunately, this patient was subsequently diagnosed as having pleurisy, but this possibility was not attended to because of the context of the morning's experience.

Hindsight

Incidentally, you may feel that this doctor deserves some kind of severe reprimand for his apparent carelessness. The interview seems to be woefully inadequate, whatever the complaint eventually turned out to be. But would you feel differently if the general practitioner turned out to be correct in his diagnosis? The chances are you would. *Hindsight* has a strong influence on how we interpret past events, such that people tend to believe that an outcome could have been foreseen by anyone, once they are told what the outcome actually was. In one study[25] several surgeons were given a case description of a patient which was compatible with the diagnosis of a leaking abdominal aortic anaeurysm (AAA). One group of the surgeons was told that an anaeurysm was found and resurrected at operation, while another group was told that a tortuous aorta was noted at operation. When they were asked: 'Based on the information available *before* the operation, what would you have estimated as the probability that this person had a leaking abdominal aortic anaeurysm?', surgeons who had been told about the tortuous aorta gave a significantly lower probability than those who had been told that the AAA was found and resurrected. We tend to be unaware that we use outcome information in making judgements about past events, and this applies equally to our views of the general practitioner who failed to diagnose pleurisy as it does to our views of the results of psychology experiments.*

* The results of many studies in psychology may appear to be common sense. However this may be due to hindsight: if the results were opposite to those actually found, these too might be considered obvious. For example, there are many studies on interpersonal attraction. These have shown that attraction is strongly related to similarity — we tend to like people who have similar views and similar personalities to ourselves. This research could be dismissed because it only seems to confirm the common-sense saying, 'birds of a feather flock together'. However, if the research had found the opposite results, a similar criticism of psychology could be made since, after all, 'opposites attract'. Other examples of contradictory homilies are, 'absence makes the heart grow fonder' versus 'out of sight, out of mind', and 'look before you leap' versus 'he who hesitates is lost'.

Self-fulfilling prophecy

Fortunately, many perceptual biases based on selective attention are remedied by further experience. The patient with pleurisy was subsequently correctly diagnosed. When patients fail to respond to medication prescribed for what was originally diagnosed as organic illnesses, doctors begin to consider social and psychological problems.[26] While an incorrect diagnosis is of course to be lamented, it is easier to understand how it could occur when the complexities of interpreting a patient's symptoms are appreciated.

Other perceptual biases are not so easily corrected, particularly in social situations. An observer may selectively attend to those features of a situation or of other people that are consistent with expectations and ignore those that are inconsistent. A person who believes that everyone is unfriendly and hurtful is likely to be suspicious himself, selectively attending to instances of rejection. This perception of the world will make him difficult to live with, perhaps resulting in the very behaviour he expects — rejection. This kind of circularity in social situations has been termed the self-fulfilling prophecy.

Some of the more important studies in this area have been conducted in classrooms. Educational theorists had suggested that some pupils failed to learn because they had a history of failure, a background that teachers used in deciding how intelligent they were and how worthwhile it was to pay careful attention to their work. Meichenbaum et al.[27] studied a group of young women who had been sent by the courts to a training centre. They administered a series of tests that purported to predict intellectual 'blooming', and the teachers were told that certain girls could be expected to show remarkable gains in intellectual competence in the coming months. In fact, there was no such test, so that the only differences between these girls and those in the control group were in the expectations of the teachers. Soon the teachers began to note and comment upon relatively insignificant instances that confirmed their expectations. When Meichenbaum et al. checked the school records of exam results, they found that those who were supposedly predicted to do better did so on objective tests in mathematics and science (but not in literature and history). These girls were also more likely to show 'appropriate' behaviour in the classroom (e.g. paying attention to lessons rather than looking distracted or whispering together).

Although some researchers have failed to replicate such findings, many other studies have supported the notion of expectancy effects. It appears that the person with the expectations changes his or her behaviour to conform with predictions. Teachers with favourable expectations gave more information to supposedly bright students, which may explain why they actually learned more. Similarly, more statements were requested of 'gifted' pupils and they were praised more frequently by their teachers. Teachers who had been led to believe that some of their students were very bright leaned forward more when they were addressing them, looked them in the eye, and nodded and smiled more frequently.

At this point, perception becomes more than simply interpreting reality, it becomes part of the *construction* of social reality.

An interesting study on this aspect of the self-fulfilling prophecy is provided by Jahoda.[28] The Ashanti of West Africa believe that infants born on different days of the week have different personalities. Those born on Mondays are supposed to be quiet and even-tempered, those born on Wednesdays aggressive and quarrelsome. Jahoda consulted the police records for the district, trouble with the authorities being his dependent measure of aggression. He found that the Monday-borns had a low rate of criminal offences, Wednesday-borns a high rate. It seems possible that the parents reacted to their children in ways consistent with their expectations, and that these expectations were incorporated into the children's personalities, thus fulfilling the prophecy. There has been much discussion of the possibility that many of the differences in behaviour shown by males and females is due to such expectations, a topic considered in Chapter 8.

The self-fulfilling prophecy can play an important role in the medical setting as well. Elderly people are often considered to be in need of much assistance and may be placed in a nursing home at the first signs of mental or physical deterioration. However, there is evidence (discussed in Chapter 10) that deterioration may accelerate if they are discouraged from taking care of themselves by staff who are too keen to help. Placebo effects (discussed in Chapter 11) are based partly on patients' perceptions of the efficacy of treatment and several studies have shown that physicians who are enthusiastic about a particular course of treatment achieve better results than those who are sceptical. Beecher[29] traced the literature on a particular surgical procedure that was eventually discarded as a result of a properly controlled experiment. Beecher showed that surgeons who were sceptical about the operation and who told their patients they did not expect any change in their condition had low success rates, but that surgeons who were enthusiastic seemed to achieve good results.

The way the environment is understood, then, is only partly determined by the sensory data impinging on the person. Not only are the data sensed by a nervous system that is constantly active and that introduces 'noise', it is also interpreted. Interpretation is dependent on context, past experience and selective attention. But the process of interpretation does not end here: the way the environment is perceived can sometimes affect the way it works, resulting in a self-fulfilling prophecy. In the next section of this chapter the situation of people who enter hospital for treatment or observation is considered, extending the principles of interpretation to their circumstances. There are two aspects to this extension. First, hospitalization is an unfamiliar event to most people, making it possible to conduct research on the process of interpretation. Principles learned in this setting may apply to other situations. Second, and no less important, are the practical implications of work on hospitalization. If research can show how patients can be made more comfortable in hospital through helping them to make sense of their environment, this could result in better care and earlier recovery.

Uncertainty and medical care

The research discussed in the previous section indicates that people have a strong tendency to make interpretations about their environment. An explanation for this tendency is that interpretations simplify the complexity of incoming information, thereby leaving room (or capacity) to deal with unexpected or unfamiliar events. Interpretation also allows the perceiver to select data, attending to features that appear to be relevant and ignoring those which are not. Interpretations provide a short-hand, a way of 'chunking' information to make it easier either to assimilate or remember. It is much more difficult to remember the letters SCLOGPHYOY than PSYCHOLOGY because the word 'psychology' has a meaning, a meaning which can be remembered more efficiently than a random series of letters. In the same way, a patient may remember advice more accurately if the doctor provides some explanation of the treatment (see Chapter 13). Because people have a limited capacity for information, interpretation provides a way of organizing and simplifying data.

When an interpretation cannot be made easily, people often search for possibilities that would reduce the uncertainty. The experience of having symptoms of illness is a good example of this tendency. Symptoms are often ambiguous and carry implications of threat to health and life-style, making them a focus for hypothesis-testing for the patient, family and physician. The threat implied by symptoms cannot be realistically appraised until their cause and potential consequences have been determined. Ambiguity is high because symptoms are often novel, difficult to localize, and of varying severity.[30] Evidence suggests that the difficulty in interpreting symptoms is an important cause of delay in seeking help in the critical minutes and hours following myocardial infarction,[31,32] for example. Thus, the factors involved in the interpretation of external events (i.e. past experience, selective attention, context) often apply equally well to the perception of internal physiological events.[33]

There appears to be a relationship between uncertainty and distress, as Johnson[34] has illustrated. She asked her subjects to rate the degree of distress they experienced while a tourniquet was applied to an arm, ratings being taken every 30 seconds. She experimentally manipulated the subjects' uncertainty about how they would experience the tourniquet by giving one group of subjects relevant information (e.g. how it would feel) and the other group irrelevant information (e.g. a technical description of the tourniquet). Although the distress of the group who knew what to expect rose during the 5-minute experiment, subjects who had not been told what the tourniquet would feel like reported consistently higher levels of distress. Apparently, reducing the uncertainty about what could be expected made the experience less distressing.

Anxiety

A real-life example is the uncertainty experienced by patients on admission to hospital. Anxiety is very common and it seems this is due more to the hospital environment (anxiety being greater in large teaching hospitals than in small community-based ones, for example) than to the severity of the condition.[35] Anxiety is often measured by the State–Trait Anxiety Inventory, a scale which consists of 40 statements. Twenty of these are designed to measure trait anxiety, a personality disposition referring to how people generally feel in a wide variety of situations. An item on this scale is 'I lack self-confidence', and a person chooses one of the four alternatives ('almost never', 'sometimes', 'often' or 'almost always') which best describes their feelings. The other 20 statements are designed to measure state anxiety, referring to how the individual feels at that moment (e.g. to the item 'I feel calm' the patient could choose from 'not at all', 'somewhat', 'moderately so' and 'very much'). Typically, replies on the state anxiety scale shoot up before surgery and fall again afterwards, while trait anxiety scores remain fairly constant throughout.[36]

That patients do feel anxious is not surprising, given the disruption to their lifestyle represented by a stay in hospital.

Emotional support from family members is affected, there is a reduction in independence and a lack of privacy in hospitals. Most germane to the present discussion, patients are troubled by the difficulty of interpreting what is happening to them. Cartwright[37] asked patients to outline their complaints about the hospital they entered. The most frequently expressed complaint was: 'They didn't tell me what I wanted to know'. Another survey found that patients' anxieties centred on the operation (31 per cent) and 'not knowing what to expect' (34 per cent).

Preparing the patient (reducing uncertainty)

If these aspects of hospitalization are so important, then helping patients to interpret this unfamiliar environment and to predict what is going to happen to them should make their stay more satisfying and less stressful. A large body of evidence indicates that this is the case.

Correlational studies

Some of the evidence is based on correlational research. Correlation is a way of measuring the strength of an association between two variables, having a value between zero (no relationship at all) and 1 (one variable predicts scores on the other precisely). A correlation may be positive or negative, a negative correlation indicating that higher values of one variable occur with lower values of the other, such as the more visits to an antenatal clinic, the fewer the obstetric complications. The variables of height and weight are positively correlated, in that taller people tend to be heavier than shorter people. Knowing the height of a person allows a better prediction of his or her weight than not knowing height. Wriglesworth and Williams[38] provide an example of this kind of research. They measured patients' satisfaction with the amount of information they had been given and the degree of their confidence in the medical staff. They found a significant positive correlation, indicating that as satisfaction with information increased, so did confidence in staff.

The problem with correlational studies is in interpretation of the results. It is tempting to conclude from this study that information given to patients was responsible for their confidence. Such a conclusion is consistent with other research, but this study by itself does not necessarily lead to it. Other interpretations can be made. It is equally possible that cause and effect work the other way round, that staff members are more likely to give information if the patient has confidence in them. Alternatively, it may be that confidence and information are related to each other only indirectly, through a third variable. The correlations could be due to the patients' personalities. Perhaps some patients would report that they were satisfied with their treatment no matter what it was like, and would therefore say that they were satisfied with both the information they were given and the competence of the staff; whereas others would complain regardless of the quality of their care, and would therefore report that they were dissatisfied with both staff and information. This possibility may be made clearer if the example of height and weight is used once more. Although these two variables are correlated, it would not be reasonable to say that height causes weight, or vice versa — they are both expressions of a third process, growth.

Despite these drawbacks with the interpretation of correlational studies, they do have advantages. First, they serve as an impetus for experimental work, which is more suited to deal with competing interpretations. Second, correlational studies can be performed when experimental manipulations are ethically or practically difficult. For example, a researcher might be interested in testing the hypothesis that children's language develops more quickly when their mothers talk with them more frequently. Rather than asking one group of mothers to talk with their children more than another group, the investigator might observe the mothers and correlate their behaviour with the children's development. Although a significant correlation would be suggestive, it would not be conclusive, since it could be argued that mothers talk with their babies more when they are developing quickly.

Experimental studies

Fortunately, the area of preparing patients for hospitalization is one that is open to experimental research. Since preparation is not given in many hospitals, it would not be unethical to give some patients more attention than is routinely provided. For example, Leigh et al.[39] used a self-report questionnaire to measure patients' anxiety before and after they were given information about the anaesthetic procedures they were to undergo. One group of patients was given a booklet outlining the information, a second group was given the information personally by an anaesthetist and questions were answered. A third group, the control group*, was given no extra information. Although the anxiety of

* The importance of control groups in research will arise throughout the book. The results from studies that do not use controls are often open to several interpretations, and sometimes the control groups are not adequate. The aim is to use subjects who are as alike as possible to the experimental group subjects,

the control group patients decreased only slightly over time, the anxiety of the informed patients decreased significantly, particularly in the group who were given the information personally and who were invited to ask questions about the procedure.

These studies were concerned with patients' anxieties and their satisfaction with care. While these aspects are important, other measures could also be taken, such as days required in hospital after the operation or the amount of pain-killer requested by the patients. If preparatory information was shown to affect measures such as these, this would provide convincing evidence that information is important for patients' well-being.

The work of worrying

Much of the impetus for research in this area was given by Janis,[40] who identified three groups of patients about to undergo surgery: one group showed high anxiety about the impending operation, feeling very vulnerable, sometimes being unable to sleep and sometimes trying to postpone the operation; a second showed moderate fear, asking for information about the operation and worrying about specific features of the surgical procedure such as anaesthesia; the third showed little fear, sleeping well and tending to deny that they felt worried. These latter patients seemed to feel almost completely invulnerable.

After the operation, the first group (high fear) was found to be the most anxiety-ridden and most concerned with their future. The third group (low fear) was more likely than other groups to

---

differing only on the crucial variable. Perhaps the best way to do this is randomly to assign subjects to different groups. In some instances random assignment would not be practical or ethical, however, and other strategies would be used. Say a researcher was interested in the effects of breathing techniques on the experience of pain during childbirth. He could approach a course organizer and request permission from the organizer and the parents-to-be to do the study. But in order to have confidence in any results he might find, he would have to be careful about choosing the control group. Parents who attend these classes differ in more ways than one from parents who do not elect to attend. They are more likely to be middle-class and to do more reading about childbirth than most parents-to-be, for example. If the researcher found differences in the experience of birth in this sample as compared with another group of parents, the differences might not be due to the breathing exercises but to a better diet or to greater knowledge about birth. If the researcher were lucky, the class would be oversubscribed and he could use the parents who were unable to enter the course as his control group. If no such group of parents was available, he might resort to matching — trying to find parents who are similar to those in his experimental group on relevant variables. In general, age, sex and social class are the variables most commonly used, along with any other aspects that are relevant to the particular study (perhaps income and the number of books parents have read on childbirth, in this case).

show anger and resentment towards the staff and often complained about the treatment. For these two groups the stay in hospital was distinctly unhappy. However, the second group was less likely than the other two to display emotional disturbance and showed high morale and co-operation with the medical staff. It seemed that a moderate amount of fear about the realistic threat of the operation was associated with good recovery. These patients could cope with the pain and distress of the after-effects of the operation adequately. One patient volunteered that he knew 'there might be some bad pains, so when my side began to ache I told myself that this didn't mean that anything had gone wrong'.

The reasons why the patients in the moderately fearful group were able to cope with the operation more successfully were not altogether clear, but Janis suggested that it was because they asked for information about their treatment and were thus able to prepare for its consequences. He came to believe that it is important for people to worry about future events so that they can mentally prepare themselves. This appears to be in direct opposition to the view that patients should not be 'worried' by information lest they become upset by it. A case study is illustrative:

> . . . let us consider the reactions of a 21-year-old woman who had earlier undergone an appendectomy. At that time she had been given realistic information by her physician. Before the operation she had been moderately worried and occasionally asked the nurses for something to calm her nerves, but she showed excellent emotional adjustment throughout her convalescence. About two years later she came to the same hospital for another abdominal operation, the removal of her gall bladder. In the preoperative interview with the investigator she reported that her physician had assured her that 'there's really nothing to it; it's a less serious operation than the previous one'. This time she remained wholly unconcerned about the operation beforehand, apparently anticipating very little or no suffering. Afterwards, experiencing the usual pains and deprivations following a gall bladder operation, she became markedly upset, negativistic, and resentful towards the nursing staff.
>
> Chronic personality predispositions do not seem to account fully for this patient's reactions, since she was capable of showing an entirely different pattern of emotional response, as she had on a previous occasion. The patient's adjustment to the fear-producing situation appeared to be influenced mainly by the insufficient and misleading preparatory communications she was given before the second operation. Since nothing distressing was supposed to happen, she assumed that the hospital staff must be to blame for her post-operative suffering. (Ref. 40, p. 93)

If the information received by patients before surgery helped them in coping with pain, then a short experiment could be performed to test this hypothesis. One group of patients would be given only basic information — the time and duration of the operation and that they would awaken in the recovery room. These patients would form the control group. A second group of patients — the experimental group — would be given much more information about the operation. This experiment was actually performed by Egbert et al.[41] In addition to the standard information given to a control group, the experimental group received:

1 a description of the post-operative pain, including where it would be localized, how much could be expected and how long it would continue;
2 reassurance that post-operative pain was normal and could be expected;
3 advice on how to relax abdominal muscles and how to move without tensing them (all patients had abdominal operations);
4 assurance that they would be given pain-killing medication should they require it.

The results were striking. The experimental group required only half as much sedation during the first five post-operative days (see Fig. 6) and had an average of 2.7 fewer days of hospitalization. One patient from the control group complained, 'Why didn't you tell me it was going to be like this?'.

Since this pioneering work, many researchers have explored the importance of preparatory information. Several issues have arisen during the course of this research. Not everyone seems to benefit from this information, so that psychologists have attempted to develop ways of identifying these patients. There is some indication that those who avoid gathering information about the operation can be distressed if it is presented without their request and show somewhat worse adjustment thereafter.[42,43] There is general agreement, however, that for patients who request information it should be specific rather than vague and aimed at the individual patient's concerns and anxieties rather than simply giving the same information to all patients. In the research mentioned earlier concerning the anaesthetist's visit,[39] the opportunity to ask questions resulted in a greater reduction of anxiety than simply giving the patient a booklet to read. There is also evidence that encouraging accurate expectations about sensations forms an important component of preparation: in one study subjects who were told what sensations would follow from the procedure showed less distress than subjects who were merely

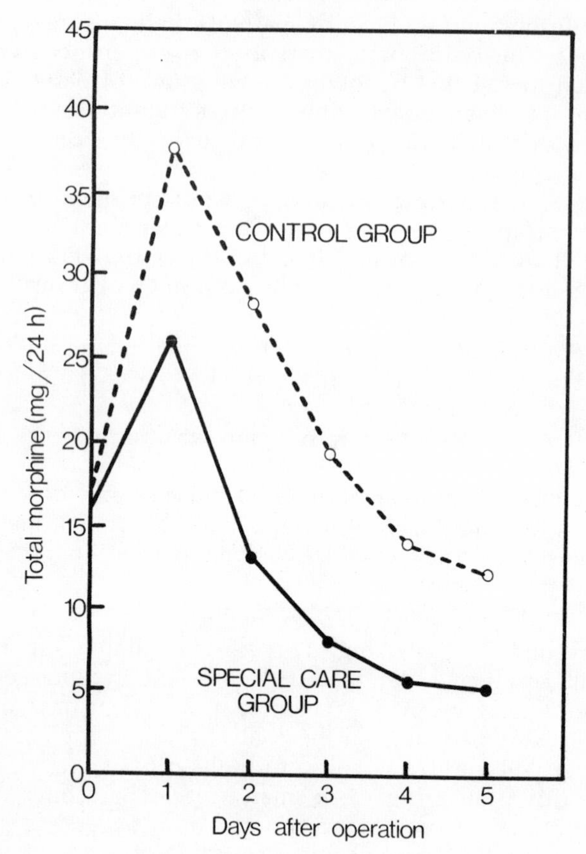

Fig. 6. Post-operative narcotic treatment of patients given routine and extra preparation for surgery. (Reproduced from Egbert, L., Battit, G., Welch, C. & Bartlett, M. (1964) *New England Journal of Medicine* **270**: 825–827, by permission.)

informed about the mechanics of the procedure. Another issue involves the relationship between pre-operative anxiety and post-operative recovery. While Janis contended that moderate anxiety is the preferred state (both high and low anxiety being less desirable), many others have provided evidence that the relationship is more simply linear, with higher anxiety associated with poorer outcome, lower anxiety with better outcome.

In general, there has been support for Janis's original recommendations:

1 To give realistic information, so that patients are able to prepare themselves and to correct unrealistic fears.
2 To provide reassurance that others (particularly the medical

staff) can be relied on to give assistance. Reassurance counteracts fears of helplessness.

3 To encourage plans for coping with future difficulties, such as the pain and social consequences of treatment.

To this list should be added a fourth recommendation:

4 To provide the patient with an opportunity to review the information given.

Memory does not function well when people are anxious, so that patients may not remember what is said if they are told only once, even if they have a strong wish to understand their treatment. This fourth recommendation can be accomplished by giving the patient a written description to keep and a chance to go over the information again with a doctor or nurse.

Investigators have also examined treatments besides surgery. For example, Wilson-Barnett[44] explored the effectiveness of explanatory information on patients who were to have a barium enema. None of the patients had experienced this before, so that they were all unfamiliar with the procedure and the sensations it produces. The experimental group received a written and verbal explanation of the investigation, an explanation based on both observation and previous patients' comments. The verbal explanation took about five minutes, the written information was given to the patients to keep, and any questions were answered. The control group was visited for the same amount of time and asked how they were getting on in hospital. (Giving the control group an equal amount of attention makes this a particularly convincing study. One criticism of research in this area is that many experimenters have neglected to talk with their control group patients, so that it is possible that patients in experimental groups find their stay in hospital less stressful simply because someone took the time to talk with them and was interested in their worries, rather than because they gained more information. This criticism does not apply to this experiment because Wilson-Barnett arranged for all patients to have a chat. She also took her measures 'blind', so that the investigator who measured anxiety did not know which condition a particular patient was in. Researchers may often find the results they expect to find, not because they 'cook' the data but rather because they are more likely to perceive what they expect to perceive.)

Measures of the patients' anxieties were taken on several occasions, as shown in Fig. 7. Before the interaction between nurse and patient, there was no difference in anxiety between the experimental and control group subjects (baseline). Since there was also no difference between the groups after the preparatory

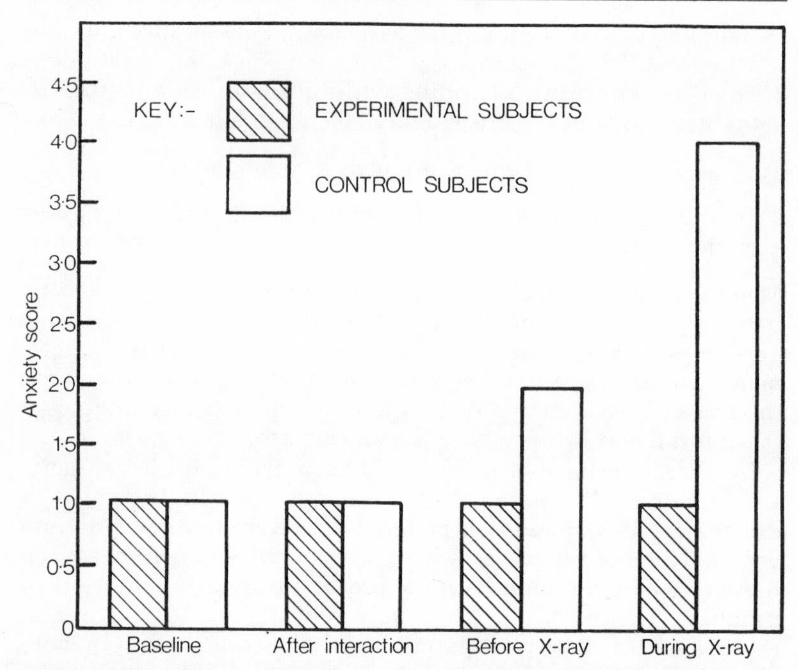

Fig. 7. Average anxiety scores of patients having a barium enema. The experimental subjects had the procedure explained to them, but the control subjects did not. The control subjects' anxiety began to rise just before the X-ray and continued to rise during it; this was not the case for the experimental subjects. (Reproduced from Wilson-Barnett, J. (1978) *Journal of Advanced Nursing* **3**: 37–40, by permission.)

information was given, it seems that this knowledge did not adversely affect the patients in the experimental group. But 30 minutes before the X-ray, differences between the groups appeared and were stronger during the X-ray. Although anxiety in the control group patients increased, the experimental subjects showed no such increase.

Research has also been conducted on timing. Johnson[45] concluded that anxiety about operations begins well before entering the hospital, indicating that preparation and support could profitably be given before admission.

Children in hospital

The difficulties that children experience in entering hospital are particularly distressing, not only for the children themselves but also for parents and staff. Helping parents is one effective method of reducing children's distress. For example, Ferguson[46] arranged a pre-admission home visit by a nurse for children about to have a tonsillectomy. The nurse completed the admission documents with the mother and gave her information about general hospital rules such as what to bring to the hospital, what tests to expect, the fasting requirements on the morning of surgery and what the operating room looked like. They were also told that the child would have a very sore throat after surgery and might vomit. The mothers were given the opportunity to ask questions and express concerns. A group of mothers who received no home visit comprised the control group.

Ferguson measured both mothers' and children's anxieties at admission and 10 days after release from hospital. For children of 6–7 years of age (but not younger) the pre-admission visit resulted in fewer indications of poor adjustment after discharge (e.g. difficulty in sleeping, eating, general anxiety) and mothers were less anxious during and after hospitalization.

Some research (see Chapter 7) has indicated that the child's family background is important, in that children from secure homes are less likely to be disturbed by the experience. Research has also indicated ways in which their difficulties could be lessened by medical and nursing staff. Ferguson took care to inform the children's mothers about hospital procedures because there is evidence that anxiety felt by the mother affects the level of anxiety in her child. Skipper and Leonard[47] asked a nurse to attend some mothers when they arrived at the hospital with their children. As in the Ferguson study, the mothers were encouraged to ask questions and express their concerns. The control group mothers received the regular introduction to the hospital with little personal contact. Behavioural and physiological measures indicated a lower level of anxiety in the *children* of the experimental group mothers, and they made a more rapid recovery and experienced fewer after-effects of their stay. The reduction of the mothers' level of anxiety was reflected in their children's recovery. Apparently, one way to help children in hospital is to help their parents make sense of the hospital routine and treatment.

The difficulties that young children experience may also be due in part to the anxiety they feel when confronted with an unfamiliar situation or unfamiliar adults. Several studies have shown these increase children's need to be close to their parents, particularly at ages between eight months and two years. Yet it appears this anxiety is strongest when an adult approaches a child, rather than allowing the child freedom to approach the adult in his or her own time. When infants are allowed to control the encounter, anxiety about strangers is much less noticeable.[48] Thus it may be possible to reduce children's distress in hospital by allowing them some control over their encounters with medical and nursing staff. The anxiety about unfamiliar environments may be alleviated if parents are encouraged to accompany their children to hospital and to the ward: children are more willing to explore their environment if there is a 'safe base' to which they can return if necessary.

A third possibility for reducing anxiety in hospital is providing the children themselves with preparatory information. However, the information needed by children may often be different from that needed by adults. Children often think of illness as a punishment for bad behaviour and their conceptions of the content and functions of the human body may be vague or false. A young child's lack of experience with large institutions could make a verbal explanation unsatisfactory, so that preparatory information may well need to be modified to take their individual interpretations and expectations into account.

One way of giving information to children is by providing films about the hospital and about treatment. This approach, which has been used with children from about four years of age, has typically included pictures of the admission of a child into hospital, aspects of the operation and post-operative recovery. This has met with considerable success. Known as 'peer-modelling', the technique will be discussed in more detail in Chapter 3, but one example is illustrative. Vernon[49] studied children about to have an injection. One group saw a realistic film of a child having an injection, a second group an unrealistic film (in which there was no indication that the injection might be distressing) and a third group saw no film. The children who saw the realistic film appeared to experience the least pain from the injection, whereas the children who saw the unrealistic film were the most upset. It would seem that many of the principles which apply to the preparation of adults may also apply to children, except that the preparatory information may need to be presented in different ways.

Summary

The way in which people make sense of their environment can be considered in three phases — the sensory, the interpretive and the memory phases — but they are interdependent. For example, the way in which a situation is interpreted depends on the memory of past experiences in similar situations. Research on both the sensory and interpretive phases has indicated that it is not possible to specify a person's experience completely from knowledge of a stimulus alone. Spontaneous neuronal firing, for example, affects the sensory phase by introducing noise into the nervous system, making detection of signals probabilistic rather than absolute. During the interpretive phase, the context in which a stimulus occurs and the past experience and purposes of the observer affect both how events are perceived and which events will be selected for attention. People tend to see what they hope and expect to see. These perceptions can result in a self-fulfilling prophecy when an observer acts on the basis of his or her interpretations.

These principles of interpretation are illustrated by the situation of patients in hospital, who find themselves striving to make sense of an environment which is both novel and threatening. Providing patients with realistic information about their treatment and the hospital procedure can reduce their anxiety and recovery time. Their individual perceptions and concerns about hospitalization should be taken into account, reassurance being given to counteract unrealistic fears. Children also benefit from such preparatory information, but their perceptions about hospitals and their own bodies are likely to be different from adults'. Their anxieties about separation from the family may also be stronger. Methods for making their stay in hospital less alarming, for instance by preparing their parents and providing films depicting other children undergoing similar treatment, have proved helpful.

Suggested reading

There are a large number of books which elaborate on the principles of perception outlined in this chapter. Reference 2 provides a good introduction, as do Coren, S., Porac, C. & Ward, L. (1978) *Sensation and Perception* London: Academic Press. C. Ray's chapter, 'The surgical patient: Psychological stress and coping resources', in Eiser, J.R. (1982) *Social Psychology and Behavioural Medicine* Chichester: Wiley, reviews in more detail the research on preparing patients for hospital care.

References

1. Yersushalmy, J. (1969) The statistical assessment of the variability in observer perception and description of roentgenographic pulmonary shadows. *Radiology Clinics of North America* **7**: 381–392.
2. Lindsay, P.H. & Norman, D. (1977) *Human Information Processing*, 2nd edn. London: Academic Press.
3. Hubel, D.H. & Wiesel, T.N. (1965) Receptive fields and functional architecture in two non-striate visual areas (18 and 19) of the cat. *Journal of Neurophysiology* **28**: 229–287.
4. Walsh, L.W. (1978) *Neuropsychology* London: Churchill Livingstone.

5. Miller, E. (1984) *Recovery and Management of Neuropsychological Impairments* Chichester: Wiley.
6. Garland, L.H. (1959) Studies in the accuracy of diagnostic procedures. *American Journal of Roentgenology* **82**: 25–38.
7. Dombal, F.T. (1972) Computer-aided diagnosis of acute abdominal pain. *British Medical Journal* **2**: 9–13.
8. Dion, K.K. (1972) Physical attractiveness and evaluations of children's transgressions. *Journal of Personality and Social Psychology* **24**: 207–213.
9. Nordholm, L.A. (1980) Beautiful patients are good patients: evidence for the physical attractiveness stereotype in first impressions of patients. *Social Science and Medicine* **14A**: 81–83.
10. Meiners, M.L. & Sheposh, J. (1977) Beauty or brains: which image for your mate? *Personality and Social Psychology Bulletin* **3**: 262–265.
11. Pendleton, D.A. & Bochner, S. (1980) The communication of medical information in general practice consultations as a function of patients' social class. *Social Science and Medicine* **14A**: 669–673.
12. Shapiro, M.C., Najman, J., Chang, A., Keeping, J., Morrison, J. & Western, J. (1983) Information control and the exercise of power in the obstetrical encounter. *Social Science and Medicine* **17**: 139–146.
13. Maguire, G.P. & Granville-Grossman, K. (1968) Physical illness in psychiatric patients. *British Journal of Psychiatry* **114**: 1365–1369.
14. Maguire, G.P., Julier, D., Hawton, K. & Bancroft, J. (1974) Psychiatric morbidity and referral on two general medical wards. *British Medical Journal* **1**: 268–270.
15. Rosenhan, D.L. (1973) On being sane in insane places. *Science* **179**: 250–258.
16. Turnbull, C. (1961) Some observations regarding the experience and behaviour of the Bambuti pygmies. *American Journal of Psychology* **74**: 304–308.
17. Gregory, R.L. (1966) *Eye and Brain* New York: McGraw-Hill.
18. Leeper, R.A. (1935) A study of a neglected portion of the field of learning. *Journal of Genetic Psychology* **46**: 42–45.
19. Luchins, A.S. (1942) Mechanization in problem-solving. The effect of *Einstellung*. *Psychological Monographs* **54**.
20. Stimson, G.V. (1974) Obeying doctors' orders: a view from the other side. *Social Science and Medicine* **8**: 97–104.
21. Maguire, G.P. & Rutter, D.R. (1976) History taking for medical students: 1. Deficiencies in performance. *Lancet* **2**: 556–558.
22. Abercrombie, M. (1969) *The Anatomy of Judgement* Harmondsworth, Middx.: Penguin.
23. Barrows, H.S. & Bennett, K. (1972) The diagnostic (problem-solving) skill of the neurologist. *Archives of Neurology* **26**: 273–277.
24. Byrne, P.S. & Long, B. (1976) *Doctors Talking to Patients* London: HMSO.
25. Deymer, D.E., Fryback, G. & Gassner, K. (1978) Heuristics and biases in medical decision-making. *Journal of Medical Education* **53**: 682–683.
26. Shepherd, M., Cooper, B., Brown, A. & Kalton, G. (1966) *Psychiatric Illness in General Practice* London: Oxford University Press.
27. Meichenbaum, D.H., Bowers, K.S. & Ross, R. (1969) A behavioural analysis of teacher expectancy effects. *Journal of Personality and Social Psychology* **13**: 306–316.
28. Jahoda, G. (1954) A note on Ashanti names and their relation to personality. *British Journal of Psychology* **45**: 192–195.
29. Beecher, K.K. (1961) Surgery as placebo: a quantitative study of bias. *Journal of the American Medical Association* **176**: 1102–1107.
30. Leventhal, H. (1975) The consequences of depersonalisation during illness and treatment. In: Howard, J. & Strauss, A. (eds.) *Humanizing Health Care* New York: Wiley.
31. Croog, S.H. & Levine, S. (1969) Social status and subjective perceptions of 250 men after myocardial infarction. *Public Health Reports* **84**: 984–997.

32. Hackett, T.P. & Cassem, N. (1969) Factors contributing to delay in responding to the signs and symptoms of acute myocardial infarction. *American Journal of Cardiology* **24**: 651–658.
33. Skelton, J.A. & Pennebaker, J. (1982) The psychology of physical symptoms and sensations. In: Sanders, G.S. & Suls, J. (eds.) *The Social Psychology of Health and Illness* London: Laurence Erlbaum.
34. Johnson, J.E. (1973) Effects of accurate expectations about sensations. *Journal of Personality and Social Psychology* **27**: 261–275.
35. Lucente, F.E. & Fleck, S. (1972) A study of hospitalisation anxiety in 408 medical and surgical patients. *Psychosomatic Medicine* **34**: 304–312.
36. Speilberger, C.D., Auerbach, S., Wadsworth, A., Dunn, T. & Taulbee, E. (1973) Emotional reactions to surgery. *Journal of Consulting and Clinical Psychology* **40**: 33–38.
37. Cartwright, A. (1964) *Human Relations and Hospital Care* London: Routledge and Kegan Paul.
38. Wriglesworth, J.M. & Williams, J. (1975) The construction of an objective test to measure patient satisfaction. *International Journal of Nursing Studies* **12**: 123–132.
39. Leigh, J.M., Walker, J. & Janaganathan, P. (1977) Effects of a preoperative anaesthetic visit on anxiety. *British Medical Journal* **2**: 987–989.
40. Janis, I.L. (1971) *Stress and Frustration* New York: Harcourt Brace Jovanovich.
41. Egbert, L., Battit, G., Welch, C. & Bartlett, M. (1964) Reduction of postoperative pain by encouragement and instruction of patients. *New England Journal of Medicine* **270**: 825–827.
42. Auerbach, S.M. & Kilman, P. (1977) Crisis intervention: a review of outcome research. *Psychological Bulletin* **84**: 1189-1217.
43. Miller, S.M. & Mangan, C. (1983) Interacting effects of information and coping style in adapting to gynecologic stress: should the doctor tell all? *Journal of Personality and Social Psychology* **45**: 223–236.
44. Wilson-Barnett, J. (1978) Patients' emotional responses to barium X-rays. *Journal of Advanced Nursing* **3**: 37–40.
45. Johnson, M. (1980) Anxiety in surgical patients. *Psychological Medicine* **10**: 145–152.
46. Ferguson, B.F. (1979) Preparing young children for hospitalisation. *Pediatrics* **64**: 656–664.
47. Skipper, J.K. & Leonard, R. (1968) Children, stress and hospitalisation: a field experiment. *Journal of Health and Social Behaviour* **9**: 275–287.
48. Horner, T.M. (1980) Two methods of studying stranger reactivity in infants: a review. *Journal of Child Psychology and Psychiatry* **21**: 203–219.
49. Vernon, D.T. (1974) Modelling and birth order in response to painful stimuli. *Journal of Personality and Social Psychology* **24**: 794–799.

2

Personality and Psychopathology

Introduction

There are many ways of predicting how people will act in a particular situation. One source of information is the role or place in society which a person holds. If an individual is a teacher, for example, it is possible to predict that he or she will talk in front of a class of students occasionally. A doctor is likely to take medical histories, perform physical examinations and to prescribe drugs. However, all teachers have their own individual manner of teaching, although they may impart the same facts to their students: equally, two doctors may have very different styles of consultation although they may recommend the same course of treatment. These differences between people, which make each individual unique, are usually put down to the person's personality. Just as some researchers have been interested in studying the similarities between people, employing concepts such as roles and socialization to account for the consistencies (see Chapter 6 and Part II of this book), others have developed concepts and theories to account for these individual differences in personality. It is this latter work with which this chapter is concerned.

Individual differences are due to both genetic and environmental factors. Since each person's genetic code predisposes him or her to behave in certain ways and genetic factors interact with the environment, each person's behaviour is the result of both kinds of influence. Some personality theorists place more emphasis on one than the other. Freud, for example, considered people to be primarily biological machines: in his early work the influence of the environment was thought to be secondary. For other theorists, people are seen to be motivated by a search for personal meaning arising largely from environmental factors, and little attention is given to biology.

Similarly, some psychiatrists* consider personality disturbances to be due to chemical imbalances and that the difficulties can be remedied through the use of medication. This area of research falls outside the domain of this book. Others consider personal problems to be due to disturbances in relationships with other people, so that personal psychotherapy is seen to be the answer. In practice, both methods are often used: a patient who is depressed, for example, may be prescribed medication as well as being given personal therapy.

There are therefore many approaches to personality and it is beyond the scope of this book to consider them all. Those selected for discussion here reflect three important trends in personality research. These are the psychodynamic and cognitive approaches (both of which have been developed by therapists through their experience with patients) and descriptive theories. First, however, it is appropriate to outline the classification of psychological difficulties in current use.

The classification of psychological difficulties

Psychological problems can be classified in several ways. Current schemes emphasize symptomatology rather than aetiology, so that all those people who show a particular symptom or set of symptoms are usually considered to have the same disorder. The three main categories are neurosis, psychosis and personality disorders. The following is a brief and simplified account.

Neurosis

People who are classified as neurotic are characterized as engaging in self-defeating patterns of behaviour and as having high levels of anxiety. There are several sub-classifications, including phobic neurosis, hypochondriacal neurosis and neurotic depression.

---

* It may be useful to distinguish between the psychiatrists and psychologists who work in the area. Psychiatry is a speciality, like surgery or paediatrics, which is followed after training in general medicine. Psychologists, on the other hand, will have completed an undergraduate course in psychology, covering in depth many of the topics discussed in Parts I and II of this book, and usually a postgraduate course in a specialist discipline. Clinical psychologists attempt to assist people who seek help for a wide range of psychological problems, which could include fears of specific objects (e.g. of spiders or leaving home alone) or more generalized anxieties. Psychiatrists and psychologists often share the same theoretical positions and use the same methods, medication being the exception: since psychologists are not medically trained they cannot prescribe drugs.

When someone has an unrealistic fear of a situation, so intense that the situation is avoided for no apparently reasonable cause, a phobia is said to be present. Some common phobias are fear of heights (acrophobia) and of crowded or open spaces away from home (agoraphobia). Hypochondriasis is the term given to the condition in which the person is over-concerned with his or her own physical health, perhaps visiting the doctor frequently with complaints of illness, although no physical cause for the complaints can be found. A person is said to be neurotically depressed when dejection and feelings of hopelessness out of proportion to events is shown.

Psychosis

This term is applied to people who are characterized as being out of touch with reality in some way and whose social relationships are seriously impaired. Hallucinations and bizarre behaviour — both verbal and non-verbal — may be present. Types of psychosis include schizophrenia and the affective disorders. There are various types of schizophrenia: paranoid schizophrenia typified by delusions of some kind (e.g. a certainty that the patient is being followed and spied upon); hebephrenic schizophrenia characterized by disorganized and childish speech; and catatonic schizophrenia which often involves a lack of movement. All of these conditions have in common peculiar behaviour patterns which are difficult to understand. Schizophrenia is not necessarily so very obvious, partly because the symptomatology can be intermittent — patients often have lucid periods when they talk and act in an understandable way. Among the affective disorders are mania (extreme excitability) and psychotic depression (which includes extreme feelings of worthlessness and lack of motivation).

Personality disorders

Originally, difficulties such as alcoholism and drug addiction were classified under personality disorders since these problems were seen to be primarily due to personality factors. With the awareness that these conditions are strongly influenced by social factors, the classification of personality disorder is now often limited to those people whose behaviour is antisocial: they are known as sociopaths or psychopaths. Their motivations for behaviour appear to be directed towards their own needs without regard for others.

Problems with classification

While this classification of psychological difficulties is commonly applied, it is becoming increasingly controversial. First, there is reason to doubt whether different diagnosticians use the scheme in the same way. Although therapists tend to agree on broad categories (e.g. neurosis or psychosis), there is much less agreement within a category. Among psychoses, for instance, many symptoms overlap, and since patients show different symptoms at different times, one therapist might diagnose hebephrenic schizophrenia while another suggests paranoid schizophrenia. Schizophrenia is diagnosed more frequently in the United States than in Britain, where affective disorders are more commonly found. There is evidence that at least part of this difference is due to the diagnostic procedures used by the doctors involved. The DSM-III classification, recently developed in the United States, attempts to reduce such difficulties by classifying patients along several dimensions.[1]

A second difficulty of the classification scheme is that it is primarily descriptive, so that the presenting complaints of patients are often used not to discover the aetiological basis of the symptoms but rather to classify the patient. This is not a problem for those psychologists and psychiatrists who believe that each disorder has a biochemical cause, but for others such a classification is incomplete on its own. For them, a satisfactory system would involve an explanation of how the condition arose during the patient's psychological development.

A third and related problem is that, by considering all the people who show a set of symptoms as a homogeneous group, there has been a tendency to search for a single cause. To take schizophrenia as an example, some researchers have presented evidence that vulnerability to schizophrenia has a genetic base (e.g. if one twin is diagnosed as schizophrenic the other twin is more likely to be schizophrenic if they are monozygotic than dizygotic),[2] while others have argued that it results from family difficulties and disturbances in communication. Evidence for both positions can be found, yet neither can account fully for the onset of schizophrenia. This has led some researchers to consider the interaction between genetic predisposition and environment. The contention is that although schizophrenia has a genetic component, it only becomes evident when the family does not provide a sound and secure environment.[3]

Normality

There is a further difficulty with the classification, one that is common to all such schemes. It implies that there are basic differences between people who are neurotic or psychotic, and people who are normal. However, normality is a difficult concept to define. A statistical definition is a possibility: behaviour which is unusual could be defined as abnormal. The problem with this criterion is that the meaning of the behaviour is not taken into account. Playing a violin is statistically infrequent, for example, yet it would be absurd to consider a violinist to be in need of help simply because the behaviour is unusual. Further, since most people will ask for some kind of psychological assistance at some time in their lives, the statistical definition is not an adequate one in any case.

Another possible definition of normality concerns the violation of social norms: people who do not conform to the rules and customs of society might be considered abnormal. The difficulty with this criterion is that social norms change, so that behaviour that was considered to require psychiatric assistance in our society at one time (such as homosexuality) is no longer considered a symptom of psychopathology. Social norms also vary between cultures so that, for example, although experiencing visions is the norm among Australian aboriginals, Western psychiatrists might diagnose schizophrenia.

The criterion which is actually used seems to be one of the meaning of behaviour rather than the behaviour itself. It is the meaning given to actions by the individual and the group of people around him which is significant. A person may seek help when, to others, the difficulty may seem a minor one or, alternatively, refuse assistance when the problem seems a major one to friends, family and professionals. This principle applies not only to psychological difficulties but physical problems as well, a topic given further consideration in Chapter 6. Many prefer to consider the problems that require the assistance of a therapist to be only a magnification of the kinds of difficulties that everyone faces, rather than a qualitative difference. The contention is that everyone is neurotic to some extent, for example, having unrealistic fears of some kind, and it is only when these fears have a disabling effect that assistance is sought. According to this approach, there is a continuum between normality and neurosis and between normality and psychosis, rather than sharp distinctions between them.

One final difficulty with the classification approach merits attention. This involves the tendency for people to define themselves according to the reactions they receive from others. The reader, if he or she has recently entered medical school, may have noticed a change in self-evaluation. Since one of the criteria for selection into medicine involves academic performance, most students about to enter the medical course evaluate their performance and academic competence highly. However, with experience of low grades and sometimes failure in exams, self-evaluations tend to decrease in the first years, rising again later in training.[4] A similar process could be expected to occur in mental health. Psychological difficulties are not well accepted in the community, often resulting in rejection and distrust.[5] Behaviour that has been previously interpreted as eccentric is often reinterpreted when the person is classified as disturbed. Once a person has had therapeutic assistance in hospital, acceptance back into the community can be hindered.[6] This is illustrated by one experiment where subjects were asked to engage in a co-operative task with a stranger. Some of the subjects were led to believe that their partners had a history of psychological disturbances, whereas others were not given this inaccurate information. Although no objective differences were found between the groups in how well they performed the task, those who were told that their partner had psychological difficulties later described them as being less able to understand others, less able to understand themselves and less able to get along with others.[7] In so far as self-evaluations are dependent on the reactions of others,[8] classification and the labelling it entails may affect the well-being and behaviour of patients.

Thus, it can be argued that the classification of a patient's problem is less important than the steps taken to provide help. Because many people have psychological difficulties, it is often inappropriate to consider a person who needs to consult a psychiatrist or clinical psychologist as being fundamentally different from everybody else: most psychological difficulties are a matter of degree.

Psychodynamic approaches

Freud

Sigmund Freud is considered to be the father of the psychodynamic approach to personality. Although many aspects of his original theory have been modified by later therapists, his contribution to psychiatry and psychology is enormous and it is important to give at least a brief outline of his thinking. His perspective grew out of experiences with the patients he treated in Vienna at the turn of the century, and his theory is much easier to understand in the context of this cultural background.

Trained as a neurologist, Freud was steeped in the medical model. One tenet of medical training is that complaints are symptoms of an underlying cause and important only in so far as they point to an underlying pathology of some kind: if this pathology is treated then the symptoms will disappear of their own accord. Freud was more interested in discovering what his patients' symptoms indicated than in the symptoms themselves.

The unconscious

Freud was born in 1856, and his training and thinking originated in the nineteenth century. Many contemporary ideas were included in his theory, such as the unconscious. Although Freud is sometimes credited with discovering the unconscious, the idea seems to have been present in Victorian culture. Stevenson's *Dr. Jekyll and Mr. Hyde* provides an example: by drinking a potion, a hidden side of the doctor's personality was expressed. Further, this unknown personality was destructive and needed to be controlled. Freud argued that the unconscious formed the greater proportion of everyone's personality, with consciousness being like the tip of an iceberg. The unconscious contained feelings and experiences of which, under ordinary circumstances, the person was unaware but which motivated actions or desires.

Freud's theory was also consistent with an important trend in Western thinking — biological determinism, the idea that what people do and think is determined by their biology. Harvey's contention that the heart was not a 'vital' organ (i.e. not the seat of life) but simply a pump, was one example; Darwin's theory of evolution was another. Freud saw no reason to believe that thinking and perceiving were any different from breathing or walking. Both kinds of process were seen to be manifestations of the same underlying biological machine. Like physical energy, he contended that psychic energy (which he called libidinal energy) was present in finite amounts and could be neither created nor destroyed. Since intake of food resulted in the production of energy, if the personality were to be kept in some kind of equilibrium, then this energy must find expression. If for some reason the expression of energy was blocked, then, like a hydraulic system, the energy found expression elsewhere. If someone had the compulsion to wash his hands repeatedly, then Freud might suggest that he was using up the energy from a blocked impulse. There would be little point in treating the hand-washing alone since the energy would simply find expression elsewhere — *symptom substitution*.

The components of personality

Freud postulated three systems within the personality. The most basic was the *id*. The id was like a reservoir, supplying the energy required for human behaviour. Freud argued that the *ego* developed as a system that was responsible for mediating between the id's demands for pleasure and the demands of external reality. The ego did not have energy of its own but only borrowed it from the id in return for satisfying the id whenever possible. He also postulated the existence of a third system, the *superego*, as a means of incorporating society's values into the individual. The superego developed in two ways, through rewards and through punishment. Punishments given by others, parents in the first instance, resulted in the conscience which inhibited transgression of rules. Rewards resulted in the development of the positive side of the superego, the ego-ideal. This was responsible for endeavours to please parents, friends and self. When the superego was fully developed, parental and societal values were internalized so a person no longer needed direct control from others but was self-controlled.

These three systems, the id, ego and superego, interacted with and counterbalanced each other in Freud's theory. The ego was a kind of executive, trying to satisfy the often conflicting demands of the id and the superego. Symptoms were said to arise when one or two systems contained an undue share of libidinal energy, so that someone who had too much energy in the conscience may be over-inhibited and fearful lest he or she be punished for allowing the id to express itself. Many of the patients that Freud originally treated, who would be classified as 'neurotic', seemed to have an undue amount of energy invested in the superego. They showed hysterical symptoms such as paralysis for which no physical cause could be discovered. Freud found that by 'working through' patients' emotions and helping them gain insight about themselves, these symptoms would disappear. 'Working through' involved an exploration of childhood experiences, particularly those that were emotionally painful. This was considered to be difficult because many of these childhood memories were no longer conscious but could only be rediscovered through the use of analytic techniques.

Defence mechanisms

Freud argued that memories became unconscious because the ego, in its attempts to satisfy the demands of both the id and the superego, used *defence mechanisms*. All of these mechanisms involved distortion of some kind, either of reality or of one's own impulses. For example, *repression* might be an ego-response to a painful memory: the memory might be of being hurt by a parent as a child, but this would be unacceptable to a superego which demanded that parents should always be loved and respected in an unambivalent way. *Denial* was a refusal to accept the existence of a situation which was too painful to tolerate, such as inscribing 'Only Sleeping' on a gravestone. *Rationalization* was the attempt to find socially and personally acceptable reasons for behaviour that would otherwise be threatening in some way. If, for instance, you have ever cheated in an exam (behaviour which might be unacceptable to the superego), the rationalization 'Well, it's all right to cheat if they make the examinations so ridiculously difficult' might be used. Freud believed that these and the other defence mechanisms had two properties in common. First, they were present in everyone, not only those with psychological difficulties. Second, the individual was not aware that he or she was using them. These mechanisms were usually unconscious but could be explored during psychoanalysis.

Freud understood his patients' difficulties in terms of different kinds of conflict between the id, ego and superego. For some patients, the problem was seen as being due to a damming-up of libidinal energy: failure to discharge the energy adequately left a residue that could result in a state of anxiety. The problem could be quite transitory and deep psychoanalysis not needed. For other patients, however, a detailed analysis of personality development was needed. The growing individual was said to pass through oral, anal, phallic and genital stages, each of which marked a particular kind of libidinal expression. During the oral phase, for example, libidinal energy was expressed through the mouth: this is exemplified by the first months of an infant's life, where sucking is the main activity. Gradually, libidinal energy was transferred to the anal zone, and so on. When patients consulted Freud, he saw their difficulties as manifestations of incomplete or inadequate transfer of energy from one bodily zone to the next, and the kinds of problems they presented as being a result of regression to this earlier phase. This model of psychological growth is analogous to the development of the foetus *in utero*. If an infant is born with some physical handicap, it is possible to specify the time when something went wrong in its development. For example, the limb defects caused by thalidomide were due to prescription of the drug during the critical weeks of limb growth in the foetus. Similarly, Freud attempted to discover what 'went wrong' in a patient's psychological development by exploring the relevant phase. Someone who presented with an hysterical complaint (such as paralysis of a limb with no physical cause), for example, was said to have regressed to the phallic phase.

Developments in psychodynamic theory

It would be a mistake to consider psychodynamic theory and therapy as currently practised to be the same as Freud originally outlined. Although many of his concepts are still in common use, their meaning has been modified in the light of further clinical experience. Many of Freud's students broke with him early on, particularly over his emphasis on sex and aggression as motivators of behaviour, and there is now a wide range of psychodynamic theories. During the 1940s and 1950s there was an increasing emphasis on the interpersonal aspects of personality and personality growth. The infant's first and intense relationship with a mother or mother-figure became all important. The quality of mothering was seen to be crucial, providing the context in which the child first begins to form ideas about the self and the world. If the world (i.e. the mother) were frustrating and inconsistent, then the infant was thought to internalize these experiences and use them as a basis for all later relationships. One result of the increased emphasis on the mother–infant relationship is the concern with attachment and maternal deprivation, a topic raised in Chapter 7.

Some psychiatrists and psychologists have gone so far as to question the validity and usefulness of the idea of personality residing solely within the person, arguing that it is a meaningful concept only when seen in relation to other people. The American psychiatrist, Sullivan, contended that 'personality is the relatively enduring pattern of recurrent interpersonal situations which characterize a human life' (Ref. 9, pp. 110–11). According to this position, personality has to do with the individual's relationship to his or her world, particularly with other people, and psychological difficulties are mainly disturbances of communication in interpersonal relationships.

In fact, there is now a great diversity of psychodynamic approaches to personality,[10] but despite this there are some broad areas of agreement about therapeutic principles. One important principle concerns acceptance of the patient's statements, wishes and concerns without condemnation or castigation. In order for people to change, it is argued, it is first necessary to develop an open and trusting relationship with another person. The aim is not to change the person in ways that the therapist thinks are correct, but to allow the patient an opportunity to develop in ways that are personally helpful. Acceptance is regarded as a crucial aspect of psychotherapy because as soon as someone is penalized for their feelings, these feelings cannot be explored satisfactorily. This does not usually mean that patients are simply allowed to talk while the therapist listens passively. Psychotherapy often involves a degree of confrontation and challenge, except that these challenges may be termed 'interpretations'. A therapist might challenge his patient with the observation that, while the patient is professing relaxation, he is moving or sitting uncomfortably. Or that he is talking about the death of a parent intellectually, without depth of feeling. Most psychotherapists would also agree that giving advice is inappropriate, since this implies taking responsibility away from the patient. One aim of therapy is to help patients cope with their 'problems of living' in ways of their own choosing, and this is impeded if the therapist advises or makes value-judgements.

Psychotherapists often place strong emphasis on the need for therapy for themselves as well as their patients. Just like everyone else, psychotherapists have problems in their relationships with others — parents, friends and spouse. They, too, have 'problems of living' and these will affect their relationships with patients. Psychotherapy can involve strong emotional reactions, both positive and negative, from patients. It is not uncommon for a patient to become very dependent on the therapist during treatment, for example, and the ways such dependency is dealt with may well affect the course of treatment. A therapist who fosters inordinate dependency may make it difficult for the patient to progress or end therapy. Anger is another commonly aroused feeling in therapy: a therapist who finds anger particularly distressing may not be able to help the patient explore his or her feelings of hostility.

There seems little doubt that the way therapists approach their patients has an effect on the course of treatment. Whitehorn and Betz[11] examined the importance of the therapist's approach in a psychiatric hospital by comparing seven doctors whose patients showed good improvement with seven doctors whose patients showed least improvement. Several differences were found between the two groups of physicians. The first group tended to see their patients' behaviour in terms of personal meanings, rather than a way of arriving at a descriptive diagnosis. When case histories were taken, the personal relevance of past experiences was considered and discussed. They worked towards goals which were oriented towards the perceptions of the patients, rather than curing symptoms, and they were more likely to build trusting relationships with their patients.

It is sometimes difficult to see how psychotherapy differs from a close friendship and, indeed, there are many similarities. Caring, attention and commitment are common to both, but they are different in psychotherapy compared with a friendship. Contact between therapist and patient is usually limited to hourly sessions (often once a week) and there is an inevitable difference in power.

A degree of objectivity is important lest the therapist becomes so involved that he or she is unable to see where the relationship is floundering. The people involved in a friendship also have vested interests in keeping the relationship fairly constant, whereas the essence of psychotherapy is change. While few people in their everyday lives set out to end a relationship, an important aim in psychotherapy is to help the patient eventually cope with his or her difficulties without the assistance of the therapist.

While these broad areas of agreement exist between therapists, there are many differences in how they encourage patients to express and come to terms with their feelings and relationships with others. Many therapists trained in the Freudian and neo-Freudian schools emphasize the importance of *transference*. The argument is that, if our first relationship (especially with parents) forms the pattern for all later ones, then a patient coming for therapy can be expected to bring these patterns to his relationship with the therapist, reacting to him or to her as if to the parent. The therapist's job is to help the patient understand these reactions, thus assisting in the understanding of difficulties experienced in relationships outside the consultation. Therapists who use transference tend to be rather unforthcoming in talking about themselves, preferring to present a kind of 'mirror' that reflects the patient's personality.

This method has been rejected by many therapists who believe that mirroring is impossible to achieve. Inevitably, they contend, the therapist's personality is an important aspect of the treatment and can be a helpful addition to psychotherapy. The use of the therapist's own experiences and views is closely associated with humanistic and existential forms of psychotherapy. In order to help people in their search, therapists from these schools place strong emphasis on self-disclosure, genuineness and warmth. Only if the patient comes to understand the reactions his behaviour engenders in others, it is felt, can he be helped to grow. Two quotations from Carl Rogers illustrate the viewpoint:

> The relationship which I have found helpful is characterized by a sort of transparency on my part, in which my real feelings are evident. . . . I become a companion for my client, accompanying him in the frightening search for himself. (Ref. 12, p. 34)

> . . . so if I sense that I am feeling bored by my contact with this client and this feeling persists, I think I owe it to him and to our relationship to share this feeling with him. The same would hold if my feeling is one of being afraid of this client, or if my attention is so focused on my own problems that I can scarcely listen to him. But as I attempt to share these feelings I also want to be constantly in touch with what is going on in me. . . . I also feel a new sensitivity to him now that I have shared this feeling which has

> been a barrier between us. I am very much more able to hear the surprise or perhaps the hurt in his voice because I have dared be real to him. I have let myself be a person — real, imperfect — in my relationship to him. (Ref. 13, p. 57)

The problem of cures

A complex but fundamental point in psychotherapy concerns the problem of defining a successful outcome. For many physical illnesses, a patient is said to be cured when the presenting symptom is successfully treated. Similarly, some psychologists have taken removal of the presenting complaint as an indication that psychotherapy has been successful. If this criterion is used, then many patients improve without psychological care, and it has been argued that much of the improvement in patients who have received psychotherapy is due to this spontaneous remission.

Others contend that an emphasis on the disappearance of symptoms misses the point of psychotherapy. They are less interested in symptoms than in underlying difficulties and consider the quality of the therapist–patient relationship to be the important criterion of success. Rogers puts the problem in this way:

> . . . in my early professional years I was asking the question: How can I treat, or cure, this person? Now I would phrase the question in this way: How can I provide a relationship which this person may use for his own personal growth? (Ref. 13, p. 32)

Storr, a therapist who is more closely identified with a traditional psychodynamic approach, makes a similar point:

> Some time ago I had a letter from a man whom I had treated some twenty-five years previously asking whether I would see . . . his daughter. . . . in the course of his letter, he wrote as follows: 'I can quite truthfully say that six months of your patient listening to my woes made a most important contribution to my life-style. Although my transvestism was not cured my approach to life and to other people was re-oriented and for that I am most grateful. It is part of my life that I have never forgotten.'
>
> Looked at from one point of view, my treatment of this man was a failure. His major symptom, the complaint which drove him to seek my help, was not abolished. And yet I think it is clear that he did get something from his short period of psychotherapy which was of considerable value to him. A man does not write to a psychotherapist asking him to see his daughter, twenty-five years after his own treatment was over, using the terms employed in this letter, unless he believes that what happened during his period of treatment was important. (Ref. 14, p. 146)

There are, however, some more objective ways of measuring the progress of therapy. One method, content analysis, categorizes the patient's statements according to certain criteria. For example, Raimy[15] divided patients' comments into three categories: (1) positive or approving self-references, (2) negative or disapproving self-references, and (3) ambivalent self-references. At the beginning of therapy most of the statements were of the second kind, indicating that the patients had negative views about themselves. As therapy progressed, there was a greater frequency of ambivalent statements. At the end of therapy, those patients who were considered to have improved gave comments mostly of the first kind, suggesting a greater acceptance of themselves, while those who were considered not to have improved continued to present ambivalent or negative statements about themselves. It seemed from this study that improvement in psychotherapy was reflected in an increase in positive feelings about oneself. Thus, while it may be difficult to define what a 'cure' may be for many patients in psychotherapy, there are measures that allow the progress of therapy to be monitored.

In summary, the psychodynamic approach to personality emphasizes the unconscious workings of the mind. Although people may believe that they are aware of their hopes, desires and motivations, Freud and his followers explored the ways in which unconscious conflicts between the id, ego and superego can determine feelings and behaviour. While Freud concentrated upon the biological basis of personality and personality development, later therapists have been more concerned with the ways in which relationships develop. A psychological problem is now often seen to be a difficulty in relating to others, a difficulty which has its source in an individual's early relationships, particularly with parents. It may be inappropriate to expect to cure someone with a long-standing problem: it may be more useful to see psychotherapy as a way of encouraging the development of new and less uncomfortable ways of relating to others.

Cognitive theories

There are many similarities between the psychodynamic and cognitive approaches to personality. In both, past experience plays an important role and both types of therapy aim to give patients the means to solve their difficulties in the future. Therapists of both schools would agree that feelings about oneself and one's relationships are crucial. However, the emphasis in cognitive therapy is on the conscious workings of the mind rather than the unconscious. For these psychologists personality is the way the person interprets the world. The assumptions and expectations made about the environment determine behaviour and reactions. Two examples of therapists who take this position are George Kelly and Aaron Beck.

George Kelly

Just as a scientist makes observations, has expectations about what will be found and modifies theories in the light of new results, Kelly suggested that people use the scientific method in their everyday lives. Personal theories about how the world works help the individual to make sense of the environment and lead to certain predictions about future events. For example, someone might have the theory that the world is a kind place and that everyone can be trusted. This theory could lead to the prediction that if money is left on a table in a public place, it would still be there when the owner returns. If the money is not there, the person might predict that someone found it and turned it in to a Lost Property Office — a way of fitting the event into the theory. If the money could not be traced, the person may decide the theory is not a good one and change it. Not only do people have theories about the actions of others, they also have theories about themselves. To say 'I'm not the sort of person who does that kind of thing' indicates a theory about oneself that will determine to some extent how events are perceived and which behaviour will be shown.

Existence is said to be like a series of experiments and each person holds theories about how life works, selectively attending to some phenomena and ignoring others. Scientists work first by inductive reasoning, looking for a general rule that explains or accounts for their observations. In the same way, infants initially perceive the world with no theory, but gradually build up a view which can be used to explain why people react to them in the way they do. If adults react negatively towards a child, he or she might conclude: 'I am worthless' or 'the world is essentially a hurtful place'. These conclusions eventually become premises upon which behaviour and interpretations of others' behaviour are based.

Personal constructs

Different people have different ways of understanding their world (their theories) and place emphasis on different aspects of it. For one person, generosity may be important, for another, happiness. When asked to describe someone, the first person might be more likely to use a generosity–miserliness dimension, while the second would tend to select happiness–sadness. These descriptions are known as *constructs*. In order to make a person's constructs explicit, Kelly devised a technique which involved the individual naming three objects: three cars, for example, or three people. The person is then asked to say how two of the objects are similar to each other but different from the third. Through questioning, the terms in which the world is viewed can be discovered. Rowe[16] provides an illustration, in which a student is asked to name three cars:

> Let us suppose the student names a Rolls-Royce, a Lamborghini and a Ford Popular. Then the psychologist asks the student to tell him one way in which two of these are the same and the other different. The student could reply in a number of ways. He could say that two are fast and one is slow or two are elegant and one ordinary, or two are expensive and one cheap . . . .
>
> Suppose the student replies that two are fast and one slow. Then the psychologist asks, 'Which would you prefer, the fast or the slow?'
>
> Suppose the student replies 'The fast'. Then the psychologist asks, 'Why is it important for you to have the fast one?'
>
> 'Because', the student might reply, 'I like driving fast. I'm really feeling alive when I'm driving fast.'
>
> 'Why', the psychologist will then ask, 'is it important to feel really alive?'
>
> 'Because I want to make the most of my life while I'm here to enjoy it,' says the student, thereby defining an aspect of his philosophy of life. (p. 14)

The last statement made by the student seems to be an important rule for him and could be expected to influence his approach to many situations.

When applied to patients in therapy, the objects (or *elements* as they are termed) are often people (mother, father, self, for example) and the terms the patient chooses to distinguish between them are taken as important constructs. Additional elements can then be added — usually individuals important in the patient's life — and each categorized in terms of the previously elicited constructs, to provide a grid (a 'repertory grid').

Figure 8 illustrates how this information can be presented, being the result of a statistical analysis of information obtained from a repertory grid. In this particular case, five elements were elicited — mother, father, sister, self and ideal self (how the patient wishes to be). There were also a number of constructs, including depressed, happy, careful with money. The distance between elements and constructs is taken as a measure of their similarity. Thus, the self is similar to the mother and both are careful about money. By contrast, the sister is quite different,

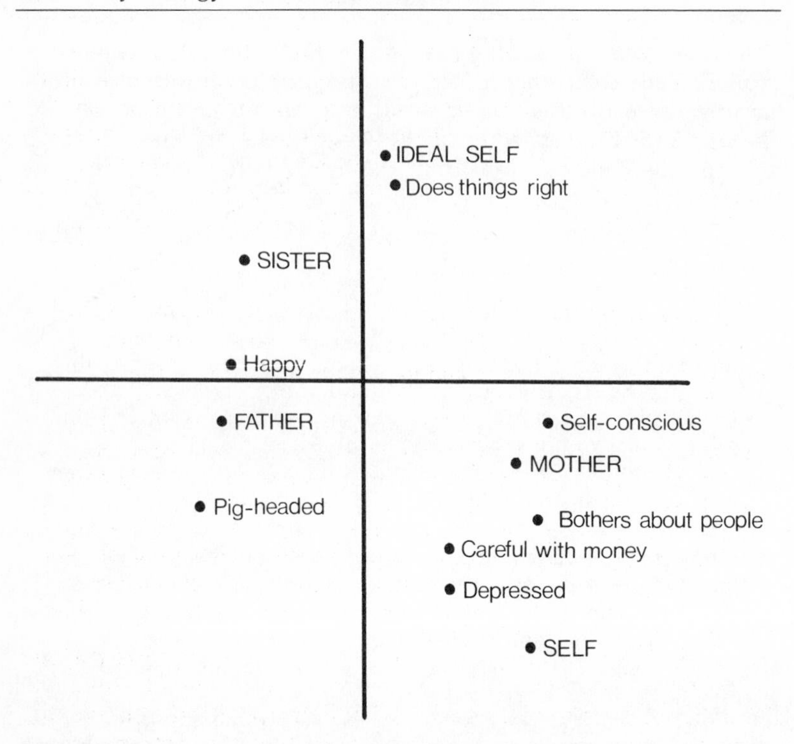

Fig. 8. An example of a repertory grid analysis. (Reproduced from Rowe, D. (1978) *The Experience of Depression*, John Wiley & Sons, by permission.)

being happy rather than depressed and perceived as being more similar to the patient's ideal self than is the patient.

Therapy

This first step then leads to a consideration of how the patient might alter his or her perceptions. Personal change is difficult because change implies an alteration in the way the person sees the world, a frightening and anxiety-provoking prospect. This may be particularly so when 'core' constructs are involved, those that deal specifically with perceptions of the self. The idea in this kind of therapy is to loosen the patient's theories so that new and more helpful ones can be formed. Conversation plays an important part, with the therapist challenging and adding to the patient's constructs, but Kelly advocated more active methods as well. The patient might be encouraged to 'role play', being given a personality sketch of an individual and asked to act as if he were that person for a brief period:

> The client is to eat the kind of food they think this person would eat, read the books they would read, respond to other people in the way in which this person would respond, dream the dreams this person would dream, and try to interpret their experiences entirely in terms of this 'person'. It should be made clear to the client that this is a limited venture and that after a fixed period it will come to an end and they will revert 'to being themselves'. It must be made clear that the fixed role is in no sense being set up as an ideal, it is merely a hypothesis for them to experiment with, a possibility for them to experience. During the short period of fixed role enactment the client sees the therapist frequently to discuss the interpretation of the fixed role, to consider the kind of experiences they are getting and to play the role with the therapist.
>
> At the end of the fixed role enactment it is hoped that the client will have experienced behaviours from people of a kind not likely to have been elicited by their usual 'self'. They will have been forced into a detailed psychological examination of this imaginary person and thereby have been less centred on themselves. Above all, they may have begun to suspect that a person is self-inventing and that they are not necessarily trapped forever inside their own autobiography and their own customary thought and behaviour. (Ref. 16, p. 14)

An appealing aspect of the repertory grid technique is that it can be used to assess the progress and outcome of therapy. The distance between elements and their position relative to constructs might change, for example, so that the 'self' matches the 'ideal self' more closely. Furthermore, the actual constructs elicited by the grid may alter, providing further evidence of change.

Aaron Beck

Kelly's Repertory Grid technique provides a way of making explicit an individual's personal theories about the world. The notion of personal theories is also central to Beck's work, but, unlike Kelly, Beck[17] argues that some theories are better than others, and that 'erroneous' perceptions can be identified. Just as a psychodynamic therapist would argue that no one has a perfect upbringing and that a certain amount of internal conflict is inevitable, Beck contends that everyone operates on some premises that are mistaken and that distort reality. The problem for both the therapist and the patient is to find these premises, examine them, and to make changes if need be. An analogy can be drawn here between the use of rules of grammar and the use of these premises. When talking, people do not consciously form their sentences. They do not have to take care to place the subject before the verb because this rule is so well learned. Similarly, when interpreting a situation, people do not consciously reflect on the rules they use in making sense of that event. But when learning a new language, it is necessary to consider what is being said very carefully, taking time to place the parts of speech in their correct order, for instance. In Beck's therapy, the patient is encouraged to consider the rules he uses: first, to see how premises can be self-defeating, and second, to experiment with new premises that had not been previously considered.

Some of the mistaken assumptions that many people hold include:

1 In order to be happy they have to be successful in whatever they do.
2 If they make an occasional mistake it means they are inept.
3 If they don't take advantage of every opportunity they will regret it later.
4 That their value as people depends on what others think of them.

In particular, Beck has been interested in depression. This difficulty can be seen in many ways (for example, some psychologists consider it to be due to feelings of helplessness learned through lack of success in affecting the environment),[18] but Beck prefers to see it in terms of faulty premises. He suggests that there is a triad of cognitive patterns which forces the person to view events in a particular way. The first component is the pattern of interpreting experiences in a negative way. Life is seen as a series of burdens and obstacles, all of which detract from the quality of life. This cognition is often associated with loss of friends, time or money. The second component involves negative self-perceptions — of being inadequate or unworthy in some way — and is often associated with self-reproach and self-castigation. The third component consists of negative views about the future, which seems unremittingly difficult and full of continuing deprivation. Beck contends that if depressed people are given evidence to illustrate that they can, indeed, attain goals, or if they can be helped to re-evaluate their present performance, their depression will be lessened.[19,20] Some preliminary results suggest that therapy based on this view might be more effective than chemotherapy.[21]

Kelly and Beck represent two examples of the cognitive approach to personality. They both concentrate on the ways that people perceive their environment, but Kelly was more concerned about how these perceptions relate to one another whereas Beck has been interested in what assumptions people make about themselves and their experiences. Much of the therapy based on

Beck's approach is a process of identifying erroneous assumptions, while Kelly encouraged his patients to explore their personal constructs.

Personality tests

This third section of the chapter considers ways of assessing personality. Neither the psychodynamic nor the cognitive theorists have been particularly concerned with *measuring* personality. For them, the interest has been in identifying psychological problems and finding ways to alleviate them. Other psychologists have developed ways of measuring personality in order to predict how different types of people might act in certain situations. Such measures are used in, for example, personnel selection, as well as in research studies — e.g. identifying people who are most susceptible to certain kinds of illness. Although there is a brief description of projective techniques here, most of the research in this area has been conducted using self-report questionnaires and this will form the main discussion.

Projective techniques

Two of the best-known projective tests are the Thematic Apperception Test (TAT) and the Rorschach Inkblot Test. In both instruments the person is presented with vague and ambiguous pictures and asked to describe them. The TAT consists of 20 cards, one of which is actually blank. The examiner asks the person to concoct a story that suggests what led up to the event shown, what is presently occurring, and what the outcome might be. There are no right or wrong descriptions, the assumption being that the way the person makes sense of the pictures is a reflection of personality, aspirations and needs. These are said to be shown through the use of repeated themes. If, for example, an individual often describes the pictures in terms of parent–child relationships, then the relationship with his or her parents might be particularly important for that person. The Rorschach includes 10 inkblots in reds, greens and blacks. People are asked to suggest what the inkblots might represent and the responses are coded in terms of their number and the parts of the inkblot that are included in the description. The actual content is not considered to be so important unless the description is very unusual.

Projective techniques have not been well accepted by psychologists for several reasons. One requirement of a measuring instrument is that observations taken at one time are similar to observations taken at another. In addition, it is important to have agreement between different observers when applying the measure in the same circumstances. The *reliability* of projective techniques is not good since the same description of the TAT or Rorschach materials produces differing interpretations from different examiners. Another important requirement of personality instruments is that they measure what they purport to measure (i.e. underlying personality factors) rather than something else (e.g. what the examiner wants to hear). This is termed *construct validity*. There is evidence that responses on projective techniques are subject to temporary mood changes in the individual: if, for example, people are asked not to eat breakfast before describing the pictures on the TAT, they are more likely to give responses concerning food. Projective techniques seem to be sensitive to transient states as well as to longer-term ones. A further difficulty is that they are not particularly suitable for research purposes. Examiners require long training in order to interpret the responses and even then the materials do not lend themselves easily to numerical assessment. For testing large numbers of people, instruments that can be scored easily and provide data which can be readily analysed using statistical techniques are preferred.

Such difficulties with projective materials have led many psychologists to question their usefulness in assessing personality. On the other hand, it has been argued that they can be helpful in providing a global view of individuals when precise descriptions are not needed. They may, for instance, be useful in opening conversation between a therapist and a patient when the patient is feeling unsure or hesitant.[22,23]

Personality questionnaires

When describing a person, the reader may well use a series of adjectives — honest, shy and hardworking, for example. Someone else might be described as less honest and shy but more outgoing and independent. Such descriptions illustrate that people have everyday ways of understanding personality which not only include adjectives but also scales as well — one individual might be more or less shy than another. Psychologists have systematized this approach in studying personality by attempting to provide instruments which measure the extent to which a person possesses certain characteristics, or traits, and to compare the results with others.

The method of personality assessment that has generated most research is the self-report questionnaire, in which subjects are asked a number of questions about their behaviour or their thoughts, and are given a choice of answers, often a simple 'Yes' or 'No'. The decision about which questions (or items as they are usually called) are included depends on the purpose of the questionnaire. There are three main ways of selecting items..

Observation

First, the items may be suggested through observation. For example, several clinicians have noted that patients with coronary heart disease often have distinctive personalities, characterized by striving for achievement, competitiveness and impatience. This constellation of traits has become known as the Type A personality, as compared to those who do not have these characteristics (known as Type B personalities). Jenkins et al.[24] constructed a number of items from interviews and observations which seemed to tap this distinction, arriving at the Jenkins Activity Survey. In this questionnaire people are given a number of situations (e.g. waiting to be served in a restaurant or post office) and asked how they typically react in them (e.g. a choice between 'accept it calmly', 'feel impatient but do not show it', 'feel so impatient that someone watching could tell that you are restless' and 'refuse to wait, and find ways to avoid such delays').

Criterion groups

Second, items may be selected empirically. Perhaps a researcher aims to distinguish people who belong to different groups, such as those who have been diagnosed as neurotic and those who have not been so diagnosed. The investigator could ask a large number of questions of the people in each group and then subsequently use only those items which a majority of one group answered one way and the other group the other way. These items could then be later used as a diagnostic tool, assuming, of course, that the diagnosis of the original criterion group was a valid and reliable one and that the selection of the original control group was representative of the general population. This empirical approach was used in the development of the Minnesota Multiphasic Personality Inventory (the MMPI) which is widely used in the United States. The MMPI contains 13 scales, each of which is intended to differentiate between various criteria and control groups. The scales include hypochondriasis, depression and social introversion–extraversion. Like the Jenkins Activity Scale, the MMPI is purely descriptive and there is no explanation given why the people in the various groups answer in particular ways or why they came to enter that group in the first place. While some of the items are obvious (e.g. 'I am happy most of the time' is an item on the depression scale), others are less so (e.g. 'It takes a lot of argument to convince most people of the truth' in the same scale). The inclusion of an item is not dependent on being obviously applicable but only on whether or not it discriminates.

An example of how the MMPI could be used in practice is given by a study on reactions of cancer patients to their diagnosis. The questionnaire was given to 133 newly diagnosed patients who were followed up monthly for the next six months. A social worker, who did not know the MMPI results, took several measures of their emotional distress, so that the patients could be divided into those who showed a high degree of emotional distress and those who showed a low degree of distress. The highly distressed group scored higher on several scales of the MMPI, including emphasis on physical complaints, depression, anxiety and withdrawal. About 75 per cent of the patients could be classified as showing high or low distress by the MMPI results gathered six months previously, suggesting that the questionnaire might be used to predict patients' reactions to the diagnosis.[25]

Factor analysis

A third approach to the design of personality questionnaires is based on factor analysis. Essentially, this method involves correlating subjects' answers on one item with their answers on all other items. In some cases the subjects would give similar responses to a group of questions: if they scored high on one they would score high on others. In other cases, the scores on one item would not correlate with scores on others. Each group of items which correlate or cluster together constitute a factor, and this factor is given a label which reflects the kinds of items which were found to cluster together. For example, people might respond to items about their relationship with parents and with friends in similar ways that may be appropriately subsumed under a factor labelled dependency. Factors may be selected to be independent of each other, so that an individual's score on one factor should not be related to his score on others.

In practice, the development of personality questionnaires often involves all three approaches. The Jenkins Activity Survey was first developed on the basis of observations, but later, items found not to discriminate between coronary and non-coronary patients were dropped. In the development of the Maudsley Personality Inventory (and the later versions, the Eysenck Personality Inventory and the Eysenck Personality Questionnaire),[26,27] Eysenck originally chose many items on the basis of observation, factor-analysed them, and finally made adjustments according to the criterion group approach. He suggests that there are three important factors — psychoticism, neuroticism and introversion–extraversion. The Eysenck Personality Questionnaire (EPQ) consists of 90 items, each of which is answered by a 'Yes' or 'No'. The individual's responses are compared to a large sample of others' answers in order to discover how unusual the responses are, so that this questionnaire, like the others mentioned, does not give an absolute measure of personality but simply a relative one. Someone is said to be extraverted, for example, if he or she replies to more of the items in an extraverted way than most other people. The responses of this large sample are called 'norms' and it is important to take account of the characteristics of the normative population when making the comparison: the individual should be similar in age, sex and cultural background to the comparison group. Another feature of this questionnaire, again shared by others, is that psychoticism, neuroticism and extraversion–introversion are considered to be continuous rather than discrete entities. The assumption is that everyone possesses these traits to some extent.

Lie scales

One further aspect of personality questionnaires merits attention. It is important that the examiner has some idea of how honestly and carefully the person has answered the items. For several reasons, people may present a picture of themselves which is not an accurate one but, rather, a picture that is socially desirable. Some people may not want to admit, even to themselves, their foibles and embarrassing thoughts, so that questionnaires often include some indication of how honestly the person is reporting his personality. Most questionnaires include one or more 'Lie' scales, in which questions about common frailties are asked. For example, on the EPQ, questions such as 'Have you ever taken advantage of someone?' are included. If the person answers too many of these kinds of items in a socially desirable way, then the validity of the answers on the other scales is called into question.

Biological explanations for personality

There is a common tendency to use traits to explain behaviour but this is logically incorrect. Traits are inferred from behaviour and cannot, therefore, be used to explain it. For example, if someone behaves in an honest way, people are likely to attribute this behaviour to an underlying trait of honesty. If this person returns some money which he had found, his friends may explain this by saying, 'Well, he returned the money because he is honest'.

This is a tempting mistake to make, one which Eysenck has avoided. He considers the responses on the EPI and EPQ to be strongly influenced by genetic factors. Vulnerability to psychotic behaviour is considered to be inherited,[2] the predisposition becoming apparent in disturbed environments. High scorers on the neuroticism scale (who are easily upset and lack confidence) are thought to have over-reactive autonomic nervous systems, whereas high scorers on the extraversion scale (who are impulsive and sociable) are said to be cortically inhibited.

The attraction of Eysenck's position is that he has attempted to provide an understanding of why people have certain traits rather than simply describing them. There is some evidence that there are biological differences between Type As and Type Bs as well. At admission to hospital, Kahn et al.[28] assessed the personality of patients due to have coronary bypass surgery. During the operation, the Type As were more likely to show rises in systolic and diastolic blood pressure than Type Bs. Since the anaesthetized patients were presumably free from consciously mediated determinants of blood pressure, these results suggest that there are constitutional differences between As and Bs.

Validating personality questionnaires

It may seem that the best way to validate a personality questionnaire is simply to administer and score it and then go back to the individual and ask if the results reflect his or her personality accurately. If the person were to say yes, then the examiner might conclude that the instrument is a valid one. There is a major problem with this approach, however, as shown by a study[29] in which subjects were asked to fill out a questionnaire and then some days later were given a summary of their personalities. They were then asked to evaluate the summary's accuracy, and most thought it was a good description of them. Although the subjects could not know it, all the summaries were the same, containing such vague statements as 'You have a tendency to be critical of yourself' and 'Your sexual adjustment has presented problems for you'. These statements could apply to anyone. Subjects' assessments of accuracy are unlikely, then, to provide a good indication of construct validity (a term mentioned earlier with respect to projective techniques).

Perhaps a better indication of the validity of a personality test would be if it could predict how someone behaves. There are two basic assumptions behind the use of personality questionnaires: (1) that they tap underlying dispositions which are relatively independent of circumstances, and (2) that people act consistently in different situations. If person A is more assertive, aggressive and honest than person B in one situation, then A should be more assertive, aggressive and honest in other situations as well. If a theory is unable to predict how someone will act (i.e. it has little *predictive validity*), then it could be argued that it should be discarded.

Eysenck's theory has met with some success in these respects. In several objective tests (e.g. under experimentally imposed stress) high scorers on the extraversion and neuroticism scales give different results from low scorers. Reactions to analgesics vary along lines similar to those which Eysenck's theory would predict (see Chapter 11) and high scorers on the neuroticism scale are more likely to have complications and to recover less well after surgery than those who score low.[30] Other personality questionnaires which have been designed for specific purposes have also been useful. The Jenkins Activity Survey, for example, has been validated in a prospective study. Over 3000 people were monitored in a long-term study of the correlates of coronary heart disease. Some $8\frac{1}{2}$ years after the initial tests were given, 257 males in the sample who were initially healthy had some kind of heart complaint. Even when serum lipids, blood pressure, obesity and smoking were taken into account, Type A men had over twice the risk of heart disease than Type B men. Of course, many of the Type As did not report heart disease and many Type Bs did, indicating that other factors besides personality were also significant.[31,32]

Limitations of personality tests

However, the relationship between scores on personality tests and observations of behaviour have often been found to be tenuous, correlations being quite low.[33] A similar lack of correspondence between what people say they would do and what they actually do in practice has been found in research on attitudes. Attitudes are said to be general predispositions to respond towards objects or people in positive or negative ways, but they have been found to be poor predictors of behaviour.[34]

Similarly, there is evidence that how a person behaves in one set of circumstances often provides a poor predictor of behaviour in dissimilar situations. Ellsworth et al.[35] asked both the staff of a psychiatric hospital and the patients' family and friends for assessments of patients' behaviour: the way in which they acted in hospital showed little congruence with the ways they acted outside it. Patients who showed improvements in hospital were not necessarily those who were improved once they rejoined the community. Such studies have important implications for medical care. Simply because a patient appears hostile in a hospital or a consulting room may not provide clues as to his or her behaviour elsewhere. As mentioned above, there seems to be a strong tendency for people to cite personality variables as causes of behaviour, a tendency that may often be misplaced.[36] For example, physicians often attribute lack of compliance in their patients to an uncooperative personality, but there are few indications that this provides an accurate assessment of the reasons for their behaviour (see Chapter 13).

Such results have thrown personality and attitude theorists into some disarray. Many psychologists have argued that personality is simply an illusion and advocated rejection of the concept. Although people do act consistently, perhaps this consistency is not due to personality factors but to recurring patterns in the environment. For example, people tend to appear the same over time because their physical appearance changes only slightly and they have many routines they repeat daily. For some of these psychologists it is the consequences of behaviour which are significant and an analysis of these consequences will provide good predictors of how people will act (a possibility discussed in the next chapter). For others, the expectations that people have of behaviour form the important variables: the roles that people play are seen to be of prime importance (see Chapter 6).

Other psychologists have advocated an intermediate position between those who argue that traits are significant (if only the important ones were isolated)[37] and those who argue that the environment is crucial. They suggest that a useful approach is to consider behaviour as influenced by the environment, but also that people choose the situations in which they act and select the significant aspects of the situation upon which to respond. These responses subsequently affect the character and course of these situations. Instead of considering behaviour to be the product of either personality traits or situational determinants, the argument is that they interact, mutually influencing behaviour.[38] This position implies that, as advocated by the cognitive theorists discussed early in this chapter, it is the meaning of each situation that is important, and if psychologists are to predict behaviour, it is these idiosyncratic meanings which need to be explored.

Summary

Three major trends in the study of personality are considered in this chapter, psychodynamic, cognitive and descriptive approaches. Nowadays, a distinction is made between three types of psychological problems: neurosis, psychosis and personality disorders. This scheme implies that a state of normality can be identified, although in practice normality can be defined in many ways.

Although psychodynamic theories have developed significantly since the work of Freud, with greater emphasis on interpersonal relationships rather than considering an individual in isolation, many of his original concepts remain influential. Many psychodynamic theorists believe that normal development can be considered as a series of stages. Each stage places new demands on the individual, many of which are concerned with relationships with others, particularly with parents. Psychological problems are said to arise when these demands are too difficult to cope with. These problems are 'worked through' in psychotherapy, a term encompassing a variety of techniques by which a patient is able to gain insight about his or her feelings. Measuring the success of psychotherapy is problematic because of difficulties in defining what a cure might be. However, some ways of evaluating progress do exist.

While psychodynamic theorists place emphasis on the unconscious, cognitive theorists are more concerned with the conscious workings of the mind. Some, like Kelly, liken people to scientists who try to make sense of and predict events in their everyday lives. Everyone has his or her own theory, which is said to be the individual's personality. Beck believes that psychological problems are associated with certain erroneous beliefs. Treatment consists of helping the patient to identify and correct such beliefs.

Unlike the first two approaches which were developed by therapists through their work with patients, descriptive approaches to personality have been developed for ease of measurement and statistical analysis. Personality questionnaires are composed of statements or items which are selected either by observing differences between groups, identifying differences between groups by research, or through factor-analytic methods. Although these questionnaires often simply describe people as possessing certain traits without explaining why they behave as they do, Eysenck has developed a theory to account for the differences, based on genetic factors. Although these questionnaires have proved useful in identifying individuals who are susceptible to certain types of illness or problems, difficulties in validating questionnaires have led some psychologists to consider the situation in which the behaviour takes place as well as the particular individual.

Suggested reading

Two books which provide introductions to psychotherapy are References 10 and 14.

References

1. American Psychiatric Association (1980) *Diagnostic and Statistical Manual of Mental Disorders*, 3rd edn. Washington: APA.
2. Slater, E. & Cowie, V. (1971) *Genetics of Mental Disorders* London: Oxford University Press.
3. Hirsch, S.R. (1983) Psychosocial factors in the cause and prevention of relapse in schizophrenia. *British Medical Journal* **286**: 1600–1601.
4. Preiss, J.J. (1968) Self and role in medical education. In: C. Gordon and K.J. Gergen (eds.) *The Self in Social Interaction* London: Wiley.
5. Brockman, J., D'Arcy, C. & Edmonds, L. (1979) Facts or artifacts? Changing public attitudes towards the mentally ill. *Social Science and Medicine* **13A**: 673–682.
6. Whatley, C.D. (1959) Social attitudes towards discharged mental patients. *Social Problems* **6**: 313–320.
7. Farina, A. & Ring, K. (1965) The influence of perceived mental illness on interpersonal relations. *Journal of Abnormal Psychology* **70**: 47–51.
8. Fazio, R.H., Effrein, E.A. & Falender, V.J. (1981) Self-perceptions following social interaction. *Journal of Personality and Social Psychology* **41**: 232–242.
9. Sullivan, H.S. (1953) *The Interpersonal Theory of Psychiatry* New York: W.W. Norton.
10. Brown, D. & Pedder, J. (1979) *Introduction to Psychotherapy* London: Tavistock.
11. Whitehorn, J.C. & Betz, B.J. (1954) A study of psychotherapeutic relationships between physicians and schizophrenic patients. *American Journal of Psychiatry* **111**: 321–31.
12. Rogers, C.R. (1967) *On Becoming a Person* London: Constable.
13. Rogers, C.R. & Truax, C.B. (1967) The therapeutic conditions antecedent to change. In: Rogers, C.R. (ed.) *The Therapeutic Relationship and its Impact* Madison: University of Wisconsin Press; © 1967 by the Board of Regents of the University of Wisconsin System.
14. Storr, A. (1979) *The Art of Psychotherapy* London: Secker and Warburg.
15. Raimy, V.C. (1948) Self-reference in counselling interviews. *Journal of Consulting Psychology* **12**: 153–163.
16. Rowe, D. (1978) *The Experience of Depression* Chichester: Wiley.
17. Beck, A.T. (1976) *Cognitive Therapy and the Emotional Disorders* New York: International Universities Press.
18. Garber, J. & Seligman, M. (eds.) (1980) *Human Helplessness: Theory and Applications* New York: Academic Press.
19. Loeb, A., Beck, A.T. & Diggory, J. (1971) Differential effects of success and failure on depressed and non-depressed patients. *Journal of Nervous and Mental Disease* **152**: 106–114.
20. Beck, A.T., Rush, J., Shaw, B. & Emery, G. (1979) *Cognitive Therapy of Depression* London: Wiley.
21. Goldberg, D.(1982) Cognitive therapy of depression. *British Medical Journal* **284**: 143–144.
22. Anastasi, A. (1968) *Psychological Testing*, 3rd edn. London: Macmillan.
23. Cronbach, L.J. (1970) *Essentials of Psychological Testing*, 3rd edn. London: Harper and Row.
24. Jenkins, C.D., Rosenman, R.H. & Friedman, M. (1967) Development of an objective psychological test for the determination of the coronary-prone behaviour pattern in employed men. *Journal of Chronic Diseases* **20**: 371–379.
25. Sobel, H.J. and Worden, J.W. (1979) The MMPI as a predictor of psychosocial adaptation to cancer. *Journal of Consulting and Clinical Psychology* **47**: 716–724.

26. Eysenck, J.H. (1952) *The Scientific Study of Personality* London: Routledge and Kegan Paul.
27. Eysenck, J.H. & Eysenck, S. (1976) *Psychoticism as a Dimension of Personality* London: Hodder and Stoughton.
28. Kahn, J.P., Kornfeld, D.S., Frank, K.A., Heller, S.S. & Horr, P.F. (1980) Type A behaviour and blood pressure during coronary artery bypass surgery. *Psychosomatic Medicine* **42**: 407–414.
29. Forer, B.R. (1949) The fallacy of personality validation: A classroom demonstration of gullibility. *Journal of Abnormal and Social Psychology* **44**: 118–123.
30. Mathews, A. & Ridgeway, V. (1981) Personality and surgical recovery. *British Journal of Clinical Psychology* **20**: 243–260.
31. Rosenman, R.H., Brand, R.J., Jenkins, C.D., Friedman, M., Straus, R. & Wurm, M. (1975) Coronary heart disease in the Western Collaborative Group Study. *Journal of the American Medical Association* **233**: 872–877.
32. Dembroski, T.M. & MacDougall, J.M. (1982) Coronary-prone behaviour, social psycho-physiology and coronary heart disease. In: J.R. Eiser (ed.) *Social Psychology and Behavioural Medicine* Chichester: Wiley.
33. Mischel, W. (1973) Towards a cognitive social learning reconceptualisation of personality. *Psychological Review* **80**: 252–283.
34. Wicker, A.W. (1969) Attitudes versus actions. *Journal of Social Issues* **25**: 41–78.
35. Ellsworth, R.B., Foster, L., Childers, B., Arthur, G. & Kroeker, D. (1968) Hospital and community adjustment as perceived by psychiatric patients, their families and staff. *Journal of Consulting and Clinical Psychology, Monograph Supplement* **32**.
36. Ross, L. (1977) The intuitive psychologist and his shortcomings: Distortions in the attribution process. In: L. Berkowitz, (ed.) *Advances in Experimental Social Psychology 10* New York: Academic Press.
37. Bem, D.J. & Allen, A. (1974) On predicting some of the people some of the time. *Psychological Review* **81**: 506–520.
38. Endler, N.S. & Magnusson, D. (1976) *Interactional Psychology and Personality* London: Wiley.

3

The Behavioural Approach

Introduction

The previous chapter discussed three trends in personality research — psychodynamic, trait and cognitive theories. Common to all three approaches is the notion that 'personality *is* something and *does* something . . . . It is what lies *behind* specific acts and *within* the individual' (Ref. 1, p. 48). Behaviour was considered to be an outward manifestation of inner drives, traits or cognitions. Unusual or maladaptive behaviour would therefore reflect an underlying problem, only 'signalling' the real difficulty. Although theorists in this tradition have become increasingly concerned with environmental influences on behaviour, the focus of interest has been on individual differences and inner predispositions to behave in certain ways.

Some psychologists were dissatisfied with the personality approach, arguing that the postulated inner states that were said to underly behaviour could never be understood scientifically. They found that when the symptom alone was treated, only infrequently did the patient return with another manifestation of a problem: little evidence was found for symptom substitution. Although the psychodynamic approach implied that deviant behaviour was in some way fundamentally different from normal behaviour, and the experiences involved in normal development differed from those of abnormal development, the approach advocated by the psychologists discussed in the present chapter implied the opposite: that behaviour which could be considered unusual or maladaptive was acquired in the same way as other, more desirable, behaviour. Instead of developing principles in clinical settings with small samples of patients and uncontrolled case studies, they argued, the science of psychology should be firmly based in the laboratory. Only experimental studies could be used critically to evaluate the validity of a theory or the efficacy of a therapy.

Some of the studies mentioned in this chapter are based on experiments with non-human animals, such as rats and pigeons, in artificial laboratory situations, such as learning to press a lever in order to gain a drink or a pellet of food. The reader may feel that this work provides a poor basis for forming conclusions about how humans learn, with their greater ability to understand and interpret situations. Simply because rats seem to learn in a certain way does not necessarily mean people learn in the same way. What similarities could there be between pressing a lever and studying for an exam?

There are several answers to such criticisms. First, the use of lower animals in experiments means that some of the ethical problems involved in experimenting with humans can be overcome. Just as society considers it more acceptable to test drugs first on rats before trying them out on humans, so too is it more accepting towards keeping rats hungry or thirsty or giving them electric shocks. It seems likely that many of the methods which can be used to alleviate human distress described in this chapter would not have been discovered if only human subjects had been used. (Of course, many people in our society argue that animals should not be used for any kind of experimentation.)

A second reply to this criticism is empirical: many of the principles and theories developed through work with rats do seem to apply to humans as well. However dissimilar humans and non-humans may be, there are also many similarities. For psychologists, the term 'learning' is used in a wide sense, applying to many kinds of adaptive changes. The argument is that, in principle, there is little difference between lever-pressing and studying, since they result in consequences that aid the organism. In the first case it is food to relieve hunger, whereas in the second a pass mark provides a qualification that, in turn, might lead to a job.

The first part of this chapter examines approaches where behaviour and behavioural difficulties are considered to be due to environmental influences rather than intrapsychic variables. In chronological order, the respondent (or classical) model, the instrumental (or operant) model and the observational model have been suggested as ways of explaining how the environment influences behaviour. Most recently, these theories have been expanded to include cognitions. Applications from these theories are termed behaviour therapy or behaviour modification to distinguish them from psychotherapies that involve techniques based on the personality theories of the previous chapter (but note that some writers use the term psychotherapy to include behavioural treatments). These behaviour therapies are relevant because they may be used by clinical psychologists who form part of the paramedical services increasingly associated with general practitioners and hospitals.

Clinical psychologists have much to offer to the medical profession, often being able to help doctors who either do not have the time or the expertise to apply the therapies outlined in this chapter. For instance, Koch[2] describes how he used these approaches on 30 patients who had been referred by a general practitioner. All the patients (who suffered from a variety of problems including psychosomatic disorders, anxiety, smoking, drinking and eating disorders) were seen at the surgery. Before the intervention, these patients made an average of 9.27 consultations (as opposed to the practice's average of 3.31) in the year before referral, but in the year after treatment this dropped to 5.46 and the repeat prescription rate for psychotropic drugs also dropped significantly. Although some of this improvement could have been due to spontaneous recovery, it seemed as though contact with clinical psychology services considerably reduced the demand made by these patients for general practitioner time.

Respondent conditioning

Pavlov's experiments

The origins of the respondent or classical conditioning approach are considered to lie with Pavlov (1849–1936), a Russian physiologist who studied the digestive system of dogs. He used the concept of a 'reflex' to describe the unlearned and predictable response of producing saliva and stomach digestive juices when food was tasted. All reflexes (others include withdrawal from a painful stimulus and eye-blinking in response to a puff of wind) were thought to have adjustment or protective purposes. He noticed that after several feedings his dogs would begin salivating not only at the taste of food but also at the sight of food and even at the sight of the handler who regularly fed them. It seemed as though a connection or association had been made between the sight of food (and the handler) and salivation. He called salivation in this instance a conditioned reflex, because its occurrence was conditional upon a prior association between seeing the food and tasting it.

Pavlov hypothesized that many such associations could be learned, and performed several experiments to test the limits of this prediction. Typically, a stimulus that the animal was likely to notice but that had no prior association with salivation was presented – a light, for example. This stimulus was then followed closely in time by food, which normally elicited salivation. Several pairings, or acquisition trials, were conducted in this way. In order to test for the presence of an association, the light was turned on but no food presented: if salivation occurred, a conditioned reflex had been formed. Pavlov showed that many previously neutral stimuli could come to elicit salivation, even though the response may be somewhat weaker (fewer drops of saliva) compared to the original unconditioned stimulus (the food). The more pairings made, the more similar did the conditioned reflex become to the unconditioned one (i.e. the quantity of saliva increased). After a period of time, the response to the conditioned stimulus alone became progressively weaker. Gradually, fewer and fewer drops of saliva were elicited by the light. These trials are known as *extinction* trials. Pavlov came to view the learning of associations between unconditioned and conditioned stimuli as the fundamental building-block of all behaviour, contending that all learning could be reduced to associations between unlearned reflexes and previously neutral stimuli.

Behaviourism

Although Pavlov's results were important in their own right, perhaps his greatest influence has been in providing a method of studying *behaviour,* as distinct from inner thoughts, images and imagination. An important debate at the turn of the century was between those philosophers and psychologists who thought that man's inner life was the proper area of study and those who disputed this, arguing that these inner states could never be scientifically validated or measured. It was impossible, they claimed, to know if one person has the same image of an event as another person, or to prove that such images exist at all. The only way anything could be discovered about people was from their behaviour; everything else is inferred. Taking classical physics as their model, these psychologists wanted to find mathematical equations that could predict how someone would behave in a given situation. It was behaviour which was important, not the subjective feelings of an individual. This school of thought came to be known as *behaviourism.*

Pavlov's experiments explored many questions consistent with behaviourism. For example, did the timing of presentation of the unconditioned and conditioned stimuli affect the strength of the conditioned reflex? Or, can an animal learn to discriminate between two very similar stimuli? However important the answers to these questions might be, the exciting prospect for psychologists was that they could be answered at all. Unanswerable questions about inaccessible thoughts need not be considered. Here was a method for understanding how an animal adapts to its environment during its lifetime — a contribution that seemed as important as Darwin's.

Perhaps the best-known example of the application of his methods to the study of human learning is provided by Watson and Raynor[3] in their study of an 11-month-old boy called Albert and a white rat. Originally, Albert was shown the rat: he seemed interested in it and wanted to play with it, showing no obvious aversive behaviour towards the animal. Although it may be proper to question the ethics of this study, Watson and Raynor showed how a fear of situations could be learned. They did this by pairing a loud noise (a hammer striking a steel bar) with presentation of the rat, so that each time Albert saw the rat he would also hear the unpleasant noise. Very quickly (after six trials) Albert's behaviour changed: he began to show distress at the sight of the rat in the absence of the noise. Further, the distressful behaviour seemed to generalize to other objects similar in appearance to the rat, so that white rabbits, cotton wool and fur coats also elicited the distress. Thus, stimuli that had a similar physical appearance to the original conditioned stimulus also elicited the fear response, a phenomenon termed *generalization*.

Owing to experiments such as this, the classical conditioning model and the behaviourist perspective gained many adherents. Although conditioned fear responses could not always be shown to be learned in this way,[4] it was argued that many fears could be the result of conditioning. Classical conditioning can also be used to explain a wide range of behaviours besides fear, such as the anticipatory nausea and emesis shown by some cancer patients given chemotherapy. Chemotherapy often has the side-effect of inducing nausea and vomiting, a problem which had been recognized for some time. Recently, clinicians have become aware that many patients experience these side-effects prior to their visit to the hospital. Environmental events associated with the treatment (e.g. the waiting-room or the drive to the hospital) can become conditioned stimuli for the nausea and vomiting. About 45 per cent of cancer chemotherapy patients experience anticipatory nausea, with about 18 per cent actually vomiting before their appointment.[5]

Treatments based on respondent conditioning

This approach to psychological difficulties considers it unnecessary to examine a patient's personality or to discover any unconscious conflicts that might have led him or her into difficulty. Instead, principles discovered and validated in the laboratory such as extinction, generalization and the pairing of conditioned and unconditioned stimuli would be employed. Several methods have been developed within this orientation, including aversion therapy, flooding and systematic desensitization.

Aversion therapy

This kind of therapy is designed to reduce the frequency of behaviour that is considered undesirable. The idea is to pair the undesired behaviour with a noxious stimulus, thus making the behaviour unpleasant and likely to be avoided, just as little Albert avoided the white rat. Any aversive stimulus could be paired with any undesired behaviour in theory, but in practice there are cultural and methodological constraints. A particular behaviour may become more or less acceptable depending on current social values and knowledge. In the 1960s and early 1970s homosexuality was considered undesirable and there are many papers in the literature from this time exploring the effect of aversion therapy on homosexuals. But as this sexual practice has become more acceptable fewer reports have been published. Conversely, smoking has only been viewed as undesirable in recent years, reflected by an increase in the number of studies attempting to modify this behaviour.

The ethics of aversion therapy have played an important role in the reluctance of many psychologists to use this technique. It is not always clear why someone seeks therapy for a problem. Many of the people who seek assistance for socially unacceptable difficulties only do so after they have been detained by law or have been isolated by family and society. It is important to question whether it is reasonable to subject patients to aversive stimuli for the sake of society rather than the individual. Given the cultural relativity of many behaviours, psychologists are often unwilling to pursue this kind of treatment.

An interesting form of aversion therapy that reduces this ethical problem somewhat is covert sensitization, in which the patient is asked to imagine the aversive stimulus, rather than experience it. There is evidence that this approach is effective. An example of the technique is the following, used in the treatment of an obese woman with a particular liking for apple pie:

> I want you to imagine you've just had your main meal and you are about to eat your dessert, which is apple pie. As you are about to reach for the fork, you get a funny feeling in the pit of your stomach. You start to feel queasy, nauseous, and sick all over. As you touch the fork, you can feel food particles inching up your throat. You're just about to vomit. As you put the fork into the pie, the food comes up into your mouth. You try to keep your mouth closed because you are afraid that you'll spit the food out all over

> the place. You bring the piece of pie to your mouth. As you're about to open your mouth, you puke; you vomit all over your hands, the fork, over the pie. It goes all over the table, over the other people's food. Your eyes are watering. Snot and mucus are all over your mouth and nose. Your hands feel sticky. There is an awful smell. As you look at this mess you just can't help but vomit again and again until just watery stuff is coming out. Everybody is looking at you with shocked expressions. You turn away from the food and immediately start to feel better. You run out of the room and, as you run out, you feel better and better. You wash and clean yourself up, and it feels wonderful. (Ref. 6, p. 462)

Flooding

This is another technique which uses the classical conditioning model. The approach is based on the possibility that once fears and phobias are learned they are not extinguished because patients never place themselves in the fear-eliciting situation again. For example, a person who is afraid of the dark will avoid dark places and thus the strength of the response will not diminish. Therapists who use flooding encourage patients to confront the situation repeatedly until they discover that dark places (or spiders or snakes) are not really all that frightening.

Sreenivasan et al.[7] report the effects of flooding on a young girl who had been extremely fearful of dogs for about five years. The fear did not lessen in response to other kinds of therapy and flooding seemed justified in this case. A passive and friendly dog was chosen and taken off the leash while the girl was in the room:

> For the first session, Colleen was apprehensive for several hours before. On arrival in the treatment room she was anxiously scanning the area for the dog. When the dog was led in she froze, visibly paled and her pupils were dilated. Staff talked reassuringly to Colleen, but when the dog was freed she jumped on a chair. She cried and pleaded that the dog should be placed on its leash. Gradually she relaxed slightly but stayed on the chair, becoming anxious and entreating if the dog moved towards the chair. Two of the staff played table tennis and tried unsuccessfully to persuade Colleen to join them. In the second session she was equally anxious but would get down from the chair or table she stood on for a few seconds but was never at ease. Prior to the third session Colleen appeared excited, although she expressed fear and dislike of the sessions. She managed to take part in the table tennis game for brief periods, sitting on the table if the dog ambled towards the table. In the fourth session she could pat the dog if it was not facing her. In the sixth session she tolerated the dog in her lap, and then took the dog for a walk holding the leash to the amazement of her parents who happened to arrive. After this, she was able to

> take the family pet for a walk and then to go for a drive with the puppy in the car. (Ref. 7, pp. 257–258)

After only six sessions of about an hour each her fears appeared to subside, as measured by the therapist and subjectively validated by the girl herself. Further, she was no longer troubled by thoughts about dogs attacking her and was now doing well in school. Although flooding was effective in this case, systematic desensitization (discussed next) is generally preferred because it is less stressful for the patient.

Systematic desensitization

Whereas flooding involves long periods of intense experience with the feared object, systematic desensitization (or SD) involves a gradual approach to the feared object. Developed by Wolpe,[8] it may best be described by outlining a case study of a patient who had a phobia about visiting the dentist.[9] This 32-year-old man had been taken to the dentist at the age of 5 or 6 but tried to flee from the office. At 8 years of age, he refused to have any dental work done and at 18 he had one filling and then refused to return. Later, after a toothache lasting three weeks, he finally went to a dentist who placed him under a general anaesthetic. Several teeth were removed and several restorations completed at this time. Over the next 12 years or so he suffered repeated toothaches but had not seen a dentist.

During SD, the patient was seen by a therapist for nine sessions of one hour each. At the first session his history was taken and the therapist began to give relaxation training. The idea behind this training is that anxiety is associated with physiological arousal — high heart rate, muscular tension and sweating. If a patient could be taught to relax, these signs of arousal could be reduced and anxiety alleviated. The most common method for teaching relaxation is called progressive muscle relaxation. The patient is asked to sit in a comfortable reclining chair. The therapist then asks the patient first to tense and then relax the major muscle groups in the body. This often starts with the toes, progressing through the ankles, calves, thighs, and so on. Slow and controlled breathing with the eyes shut is finally achieved. The exercise takes 15–25 minutes to complete and for most people it results in a general feeling of calm and relaxation, a feeling very different from that engendered by anxiety. The patient would be asked to remain in this state for a further 10 minutes or so. After several training sessions people can generally relax themselves fairly quickly without the therapist's instructions. In the second session, further relaxation training was given to this patient and he was

Table 2. Hierarchy of patient's fears from least (1) to most (13) feared situations. Reproduced from Gale, E.N. and Ayer, W.A. (1969) *Journal of the American Dental Association* **78**, 1306. Reprinted by permission.

1	Thinking about going to the dentist
2	Getting in your car to go to the dentist
3	Calling for an appointment with the dentist
4	Sitting in the waiting room of the dentist's office
5	Having the nurse tell you it's your turn
6	Getting in the dentist's chair
7	Seeing the dentist lay out his instruments, one of which is a probe
8	Having a probe held in front of you while you look at it
9	Having a probe placed on the side of a tooth
10	Having a probe placed in a cavity
11	Getting an injection in your gums on one side
12	Having your teeth drilled and worrying that the anaesthetic will wear off
13	Getting two injections, one on each side.

asked to list his fears about the restoration of his teeth. These fears were ordered in a hierarchy, as shown in Table 2. The least anxiety-provoking situation was thinking about going to the dentist, while the worst was receiving two injections, one on each side. In the third session relaxation training was completed.

The next six sessions were devoted to pairing the relaxation with the items in the hierarchy. In SD this is done by asking the patient first to relax as fully as possible. He is then requested to visualize the situations which he finds frightening, starting with the least frightening one. Whenever he begins to feel anxious, the therapist instructs him to stop thinking about the situation and concentrate again on the relaxation. By pairing relaxation with the image, the situation begins to lose its anxiety-provoking properties. When the patient can visualize the least frightening situation without feeling anxious, he moves on to the next step of the hierarchy. This is repeated until he can think of the most frightening situation without anxiety. SD was very successful with this particular patient. Just before the ninth session, he made and kept an appointment with a dentist. Afterwards, all dental treatment was completed and he found the experience 'relaxing'.

Instrumental conditioning

Pavlov argued that learning comes about because events happen to occur at about the same time and these become associated within the organism. But this point of view neglects the fact that animals often actively explore their environment and appear to make attempts to influence events. They are active operators as well as passive recipients and rarely wait for a stimulus to occur. It was the recognition of the importance of this aspect of behaviour that led psychologists in the 1930s to explore another area of learning.

This approach has come to be known as instrumental or operant learning. According to this viewpoint, it is the consequences of behaviour which determine what an animal will do. When a positive consequence occurs, the animal is more likely to repeat the behaviour; if the consequences are negative, it is less likely to repeat it. Usually, the behaviour is random in the first instance.

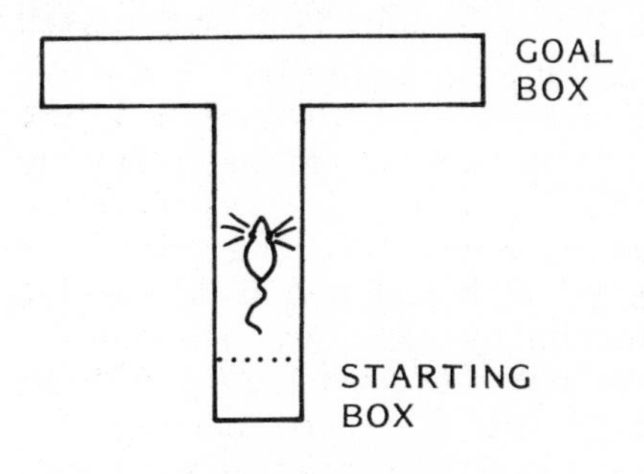

Fig. 9. A T-maze.

For example, a rat running through a T-maze (Fig. 9) is equally likely to turn right or left as it runs up from the starting box. But when it happens to turn right, it finds food, and if it is hungry this is a gratifying result. In time, it will learn that a right turn results in food and will turn that way more often. The speed of learning would be affected by the intensity of the rat's hunger (which could be manipulated by denying it access to food for a specified time) and by the amount of food it would find.

Reinforcement

The food in this example is called a *reinforcer*, a concept that plays an important part in understanding operant behaviour. A reinforcer could be any experience (food, water, praise) which increases the probability of a behaviour. If the reader has attempted to train a dog by giving the animal biscuits when the desired behaviour is shown, positive reinforcement has been used. By giving a biscuit when a stick is retrieved, for example, the dog is more likely to fetch the stick again. Similarly, if the reader has been rewarded in any way for behaviour in the past (e.g. relieving a headache by taking an Aspirin) operant conditioning could be said to have occurred. Any relief of the headache would make it more likely that Aspirin would be taken again on another occasion. B.F. Skinner, a leading proponent of operant learning, has written extensively about the ways that the principle of reinforcement can be applied to humans, notably in his novel about the utopia *Walden Two*.[10]

Reinforcers can be positive or negative. In the case of a positive reinforcer, *presentation* increases the probability of a response, whereas the *removal* of a negative reinforcer increases the chance that a response will occur. A hungry rat will learn to press a bar in order to obtain food through positive reinforcement if, when the bar is pressed, food arrives. The rat will also learn to press the bar through negative reinforcement, if an aversive stimulus like an electric shock is terminated by bar-pressing. An everyday example of this is a mother picking up a crying infant. If the baby stops crying when picked up, the probability of the mother repeating the same behaviour increases since the cessation of the baby's crying is reinforcing. Punishment is not the same as negative reinforcement. Technically, punishment is an event that *reduces* the probability of behaviour. This can occur when a positive event is withdrawn (e.g. a parent might refuse to allow a child to watch a favourite TV programme when he has been badly behaved) or when an aversive stimulus is presented (e.g. a parent might reprimand a child).

Reinforcers can also be primary or secondary. Primary reinforcers are those which satisfy basic biological needs, such as hunger or thirst. Secondary reinforcers are events that have become rewarding through their association with primaries. Money is an obvious example: cash will increase the probability of behaviour not because it is innately reinforcing, but because people have learned that they can satisfy their needs with it. It then takes on reinforcing characteristics of its own.

Treatments based on instrumental conditioning

Operant learning procedures thus gave psychologists another powerful tool for predicting and changing behaviour. The theory suggested that, by discovering the reinforcement contingencies involved in maladaptive behaviour, it would be possible to change these contingencies and substitute more appropriate reinforcement patterns. For example, some children become disruptive, disturbing classes at school and being difficult to control at home. Although many children do this occasionally, constant disruption is a problem for teachers and parents and, in the long run, for the children themselves. Some children become very isolated, refusing to take part in social play and preferring to stay on their own. Again, although such behaviour is sometimes desirable, prolonged isolation from others may be considered maladaptive.

Where a psychotherapist might see the children and their families in such cases for verbal psychotherapy, a behaviour therapist using the operant model might confront such difficulties directly, first observing the child's behaviour and the behaviour of others around him. The aim would be to discover the frequency of the problem behaviour and its function: the context in which it occurs and the reactions it evokes from others. For example, whenever one particular child sat alone, teachers talked to him and showed concern but whenever he joined the other children his contact with the teachers lessened. Effectively, the teachers were punishing the child's social behaviour by withdrawing the social reinforcements he received when alone. When this was pointed out, they stopped rewarding seclusion and began to reward co-operation with other children. As a result, the child's tendency to play alone lessened and he began to play with the other children.[11]

This study illustrates several important features of operant behaviour therapy. First, there is the functional analysis of the behaviour to be modified, depending upon careful observation and description. Behaviour must be described in very specific terms and small steps towards the desired (or target) behaviours rewarded. Second, the reinforcers must be chosen to suit each individual, since what might be reinforcing for one person might be aversive to another. If a person is particularly fond of a food, that food may be a suitable reinforcer: if he or she chooses to sit on a particular chair whenever possible, an opportunity to do so is a reinforcer. Parents use this regularly. Since children often play when they have the opportunity, play can be used as a reward, as in 'if you finish your supper you can go out and play'.

Once the target behaviours and the reinforcers appropriate to the individual case are chosen, the treatment procedures can be started. Generally, positive aspects of behaviour are emphasized by the introduction of the reinforcers at the appropriate times. Decreasing the probability of undesirable behaviour is a secondary consideration. Coercive procedures (e.g. threats) are rarely used, and undesirable behaviour is left to extinguish. Besides, if positive behaviour is being produced, there is less time available for undesirable behaviour and this kind of behaviour is effectively punished since it delays the availability of positive reinforcements.

Punishment *per se* has its effects on behaviour, however, and has been used in extreme circumstances. Lang and Melamed[12] describe a case in which a 9-month-old child was vomiting persistently, weighing only 12 lb. When various physical and psychological treatments were unable to discover the cause or alleviate the problem, punishment was used. In an attempt to save the child's life, an electric shock was administered to the infant's leg when he was about to vomit. This treatment had quick and dramatic effects: the vomiting ceased almost immediately and the child began to gain weight.

Shaping

When attempting to make complex changes in behaviour, a procedure called *shaping* is used. Horner and Keilitz[13] describe how they used shaping to teach people with severe intellectual impairments how to brush their teeth. Toothbrushing involves a complex series of behaviours which can be a formidable task for them, although it is relatively easy for most people. Horner and Keilitz first videotaped a person skilled at brushing his teeth. This allowed them to analyse the task closely and from this tape they identified several small steps:

1 Pick up and hold the toothbrush.
2 Wet the toothbrush.
3 Remove the cap of the toothpaste.
4 Apply the toothpaste to brush.
5 Replace the cap on the toothpaste.

Steps 6 to 15 involved brushing parts of the mouth, rinsing the toothbrush and putting the equipment away. The teaching of each of these steps was accomplished by giving rewards. When the patient picked up and held the toothbrush, for example, he or she was praised or given tokens which could be later exchanged for sugarless gum, and was therefore more likely to repeat this action again. When this learning was accomplished, the next step was taught: rewards were given only when the toothbrush was wetted. These two pieces of behaviour were then *chained* together so that the reward was given only when the patient both picked up the toothbrush and wetted it. Then the next step was taught. This procedure was followed until the whole series of actions could be accomplished. Brushing one's teeth might form only a small part of an overall programme of self-care which might also include such skills as dressing, eating with utensils, and so forth.

Compliance

These operant techniques have gained wide acceptance amongst clinical psychologists. They can be adapted to fit individual cases and provide reasonably clear guidelines about how to perform therapy. There is an increasing interest in their application to encourage patients to follow their doctor's advice. Compliance with medical instructions is surprisingly low and is considered in detail in Chapter 13. An operant analysis can be used to enhance compliance as outlined by Zifferblatt.[14] He argues that whether or not a patient follows advice is a function of the environmental events which immediately precede and follow the prescribed behaviour. If the patient can feel or observe that 'this is the time to take my medication' easily and unambiguously, compliance would tend to be high. A headache or an upset stomach, for example, would provide these clues. If, however, there is no obvious signal the probability of compliance would be low. This could occur if a drug is given as a preventive measure: by the time the patient realizes medication is necessary it is already too late. The events which follow the prescribed behaviour are also seen as significant. If taking medication is followed by pleasant consequences, for example pain relief, it is likely to occur. If there are no immediate and pleasant consequences, then the probability of following advice would be low. An individual on a weight-reducing diet may find it difficult because any loss of weight will occur in the long term; in the short term the consequences are unpleasant. Thus Zifferblatt argues that compliance can be increased if the signals are made explicit and unambiguous (perhaps by using a buzzer) and by providing rewards (perhaps money) when the medications themselves are not intrinsically pleasant. An example of the application of these principles is given by a study on haemodialysis patients. Each time their weight or potassium level was within acceptable standards, they were given coupons that could be redeemed for such rewards as a shorter dialysis session, forgoing a complete dialysis session or purchasing material goods. Over the seven-week study, the patients' weights changed in the desired direction.[15]

Biofeedback

Biofeedback is another technique that can be considered in terms of operant conditioning principles, in that a person is rewarded each time a certain behaviour is shown. The important distinction is that this required behaviour is internal rather than external: lower muscular tension, for example, rather than pressing a lever. The internal behaviour is monitored and rewards are given to people via lights or tones, which reflect changes in the internal behaviour. Biofeedback thus provides a way of controlling certain internal states.

The technique has aroused considerable interest. It has indicated that some functions that had previously been thought to be autonomic (e.g. heart rate, blood pressure) can be controlled through higher-level processes. This implies that a patient with, say, high blood pressure might be helped to lower it without the use of drugs. Since there is concern about placing people on hypertensive drugs indefinitely, biofeedback provides an attractive alternative. Kristt and Engel[16] studied a few patients whose high blood pressure had required doctors' care for the previous ten years. The patients were asked to control their systolic blood pressure — sometimes they were asked to lower it, sometimes to raise it. Keeping a light illuminated provided the patients with the information that they were exerting control. All patients were able to alter their systolic blood pressure, some more effectively than others. Kristt and Engel also took measures several months later and found that the effects of biofeedback were not transient.

There are several methodological problems with many studies of biofeedback, including the study discussed above. In order to say that the effects are directly attributable to biofeedback, there would need to be a control group of subjects who were treated in exactly the same way as the 'treatment' group (hooked up to the biofeedback equipment, asked to concentrate on the light, and so forth), but whose feedback was not contingent on changes in internal state. If no such placebo control groups were used, any beneficial effects might have resulted from some other aspect of the therapy sessions, such as concentrating on the light or being hooked up to the apparatus. Biofeedback is often used in conjunction with relaxation techniques similar to those mentioned earlier under systematic desensitization, and there are some encouraging results.[15]

In summary, the instrumental approach to learning emphasizes the active, exploring nature of animals, including man. The consequences of behaviour determine subsequent actions, such that when a positive consequence occurs as a result of someone's action, this action is likely to be repeated, whereas if the consequences are negative or neutral the probability of this behaviour occurring again will tend to decrease. This approach has been used with much success in a wide variety of situations, such as helping mentally handicapped people, in understanding patient non-compliance, and in biofeedback.

Observational learning

A type of learning which neither the classical nor the operant approach explains adequately is observational learning. Albert

Bandura was interested in the fact that people were able to repeat a performance, often without error, when there was no obvious reinforcement for this learning provided to the subject. Even when children in one study were not informed in advance that correct imitations would be rewarded, as much learning was displayed as when incentives were promised.[17]

There are several reports of dolphins and chimpanzees also learning in this way. For example, chimps raised in psychologists' homes have been seen to sit at typewriters striking the keys and to apply lipstick in front of a mirror without prior tutoring.[18] Particularly charming are the descriptions of dolphins kept in zoos, who often imitate their handlers' behaviour. For example, just as divers use scrapers to remove algae growth from their tanks, dolphins have been known to grasp loose tiles in their mouths and to scrape the viewports of the tanks. They have also been seen to release air bubbles, just like the divers. There are many examples of such learning in humans. For instance, much of the learning involved in becoming a member of a profession involves observation. Watching a consultant during his or her rounds provides much information for a medical student about behaviour with patients.

It may be the case that imitation is in itself pleasurable and so external rewards or punishments are not necessary for learning. Another explanation is that the observer expects to be treated in a similar way to the person watched, so there is 'vicarious' reinforcement. For example, children in one study viewed aggressive behaviour that was sometimes rewarded and sometimes punished. When given an opportunity to imitate, the children acted as if vicarious reinforcement were taking place: those who saw aggression rewarded tended to be aggressive whereas those who saw it punished showed no imitative behaviour.[19] Other studies have indicated that when a prohibited behaviour is not punished, it is as if it were rewarded, since imitation increases in this circumstance.

Treatments based on observational learning

The emphasis in this kind of social learning is on the importance of models, their behaviour and the consequences of their behaviour. Extensive research has been conducted in various situations on the characteristics of models which are effective in encouraging imitation (high prestige and similarity to the observer are important), on how the modelling should be accomplished (e.g. phobic patients benefit more from watching initially fearful models gradually overcoming their fear than initially confident models), and on how this type of learning could be used clinically. The latter has resulted in two important techniques: the use of models in helping patients cope with anxieties (such as phobias and hospitalization) and social skills training.

Coping with anxieties

The idea behind the use of observational learning in treating anxieties and phobias is that behaviour which the observer has previously regarded as hazardous in some way is repeatedly shown, under various circumstances, to be safe. Through vicarious reinforcement, the observer is encouraged to perform the actions that he had previously shunned. Someone with a phobia about snakes, for example, is more likely to approach snakes after seeing a model handle one without negative consequences. A variation of this method is participant modelling, which involves the therapist first modelling the desired behaviour and then the patient repeating the performance, at his own pace, until imitation is achieved. This combination of modelling and participation seems particularly effective.

More relevant here perhaps is one study that has used the technique to help patients cope with their fears of medical treatment. Some methods for assisting the patient in hospital were discussed in Chapter 1, and the idea of peer-modelling was mentioned there: children who watched a realistic film of another child receiving an injection were able to cope with the procedure better than children who watched an unrealistic film or who saw no film. Similar research has been conducted on admission to hospital and surgery.[20] Films were shown to children between 4 and 12 years of age, who were about to enter hospital for surgery (e.g. tonsillectomy). None of the children had been in hospital previously and two groups of children were matched for sex, age, race and type of operation. One group saw a film of a child who hesitated before entering hospital, who showed some anxiety during the admission procedure and who talked with the surgeon and anaesthetist about what to expect. After waking in the recovery room, he regained his composure as he prepared to go home. He talked about his feelings about his stay, as did other children in the hospital playroom. The uncomfortable aspects of the operation were balanced by a rewarding atmosphere, with medical staff and the mother on hand to give comfort and support. The model was given a present after the operation and was shown leaving the same way as he arrived, which included carrying his toy dog, Ruffy. The control children were also shown a film but it was not related to hospitals. This film, about a fishing trip, controlled for length of time, interest value and a peer model coping with a new experience. Several measures were taken, including the palmar sweat index (a measure of emotional factors) and observers' ratings of anxiety (as shown by crying and trembling hands). On both these measures, the children who were able to observe a model go through the hospital procedure and arrive safely home again showed better adjustment both just before the operation and after it (some 3 to 4 weeks later). Results such as these indicate that modelling is a powerful procedure in helping patients to overcome their anxieties about medical care.

Social skills training (SST)

SST has been used with considerable success with people whose relationships with others are in some way inadequate. As in the behaviour therapies previously mentioned, this type of learning is not primarily concerned with bringing about changes in inner personality states but in learning useful behavioural skills. This could apply equally to a manager who alienates employees as to a patient who complains of an inability to get along with other people.

Several methods are used. *Role playing* involves the person acting in situations which approximate to the real ones. An excessively shy person, for example, might role play someone who engages another in conversation. By practising the skill in a relatively non-threatening situation, some of the anxieties can be allayed. *Role reversal* is similar in that an artificial role play is used, but in this case the person takes the role of the other individual with whom he has difficulty. In many medical schools, students are asked to role play patients, to help them appreciate patients' reactions to medical care. Another technique is *modelling*, in which actors or therapists demonstrate effective ways of behaving. Watching a peer handle a difficult situation seems particularly effective.

The *instructional* component of SST entails giving information about non-verbal communication. For instance, eye gaze is very important in conversation, indicating interest and attention. Someone who does not look at his conversational partner may seem disinterested and unfriendly, making it difficult to achieve satisfactory social relationships. The instructor might suggest to the patient, 'When you're listening to people, show that you're interested by looking at them more often'.

Finally, there is the *feedback* component. Social skills can be likened to other kinds of skill, such as riding a bicycle. In order to learn to ride a bike, it is necessary to acquire knowledge of results — the effect of a shift of weight on balance, for example. Similarly, videotapes provide an opportunity for patients to see and hear themselves less subjectively, and when they cannot see where they have gone 'wrong' the instructor can point out the difficulty. The uses of this training are various, including marriage guidance and the rehabilitation of adolescent offenders and psychiatric patients.[21] A method which uses social skills training in helping students and medical staff learn to interview patients is discussed in Chapter 12.

Cognitive learning

Although advocates of the kinds of learning previously discussed may disagree about the relative importance of different environmental characteristics, little or no emphasis is placed on the inner workings of the mind. In many respects, this is quite satisfactory, since they are able to account for man's behaviour much of the time (at least in restricted environments). This is a valid criterion for any theory. In other respects, their theories are not as appealing. Cognitive factors appear to play a role in some learning, such as in the case of covert sensitization where the patient is asked to imagine an aversive situation, and even in classical conditioning.[22,23]

Latent learning provides another example of the importance of inner states. This kind of learning is shown when a subject is able to perform a task well, not because he has been reinforced for it previously but simply because he has had an opportunity to explore the task requirements beforehand. In this case, reinforcement seems to be responsible not for learning, but only for the performance of a task. In the classic experiments, some rats were allowed several days to wander around a complicated maze, while another group of rats was regularly rewarded with food if they found their way to the goal box. As soon as the first group of rats were similarly rewarded they were able to find their way through the maze as quickly as the always-rewarded rats, indicating that learning had taken place without reinforcement.[24] This finding suggests that inner maps or cognitive structures are learned through experience, but that this learning becomes apparent only if some incentive is given for performance.

One explanation for these findings has been given by Bandura.[25] He suggests that the critical factor in learning is not simply that events occur together in time, but that people become able to predict them and summon up appropriate actions. Thus, the CS in Pavlov's experiments provides a predictive signal for the presentation of food. Extinction occurs when the animal discovers that the signal is no longer predictive. Similarly, it may be that operant methods are useful in changing behaviour because the subject learns that the consequences of his behaviour depend on his actions in a predictable way: if he performs X in all probability Y will occur.

Treatments based on cognitive learning

Such an argument has important consequences for those who hold that only behaviour should be studied in psychology. Since studies have shown that inner mental states play a significant role in behaviour, there has been a major and important shift in learning theory, a shift away from changing behaviour alone towards changing beliefs and cognitive structures as well. If it is people's assumptions about how the world operates that are critical, then these assumptions should be considered and changed where appropriate. The similarity between this position and that advocated by Kelly and Beck discussed in Chapter 2 is striking. Although there are many differences in their approaches and theories, both they and the cognitive learning theorists contend that it is the individual's perceptions of the environment and of himself which are significant in changing behaviour. This recent shift in learning theory thus approaches the position that considers personality variables important in therapy.[26]

Self-instruction

In a new or stressful situation, people often talk to themselves, reflecting on how they feel and giving themselves instructions on how to behave. Before going into an examination, for example, a student may be thinking: 'I wonder what the exam will be like' and 'Remember to read each question carefully'. If feeling confident, he or she might be saying: 'I know all about this subject so calm down and relax'; but if lacking in confidence, something like: 'I'm going to make a mess of this' or 'I don't know enough to pass' might be going through the student's mind. The self-statements used by patients in clinical settings are also associated with their levels of anxiety. Kendall et al.[27] examined the self-statements of patients who were undergoing cardiac catheterization, asking them to indicate the kinds of thought they experienced during the procedure. Some of the thoughts were positive (e.g. how little pain the procedure caused and how easy it was to go through it) but many more were negative (e.g. thinking about the possibility of the catheter breaking off). When the attending physicians' and technicians' ratings of adjustment made during the procedure were compared with the patients' self-statements, there were significant relationships between them, with poor adjustment being correlated with the frequency of negative self-statements.

Cognitive theorists argue that such self-statements are not simply the result of any anxiety felt by a student before an exam or a patient during cardiac catheterization, but actually contribute to the anxiety. The implication is that if these self-statements can be modified, the anxiety level will be changed. Kendall et al. (1979) tested this possibility by giving some catheterization patients a short introduction to the idea that what people say to themselves can affect their level of anxiety. The patients' specific fears were addressed. If, for example, a particular patient was to say that he was anxious about all the machinery at the hospital, a new self-statement such as 'science has come such a long way to be able to have and to use all of this expensive equipment, and the doctors are very skilled in their use' would be encouraged. Other patients formed a control group: they were given a chat which was generally supportive of their concerns, but no specific coping skills were discussed. Both the doctors' and technicians' ratings of adjustment and the patients' reports of anxiety experienced during the subsequent procedure indicated that the patients encouraged to use coping self-statements fared better during the catheterization. Thus, positive self-talk modified the level of anxiety.

An application of self-instructional training which may be of personal relevance to the reader concerns test anxiety. The deleterious effects of high anxiety in the performance of complex tasks are well documented, and are a problem often encountered by students taking important exams. Part of the difficulty seems to be that highly anxious students tend to be self-deprecating about their performance and ruminate on the performance of others in the examination hall. There seems to be a failure to attend to the relevant aspects of the task, with irrelevant thoughts intruding frequently. In an attempt to help with this problem, students were encouraged to become aware of their thoughts and self-verbalizations during exams. They were then asked to imagine themselves taking an exam, but instead of ruminating on irrelevant thoughts, to instruct themselves positively, for instance, to say to themselves, 'This is a difficult exam, I'd better start working at it' rather than 'I'm really nervous. I can't handle this'. Compared with students who were waiting to take the cognitive modification programme, this procedure had a significant effect on grades and self-reports of improvement.[28]

Self-control

Self-control techniques do not involve 'use your willpower' or 'pull yourself together' admonitions. Self-control methods are much more detailed and structured than these kinds of advice. There are two main components. First, there is careful observation of the conditions that evoke the undesired behaviour. Someone who wants to stop smoking, for instance, would be encouraged to monitor the occasions when a cigarette is taken. This could be done by keeping a diary of the circumstances in which smoking occurs, the number of cigarettes smoked, and so on. Since people are not particularly accurate at observing their own behaviour, the therapist would provide instructions on how this charting could be accomplished.

The second component of self-control involves the idea of self-reward, in which patients give themselves rewards contingent on their behaviour. This can be encouraged by either direct instruction or by modelling. In the case of direct instruction, the therapist tells the patient to choose something pleasant whenever a certain standard of behaviour is reached. When the patient has no cigarette with morning coffee he or she could have a piece of cake, for instance. In modelling, the individual observes models rewarding themselves for performing a certain action and is encouraged to do the same. Once people have learned to reward themselves in this way, the behaviour is typically maintained for longer periods of time than when reinforcement is always given by the experimenter or therapist. Self-punishment, by contrast, has relatively little effect on self-control.[29]

This approach is nicely illustrated by some research that explored the self-control shown by students attempting to study. Students were initially asked to examine their own study methods, noting when and where they usually revised. To increase motivation, the students were also requested to make lists of all the reasons why they should study. Two methods were used to increase self-control. The first involved stimulus control: the students were encouraged to use only one or two places for study, places not associated with behaviour incompatible with studying. This method was based on the notion that the environment has an important effect on behaviour.

The second method involved asking the students to reward themselves whenever they studied for a specified length of time. At first, this time was short, about 20 minutes, but this increased as the programme progressed. They chose their own reinforcers, which could have been food, or watching TV. The students were also taught to graph the number of hours they spent studying, so that they could see the results of their efforts. The programme was supplemented by information about the SQ3R, a method outlined in Chapter 4. The results were very encouraging. A significant improvement in grades in the university exams was found for these students, compared with those not involved in

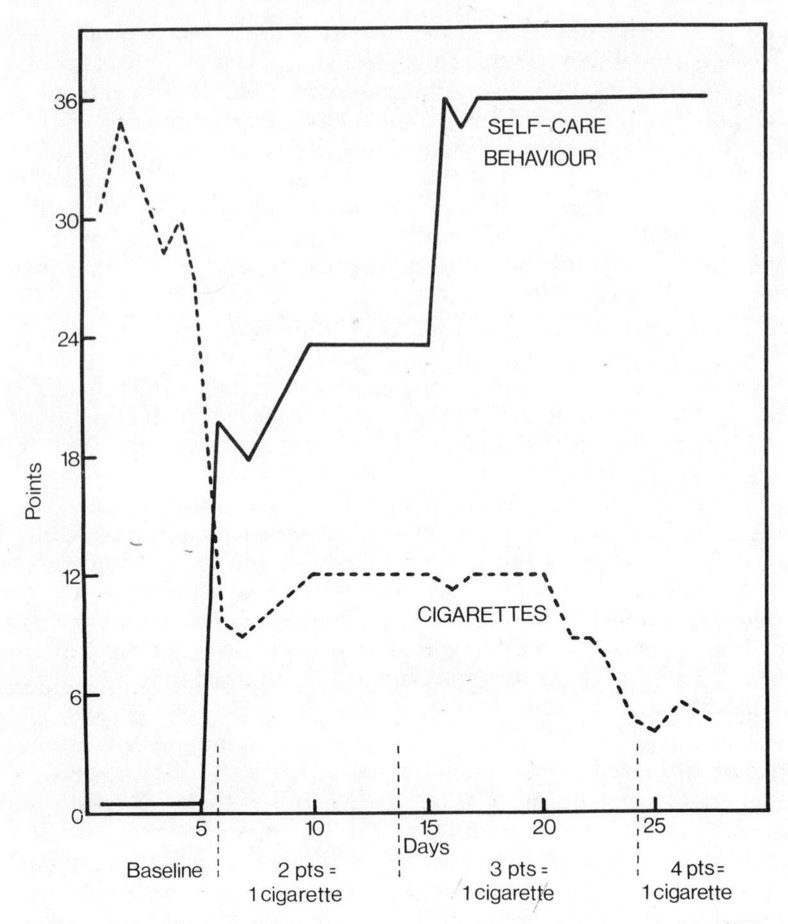

Fig. 10. The effect of self-reinforcement on self-care for one diabetic patient. (Reproduced from Karasu, T. B. & Steinmuller, R. I. (1978) *Psychotherapeutics in Medicine*, by permission of Grune and Stratton.)

the programme and those who dropped out after the introduction. While these researchers could not attribute the results to self-reinforcement alone owing to the design of the experiment, others have shown more clearly that self-reinforcement is effective in changing study patterns.

Self-reinforcement has proved effective in modifying many problem behaviours, such as eating and speech disorders. Compliance with medical advice has recently become an increasingly important topic of study. One diabetic patient, who had been admitted to hospital on three previous occasions for hypoglycaemia, was encouraged to maintain self-care procedures through the use of self-reinforcement. Finding cigarettes pleasurable, he was instructed to reward himself whenever he performed his self-care tasks (testing his urine, adjusting his insulin supply and keeping to an appropriate diet). Gradually, more and more tasks were required before he could reward himself. The results of this reinforcement scheme are shown in Fig. 10, which indicates a clear increase in self-care.[30] Interestingly, a corresponding decrease in the number of cigarettes was also found.

Thus, the cognitive approach to learning emphasizes the ways that people perceive their environment and themselves. Their thoughts are seen to be crucial, with self-statements about feelings and about what to do in new situations affecting behaviour. The argument is that if these self-statements can be modified, then behaviour and feelings will also change, an idea that is gaining much support in a variety of situations from encouraging compliance to helping students take exams.

Comparing therapies

The search for evidence that indicates that one kind of therapy is superior to others is relatively recent, but there are perhaps thousands of studies addressed to the issue of treatment efficacy. The topic is an important one, having many practical implications. If one treatment can be shown to be more effective than another, then therapists would have a responsibility to use the superior treatment for the good of their patients. The type of approach a therapist advocates may not only affect the treatment used but also which signs and symptoms will be observed.[31] Broadly speaking, studies in this area have been concerned with distinguishing between different behaviour therapies or with distinguishing between behaviour therapy and verbal psychotherapy.

Different behaviour therapies

The usual approach is to assign patients, with similar severity and types of difficulties, randomly to one of three groups. Two of the groups would be treated by two different methods (for example systematic desensitization and modelling), whereas the patients in the third group would serve as waiting-list controls. Baseline measures would be taken before treatment, and a follow-up conducted some months after treatment is completed. As well as experiments which have considered differences between treatments, researchers have been interested in ascertaining the most important aspects of any one procedure.[32] Several general principles have appeared:

1 Generally, behaviour therapies have proved effective as compared with waiting-list control groups in the treatment of phobias, some sexual dysfunctions and compulsions. However, many of these comparative studies have relied on university undergraduate recruits — volunteers who might not ordinarily have sought help for their difficulties.
2 There are many individual case studies in the literature testifying to the efficacy of behaviour therapy. While these cases provide evidence, a therapist is unlikely to seek to publish instances where his or her therapy has not been successful.
3 Treatments that involve the patient in actually engaging in the feared behaviour are more effective than those which rely on imagination. *In vivo* treatments, such as participant-modelling, produce more change than, say, modelling alone.
4 Studies using cognitive behaviour modification have generally proved superior to the more traditional kinds of behaviour therapies, providing better generalization with less cost in therapists' time.
5 Programmes which use multiple treatments have tended to be more effective than those that use a single method. This may be because many psychological difficulties have several components and each approach is best suited to a different component. Fear of a spider, for example, can involve physiological reactions, subjective perceptions and behavioural actions. Each component might best be altered by a different kind of therapy: a classical approach for the physiological component, a cognitive approach for the subjective one and an operant approach for the behaviour. Perhaps a fear is caused via the classical conditioning model but is maintained through the operant: for example, a person may run out of a room whenever a spider is sighted, thus gaining some relief from the feared stimulus. By combining several methods, each component is treated.

Psychotherapy versus behaviour therapy

The important distinction made in this book between these two broad types of therapy is that the former conceives of the patient's presenting complaint as only a symptom of the underlying 'real' difficulty, while the latter considers the presenting complaint *as* the real difficulty, with little attention paid to inner states. There have been few areas in psychology that have been so extensively researched or passionately debated as these alternative viewpoints. The controversy reached its height in the 1960s and early 1970s, when several researchers who saw behaviour therapy as the most efficacious challenged the psychotherapists to justify their treatments. Those who believed in the importance of insight and interpersonal relationships cited evidence indicating that it was the interest and concern shown by the behaviour therapists that were the ingredients of change, and argued that the practitioners of behaviour therapy were unaware of the role that their warmth and caring had on patients' improvements. For example, when behavioural techniques are used, 'warm' therapists obtain better results than 'cold' ones, indicating that the personality of the therapist and the relationship with his or her patient has an effect on recovery. Behaviourists countered this by arguing that psychotherapy involved positive reinforcement of certain behaviours by the therapist, punishment of others, and attempted to redefine psychotherapy in learning theory terms. Who is right?

At first sight, the question seems to be an easy one to answer. Simply assign patients to either psychotherapeutic or behavioural treatments and compare their recovery rates. A particularly good example of research of this kind has been conducted by Sloane.[33] Unlike most studies, there was a fairly large sample (N = 94) and a follow-up was conducted one year after the completion of treatment. He used therapists clinically experienced in both behavioural and psychotherapeutic groups, and there was little subject attrition. (This is important since those who leave therapy may differ from those who remain. If there were a high drop-out rate in one condition but not the other, the comparison may be biased in some way.) The patients were moderately disturbed (neurotic) and were given four months of treatment. Assessments were taken from the therapists, their patients, an independent assessor and the patients' relations both before and after treatment.

In general, there were many similarities in the outcomes of the two patient groups, both of whom did better than the waiting-list controls. About 80 per cent of the treated patients showed improvement for the *target* symptoms according to the independent assessor four months after treatment ended. This study has been widely cited by psychotherapists in defence of insight therapies, but there have been criticisms from the other side. Behaviour therapists have noted that the independent assessor was a psychiatrist who was likely to favour psychotherapy. Even though he assessed the patients blind (that is, without knowing their treatment condition), it was possible that he gained some knowledge about the treatment during the assessment interview, perhaps introducing some bias. Another criticism was that the patients in this study were mostly young, articulate, intelligent and successful — the kinds of patients who traditionally do well in psychotherapy. A more representative sample of the population may have given different results. A third criticism has been that, although there was little difference between the treatment groups on most measures, those significant differences which were found favoured behaviour therapy. For example, when the patients' *overall* adjustment was measured, 93 per cent of the behaviour therapy group were considered to be improved or recovered, as compared to only 77 per cent of the patients given psychotherapy.

The history of other similar studies has been that one side or the other has found something to criticize in the experimental design or in the interpretation of the results. An alternative to designing the 'perfect' experiment has been suggested by Smith and Glass.[34] They conducted a statistical review of about 350 studies that examined this issue, of which about 50 had adequate control groups. Most reviewers take a 'voting' system approach: if 15 studies support a viewpoint, while 5 are against, the reviewer might conclude that the evidence is weak but supportive. Such an approach does not take the *size* of any effect into account, however. If, for instance, the 5 against showed highly significant results whereas the effects in the other 15 were much less strong, the voting system could be quite misleading. Smith and Glass took the effect size into account in their analysis, so that a study which strongly supported one side or the other was weighted more heavily than a study which found only slight differences. Overall, their analysis showed the difference between treatments to be very small indeed, suggesting that psychotherapies and behaviour therapies were equally effective. However, this approach has two major drawbacks. First, it relies on the comparability of different assessment measures, assuming that self-report questionnaires, interviews and observations are equally valid and reliable, an assumption questioned in the previous chapter. Second, the quality of the studies was not taken into account. Many of Smith and Glass's sample of studies were not as well designed as the Sloane study mentioned above. Nevertheless, there was little evidence that one approach was superior to the other.

Why the similarity?

Several suggestions have been put forward to account for the similarity in effectiveness of the psychotherapies and the behaviour therapies. One contention is that different approaches have *specific effects*;[35] that is, a particular type of therapy would be more appropriate for certain conditions but less so for others. The cognitive approach could, for example, be most effective for helping patients who are having trouble succeeding at work or school; the psychodynamic approach could be best for altering personality traits; while the more traditional behaviour therapies could be most useful for helping anxious or fearful patients.[36]

An alternative view is that, rather than psychotherapies and behaviour therapies having different strengths and weaknesses, they are both effective because they have many similar features.[37] The *common behaviours* used by the two types of therapist may be responsible for changes in their patients. If it is these common behaviours that are significant, then a therapist may not require specific training and long experience in order to be helpful. Several features found in both types of therapy have been outlined:

1 Motivation of client. Whatever the therapeutic method, patients who are motivated to succeed do better. Patients entering therapy on their own initiative are more likely to benefit than those who have been referred (from school or the courts, for instance).
2 Socially sanctioned healer. All forms of therapy involve a 'healer' who is recognized by society. Whether the therapist uses behavioural or verbal techniques, the patient comes to someone who society has sanctioned to help others.
3 Some verbal relationship. A behavioural psychologist involves patients in verbal exchanges even if the techniques are non-verbal in nature. In order to elicit the patient's difficulties the therapist must show concern, caring and willingness to help. Understanding, acceptance and respect are central to all therapies.
4 Some kind of rationale for therapy. Each therapeutic procedure is underpinned by a theory. When people seek help, they are often confused and unable to make sense of feelings. It may be the case that any explanation will do, as long as it provides some rationale for being depressed, phobic, or whatever. This belief system removes some of the mystery surrounding the complaint.
5 Hope. One characteristic distinguishing people who seek assistance for their difficulties from those who do not is their sense of helplessness and demoralization. All therapies hold out hope that suffering will be diminished. Many patients improve spontaneously after an initial interview: perhaps the expectation that assistance will be given is responsible for this effect.
6 Opportunity to confide in a trusted individual. The opportunity to confide in another person seems to have particularly important consequences in therapy. Behavioural therapists often find their patients talking about many aspects of their lives not specifically being considered in treatment.

Summary

The theories we hold about how behaviour is acquired affect how we attempt to help people who experience psychological difficulties. Some psychologists believe that behaviour is guided mainly by an individual's personality (inner drives, conflicts, etc.), leading to the psychotherapies; others believe that such a subjective view is unscientific and rely mainly on external, observable events to account for learning. This chapter considered the theories held by the latter group of psychologists and their resulting treatments.

In classical conditioning, associations between unconditioned and conditioned stimuli are viewed as the fundamental building blocks of all behaviour. Various treatments are based on this model: aversion therapy, where an undesired behaviour is paired with a noxious stimulus; flooding, where patients confront the feared stimulus; and systematic desensitization, where an incompatible response, such as relaxation, is paired with the anxiety-provoking situation. Classical or respondent conditioning theories view behaviour as being acquired passively, but it is clear that individuals learn actively as well, by relating actions to consequences. This is recognized in instrumental learning theories, where actions which are reinforced or rewarded are repeated, while those which are not die out. Some learning seems to come about through observing the actions of others and this is not accounted for by either classical or operant learning. Imitating others' behaviour has helped individuals cope with stressful situations or in developing social skills. In the latter case, observation of their own videotaped interactions provides important feedback.

Although these theories are able to predict behaviour most of the time, they do not consider beliefs and values. In addition, learning occurs when there are no apparent rewards. These considerations have led to methods of helping patients which take cognitive factors into account, such as structured self-instruction and self-control techniques.

These different forms of behaviour therapy have been shown to be effective, with those incorporating real-life situations and those involving a cognitive element being superior to others. Their value compared with the psychotherapies has proved difficult to assess. This may be because each is effective but only in specific situations, or because the common aspects involved in both, such as the opportunity to talk to somebody, are actually what is relevant.

Suggested reading

S. Rachman and G. Wilson (1980) *The Effects of Psychological Therapy* Oxford: Pergamon, and R. Williams & W. Gentry (eds.) (1977) *Behavioural Approaches to Medical Treatment* Cambridge, Mass.: Ballinger, provide reviews of a variety of applications of behaviour therapy, the latter being more medically oriented. P.C. Kendall & S.D. Hollon (eds.) (1979) *Cognitive–Behavioural Interventions* London: Academic Press, show how the cognitive approach can be applied to psychological difficulties. Many of the issues raised in the last part of this chapter are considered in S. Garfield & A. Bergin (eds.) (1978) *Handbook of Psychotherapy and Behaviour Change* Chichester: Wiley.

References

1. Allport, G.W. (1937) *Personality: A Psychological Interpretation* New York: Holt.
2. Koch, H.C.H. (1979) Evaluation of behaviour therapy intervention in general practice. *Journal of the Royal College of General Practitioners* **29**: 337–340.
3. Watson, J.B. & Raynor, R. (1920) Conditioned emotional reactions. *Journal of Experimental Psychology* **3**: 1–14.
4. Harris, B. (1979) Whatever happened to Little Albert?. *American Psychologist* **34**: 151–160.
5. Nicholas, D.R. (1982) Prevalence of anticipatory nausea and emesis in cancer chemotherapy patients. *Journal of Behavioural Medicine* **5**: 461–463.
6. Cautela, J.R. (1967) Covert sensitization. *Psychological Reports* **20**, 462.
7. Sreenivasan, U., Manocha, S.N. & Jain, V.K. (1979) Treatment of severe dog phobia in childhood by flooding: A case report. *Journal of Child Psychology and Psychiatry* **20**: 255–260.
8. Wolpe, J. (1969) *The Practice of Behavior Therapy* New York: Pergamon.
9. Gale, E.N. & Ayer, W.A. (1969) Treatment of dental phobias. *Journal of the American Dental Association* **78**: 1304–1307.
10. Skinner, B.F. (1976) *Walden Two* London: Collier Macmillan.
11. Harris, F.R., Wolfe, M.M. & Baer, D.M. (1964) Effects of adult social reinforcement on child behaviour. *Young Children* **20**: 8–17.
12. Lang, P.J. & Melamed, B.G.(1968) Case report: Avoidance conditioning therapy of an infant with chronic ruminative vomiting. *Journal of Abnormal Psychology* **74**: 1–8.
13. Horner, R.D. & Keilitz, I. (1975) Training mentally retarded adolescents to brush their teeth. *Journal of Applied Behaviour Analysis* **8**: 301–309.
14. Zifferblatt, S.M. (1975) Increasing patient compliance through the applied analysis of behaviour. *Preventative Medicine* **4**: 173–182.
15. Hart, R.R. (1979) Utilisation of token economy within a chronic dialysis unit. *Journal of Consulting and Clinical Psychology* **47**: 646–648.
16. Kristt, D.A. & Engel, B.T. (1975) Learned control of blood pressure. *Circulation* **51**: 370–378.
17. Bandura, A., Grusec, J.E. & Menlove, F.L. (1966) Observational learning as a function of symbolisation and incentive set. *Child Development* **37**: 499–506.
18. Hayes, K.J. & Hayes, C. (1952) Imitation in a home-raised chimpanzee. *Journal of Comparative Physiological Psychology*. **45**: 450–459.
19. Rosekrans, M.A. & Hartup, W.W. (1967) Imitative influences of consistent and inconsistent response consequences to a model on aggressive behaviour in children. *Journal of Personality and Social Psychology* **7**: 429–434.

20. Melamed, B.G. & Siegel, L.J. (1975) Reduction of anxiety in children facing surgery by modelling. *Journal of Consulting and Clinical Psychology* **43**: 511–521.
21. Argyle, M. (ed.) (1981) *Social Skills and Health* London: Methuen.
22. Chatterjee, B.B. & Eriksen, C.W. (1962) Cognitive factors in heart rate conditioning. *Journal of Experimental Psychology* **64**: 272–279.
23. Grings, W.W. (1973) The role of consciousness and cognition in autonomic behaviour change. In: McGuigan, F.J. & Schoonover, R. (eds.) *The Psychophysiology of Thinking* New York: Academic Press.
24. Tolman, E.C. (1948) Cognitive maps in rats and men. *Psychological Review* **55**: 189–208.
25. Bandura, A. (1977) *Social Learning Theory* Englewood Cliffs, New Jersey: Prentice-Hall.
26. Meichenbaum, D. (1977) *Cognitive Behavior Modification* New York: Plenum.
27. Kendall, P.C., Williams, L., Pechacek, T.F., Graham, L.E., Shisslak, C. & Herzoff, N. (1979) Cognitive–behavioural and patient education interventions in cardiac catheterization procedures. *Journal of Consulting and Clinical Psychology* **47**: 49–58.
28. Meichenbaum, D. (1972) Cognitive modification of test-anxious college students. *Journal of Consulting and Clinical Psychology* **39**: 370–380.
29. Thorensen, C.E. & Mahoney, M.J. (1974) *Behavioural Self-control* New York: Holt, Rinehart and Winston.
30. Fordyce, W.E. (1978) Behavioural methods in medical practice. In: Karasu, T.B. & Steinmuller, R.I. (eds.) *Psychotherapeutics in Medicine* London: Grune and Stratton.
31. Langer, E.J. & Abelson, R.P. (1974) A patient by any other name. *Journal of Consulting and Clinical Psychology* **42**: 4–9.
32. Kazdin, A.E. & Wilson, G.T. (1978) *Evaluation of Behavior Therapy* Cambridge, Mass.: Ballinger.
33. Sloane, R.B., Staples, F.R., Cristol, A.H., Yorkston, N.J. & Whipple, K. (1975) *Psychotherapy versus Behaviour Therapy* Cambridge, Mass.: Harvard University Press.
34. Smith, M.L. & Glass, G.V. (1977) Meta-analysis of psychotherapy outcome studies. *American Psychologist* **32**: 752–760.
35. Kiesler, D.J. (1971) Experimental designs in psychotherapy research. In: Bergin, A.E. & Garfield, S.L. *Handbook of Psychotherapy and Behaviour Change* London: Wiley.
36. Shapiro, D.A. & Shapiro, D. (1982) Meta-analysis of comparative therapy outcome studies: A replication and refinement. *Psychological Bulletin* **92**: 581–604.
37. Garfield, S.L. (1971) Research on client variables in psychotherapy. In: Bergin, A.E. & Garfield, S.L. *Handbook of Psychotherapy and Behaviour Change* London: Wiley.

4

Memory

Introduction

In Chapter 1 an information processing model of perception was outlined. According to this model, there are three stages involved in perception – sensation, interpretation and memory. The aim of this chapter is to consider some aspects of memory, particularly as they apply to learning information, as in studying for examinations; and to clinical practice, as in giving information to patients.

The hippocampus and the Papez circuit generally (hippocampus–fornix–mammillary bodies–thalamus–ungulate cortex–hippocampus) have been implicated by several studies exploring the effect of brain lesions on memory. It seems that bilateral damage of any part of this circuit will disrupt memory. Some of the more striking case studies are those reported by Milner.[1] In an attempt to relieve patients of severe epilepsy, and when more conservative treatments had little effect, the mesial parts of both temporal lobes were removed, thus destroying two-thirds of the hippocampus bilaterally. Unfortunately, the operation led to severe memory impairment in several patients. For example:

> . . . ten months after the operation the family moved to a new house which was situated only a few blocks away from their old one, on the same street. When examined nearly a year later, H.M. had not yet learned the new address, nor could he be trusted to find his way home alone, because he would go to the old house. Six years ago the family moved again, and H.M. is still unsure of his present address, although he does seem to know that he has moved. Moreover, his mother states that he is unable to learn where objects constantly in use are kept; for example, although he mows the lawn regularly, and quite expertly, she still has to tell him where to find the lawnmower, even when he has been using it only the day before. His mother also observes that he will do the same jigsaw puzzles day after day without showing any practice effect, and read the same magazines over and over again without ever finding their contents familiar. The same forgetfulness applies to people he has met since the operation, even to those neighbours

who have been visiting the house regularly for the past six years. He has not learned their names and he does not recognize any of them if he meets them in the street. Conversely, he cannot now be left alone in the house, because he has been known to invite total strangers in to await his mother's return, thinking that they must be friends of the family whom he has failed to recognize. (Ref. 1, pp. 113–114)

While it is clear that memory is vital to our everyday functioning, it is tempting to consider it as a rather straightforward process: information is learned and either remembered or forgotten. However, such a view is not consistent with either personal experience or experimental evidence. Sometimes information cannot be recalled when every effort is made (say, during an examination), only for it to pop up later (during the walk home afterwards). Some kinds of information are very difficult to learn, whereas other kinds can be recalled without any intention to remember. Further, over time the information stored in memory can change. In trying to understand what is, in fact, a very complex process, it has proved useful to consider memory in three stages: learning information (encoding), storing it and retrieving it.

The three stages of memory

Encoding information

The way in which information is learned has an important influence on how easy it is to recall. Perhaps the most important figure in the study of memory has been Ebbinghaus who, in the nineteenth century, studied his own memory processes by learning long lists of what are called 'nonsense syllables', such as KYH or ZIW. He found that syllables in the middle of these long lists were recalled less easily than those at the beginning (the primacy effect) and those at the end (the recency effect). He also found that most forgetting occurred within the first few hours and that it was reduced if the list was 'over-learned' (i.e. instead of stopping his reviews of the lists when the syllables were accurately recited for the first time, he would recite them once or twice more). Material that was repeated soon after it was first encountered was also more likely to be recalled later. More recent research has indicated that the timing of such rehearsals is very important. For example, one investigator had two groups of subjects read a passage five times. For half of the subjects, the readings were all done at one sitting, whereas for the other subjects they were spaced over five days. Retention was tested three times: immediately after the fifth reading there was little difference between the groups. After two weeks, however, the second group performed some 20 per cent better than the first; and after four weeks some 25 per cent. By spacing the repetitions over time, more information was retrieved. Thus, although an immediate rehearsal is helpful, subsequent repetitions should be spaced over time for maximum learning, rather than being massed into a short time-interval.

Recall can also be enhanced by some preparation for learning by first skimming over the material. This gives an overall idea of the content so that expectations about the information can be raised and the material more easily organized. For the reader of this book, some of the organizational work has already been done. Since this chapter is entitled Memory, the reader will expect to learn about factors affecting memory. There is much evidence that such preparations are effective. In one study subjects were shown how to skim over the headings and summaries of the passages they were to learn before they settled down to read. When given a new passage to learn, this group read 24 per cent faster, and as accurately as subjects not shown how to prepare themselves.

Another method for maximizing learning is through the use of mnemonics. Many people use this technique, such as in the rhyme '30 days has September, April, June and November . . .'. But there is little experimental evidence to evaluate its effectiveness as a general learning strategy. Nevertheless there are several popular books on the topic and some applications of mnemonics to medicine. For example, the causes of dementia might be remembered by using the mnemonic device DEMENTIAS, in which each letter stands for a cause:[2]

Deficiency disorders
Ethanol (alcohol) and other drugs
Myxoedema
Encephalitis
Neoplasm
Trauma
Inflammation
Atherosclerosis
Sugar low: hypoglycaemia. Senility. Schizophrenia.

It is important, of course, that the mnemonic vehicle be readily accessible and unlikely to be forgotten itself.

Storing information

Memory seems to have three kinds of store. The first type — sensory store — may last less than a second and seems to be based on an auditory or visual after-image. If this information is not attended to, it fades and seems to be permanently lost. If attention is paid to the information, it enters the second type of storage — short-term storage (STS). As this sentence is read, the previous one will be in STS and will be available for only about 20–30 seconds if it is not rehearsed or reviewed.

The reconstruction of memories

Long-term store (LTS) holds past experiences which have been integrated from the STS. The methods outlined in the previous section on learning information facilitate this process. Whatever biochemical or anatomical changes are involved in transfer to the LTS,[3] forgetting from this store seems to be very slow and its capacity is considered to be very large. An important feature of the LTS is its active nature. It is not simply a warehouse full of past experiences, holding memories that correspond exactly to what was learned. Rather, memories can change or be reconstructed in LTS. After a period of time, material recalled from the LTS may not necessarily correspond to that which was originally learned but may be distorted to fit into themes or ideas. It is as if the gaps in memory are filled with pieces of general information about the world. Inferences are made and integrated into memory.

An illustration of how memory is a constructive process is provided by Loftus and Palmer.[4] They showed subjects a film of a traffic accident and then asked them questions about the speed of the vehicles in different ways. Some subjects were asked: 'About how fast were the cars going when they *smashed* into each other?'; whereas another group heard the question: 'About how fast were the cars going when they *hit* each other?'. The first question elicited a much higher estimate of speed. This difference could have been due to response bias (i.e. the subjects in the 'smashed' condition might have thought the researcher wanted a high estimate and so provided it). Alternatively, the wording of the question may have actually affected the memory of the event. In order to test between these possibilities, the experimenters asked the subjects to return a week later. Without viewing the film again, they were asked some more questions about the accident. The hypothesis that the original questioning had actually affected the memory was tested by asking about details that had not occurred in the film. There was no broken glass shown, but over twice as many of the subjects in the 'smashed' condition remembered broken glass than those in the 'hit' condition. This suggests that our memories of events are determined not only by the perception of the event itself, but also by information gained after it.

Other studies have indicated that prior expectations can also modify memories. One of the more puzzling features of some kinds of anxiety is that people remain anxious about a situation despite repeated experiences with it when nothing aversive occurs. That is, anxiety can be slow to extinguish in real-life settings. Dental anxiety is a good example: anxious patients typically expect considerable pain when they visit the dentist, but experience does not bear this out. Why, then, do they continue to expect discomfort on their next visit? It seems to be due in part to the reconstruction of memory. In one study,[5] patients who were attending a dentist were asked to fill out a questionnaire designed to measure their degree of dental anxiety and the amount of pain they expected. After the appointment, they were asked about the amount of pain actually experienced. When the patients were contacted three months later and asked to recall the amount of pain they had felt at the appointment, the anxious patients recalled much more pain than they had originally reported, whereas the less anxious patients were more accurate in their recall. It seemed that the memories of the anxious patients had changed in order to become consistent with what they had expected their appointment to be like, rather than reflecting actual experience.

These distortions of memory are due to a tendency that we all share to fit what we experience into what we believe. This process, called 'effort after meaning', is important in much psychological research and medical practice. Whenever a subject in a psychological study or a patient under the care of a doctor is asked for retrospective data, there is the possibility that the memories will be matched not simply to events but also to previous and subsequent experiences. People may be more likely to remember and embellish an event if it is followed by a change in health, for example (see Chapter 10 on stress), or to forget a doctor's advice if it does not fit into a pre-existing pattern of memories and expectations (see Chapter 13).

Retrieving information

Not all information stored in LTS can be recalled. Ebbinghaus distinguished two types of retrieval — recall and recognition. You may have experienced the 'tip of the tongue' phenomenon, the certainty that you know a piece of information, but cannot recall it: someone's name, perhaps, or an important fact on an examination. Once the name or fact is given, it can be immediately recognized. This distinction between types of retrieval has implications for studying, since the type of examination should influence how the material is studied. Multiple-choice questions rely mainly on recognition, while essay-type examinations require accurate recall. In one experiment, students were given a passage to read and then examined on it. One group of the subjects was told that they would receive short-answer, open questions, whereas the other expected multiple-choice questions. However, half of each group was given the kind of test they did not expect, so that their preparation may have been inappropriate. As predicted, those who received the expected type of test did better than those who received the unexpected one.[6] Preparation and retrieval can be aided by checking the type of questions used in past examinations in a subject.

Incidentally, even when information has been successfully retrieved during an examination, the manner of presentation can affect the mark obtained. Legibility of writing is a particularly important factor in essay-type questions. By giving different groups of teachers the same essay written either clearly or illegibly, several studies have shown that legibly written work receives higher grades.

In summary, there are three stages involved in memory — learning the information, storing it and retrieving it. Two of the more useful methods for learning material are to 'over-learn' it and to repeat it several times over a period of weeks or months. This ensures that the material will enter long-term storage, but it is important to realize that this store is not static; memories change over time to become consistent with beliefs and feelings. Even if material is in store it may be difficult to retrieve, with recognition being easier than recall.

Applications

Effective study

Several suggestions for more effective study have already been made in this chapter. These include over-learning, the spacing of reviews, and skimming over the material before settling down to read it thoroughly. These suggestions have been formalized in the SQ3R method: Survey, Question, Read, Recite, Review.[7] This package as a whole has been shown to be effective in helping students (see 'Self-control' in Chapter 3).

Survey: The first step is to read the main headings of a chapter in order to prepare yourself for the information to be learned. In this book, the major headings are given in the Contents. This initial step should not take more than a minute.

Question: Turn the heading into a question before you read the section of the chapter. For example, the heading to this section, **Effective study**, could be turned into the question: 'How can research into memory help me to study more effectively?'

Read: Now read to answer the question. Particular words or phrases which contribute to the answer can be jotted down, as briefly as possible.

Recite: Now look away from the book and try to recite your answer to the question. If possible, use your own words and give an example. If you can't answer the question, read the material over again quickly.

The last three steps (turning the heading into a question; reading to answer the question while making brief notes; reciting the answer) can be repeated for each section of the chapter.

Review: Finally, when all the information has been learned in this way, look over your notes once more to gain an overall view of the material. Check your memory by reciting the major points again.

Clinical applications

There are two main ways in which memory research is relevant to clinical practice: first, in understanding how doctors might impart information to aid patients' recall; and second, in the diagnosis and monitoring of people with certain types of brain damage.

Imparting information to patients

As discussed above, one important aspect of memory is that simply because someone has been told something, it cannot be assumed that the information will be remembered. This could be because patients are given material which is unfamiliar and difficult to link with already existing ideas and beliefs, or because they are anxious and find it difficult to attend to everything a doctor says. These problems are illustrated by a study in one hospital where patients were given a tape-recording of the final dismissal interview. At this time the history was reviewed, a final physical examination was given, the laboratory findings were outlined and the treatment discussed. When asked about the usefulness of the tape-recording later, the patients reported that they had listened to it 3½ times on average, indicating that most were unable to assimilate all the information on first or even second hearing.[8] In Chapter 13 ways in which doctors can present advice to patients to make it more likely to be retained are described. These include being aware of the primacy effect (material given early in the consultation is more likely to be remembered), stressing the crucial aspects, and not giving patients too much to remember.

For doctors who have to transmit bad news to their patients, it seems to be the case that people in a shocked state retain little of what is said to them. This could apply equally to informing someone of a terminal prognosis as to telling parents that their child is handicapped. As one mother recalls, when asked what she was told during the consultation when she first heard her child had Down's syndrome: ' . . . I can't really remember; I think we were too shocked at the time that anything else he said just went into one ear and out the other' (Ref. 9, p. 26). This implies that it would be important for doctors to make themselves available on subsequent occasions and to be prepared to repeat information which has already been given.

Memory impairment

Apart from understanding these 'normal' memory processes, techniques developed from memory research have proved useful with patients suffering from memory impairments. Like personality and intelligence tests, tests of memory can provide significant clinical data. They can assist in diagnosis;[10] they can be used to monitor changes in a patient's condition; and they can give the patient some insight into his difficulties and suggest ways in which these might be overcome.[11,12] Brain injury can lead to amnesia. Retrograde amnesia refers to the difficulty in remembering events before the injury: concussed patients are often unable to recall the incident causing the concussion or the events just preceding it. Anterograde amnesia is an inability to retain new experiences, as occurs following the brain injury or during recovery from a general anaesthetic. The degree of such post-traumatic amnesia is often used as an index of the severity of a closed head injury. Patients usually recover their ability to remember new experiences but rarely completely fill the retrograde gap.

Memory difficulties in general are considered to be early warning signs of organic disorders with problems occurring at the learning, storage or retrieval stages. In Korsakoff's amnesia syndrome, due to chronic alcoholism, there is an almost complete inability to learn new material and much difficulty in recalling past events. Dementia is the term given to a profound and progressive deterioration of all intellectual faculties. It is most commonly found in elderly people, and is known as senile dementia.

While deficits in memory can indicate organic damage, there are other possible explanations for any deterioration. Anyone who is severely emotionally disturbed may be troubled by forgetfulness. Memory can also decline due to social and environmental factors, as in the case of some elderly people who are resident in nursing homes where there can be little stimulation and few opportunities to practise memory skills. Langer et al.[13] argued that many cognitive abilities can diminish with disuse. They reasoned that if nursing home residents could be encouraged to practise such skills then any deterioration could be stopped or even reversed. They motivated some residents to attend to and try to remember their experiences by using reinforcements: if the patients could, for example, discover and remember the names of some of their nurses they would be given tokens which could be redeemed for gifts. Other residents were also given the tokens, but these were described simply as presents. There were several clear differences in the abilities of the two groups when their memory was later tested. Not only could those in the first group recall more information about their activities but they could also remember new material more accurately. Furthermore, these patients showed an improvement in their general alertness while others showed a decline. Thus, this study suggests that the memory loss shown by some elderly patients is, at least in part, due to their unchallenging environment rather than to organic deterioration. This point is taken up again in Chapter 10 when old age is discussed in more detail.

Summary

Memory involves three interdependent stages — encoding, storage and retrieval. In attempting to learn new material, it is important to realize that preparation is useful. Mnemonics provide one method, where information is linked in some way with a word or phrase, and skimming over the information before reading in depth is also useful. Perhaps the best way of ensuring that material will be stored, however, is to 'over-learn' it and to repeat it several times over a period of weeks or months.

Sensory and short-term stores operate for short periods of time and have limited capacity, whereas long-term store can contain information for decades and has no easily measured limits. A notable feature of long-term store is its dynamic nature: memories seem to change in order to become consistent with past experiences and expectations. The third stage, retrieval, involves the recall of information from store or the recognition of information when it is encountered again.

Research in memory has many implications for patient care. Patients are often highly anxious when talking with a doctor and there may be too many ideas to assimilate all at once. There is also evidence that the deterioration of memory sometimes found in elderly people is due to a lack of stimulation and encouragement to use their memory — if they can be motivated to remember aspects of their environment any deterioration can be minimized. Memory deficits can also be due to brain damage and result in an inability to learn new material or recall past events.

Suggested reading

Loftus, G.R. & Loftus, E.F. (1976) *Human Memory: The Processing of Information* London: Wiley, consider many of the points discussed in this chapter in more detail.

References

1. Milner, B. (1966) Amnesia following operation on the temporal lobes. In: Whitty, C. & Zangwill, O. *Amnesia* London: Butterworth.
2. Shipman, J.J. (1978) *Mnemonics and Tactics in Surgery and Medicine* London: Lloyd-Luke.
3. Dunn, A.J. (1980) Neurochemistry of learning and memory: an evaluation of recent data. *Annual Review of Psychology* **31**: 343–390.
4. Loftus, G.R. & Palmer, J.C. (1974) Reconstruction of automobile destruction: an example of the interaction between language and memory. *Journal of Verbal Learning and Verbal Behaviour* **13**: 585–589.
5. Kent, G. (1985) Memory of dental pain. *Pain* **21**: 187–194.
6. d'Ydewalle, G. & Rosselle, H. (1978) Text expectations in text learning. In: Gruneberg, M.M., Morris, P.E. & Sykes, R.N. (eds.) *Practical Aspects of Memory* London: Academic Press.
7. Robinson, F.P. (1946) *Effective Study* London: Harper.
8. Butt, H.R. (1977) A method for better physician–patient communication. *Annals of Internal Medicine* **86**: 478–480.
9. Hannam, C. (1975) *Parents and Mentally Handicapped Children* Harmondsworth, Middlesex: Penguin Books.
10. Walsh, K.W. (1978) *Neuropsychology* London: Churchill Livingstone.
11. Grafman, J. & Mathews, C.G. (1978) Assessment and remediation of memory

deficits in brain-injured patients. In: Gruneberg, M.M., Morris, P.E. & Sykes, R.N. (eds.) *Practical Aspects of Memory* London: Academic Press.
12. McDowall, J. (1979) Effects of encoding instruction and retrieval cuing in recall in Korsakoff patients. *Memory and Cognition* 7: 232–239.
13. Langer, E.J., Rodin, J., Beck, P., Weinman, C. & Spitzer, L. (1979) Environmental determinants of memory improvement in late adulthood. *Journal of Personality and Social Psychology* **37**: 2003–2013.

5

Intelligence

Introduction

Most people, at some time in their lives, undergo tests of ability. They may be overt, such as an examination at school designed to give an indication of how well a student has learned a subject, or they may be less obvious, such as a manager unobtrusively assessing the ability of a worker. These kinds of test are very specific: the interest is only in one aspect of a person's life, often at a particular time. Psychologists have attempted to gain a more general measure of ability through the development of IQ (Intelligence Quotient) tests. These are used by many educational and clinical psychologists in their assessments of, say, a child who is not doing well in school or an adult whose capacities may have been damaged by a stroke or an accident. In such cases, IQ tests may aid diagnosis. The child whose school grades are low might have difficulties in learning or, alternatively, have emotional or interpersonal problems. If a high score were achieved on an IQ test, this could effectively rule out the former possibility. Since IQ tests measure various abilities, the particular difficulties experienced by a patient who has suffered a stroke can sometimes be pinpointed and rehabilitation programmes devised.[1]

Although there is a wide variety of suggested definitions of 'intelligence', as measured by IQ tests it basically refers to an ability to solve problems and to think in the abstract. Measurements of this ability run into numerous problems: for instance, can it meaningfully be regarded as one global ability or does it refer to several independent abilities such as perceptual acuity, memory and word fluency? Can it be measured without taking into account a person's motivation to succeed at the task? Is it possible to devise tests which measure aptitude rather than prior learning? Once a measurement has been made, does it show that a person has inherited greater intellectual endowment or does it reflect the individual's experiences? What, if anything, does current performance indicate about a person's future capabilities?

In this chapter we look at how people have studied intelligence, with particular attention to the development and use of IQ tests. The various factors affecting people's scores on these tests, such as age, experience and genetics are examined and the usefulness of the concept is explored. In addition to their use in educational settings, IQ tests can identify people with degenerative diseases as well as those with intellectual impairments (mental handicaps) and can be used as a way of monitoring their progress.

Measurement of IQ

Several ways of measuring intelligence have been explored. As far back as 1884, Galton tried, unsuccessfully, to relate head size and reaction times to intellectual performance. More recently, attempts to relate the speed of brain functioning through EEG recordings to intellectual performance have had some success[2] but usually produce low correlations. The most successful approach to intellectual measurement has been the IQ test.

IQ tests

The forerunner of current individual IQ tests was a scale developed by Binet at the beginning of the century at the request of the Paris authorities. They wished to identify those children who would not benefit from the educational system. By giving a large sample of children various problems to solve, he identified items which could be done by, on average, half the children of each age. For example, he found that half the eight-year-olds could count backwards from 20 to zero, and half the ten-year-olds could name the months of the year. His test consisted of a set of these age-graded items. When the test was administered to a particular child, he or she would initially be presented with the items for an age lower than his or her chronological age and then given successively harder items until several in a row were failed in order to establish the child's mental age.

The original Binet test has been revised many times but remains in common use as the Stanford–Binet test, along with a similar test developed by Wechsler (the Wechsler Intelligence Scale for Children, or WISC). In the 1960 revision of the Stanford–Binet, an eight-year-old child would be asked to define certain words (e.g. a straw, an orange, an envelope, a puddle), to point out absurdities in statements ('An old man complained that he could no longer walk around the park as he used to; he said that now he could only go half-way round and then back again) to say how two things were alike and how they differed (e.g. sea and river) and to indicate comprehension of situations by answering questions appropriately ('What's the thing for you to do when you are on your way to school and think you are going to be late?').[3] There are also various tests for children below the age of two years, such as those devised by Griffiths and Cattell.[4] In the latter, a six-month-old infant would be expected to pick a cube off a table; to lift a cup from a table; to finger his or her reflection in a mirror; to reach out for objects with one hand and to stretch persistently towards an object which was just out of reach.

All of these are individual tests — the examiner tests one person at a time. Some IQ tests have been devised for groups, such as Raven's Progressive Matrices, a non-verbal test in which a pattern has to be selected to complete a sequence.[5] This is often used in conjunction with the Mill Hill Vocabulary Scale, another paper-and-pencil test that can easily be given to large groups of people at one time. Respondents are asked to write the meanings of several words, such as 'continue' and 'putative'. A second section of the test requires choosing the correct meaning of a target word; for instance, for the word WHIM, a synonym has to be selected from the list: complain, tonic, wind, noise, fancy, wish.

Calculating IQ

For children, the intelligence quotient or IQ is derived from the formula Mental Age (MA)/Chronological Age (CA) × 100. To simplify somewhat, in the case of an 8-year-old child who passed only the items expected of an average 6-year-old, the IQ would be $6/8 \times 100 = 75$, whereas the IQ of the child whose answers indicated the ability of a 10-year-old would be $10/8 \times 100 = 125$. An 'average' child, with a mental age equivalent to the chronological age, would have an IQ of 100.

Beyond the age of 16 to 18 years, chronological age is no longer used to calculate IQ. It is not easy, for example, to find items that can be done by a 23-year-old but not by a 22-year-old: for adults, mental age ceases to maintain its relation to chronological age. An IQ can still be calculated for an adult, however, by comparing his performance with that of a large group of people of similar age. This is the same principle that many personality theorists have used in developing their tests for assessing personality. It is not the absolute score which is important, but how this compares with others' scores, so it is important to use a comparison group that is similar to the person being tested. It would make little sense, for example, to compare the IQ scores of an American astronaut with those of a rural farm worker in England, or to compare either of these with the scores of an Australian aborigine. Although the astronaut would be likely to score higher on IQ tests than the aboriginal, the former could not be said to be more intelligent. Only if people come from similar social backgrounds can the comparison be made. When an IQ test has been given to a large group of people it is said to be 'standardized' for that population and their results are called 'norms'.

IQ tests for adults are designed so that the average is 100, as in the children's versions. IQ is considered to be normally distributed in the population and this knowledge allows a curve to be constructed which indicates the number of individuals likely to obtain a particular score. To do this, it is also necessary to know the range of scores in the population: i.e. whether there could be individuals with IQs of 200 or −10. In fact, standard IQ tests are devised so that almost everybody lies within a range of 90 IQ points, from 55 to 145. For those scoring less than 85, there have been several classifications, new terms being adopted as the old ones have developed negative connotations. Intellectual impairment is considered profound with an IQ of 0–20, severe 20–35, moderate 35–50, mild 50–70, and borderline 70–85.

Reliability and validity

The results of IQ tests can only be taken seriously if they can be shown to be *reliable* (i.e. the same result would be obtained by different testers or on different occasions) and *valid* (i.e. the tests are measuring problem-solving abilities and abstract thinking rather than, say, prior experience and training).

Reliability

Reliability can be measured in various ways: by seeing if people achieve a similar score on subsequent administrations of the test; by preparing alternative or parallel forms of the test and seeing whether people score similarly on both which eliminates the practice element involved in doing the same test again; or by comparing scores on one half of the test with scores on the other half (split-half reliability).

One way in which reliability is maintained is by standardizing the way the tests are given, so that each testing is seen as a well-controlled experiment. Manuals describe precisely how the tests must be administered and the psychologists must follow this agreed procedure, down to the exact words. Instructions are given about establishing rapport with the testee and there is evidence[6] that feeling comfortable with the examiner does improve test score results. The sex and race of the examiner also influence the results obtained.[7,8]

Validity

As far as validity is concerned, IQ tests do correlate with academic achievement, the original purpose behind Binet's scale. The Stanford–Binet and Weschler Adult tests correlate between 0.40 to 0.60 with school grades. IQ test results also correlate with occupational achievement and the average IQ of people in different jobs (such as lawyer or butcher) has been found to correlate with independent rankings of how intelligent such workers would be considered to be. Within more restricted ranges, however, IQ correlates less well with achievement. Doctors in the top and bottom thirds of their graduating class displayed only very slight differences in the quality of practice thereafter and even these decreased after the first few years.[9] However, the IQ test was not designed to discriminate between people of similar high (or low) ability but rather to distinguish between the high and low scorers. Since almost everyone who goes to university will have a high IQ, this lack of correspondence would be expected. Nor are IQ tests designed to measure divergent or creative thinking, an ability that may be important in this context. There are, however, tests which have been devised to measure creativity.[10]

The validity of IQ tests in certain contexts has been brought into question because of their cultural bias. Obviously, someone with a poor grasp of the language of the test would be at a disadvantage on items which depend on understanding instructions or rely on knowledge of vocabulary. Less obviously, people from different social classes within a culture use language differently. Not only are there differences in grammar, there are also likely to be differences in vocabulary. One study[11] of the errors in IQ tests looked at an item in which subjects were asked to pick out the word that did not belong with the others in the list: 'cello, harp, drum, violin, guitar'. 85 per cent of the children from homes of high socioeconomic status chose 'drum', the intended correct answer, but only 45 per cent of the children from homes of low socioeconomic status. These children most commonly answered 'cello', an unfamiliar word that they thought did not belong. The high socioeconomic status children were more likely at least to have heard the word.

Attempts have been made to develop 'culture-fair' tests which do not rely on linguistic ability. However, it is clear that cultural influences extend beyond language: the motivation to succeed at the task may be quite different, for instance. Intelligence is highly prized in Western societies, while there is not even an equivalent concept in some other societies. It now seems apparent that, although some tests may be less culture-biased than others, no test is culture-fair. This means it is impossible on the basis of IQ tests to say people from one culture are more intelligent than people from another. This has been well demonstrated by a study[12] investigating groups of children in various parts of the world. Each group showed definite variations in the pattern of abilities. Children in underdeveloped countries sometimes surpassed Western standards on some tasks but scored very low on others. Such studies illustrate that the global concept of intelligence provides only a crude measure.

Emphasis is placed on the standardization of the way IQ tests are given because scores are open to social influences. An examiner who encourages the client to try harder, or who is warm and reassuring, may obtain different results from an examiner who does not show these qualities. At least in part, measuring IQ is a social process and this means that when doing research using IQ tests the examiner should be 'blind' to the purpose of the study. This point is illustrated by a study in which children were tested using the Stanford–Binet by graduate students in psychology. The students were asked to test two children each, being led to believe that one was capable of high academic achievement whereas the other had shown only poor academic ability. In fact, there was no such systematic sorting of children, yet the examiners' results corresponded to their expectations. Those children said to be more able attained significantly higher scores than those said to be less able.[13]

This approach to the assessment of intelligence thus concentrates on an individual's abilities to perform certain tasks. Generally speaking, the greater the number of tasks performed correctly, the higher the IQ is said to be. Because a person's intelligence refers to his or her abilities relative to others', it is important that the tests be well standardized. The average IQ in the general population is set at 100, with only a small proportion scoring below 50 or over 150. The way a test is given must also be specified very clearly, or else the reliability and validity of the results would be questionable.

Factors affecting IQ

Genetics

An individual's score on an IQ test is generally considered to be a function of both heredity and environment. Certainly a defect in an individual's genetic make-up can lead to impaired intelligence: a genetic defect that affects one in every 2000 babies born to women in their twenties but one in 50 babies born to women in their forties is Down's syndrome: 47 chromosomes are present instead of the usual 46 and the condition is always associated with severe mental handicaps.

The role of the environment is also of consequence since genes provide only a potential for growth and do not determine its course independent of the environment. The importance of genetics in height, for example, is clear, but the general population in Western countries has been becoming appreciably taller over the last generations. This seems to be due to better diet and living conditions. Specific gene mutations that affect IQ highlight the complexity of the interrelationship between nature and nurture. Children born with phenylketonuria (PKU) used to suffer brain damage due to the build up of phenylalanine in toxic quantities in the bloodstream. Now, however, every infant is routinely tested a few days after birth (the Guthrie test) and in the rare cases that the condition is detected, amelioration is possible by the provision of a special diet, largely fruit and vegetables and as low as possible in phenylalanine. Galactosaemia is similar; a single gene defect leaves the patient unable to metabolize galactose. If not detected, this can lead to mental handicap. Once identified, the treatment is again mainly dietary. In both cases, by providing the right environment, the potentially damaging effects of the individual's genetic make-up are averted.

There is considerable disagreement about the relative importance of genetic and environmental influences. Some hold that heredity is primarily responsible for scores in IQ tests, others argue that environment is the critical factor. This debate, which is found among geneticists as well as psychologists, has been fiercely argued by both sides, with accusations (some justified) of fraudulent reporting of data. It is not possible adequately to summarize the debate here except to make some general points.

The problem in disentangling the effects of genes and environment is that people who are related to one another genetically are usually related to one another socially as well. If they live in the same household, they will have many shared experiences, so that any correlation between their IQs could just as easily be attributed to similarities in environment as to similarities in genetic endowment. Studies attempting to disentangle these effects run into many problems. For example, many studies have compared the IQs of monozygotic twins reared together with those reared apart. The similar correlations found have fuelled the genetic position. However, even for those reared apart the environments may be very similar. In one study many of the separated twins were raised in related branches of the same family, such as by the biological mother's sister. Further, criticisms of the design and statistical analysis of these original twin studies have been made, and the fact that blind testing has not always been used. There is the possibility that the examiners expected to find similar IQs amongst the twins reared apart and unconsciously biased their examination.

The debate between the two camps is likely to continue for some time yet.[14] As in other areas of psychology, it is those studies which have important social implications that are most critically examined, each side looking for flaws in the other's research.

Environment

In practice, it may be impossible to distinguish between the effects of nature and nurture, since the effects of genes depend on the environment they act in. Children who are given 'good' genes by their parents are also likely to live in an enriched environment, with plentiful books, lots of conversation and encouragement to do well at school. Any genetic potential is more likely to be fulfilled in such conditions.

The effect of a wide range of environmental circumstances on intellectual ability (again, as measured by IQ tests) have been studied, including the pre-natal environment, family, social class and education. Environment is taken to mean physical as well as social influences.

Pre-natal influences

Influences on the foetus in the womb can affect the IQ of the child, and these influences depend on their timing, an organ system being most sensitive when it is developing most rapidly. Although in the majority of cases of mental handicap no physical cause can be discovered, if the mother catches rubella (German measles) in the first three months of pregnancy, for instance, the infant's hearing may be impaired and heart defects or other physical abnormalities caused. The number of brain cells in the child is reduced if the mother's diet is inadequate (too little protein or too few calories) particularly in the final three months of pregnancy, and maternal alcoholism has been shown to lead to mental handicap in the child. Certain drugs taken by the mother during pregnancy can also affect the child. The effects of maternal smoking in pregnancy are not clear, but one study[15] found children of mothers who smoked during pregnancy were, on average, three months behind their peers on general intelligence at age 11 years. Although this is a small effect, it is also a preventable one. During the birth process itself, the infant's brain is extremely susceptible to damage. Lack of oxygen during birth (anoxia) is estimated to prevent one baby in 1000 from reaching a 12-year-old level of functioning.

Family/social class

Numerous studies have shown clear relationships between parental social class and both the IQ and scholastic achievement of their children.[16] Part of this social-class influence may be related to differences in the quality and quantity of language used in the home. In residential nurseries, the quality of children's verbal environment and the richness of their activities were significant determinants of early cognitive development. Many studies have found marked social-class differences in the language used by parents to their children[17,18] which put working-class children at a disadvantage on traditional IQ tests (and, indeed, in educational settings generally) compared to middle-class children. A review by Rutter and Madge[19] of children reared in isolated or poor communities concluded that the longer the privation, the more intellectual development was impeded. The quality of the parent–child interaction and the range of experiences available to the child were among those aspects of the environment that were most important in this connection. Further, they point out that it is not the amount of stimulation, but rather the quality, meaningfulness and range of experiences available to the child that are important.

Parental attitudes to learning and education and the literacy of the home may also be part of the social-class related influences, as, indirectly, are poor material circumstances such as poverty, overcrowding and lack of basic household facilities. More important, there is a high correlation between large family size and low attainment, larger families also tending to be those with less financial and material resources. The different forms of social disadvantage all tend to affect the same group of families. Verbal skills are particularly affected. Certainly, McCall et al.,[20] comparing children whose IQ scores increased over time with those whose IQ scores decreased, found the former had parents who stressed intellectual tasks and achievements more.

Education

Education has been shown to affect IQ, but to account for much less of the variance than features of family and home, perhaps because there is less variation between schools than between homes, and because the measures taken have tended to be rather crude. There have been various attempts to help children from disadvantaged homes by means of compensatory education, generally at pre-school level. In Garber and Heber's study,[21] 40 children were selected at birth whose mothers had an IQ of 80 or below. Twenty of the children served as a comparison group, being given no special attention. The other children were given extensive educational advantages — attending a centre for 7 hours a day, 5 days a week. The programme included assistance in language, thinking and sensori-motor skills. Their mothers, too, were included, being given vocational and child-care training. Both groups of children were periodically tested and after the age of 14 months differences between the groups became apparent. At about five years of age the experimental group children averaged 120 IQ points while the control group children had an average IQ of about 95. It seems that attempts at compensatory education that involve the family and which continue into the school years seem most likely to succeed.

Thus, intelligence is affected by both genetic endowment and experience. Those psychologists who emphasize the genetic component cite the studies on twins, where there are high correlations between monozygotic twins reared apart in separate families. On the other hand, there are clear environmental influences as well, since experiences (including pre-natal experiences) have effects on IQ.

Age

Studies on the effects of ageing do not fall easily into either the genetic or environmental categories. Since growing involves both maturational and experiential influences, both factors apply. Although IQ tests assess current intellectual functioning, the underlying assumption is that they imply something about future performance. Many studies have looked at the stability of IQ over time. Before one year of age, test results bear little relation to results a year later, not because the tests are particularly unreliable (an infant will be more likely to respond to a moving light or the sound of a bell in the same way on successive testings in the short term) but because these early tests sample a different, and greatly reduced, range of behaviours compared to tests for older children. Indeed, before one year of age, parental IQs provide a better predictor of the child's future IQ than infant tests. By two years, IQ results do correlate with those obtained, say, a year later, though they still bear little relationship to adult functioning. Even when correlations between successive testings are quite high, this can mask quite substantial changes in IQ over time. Hindley and Owen[22] point out that with a correlation as high as 0.76 from age 5 to 8 years, the median change is still expected to be 9 IQ points. Between 3 and 17 years, half of their sample changed by more than 10 points, a quarter by 20 points or more. Although test unreliability and changing test content may account for some of this change, some reflects true changes in ability over time.

Mental abilities that require speed and extensive use of short-term memory peak at about 30–40 years and then decline. Those that tap general knowledge, however, show little decline with age. The first type, which generally involves tackling novel problems, have been suggested to reflect a kind of 'fluid' or non-specialized type of intelligence which indicates an individual's capacity to adapt to new situations, in contrast with the second type, suggested to reflect 'crystallized' intelligence or ability resulting from accumulated wisdom. Two tests described previously are sometimes used to measure these two types of intelligence: Raven's Progressive Matrices, requiring the solution of new problems, is believed to reflect changes in capacity; whereas the Mill Hill Vocabulary Scale, drawing on past experience, is a more resistant test, reflecting 'crystallized' intelligence.

The exact nature of the decrement in mental processes with age depends on the methods used to collect the data. Cross-sectional studies, where a sample of the population of various ages (say, 20, 40, 60, 80) are tested on one occasion, produce different results from longitudinal studies where the same group of people are tested on successive occasions as they reach different ages. Cross-sectional studies run up against non-age-related differences between generations — younger people are more attuned to the whole ethos of intelligence testing, for example. Longitudinal studies are biased by non-random factors in drop out.[23] In addition, it appears that a relatively sudden drop in IQ may occur up to five years before death which affects results.[24] The rate of decline in IQ relates to occupation; people in intellectually demanding occupations do not decline in mental abilities as early as others in less demanding jobs.

As in the case of the controversy between geneticists and environmentalists regarding influences on IQ, there is therefore much discussion regarding the relative importance of organic deterioration versus environmental changes in the decline of intelligence in old age. Many argue that any decline is due to the fewer demands made on elderly people, who have less opportunity to practise the types of skill measured by IQ tests. (A similar point was made regarding memory in Chapter 4 and will be taken up again in more detail in Chapter 10.)

Whatever the causes of decline, the distinction between fluid and crystallized intelligence is an important one when considering the needs of elderly people. Having difficulty in adapting to new problems or strange situations may make hospitalization more stressful than for a younger person. There is some evidence that whenever possible the elderly should be treated at home in order to minimize these effects (Chapter 10). Further, simply because an elderly person may have difficulty in adapting to new surroundings does not necessarily mean that he or she cannot cope in familiar ones. Thus, assessments of ability and behaviour made outside the home may not provide a true reflection of abilities within it.

Development of intelligence

The intelligence tests so far described are empirical, simply identifying tasks that an average child of a particular age can do. The researchers who devised the early tests were not primarily concerned with explaining how such skills develop. Some theorists have argued that there is a sequence of stages through which every child progresses. The idea is that the order of these stages is common to all, although some children may pass through them more quickly than others. Again, certain theorists have placed great weight on maturation (growth processes that are governed by automatic, genetically determined signals) whereas others have placed more emphasis on learning. Both processes are involved to some extent: for example, maturation is clearly important in the infant's ability to reach or to walk, but there is evidence that both skills can be hastened by experience.[25,26]

Gesell

A major proponent of the maturational approach is Arnold Gesell who made many detailed observations of infants' and pre-school children's abilities. By examining large groups of children, Gesell charted the normal (or average) course of development. An individual child's abilities could then be compared with these data. The tests devised from this work are easy to administer, score and interpret, being concerned with the average age at which such skills as smiling, sitting without support or standing holding on to furniture emerge.[27] Such normative studies of development form the basis of routine paediatric assessments. By checking all children in this way as a matter of course, developmental lags can be monitored, allowing the early detection of sensory handicaps or intellectual impairments and early intervention to deal with these. Gesell believed behaviour unfolded in a sequence of stages, determined by inherent maturational mechanisms. Although this work shows the average ages at which skills emerge, it is important to realize that there is a large normal range of ages at which skills develop. The average age of walking is 14 months, for example, but many children do not accomplish this until some months later.

Piaget

A more active view of the developmental process is taken by Piaget. Rather than simply accumulating experiences or maturing physically, he argued, the child comes to understand the world through actively working with, modifying and organizing these experiences. Like Gesell, Piaget believed that to achieve these understandings, each child goes through a series of distinct stages: some may progress further than others, but the order remains invariant. Each stage builds on the previous one and once new concepts are mastered, allows the child to explore new aspects of the environment.

Piaget suggested that the child under the age of seven is in many ways extremely limited in his or her ability to think or reason. The Piagetian pre-school child, for example, is not supposed to know what an object would look like from the other side, being unable to consider any viewpoint other than his or her own (called egocentrism); the child is supposed to think that if you pour water from one jar into another of a different shape, you change the quantity of water (conservation of volume). These and other limitations were brought to light in a series of careful — and much replicated — observations of children in defined situations.

More recently, aspects of his theory have been called into question. It seems that children can reason in many of these ways if the situation is made more relevant and if ambiguities in language are removed. For example, one of Piaget's claims was that young children cannot reason simultaneously about a total set of objects and a subset of these objects. For instance, when children are shown four toy cows, three black and one white, and asked, 'Are there more black cows or more cows?', a 5-year-old child will typically say that there are more black cows. More recent research has indicated that this response may be due more to a failure of communication between the adult and the child than a lack of ability. If the cows are laid on their sides as though sleeping and the question is 'Are there more black cows or more sleeping cows?', making the task more explicit, many more children give the correct reply, showing that they do, in fact, understand the relationship between the subset and whole.[28]

Despite such problems with aspects of Piaget's work, his theories remain influential and have made psychologists more aware of the ways that children come to understand their world. Like adults, children respond to instructions in ways consistent with their expectations and interpretations of a situation. A child is unlikely to have clear and realistic expectations about medical settings which may be novel and anxiety-provoking. Adults involved with children need to be sensitive to the ways in which they use and interpret language. Their understanding of concepts such as health and illness may be very different from an adult's view.[29] The concept of cause and effect is a very complex one in medicine, and it may not be until the age of nine or ten that a child can understand these ideas. Children often consider illness to be a punishment for bad or prohibited behaviour. Similarly, children's views about death are often different from adults'. Below the age of about five, death may be confused with 'going away' for a short time or with sleep. It, too, might be seen as a form of punishment. Later, death becomes more final and inevitable, but it is not until adolescence that most children can view it in a philosophical way.[30]

There are also implications for asking children to participate in certain situations. Schwartz[31] examined the effects of hospitalization of a purely research nature on children from 4 to 18 years of age. The researchers gave each child and the parents careful preparation before the research work began, explaining its purposes, duration and possible benefits. Later, however, despite having been told the purpose of the hospitalization was research, there was no indication that any of the children under the age of 11 understood why they were in hospital. This abstract idea was either beyond their capacity to understand or was not explained in a way that made sense to the children, so their consent to participate could not have been 'informed'.

Piaget's theory also holds that children are motivated to explore their world. Curiosity may be as important a motivator of behaviour as the biological pressures of hunger and thirst. Besides the problems associated with separation from the parents (see Chapter 7) hospitalization may have disturbing effects on the child if these cognitive requirements are not met. The opportunity to explore and experiment with their world may be restricted in hospitals due to staff shortages, or lack of toys and space. Particularly when chronic illnesses requiring lengthy stays in hospital are involved, a chance to play may be crucial for well-being.[32]

Use of intellectual assessments

Although, as discussed above, IQ scores obtained from infants have low correlations with later scores, scales based on the work of Gesell are widely used, especially by paediatricians and health visitors to diagnose sensory and mental handicaps in infants during the first years of life. Although the earlier the diagnosis is made the better, since the environment can then be structured to optimize development, it is important to ensure that re-assessments occur: 21 per cent of one sample who were originally diagnosed as handicapped were not, at future testings, intellectually handicapped on any criterion despite their earlier scores.[33]

In educational settings, standard IQ tests such as the WISC have proved useful in assessing individual children who have problems at school. They provide a way of seeing whether a child's difficulties are due to below average intelligence, for which a remedial programme might be suggested, or whether there are sensory difficulties, such as impaired vision or hearing; or whether there are specific perceptual difficulties, such as dyslexia, that would affect a child's ability to read but not affect his score on an individually administered IQ test. The different subscales of the WISC allow a comparison between verbal and performance measures (the latter comprising manipulation or arrangement of blocks, beads, etc.) that can pinpoint more specific problems.

In psychiatric settings, individual IQ tests of adults can provide helpful information. Stress at work, for instance, could arise from lack of capacity to cope with a too demanding job or could result from a person's over-capacity in an undemanding job. Some clinical conditions cause deterioration of intellectual performance, leading to dementia. In the early stages, such conditions can resemble other psychiatric disorders. In conjunction with psychiatric evidence, IQ tests may enable elderly people with intellectual difficulties associated with functional disorders to be distinguished from those related to more severe degenerative senile processes.[34] The course of any deterioration can be charted by testing over time. It is very important to take account of the state of the patient during the testing and the nature of the referral may provide clues; for instance, someone showing signs of depression may be particularly handicapped on timed items.

Mental handicap

The use of intellectual assessments in paediatric and educational settings can identify people with mental handicaps. Care of mentally handicapped people has changed in recent years. It is now recognized that long-stay hospitals, into which they were often admitted as a matter of course, provide an unsuitable environment (see Chapter 6). Most mentally handicapped people require not medical but educational help, not institutional care but housing in ordinary, small homes within the community. Although IQ tests can be helpful in identifying mental handicaps (traditionally defined as IQs less than 70), they do not provide information on appropriate care. Despite low capacity, many mentally handicapped people can, with time, learn to cope effectively with familiar situations. Their adaptive behaviour, or ability to cope independently, is what is important, and there are tests available which attempt to measure this.[35,36] Stage approaches to intellectual development may also be helpful in assessing and treating mentally handicapped people. Early stimulation of handicapped children by parents has been found to produce significant gains compared with controls.[37] Self-help guides for parents of mentally handicapped children have been produced, based on Gesell's work. As well as enabling parents to chart their child's progress, they indicate the next likely step in development, allowing parents to provide opportunities for the child to practise the necessary skills. Piaget's stages have been taken as the basis of educational work with severely handicapped adults as well as children.[38]

Summary

Intelligence, like personality, is an abstraction. It is not possible to touch or feel intelligence, only to observe its effects. It is usually measured by IQ tests which seem to provide reliable and valid indicators of current intellectual performance. However, IQ tests are strongly geared towards white, middle-class culture despite attempts to develop 'culture fair' tests. Although predictive of the future average performance of groups of people, there are often large changes in particular individuals, indicating that caution is required in the interpretation of test results.

Although intelligence undoubtedly has some genetic basis, the importance of heredity has been fiercely disputed. There are major environmental influences, such as the pre-natal environment, a person's family, social class and education. Tests assessing intellectual performance can identify particular problems such as mental handicap or intellectual deterioration. A crucial distinction can be made between the capacity to solve novel problems and abilities amassed due to experience. Although the former deteriorates with age, the latter does not. Mentally handicapped people have limited capacity but during their development ability to handle familiar situations may continue to increase as a result of experience. Both old people and mentally handicapped people may thus be able to cope effectively in familiar situations despite low measured IQ on some tests.

IQ testing is not based on a theory of intelligence but rather on the premise that children acquire more skills as they grow older. Piaget's theory of intellectual development, however, illustrates qualitative differences between the thinking of children at different ages. This theory suggests that intelligence develops through an invariant sequence of stages and has implications for education and for the care of sick children.

Suggested reading

For a general review of influences on IQ, see N. Madge & J. Tizard, (1980) Intelligence (Chapter 21). In: Rutter, M. (ed.) *Scientific Foundations of Developmental Psychiatry* London: Heinemann Medical Books. Ref. 4 gives more detail about intelligence testing. Piaget's theory is extremely complex and more detail can be found in Donaldson (Ref. 28).

References

1. Walsh, K.W. (1978) *Neuropsychology* London: Churchill Livingstone.
2. Blinkhorn, S.F. & Hendrickson, D.E. (1982) Averaged evoked responses and psychometric intelligence. *Nature* **295**: 596–597.
3. Terman, L.M. & Merrill, M.A. (1961) *Stanford–Binet Intelligence Scale: Manual for the Third Revision* London: Harrap.
4. Anastasi, A. (ed.) (1965) *Individual Differences* London: Wiley.
5. Raven, J.C., Court, J.H. & Raven, J. (1977) *Manual for Raven's Progressive Matrices and Vocabulary Scale* London: H.K. Lewis.
6. Sacks, E. (1952) Intelligence scores as a function of experimentally established social relationships between child and examiner. *Journal of Abnormal and Social Psychology* **46**: 354–358.
7. Pederson, D.M., Shinedling, M.M. & Johnson, D.L. (1968) Effects of sex of examiner and subject on children's quantitative test performance. *Journal of Personality and Social Psychology* **10**: 251–254.
8. Watson, P. (1972) Can racial discrimination affect IQ? In: Richardson, K. & Spears, D. (eds.) *Race, Culture and Intelligence* Harmondsworth, Middlesex: Penguin Books.
9. Becker, H.S., Geer, B. & Miller, S.J. (1972) Medical education. In: Freeman, H.E., Levine, S., & Reeder, L.G. (eds.) *Handbook of Medical Sociology*, 2nd edn. Englewood Cliffs, New Jersey: Prentice-Hall.
10. Hudson, L. (1966) *Contrary Imagination* Harmondsworth, Middlesex: Penguin Books.
11. Eells, K., Davis, A., Havighurst, R.J., Herrick, V.E. & Tyler, R.W. (1951) *Intelligence and Cultural Differences* Chicago: Chicago University Press.
12. Vernon, P.E. (1969) *Intelligence and Cultural Environment* London: Methuen.
13. Hersch, J.B. (1971) Effects of referral information on testers. *Journal of Consulting and Clinical Psychology* **37**: 116–122.

14. Eysenck, H.J. & Kamin, L. (1981) *Intelligence: The Battle for the Mind* London: Pan Books.
15. Butler, N.R. & Goldstein, H. (1973) Smoking in pregnancy and subsequent child development. *British Medical Journal* **4**: 573–575.
16. Douglas, J.W.B. (1967) *The Home and the School* St Albans: Panther.
17. Hess, R.D. & Shipman, V.C. (1965) Early experience and the socialisation of cognitive modes in children. *Child Development* **36**: 869–886.
18. Bernstein, B. (1965) A sociolinguistic approach to social learning. In: Gould, J. (ed.) *Penguin Survey of the Social Sciences* Harmondsworth, Middlesex: Penguin Books.
19. Rutter, M. & Madge, N. (1976) *Cycles of Disadvantage* London: Heinemann.
20. McCall, R.B., Appelbaum, M. & Hogarty, P. (1973) Developmental changes in mental performance. *Monographs of the Society for Research in Child Development* **38**: Whole number 150.
21. Garber, H. & Heber, F. (1977) The Milwaukee project. In: Mittler, P. (ed.) *Research to Practice in Mental Retardation* Baltimore: University Park Press.
22. Hindley, C.B. & Owen, C. (1978) The extent of individual changes in IQ for ages between 6 months and 17 years in a British longitudinal sample. *Journal of Child Psychology and Psychiatry* **19**: 329–350.
23. Siegler, I.C. & Botwinick, J. (1979) A long-term longitudinal study of intellectual ability of older adults. *Journal of Gerontology* **34**: 242–245.
24. Riegel, K.R. & Riegel, R.M. (1972) Development, drop and death. *Developmental Psychology* **6**: 306–319.
25. White, B.L., Castle, P. & Held, R. (1964) Observations on the development of visually-guided reaching. *Child Development* **35**: 349–364.
26. Zelazo, P.R., Zelazo, N. & Kolb, S. (1972) 'Walking' in the newborn. *Science* **176**: 314–315.
27. Frankenburg, W.K. & Dodds, J.B. (1967) The Denver developmental screening test. *Journal of Pediatrics* **71**: 181–191.
28. Donaldson, M. (1978) *Children's Minds* Glasgow: Fontana.
29. Eiser, C. (1984) Communicating with sick and hospitalised children. *Journal of Child Psychology and Psychiatry* **25**: 181–189.
30. Blos, P. (1978) Children think about illness: their concepts and beliefs. In: Gellert, E. (ed.) *Psychosocial Aspects of Pediatric Care* London: Grune and Stratton.
31. Schwartz, A.H. (1972) Children's concepts of research hospitalisation. *New England Journal of Medicine* **287**: 589–592.
32. Crocker, E. (1978) Play programmes in pediatric settings. In: Gellert, E. (ed.) *Psychosocial Aspects of Pediatric Care* London: Grune and Stratton.
33. Illingworth, R.S. (1971) The predictive value of developmental assessment in infancy. *Developmental Medicine and Child Neurology* **13**: 721–725.
34. Savage, R.D., Britton, P., Bolton, N. & Hall, E. (1973) *Intellectual Functioning in the Aged* London: Methuen.
35. Gunzburg, H.C. (1969) *The P–A–C Manual* London: National Association on Mental Deficiency.
36. Nihira, K., Foster, R., Shellhaas, M. & Leland, H. (1974) *AAMD Adaptive Behaviour Scale for Children* American Association on Mental Deficiency.
37. Gath, A. (1979) Parents as therapists of mentally handicapped children. *Journal of Child Psychology and Psychiatry* **20**: 161–165.
38. Woodward, M. (1962) The application of Piaget's theory to the training of the subnormal. *Journal of Mental Subnormality* **8**: 17–25.

6

The Social Context

Introduction

Traditionally, many of the psychological processes discussed in previous chapters have been considered to be relatively independent of the situation in which they occur. However, it has become clear that fuller understanding of such attributes as personality, memory and intelligence can be achieved by taking into account the circumstances in which they are shown. For example, an elderly person may be quite able in his or her own home but confused and helpless in a novel environment. Similarly, when an individual's IQ is considered, it is important to take not only his or her early environment into account but also the relationship with the examiner. The setting in which people act — which includes both the physical and social setting — has important influences on their behaviour. This chapter turns to some of the research that has investigated these influences.

Sociology

Sometimes the distinction between psychology and the other social sciences becomes blurred. Some of the work described is usually considered to lie within the province of sociology, which is concerned with the behaviour of groups of people rather than individuals. Perhaps the most important observation to a sociologist is that societies manage to exist at all. Since there does not seem to be anyone who directs us to have a government, to build schools, hospitals and prisons or to develop immunization programmes, the very existence of these phenomena can be seen as a remarkable achievement. Whether a society is technologically advanced or 'primitive', it has a number of institutions and customs that ensure it continues to work. Central to the sociologist's explanation of such phenomena is the concept of *expectation*. The idea is that all of us have expectations of how others should behave and they have expectations of us. As children grow up in society, they learn what is expected of them from family, friends and in school. If these requirements are not met, then steps will be taken to sanction the individual concerned — the legal system provides one institutionalized means of sanctioning people who do not meet certain kinds of expectations. In the medical school system, teachers have expectations of students (e.g. that they will turn up to lectures and take exams) and students of teachers (e.g. that they should set fair exams and mark them justly). When a doctor is on the ward, he or she has expectations of patients, and they of the doctor. A sociologist is primarily concerned with how different groups of people have different ideas about what behaviour is appropriate and how these groups relate to each other.

In order to discover and explain these behaviours, sociologists have traditionally performed their research in real-life situations, bringing interview, questionnaire or participant observation methods to bear on the topic. (In the latter case, the investigator finds a position in the organization he wishes to study and explores it from the 'inside'.) For example, a sociologist might interview patients from general practices in order to find out about their expectations of how doctors should behave. In one such study, three different kinds of expectations were identified. *Background expectations* concerned people's ideas of what a consultation is generally like, depending on the particular illness. A thorough examination would be expected for some symptoms but not for others. *Interaction expectations* concern how the doctor will react to and assess symptoms. In a group practice, for example, a patient may come to realize that the physicians differ in their approaches and will select the doctor whose approach is most favoured for a particular problem. The third type of expectation concerns the *actions* the physician will take. Before patients arrive, they have expectations of what the doctor should do for them, which might involve writing a prescription, for example. In this study it became clear that patients were dissatisfied when their expectations were not met for any apparent reason. If the doctor did not listen to their worries or if the patient did not agree with the doctor's advice, this was a cause for complaint to the researcher. For example, one woman explained:

> I had a bout when I was not sleeping at all and I used to lay awake hours and hours in the night and it was worry about my mother it was . . . she was ill at the time . . . and I was really — worked myself to such a pitch, you know, and I was trying to tell him [the doctor] but I couldn't get the words out, you know, I was so choked inside. And he just sort of — 'Oh well, it's your mother, is it, is that what you are worried about?' And I said 'Yes', and he said, 'We're doing all we can for her', and that was all. 'Take some

tablets,' he said, and he gave me some tablets. He wasn't interested, I just got over it myself. (Ref. 1, pp. 74–75)

Sometimes, a sociologist might test the importance of an expectation by deliberately breaking the rule involved. For example, in one study in California, the investigator knocked on a bank door during business hours, waiting for someone to come and open it rather than walking straight in. This would be appropriate behaviour at a private house, but not, it seems, in a public place: the police were called.

By contrast, social psychologists have usually attempted to understand social influence in the controlled conditions of the laboratory. Although these studies often seem artificial and far removed from real life, they do have advantages. It is often easier to pinpoint those factors which are responsible for behaviour. By randomly assigning subjects to various conditions, many extraneous factors such as personality can be cancelled out. However, there can be ethical problems. In certain studies, experimenters use 'confederates' — people who have been instructed to behave in certain ways, yet subjects believe they are participants in the experiment just like themselves. Subjects may be misled in other ways as well, and such deceptions are considered unethical by many people, including many psychologists. However it is difficult to see how some of the research outlined in the first part of this chapter could have been performed in any other way, and since these studies have important social implications it can be argued that this procedure is justified in certain cases.

Social influences

In some situations, the actions of other people can elicit behaviour which may seem unlikely or surprising. Three specific aspects are considered here. The first, termed 'Bystander Intervention', concerns people's reluctance to intervene in emergencies. People's willingness to perform unkind and undesirable actions when asked to do so in an authoritative way, forms the second topic. Third, the tendency for some people to conform to others' erroneous views rather than to voice their own opinions in public is examined.

Bystander intervention

Research in this area was motivated by a particularly nasty murder in New York City in 1964. A woman was killed in the street while a large number of people in a nearby apartment block could hear her screams but made no attempt to help her, not even by telephoning the police. The assault took place over more than an hour and her distress was obvious. Reactions to this incident included condemnation of the residents and warnings of the imminent breakdown of society, but it also demonstrated to social psychologists that they lacked knowledge about how people react in such situations.

Usually this topic has been explored by staging incidents. The approach has been to recruit subjects on the basis of taking part in a psychology experiment, but they are misled as to its purpose. They might be told that the study involves filling out questionnaires. At some point the experimenter finds an excuse to leave the subjects alone in the room. After some minutes, an emergency is staged — sounds of someone falling in the next room, or smoke coming from under a door. The measure taken is whether the subjects do something about it, either trying to find the experimenter or entering the room where the incident has occurred.

Diffusion of responsibility

The question is: what factors affect whether the subjects will give help? One possibility was suggested through interviews with the witnesses of the New York murder. Many mentioned that they had thought 'someone else' would contact the police. It was as if the responsibility for helping was diffused, so that in the end nothing was done. In order to test the importance of this factor, Darley and Latané[2] led subjects to believe that they were to take part in a group discussion about personal problems. To avoid embarrassment, they were told, each person in the study would sit alone in a booth and talk with others through a microphone, each in turn. There would be several rounds of discussion and the experimenter said that he would not be listening. One group of subjects was told that they would discuss their problems with one other person, a second group was told that two others would be taking part, and a third group that there would be five others. Thus, different subjects thought that they were in groups of varying size. In fact, there was only ever one person in the experiment, the others' voices being on tape. On the first round of discussion, one of the voices indicated that he was prone to having epileptic seizures. When it was his turn on the second round, he made a few calm comments but then it seemed that he was having a seizure.

The experimenters reasoned that if diffusion of responsibility were an important factor in bystander intervention, then subjects who believed themselves to be in a large group would be less likely to leave their booth and give aid than those who believed they were part of a small group. This hypothesis was supported: 85 per cent of those who thought themselves to be the only ones listening to the seizure sought help, 62 per cent of those who thought there was one other person who could give aid, and only 31 per cent of those who thought there were four others. Thus, it seems that the decision to give aid is related to the number of others who are also available to give assistance.

Of course, it could be argued that some people did not give help because they were sceptical about the genuineness of the incident. It was, after all, a psychology experiment. However, at the end of the study all subjects were interviewed and none thought that the emergency was faked. Besides, there was no apparent reason why subjects in the large group condition would believe this more often than those in the small group condition. Nor was there any evidence that the subjects who did not help were callous, uncaring individuals — at the end of the experiment when they were asked why they had not helped, they reported feeling very upset by the experience.

Interpreting the incident

Interviews with the subjects pointed towards another possible reason why aid was not given. Several said they were unsure that the situation was, in fact, an emergency. There was some ambiguity in their minds about whether help was actually required. It seemed that since emergencies are very rare in most people's lives, it takes some time to make sense of what is going on before action is taken. In order to test the importance of interpretation, Darley and Latané introduced a confederate into an experiment. They reasoned that in times of ambiguity people look to the reactions of others to help them make sense of what is going on, and if this confederate was instructed not to react to an incident, the subject would be less likely to give help. In this next experiment, they constructed three conditions. In one, the subjects were left alone in a room; in a second condition two subjects who were strangers to each other were left together; and in the third the subject was placed with a confederate. All were told that they were part of a market survey study and the experimenter was said to be a representative of the company. After she asked the subjects to fill out several questionnaires, she indicated that she would do some work next door and would return in 10–15 minutes. The subjects saw her go into the next room, screened from them by a curtain:

> While they worked on their questionnaires, subjects heard the representative moving around in the next office, shuffling papers, and opening and closing drawers. After about four minutes, if they were listening carefully, they heard her climb up on a chair to get a book from the top shelf. Even if they were not listening carefully, they heard a loud crash and a woman's scream as the chair fell over. 'Oh my God, my foot . . . ,' cried the representative. 'I . . . I . . . can't move . . . it. Oh, my ankle. I . . . can't . . . can't . . . get . . . this thing off . . . me.' She moaned and cried for about a minute longer, getting gradually more subdued and controlled. Finally, she muttered something about getting outside, knocked the chair around as she pulled herself up, and limped out, closing the door behind her. (Ref. 3, p. 58)

In order to ensure that all subjects heard the same accident, it was recorded on tape, but they had no way of knowing this. Intervention could have been made in several ways in this study—by going into the room, by looking for help or, simply, by calling through the curtain to ask the representative if she were hurt. While the accident occurred, the confederate in the third condition was instructed to look up, to stare quizzically at the curtain, shrug his shoulders and then return to the questionnaire.

The results supported the hypothesis that interpretation was significant. In the first (alone) condition, some 70 per cent of the subjects intervened. When two strangers were working together, the number fell to 40 per cent. This is both a replication and an extension of the previous study. In the personal problems experiment, the subjects could not hear or see anyone else: apparently this was not a critical factor because the responsibility was still diffused despite subjects being able to see the reactions of someone else. In the third (confederate) condition, only 8 per cent of the subjects made an attempt to help: by seeing someone not react to the incident the subjects were less inclined to treat it as an emergency which merited assistance.

Other studies, and studies in naturalistic settings as well, have supported the influence of these two factors. In some situations there may be little ambiguity about the meaning of an incident (as in the case of the murder) and in such cases diffusion of responsibility may be significant. In others, it may be difficult for the people involved to interpret the incident. Here the reactions of others may be important. One additional point which can be made about these studies, relevant to other work in social psychology, is that once such findings become widely known, the effect itself may no longer be present. The reactions of people who had seen a film describing this research were compared with those of people who had not seen the film to a staged incident on the street: more of the informed subjects gave assistance.

Psychology can reflect back and influence society as well as provide clues about its operation.

Obedience to authority

As in the case of research on bystander intervention, that on obedience was motivated by real-life experiences, particularly the murder of Jews during the Second World War. Milgram[4] sought to gain some understanding of why so many German officials had obeyed their orders. There are likely to be many valid answers to this question, but he was interested in the relationship between obedience and authority. In his experiments, subjects were recruited from a wide range of age and social groups, so that his results cannot be said to apply only to university students. They were told that the experiment involved memory, testing the theory that people learn more quickly when they are punished for making a mistake. The subject's job was to help someone to learn some paired-associate words. For example, when the word 'blue' was given, the word 'box' was to be supplied. If this association was not recalled, the learner was to be given a shock by the subject and this shock was to be more intense the next time an error was made. Each subject saw the learner strapped into a chair and was then seated in front of a shock-generator. This had a total of 30 switches, labelled from 15 volts to 450 volts. The intensity of these shocks was also indicated, from 'slight shock' to 'danger, severe shock'. The shocks were said to be painful, but not to cause any permanent tissue damage.

Actually, the learner was a confederate and the shock-generator was fake. The confederate was instructed to protest as the level was increased, then to shout and scream and finally to fall silent. The experimenter was to prod the subject if he baulked at giving the shocks, saying that he would accept all responsibility for the consequences. But there was no physical coercion and no promise of greater payment. The experimental question was to see how far up the shock levels the subjects would go before they refused to obey the experimenter.

Before this study, Milgram canvassed colleagues', friends' and psychiatrists' predictions of the results. They felt that only a minority of subjects would continue to obey the experimenter for long and that only a tiny number would go up to the 450 volt level. You might wonder if you would agree to take part in the study at all. Nevertheless, 25 of the 40 subjects tested went all the way to 450 volts despite the apparent pain involved. Was this due to malevolent or sadistic personalities? It seemed not, since most showed clear signs of distress and conflict, despite their obedience. In other experiments, the nature of the situations was shown to have an effect. When the subject and learner sat side by side, only 16 of 40 went to 450 volts, and when the subject was actually responsible for placing the learner's hand on an electric grid, only 12 out of 40. Other factors had less effect. Many of the studies were performed within the auspicious confines of Yale University and it was thought that perhaps this may have had an influence. However, when the laboratory was transferred to an old building in the centre of the city, little difference was found.

These are not isolated results, being replicated many times. Their relevance to medical care has been illustrated by a study of nursing staff and their relationship to doctors. Here, the researchers were interested in whether or not nursing students would comply with an order from a doctor that should not have been obeyed according to the hospital's rules. While on the ward, the nurse received a telephone call from the ward doctor requesting her to give some tablets. There were two problems with this call. First, it was against hospital policy for medication to be given on the basis of a telephone call: the doctor should have signed the order before the drug was given. Second, the doctor requested that twice the maximum daily dosage should be given, as it was stated on the package. When a nurse received the call, she was unobtrusively observed to see if she did, in fact, intend to give the medication (she was stopped before it was administered). Twenty-one nurses would have fulfilled the request out of 22 nurses studied. This result could not have been due simply to their being unaware of the inappropriate dosage, since 11 later said that they realized the discrepancy.[5] Milgram concluded from his work that the subjects in his study were willing to apply the electric shocks because the experimenter said that he would accept responsibility for the consequences. A similar process may have been operating here. It seems that obedience to authority happens in naturally occurring situations as well as in the psychology laboratory.

These studies also indicate that people are not particularly good at predicting how they would behave in unusual circumstances. Just as the reader might predict that he or she would, of course, give help to someone who had an accident or would refuse to give apparently painful shocks in a psychology experiment, so too did another sample of student nurses indicate that they would refuse to obey the doctor's orders when they were inappropriate. Of 21 nurses who were not involved in the study, all said that they would not give the medication. Assuming that these nurses were no different than the ones who participated, and there was no reason to suspect they were, it seems likely that they, too, would have complied under the circumstances.

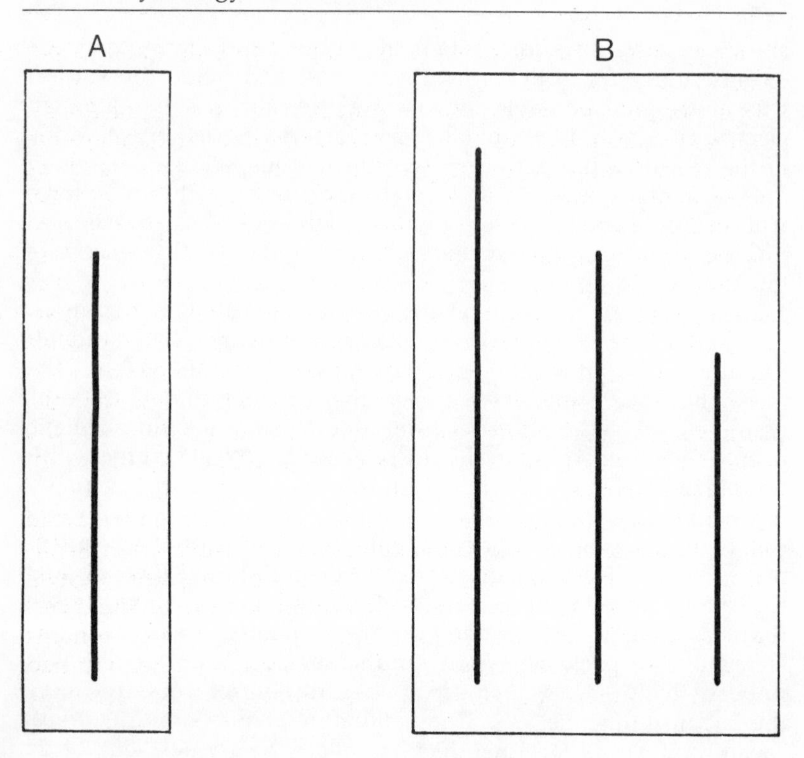

Fig. 11. Materials similar to those used in Asch's experiments.

Conformity

Another example of social influence on behaviour is provided by a series of studies performed by Asch.[6] He presented subjects with materials similar to those shown in Fig. 11. On the left is a card with one line on it. The subjects' task was to choose which of those shown on the card on the right was of the same length. Typically, one subject would give his report after four others (confederates) had given theirs. On the first two trials, all went well with no problems for the subject, but on the third trial (and occasional others) he heard the other four give a wrong answer. Faced with this clear discrepancy, the question was what would the subject do? To some extent, it seemed to depend on the subject himself. Some never conformed, others almost always. Over a large number of trials and many experiments, conformity was found on about 35 per cent of test trials. The probability of conformity could be influenced by several factors, but most especially by the presence of one other person who did not conform, where the incidence was reduced to only about 6 per cent.

It is possible to make both too much and too little of Asch's studies. Observations of the subjects indicated that they were under considerable strain, suggesting that they were aware of the oddity of the situation. However, many situations in everyday life are very ambiguous and studies suggest there is greater conformity with more ambiguous stimuli.[7] Others' responses may be important in resolving such situations, whether they be the interpretation of X-rays, the usefulness of medication for a particular patient, or diagnosis. The confederates in Asch's studies can be considered to have provided information about what kind of answer was appropriate in the situation. When, for example, diagnosis is problematic, as it often is, conformity with the opinions provided by other physicians may be significant in influencing treatment.

Most of these studies on social influences have been conducted within the laboratory and could therefore be dismissed as artificial. However, these results are similar to what happens in 'real life' in many ways: often people do not respond to emergencies when they occur and this is very similar to what the experiments suggest would happen. Similarly, people are often obedient and conform in rather surprising ways in situations when someone is in authority.

Environmental influences

Although the work discussed so far has emphasized the influence of other people on behaviour, some psychologists have concentrated on the effects of the physical environment. One application is in the design of hospitals. During the nineteenth century, many psychiatric hospitals were built on the outskirts of cities. The idea behind this was that patients should be taken away from the stresses and strains of city life and placed in quiet, isolated surroundings. Besides serving custodial functions, these conditions were thought to be conducive to rest and recovery. Many of the hospitals were large, having 1000 patients or more. Families were not encouraged to visit (if only by the distance involved). Certain policies within these hospitals were advocated. Patients' personal possessions were taken away and hospital clothing issued. This was designed to reduce the number of reminders for the patients of their past. These measures appear harsh, but for some people at least they were based on high ideals and therapeutic intentions. However, there was an unfortunate by-product of this treatment, in that many patients became dependent on the institution and indifferent or even antagonistic to leaving. They were said to be *institutionalized* and it became difficult to integrate such people back into the community. It was as if they came to consider the hospital their permanent home.

One result of this problem of institutionalization is a change in policy towards treatment procedures within existing buildings. During the 1950s and 1960s there were many attempts to minimize the difference between hospital and community. Personal possessions were allowed and more patient privacy provided. Wing and Brown[8] described how they examined three psychiatric hospitals. Hospital A was considered the most progressive, allowing most of the patients personal possessions (their own clothes instead of institutional ones, their own toothbrushes, a locker to keep books, etc.) and opportunities to engage in meaningful constructive work. Hospital B shared some of these characteristics, but there were also instances of an institutional atmosphere. Not many patients, for example, possessed scissors or a mirror, and fewer baths were screened from onlookers. Hospital C was considered the least progressive, with only few activities provided, little or no privacy and few personal possessions being allowed. The staff of this hospital were also more restrictive, the patients requiring permission to leave the ward or to use the kitchen to make a drink. Wing and Brown then took several measures of the patients' behaviour. They found that Hospital C had more severely ill patients, a result that could not be attributed to condition at admission. These patients were more likely to be socially withdrawn, isolated and passive, as well as to spend much of their time 'doing nothing'. They were also more likely to want to stay in the hospital. There seemed to be a gradation between the hospitals, so that these observations were more common in Hospital C than B than A.

Although this study was correlational, their suggestion that differences in patient behaviour were due to the effects of the hospital environment was given further support when they examined the hospitals over a period of time. As physical conditions improved, so too did the clinical condition of the schizophrenic patients. In two hospitals, conditions improved and then deteriorated again: the patients' conditions showed a similar pattern. The lack of privacy and the paucity of organized activities were thought to be responsible for these effects. Other studies have implicated drab colours on the walls and large multi-occupant bedrooms as further deleterious factors. Wing and Brown[9] argued that many of the features associated with the condition of schizophrenia were due to the under-stimulation presented by these large institutions.

Changing the environment

Influenced by such research, there have been several attempts at changing the atmosphere in psychiatric hospitals over the last decades. For example, Holahan and Saegert[10] report a study on remodelling a psychiatric ward. In this particular hospital they were able to find two nearly identical wards: in both the walls were dirty and the furniture was worn and uncomfortable. One ward was chosen for improvement. The walls were painted with bright colours and new furniture purchased. In order to create privacy, the large dormitory was divided into more personal two-bed sections and small areas of the large day ward were informally sectioned off to provide the opportunity for intimate talk. The second ward acted as a control so that the effects of the remodelling could be evaluated. Patients were randomly placed in one of the two wards and six months later the investigators returned.* Those in the remodelled ward were found to be significantly more sociable with other patients, with staff and with visitors and less likely to be passive and isolated, suggesting that the differences in environment had effects on the patients' behaviour. The researchers also took some measures of attitudes towards the ward and correlated these with the patients' activity levels. Those patients who most liked the remodelled ward tended to be those who were most active, whereas those who most liked the control ward were those who were least active (especially those who slept much of the time). Since many hospital staff place a high value on social contact, these results indicate that providing bright colours and opportunities for privacy is conducive to good treatment.

While these findings are suggestive, they are not conclusive. The behaviour of the patients in the remodelled ward may have differed from those of the control ward not because of the character of the new conditions but because they were made to feel special simply because changes had taken place. The staff, who were seemingly aware of the purpose of the experiment, might

* Instead of observing all the patients all of the time (which would be very expensive and time-consuming) they took *samples* of behaviour. Twenty-five patients on each ward were randomly selected for study and their activities at 5-minute intervals were noted over several days: whatever they were doing at this point was recorded. Sampling in this way has several advantages. Practically speaking, fewer researchers are needed, but also a better indication of the activity on the ward can be gathered. The same amount of observation time could be used observing the ward for one entire day only, but then the results might be strongly affected by unique circumstances. There might be a plan to take several residents out on a trip from one ward but not the other; some patients may be ill which could bias the results towards inactivity; the ward might be short-staffed that day due to a snowstorm. By taking several small samples of behaviour over several days, short-term influences such as these even out.

Table 3. Number of brief and sustained interactions per day when seating arrangements in a psychiatric ward were changed.

	Number of interactions	
	Brief	*Sustained*
Old arrangement	47	36
New arrangement	73	61

Reproduced from Sommer, R. (1969) *Personal Space* by permission of Prentice-Hall, Inc., Englewood Cliffs, New Jersey.

also have felt that they were special and might have made more effort to socialize with and help patients.

This problem can be found in other studies. In one experiment, a carpet was laid in one ward for disturbed women, and another ward with an old tiled floor served as a control. Both patients and staff were found to modulate their voices more in the carpeted ward, the patients were less irritable and excitable and some previously incontinent patients requested toilet facilities.[11] In another investigation, the seating arrangements on the wards of a psychiatric hospital were changed. Originally, all the chairs were lined up beside one another along the walls. In order to talk, the patients had to pivot 90 degrees and it was difficult to hold a conversation with more than one person at a time. The arrangement of chairs was then altered, so that they were grouped around small tables holding magazines. As a measure of the effect of this change, the number and length of conversations between patients were recorded. As shown in Table 3, the new arrangement was associated with more interactions, both brief and sustained, than the old one.[12] It would have been better if an adequate control ward could have been studied in both investigations (perhaps in the study on the effects of the carpet another ward could also have been given a new floor, such as linoleum), but such research has had an important effect on the environment in many hospitals.

Occasionally there are naturally occurring situations that have many of the features of well-controlled laboratory experiments. Such a situation is described in a study on the effects of ward design in a large medical hospital. Three different ward designs were incorporated into the hospital as it was built. One ward was designed in a wheel shape, with a nurses' station in the centre and the bedrooms all round it. Another ward was built in an L-shape, with the nurses' station at the junction of two corridors. A third was rectangular, containing two parallel aisles with bedrooms on either side and the station sited between them. On many measures, the circular design was found to be better than the L-shaped or rectangular wards: there were fewer absences and fewer accidents among the nursing staff and they were observed to spend more time with their patients. When the doctors and patients were asked to rate their impressions, the circular ward was again favoured.[13]

Community care

There is increasing resistance amongst those who care for psychiatrically ill and mentally handicapped people against the building of large hospitals set apart from the community. Not only does this old policy seem to be counterproductive in terms of caregiving, it also stigmatizes the patients who live in the institutions. Being set apart physically makes contact with community facilities more difficult, providing less opportunity for the development of skills required to live independently. Equally, 'ordinary' people rarely encounter the residents of such institutions and thus have little opportunity to begin to understand their problems. Accordingly, current policies stress the need to accommodate these people in smaller units sited within the community. Although there can be opposition to the provision of sheltered housing in residential communities, this may be due more to the incongruous buildings that are often constructed than to the residents themselves.[14]

Thus, research on the effects of the environment in hospitals has shown that patient improvement is strongly affected by the social and physical setting. Patients in long-stay hospitals may become institutionalized if there is a lack of privacy and opportunity to have control over their behaviour. Partly as a result of research in this area, there is now a greater emphasis on providing a more stimulating and 'home-like' atmosphere.

Some researchers have taken a broader view of the effects of the environment, being concerned with how changes in living conditions can have significant effects on the health of the general population. Indeed, it has been argued that such changes are more important than medical interventions. McKeown,[15] for example, provides evidence from various sources that the most notable improvements in health care over the last century or so are due to changes in sewage treatment, diet and housing rather than the scientific and technological advances of medicine.

Seeking medical help

The previous sections of this chapter have shown how knowledge of certain social and physical aspects of a situation can help predict how someone will behave. This section considers how people decide to request medical assistance. In order to understand the research bearing on this topic, however, it is first necessary to discuss three important concepts used by both sociologists and social psychologists, the ideas of norms, roles and socialization.

Norms

People's beliefs about what behaviour is customary and proper in a society are termed *norms.* In different societies, different norms operate. There is, for example, a norm for children to take their father's surname in our culture but this is not the case in all cultures. Within a society, there are also differences, such that different groups of people have different expectations about what behaviour is admissible. In many factories, for example, there are norms about how quickly a worker should do his or her job. If the work is done too quickly or too slowly, sanctions might be applied against the individual. Norms change over time as well. There was a time when all medical students were expected to attend lectures in very formal clothes, but now this is often required only when on the wards. This idea of norms provides one way of understanding how society operates: the relationships between people in any group can be described in terms of the expectations of how they should act. Within a family, for example, there may be norms about discussing certain topics or ways of settling arguments (see Chapter 9).

Roles

Often there is a cluster of norms associated with a particular position in society. A doctor could be expected not only to be neatly dressed, but also to be technically competent, to be interested in patients, and to go out of his or her way in an emergency. The activities that fulfil such a cluster of norms are called a *role.* Examples of other roles are father, teacher, daughter and wife. There are several features of roles:

1 *Roles have a degree of latitude.* This means that the norms connected with a role are not strictly defined. Two people could play a role adequately in quite different ways. Although a

doctor is expected to dress neatly when with patients, there is a wide variety of clothing which is acceptable; a teacher could teach in many different ways, and so on.

2 *Roles change over time.* This is another way of saying that norms change. For example, society's expectations of women have altered considerably during this century, from the expectation that they should not undertake strenuous physical and mental exercise to the belief that they can be expected to take part in sports and academic work.

3 *Roles are often complements.* To say that someone is a teacher implies that there are students to teach. A person cannot be a doctor unless there are patients, nor can someone be a parent unless there are children. In order for an individual to perform a role, there must be someone playing the complementary role.

4 *Different roles sometimes conflict.* An individual is likely to play many different roles in society; sometimes a student, sometimes a friend, sometimes a son or daughter. Each role has associated norms which can be in conflict. A person may be both a doctor and a husband or wife, having expectations from patients and a spouse that may be incompatible. Within a role there may also be conflicting expectations. Where all members of a family have the same doctor, the treatment of one member may affect others, as when a young daughter seeks contraceptive advice. It is not simply a question of what might be right or wrong in such situations, but also a problem of conflicting expectations and how these are handled.

Socialization

The process of learning, understanding and fulfilling norms and roles is a vital part of social development. During this process, people become increasingly aware of others' expectations and more skilful at fulfilling them. Known as *socialization*, this learning continues throughout life. There are expectations involved in being a patient, for example, so that when someone is admitted to hospital he or she will experience a period of uncertainty until the norms are discovered and the role can be enacted. When they enter the wards for the first time, medical students often report a similar sense of uncertainty until they find out what is expected of them. Thus, socialization can be seen in terms of predictability.[16] Once a person is familiar with norms and is adept at acting roles, his or her behaviour will be predictable to others, and if everyone has the same familiarity with requirements, then the way people act will be mutually predictable. The patient will have a good idea of how the doctor will behave and the doctor will be correct in his or her expectations of how the patient will act.

The sick role

Like other forms of behaviour, the ways someone acts when ill are regulated by norms. To some extent, these depend on the particular circumstances (one ward sister might have very different expectations of how a 'good' patient should act from another sister, for example) but there seem to be some norms which apply to most patients. As outlined by Talcott Parsons,[17] these include both rights and obligations. One right involves exemption from many social responsibilities — someone who is ill is not required to go to work or, perhaps, to take exams. This means that if an individual can manage to convince others that he or she is indeed ill, these social responsibilities can be avoided. A second right is that people cannot be expected to take care of themselves or to remove the illness by willpower. That is, they are not instructed to 'pull themselves together' and get on with social duties. When a person is admonished in this way, there is the implicit message that the presence of illness is not accepted. These rights are balanced by some obligations: the person should want to get well, should seek medical advice, should co-operate with the experts. If these obligations are not fulfilled, the individual could be said to be breaking the norms concerning illness.

Like many other roles, certain qualifications are required before the sick role can be taken up. First, the person must have a condition that has been defined by the culture to be a medical problem. Our society's views on what constitutes an illness have changed in some respects over time. Alcoholism is one example: it is increasingly being seen as a symptom of a disease rather than as a sign of moral failure. Until recently, the alcoholic could not take on the sick role because the condition was not considered to be a medical problem.[18]

A second qualification that a person will have to fulfil involves acquiring some validation of the difficulty. A physical sign is most readily accepted (e.g. a broken leg or a high temperature) but a functional complaint (e.g. a headache) will usually be acceptable as long as it does not occur too frequently. Perhaps the best method is to convince an expert of the problem. When a child, the reader may have used a parent for such validation (perhaps in order to get a day off school) but for an adult the doctor is the prime source of validation. Difficulties sometimes arise when a patient complains of a problem but the doctor can find no physical indication for it. In such circumstances, the doctor may suggest further tests, may consider psychological problems, or may decide the patient is malingering.

Third, before the sick role can be taken up, it has to be accepted by the person involved. It is tempting to assume that whenever a person has a symptom — is in ill-health — then he or she will consult a physician about it. According to this assumption, the physician would see all the people in the practice who are ill. This is mistaken. Sometimes, for instance if the condition is incapacitating, the person has little choice in the matter, but in most cases there is a decision involved. There is a problem here in defining health. If it is defined as the absence of symptoms, then it appears that most people are unhealthy much of the time. Some researchers have tried to gain some idea of the health of the general population not by consulting medical records but by screening large numbers of people in the community. In one sample of over 3000 people, only 15 per cent were considered to be free from disability, ranging from psychiatric disorders to respiratory problems.[19] Another kind of study has involved asking people to keep a diary of how they felt each day for several days or weeks. Here, again, there is strong evidence that people have symptoms much of the time. In one survey of this kind lasting for one month, symptoms (such as headaches, backaches and abdominal pains) were recorded about one day in three, lasting an average of 1.6 days.[20] There is also evidence that there is much psychiatric illness in the community that does not come to the attention of the general practitioner or psychiatrist.[21]

These studies have several implications. First, they indicate that a general practitioner will see only a proportion of the people in the practice who have a medical difficulty. In the screening study mentioned above, some 30 per cent of the difficulties found were not known to the general practitioner, some of these meriting immediate care. Second, the results mean that medical records do not provide an accurate indication of illness in the community. Third, it makes the problem of who contacts the doctor and why the choice was made at a particular time, an interesting and important one.

The decision to consult

Several factors have been identified as being important in the decision to seek medical help for both physical and psychiatric complaints. Broadly speaking, these can be grouped into those concerning the interpretation of symptoms and those concerning social and personality variables.

Interpreting symptoms

First, there is the problem of interpretation. As discussed in Chapter 1, signs and symptoms have meaning only in so far as they fit into a larger context in which past experience plays an important part. Robinson[22] asked mothers to keep diaries of the signs of illness in their families along with a description of how they reacted to and interpreted them. Clearly, there was a considerable degree of uncertainty about the meaning of these upsets. The mothers would often adopt a 'wait and see' strategy, so that a child might feel quite ill for several days or wet the bed on several occasions before a decision to see the doctor would be taken. Only once they had decided that the signs were, indeed, indications of an important illness were steps taken. Another researcher interviewed myocardial infarction patients about their perceptions at the time of the attack. Often, they first tested alternative explanations for the pains they were feeling, and only after the pains worsened was action taken.[23]

Similarly, psychiatric illness can be difficult to interpret. In one study, the process involved in interpreting psychiatric illness in the family was explored by asking the spouses of patients about their perceptions once the decision to admit to hospital was made. Initially, unusual behaviour was put down to a physical condition or to a normal response to a crisis. There were attempts to 'normalize' the behaviour by finding explanations for it or by looking for similar behaviour in others who were not ill. Only when these strategies did not work satisfactorily on several occasions was the decision taken to seek assistance.[24]

Related to the importance of interpretation are studies concerned with perceived health. Simply because a physician considers a symptom to be serious does not mean that lay members of the public do as well. The discrepancy can be large. In one study, two out of three elderly people who were rated as being in unfavourable health by their physicians gave themselves favourable reports, while one in five who saw themselves as being in poor health had physicians who considered them to be in good condition.[25] Part of this discrepancy might be due to differences in how doctors and their patients view the seriousness of symptoms. When asked about the suitability of self-care for a number of signs, doctors placed more emphasis on self-care for some (e.g. 'difficulty in sleeping for about a week'), less for others (e.g. 'more than one headache a week for a month') than did patients.[26]

Social factors

Other research has been conducted on the social factors influencing the decision to consult a doctor. The problem may be seen as one of delay: because many patients waited until the disease had been present for several weeks or months, one question was 'Why did they delay so long?'. Here, such demographic characteristics as age, sex and social class of the patients were analysed but these variables seemed only mildly related to delay. An examination of individuals' particular circumstances, however, was more informative. Through interviewing patients, it became clear that a visit to the doctor involved costs as well as gains. Although there might be some gain in physiological health, there might also be several psychological and social costs. Economics seemed to play a part, not only because of any financial fee (many studies being conducted in the United States) but also because of time taken off work. It might be difficult to find someone to look after the children, and so on.[27,28] Some of these factors are illustrated by the following quotation:

> I wish I knew what you mean by being sick. Sometimes I felt so bad I could curl up and die, but I had to go on because of the kids who have to be taken care of, and besides, we didn't have the money to spend for the doctor. How could I be sick? Some people can be sick any time with anything, but most of us can't be sick, even when we need to be. (Ref. 29, p. 30)

This kind of approach to delay has been criticized by some researchers, suggesting as it does that people would 'naturally' go and see their doctor if there weren't these obstacles in the way. This view, it is argued, does not portray the decision process at all well. In the survey study mentioned above,[20] for example, only about one in every 37 symptoms resulted in consultation with the physician. It seems unlikely that so many obstacles could be present for people so much of the time. Zola[30] described how he came to view the issue somewhat differently. While interviewing people in an out-patient department of a hospital, he noted that many were attending with difficulties that had bothered them for some time. His question became 'Why are you coming now?', rather than 'Why didn't you come before?'. He noted that they were attending not simply because there were reasons not to previously but because their symptoms were beginning to interfere with their normal activities. He suggested that people often learn to accommodate themselves to their disabilities and only when this accommodation is upset in some way (which might be the worsening of a condition or equally a new social demand) is action taken. It also seemed that a condition was sometimes used for inter-personal reasons — to relieve the person of unwanted social duties, perhaps, as in the following example:

> Carol Conte was a forty-five-year-old, single book-keeper. For a number of years she had been both the sole support and nurse for her mother. Within the past year, her mother died and shortly thereafter her relatives began insisting that she move in with them, quit her job, work in their variety store, and nurse their mother. With Carol's vacation approaching, they have stepped up their efforts to persuade her to at least try this arrangement. Although she has long had a number of minor aches and pains, her chief complaint was a small cyst on her eyelid (diagnosis: fibroma). She related her fear that it *might* be growing or could lead to something more serious and thus she felt she had better look into it now (the second day of her vacation) 'before it was too late'. 'Too late' for what was revealed only in a somewhat mumbled response to the question of what she expected or would like the doctor to do. From a list of possible outcomes to her examination, she responded, 'Maybe a "hospital"[ization]. . . . "Rest" would be all right . . . ' (and then in barely audible tone, in fact turning her head away as if she were speaking to no one at all) 'just so they [the family] would stop bothering me.' Responding to her physical concern, the examining physician acceded to her request for the removal of the fibroma, referred her for surgery, and thus removed her from the situation for the duration of her vacation. (Ref. 30, p. 683)

According to this view, social factors act as 'triggers' that set in motion the decision to seek aid.

Others have looked at factors associated with family background that affect the decision to consult. It appears that not only is the interpretation of the nature of the condition affected by the family setting, but the decision as to whether it merits professional assistance is also negotiated here. For most people, the decision to consult the doctor is an interpersonal process and, thus, affected by the needs and expectations of the family group. Almost all potential patients seek the advice of relatives about what they should do, except when there is a sudden disability or a great deal of pain. If no one advises the individual to see a doctor, symptoms are usually ignored until they disappear or until they become much worse.[31] Where psychiatric difficulties are involved, friends are more likely than relatives to suggest professional assistance. This may be because friends do not want to be bothered with the person's problems or because relatives are anxious about the stigma of psychiatric treatment.[32] For physical illnesses in children, the influence of the mother is particularly important. Mechanic[33] showed that mothers tended to treat their children's illness like their own: those mothers who were more likely to take medication or to visit the doctor for themselves, were also more likely to give medication to their children and to take them to see the doctor.

Illness behaviour

It seems possible that some people are more ready to take up the sick role than others, given the same degree of disability. This was explored in one study by giving students a questionnaire designed to measure this inclination. Briefly, they were asked to indicate how likely it was that they would report to the University health service if they had been feeling unwell or had a specified temperature. When the medical records were later consulted, those who had indicated a high tendency to adopt the sick role did, indeed, attend the health service more frequently.[34]

The same study also provided some support for Zola's triggering hypothesis. Students who reported that they were nervous or lonely made more use of the medical facilities, supporting the view that psychological difficulties make the decision to consult more likely. Another possible interpretation of this last result (discussed in more detail in Chapter 10) is that these psychological difficulties actually contributed to the onset of disease.

In summary, the evidence indicates that the relationship between symptom and action is mediated by several social and psychological factors. It seems necessary to consider the presentation of symptoms against the total background of the patient's daily life and relationships with others. In this context many writers have made a distinction between disease and 'illness behaviour'. Disease might be considered a good term for the objective pathology, while the term illness behaviour might be used to describe the processes of evaluation and action connected with the perceptions of symptoms. It may be more useful to consider the decision to consult a physician as a result of difficulties in continuing a lifestyle rather than as a result of the disease itself.[35] Seen in this way, illness becomes an indication of impaired capacity rather than an indication of disease.[36] If this is the basis upon which a person consults a doctor, it seems likely that some consultations will not be about diseases at all, but rather about interpersonal relationships and emotional difficulties. It would also seem that curing a disease is not the same as curing an illness, so that medical care would involve more than pharmacological or surgical treatments.

It is relevant to mention here the possibility that the sick role is expected of some groups of people for whom it is inappropriate. This may be especially so for those whose disability is chronic rather than acute, and for those more in need of emotional or educational assistance than medical. The disagreement about whether alcoholism is a disease was mentioned previously: similar disagreements can be found concerning mentally handicapped or blind people.

An interesting analysis of how people with visual impairments come to take on the sick role and the associated behaviours expected of them is given by Scott.[37] He suggests that blindness is a social role that people who have serious difficulty in seeing or who cannot see at all learn how to play. Blind people are often seen as a homogeneous group — docile, dependent, and reacting with gratitude to assistance. Scott argues that much of this behaviour is socially determined, in that many of the patterns which are assumed to be the result of the condition are actually the result of the socialization processes. This may be equally true of many groups of people who are placed in institutions: unusual or disturbed behaviour might owe more to this placement than to their original condition.

Relinquishing the sick role

It seems, then, that the presence of a disease is not an adequate reason to consult a doctor for many people. While it is the case that the more severe the symptom the more likely it is that the individual will consult, there is no one-to-one relationship between the two. Similarly, recovery from a condition may not automatically return the individual to the previous state of activity. Studies of patients recovering from myocardial infarction (MI) provide an example of this. About 50 per cent of MI patients never take up employment again, although this proportion has been steadily falling over recent years. Many individuals may become invalids through psychological and social rather than cardiac problems. It seems that there is long-lasting distress for a sizeable minority of patients, and if measures of distress include personality and social difficulties in adjustment as well as vocational ones, the proportion rises significantly.[38,39]

The way the patient comes to see his health appears to be the important variable, rather than the medical view. For example, Garrity[40] related the severity of the heart attack in 71 patients to various social and psychological indicators six months later. No relationship was found between severity and return to work, but the way in which the individual perceived his current health was a reasonably good predictor. When they were asked about their general morale, similar results were found: morale correlated with health perception but not with severity of attack, implying that the patient's perceived state of health is more important than the objective state of health.

There is also evidence that recovery may be related to a person's

Table 4. Follow-up condition related to prior team assessments for patients who had been given a favourable clinical prognosis. 75 per cent of the patients judged to be without distress at the initial assessment had a satisfactory outcome, but only 35 per cent of the patients considered to be in distress.

Follow-up condition	*Team assessment*		
	No distress	*Distress*	
Satisfactory	497	163	
Unsatisfactory	168	300	
Total	665	463	1128

Reproduced from Querido, A. (1959) *British Journal of Preventative and Social Medicine* **13**: 33–49, by permission.

general ability to cope with problems and difficulties in his life. Querido[41] followed up patients who had undergone hospital treatment. When admitted, two assessments were made. One was based on the medical, technical and somatic side of the problem, a decision being made by a general physician as to whether the prognosis was 'favourable' or 'unfavourable'. The second assessment was made by a team consisting of a social worker and psychiatrist as well as general physician. They looked at the patient's psycho-social case history and obtained additional information as necessary in order to judge whether the patient could be considered 'distressed', meaning the patient was hampered or burdened by his or her problems. This did not indicate the presence of problems *per se*: patients could be under stress, but if the team considered they were able to handle these problems, 'distress' was not considered to be present. Six months after discharge the patients were visited in their homes and their medical condition relating to the original hospital treatment was evaluated as satisfactory or unsatisfactory. Of the 1630 patients in the study, 1128 had been given favourable clinical prognoses. Their condition at follow-up is shown in Table 4. Patients without distress were more than twice as likely to do well as those considered to be distressed. Perhaps, with the right kind of help, more of those suffering distress might have been able to achieve a satisfactory outcome.

The self-concept

If recovery is affected by perceptions of health and ability to cope, the question arises as to what factors influence these perceptions. Many social psychologists have argued that our sense of self — our identity — results from others' reactions to us. The only way we can gain some idea of our abilities is to test them and see what effect they have on others. If other people find them praiseworthy, we are likely to have a good self-image, but if others find them lacking, we may come to consider ourselves inadequate in some respect. For example, it is likely that the reader's self-image was enhanced when an application was accepted by a medical school but perhaps would become less positive if exams were failed. Similarly, people who have suffered a disease may undergo changes in their self-image, depending on the reactions they receive from others. If the individual is expected to be incapable in some way, the sick role may become part of the self-image. Since the sick person is not responsible for performing many social duties, return to work may not be contemplated if this role has become integrated within the self-concept. If this way of seeing problems of rehabilitation has value, then the length of time a patient waits for treatment — i.e. the length of time he occupies the sick role — should be related to outcome.

An examination of patients who had undergone surgery for a coronary bypass supports this idea. Men were interviewed before the surgical procedure and again 1–2 years later. At follow-up, a large proportion continued to experience difficulty: 83 per cent were unemployed and 57 per cent sexually impaired, for example. The waiting time before surgery was associated with these rates: significantly more patients showed long-term impairment if they waited more than 8 months than if the operation was performed within this time. The researchers noted that those patients whose symptoms were prolonged showed 'damaged' self-concepts.[42]

Family support

Another way of examining the difficulties a person might experience as a result of a condition is in terms of the support given by the family. Some of the evidence that suggests that a supportive family has a protective effect against illness is discussed in Chapter 10, but there are also indications that it can either aid or hinder rehabilitation as well. For example, Litman[43] found that three-quarters of those who had a supportive family had a good response to rehabilitation from a variety of conditions, whereas three-quarters of those whose family was not considered to be a source of strength and assurance during recovery were considered to have a poor rehabilitation record. Support may be important for other family members, too, and may be obtained from outside the immediate family network. In one study,[44] the resources available to the spouses of MI patients were found to be of significance. Those women who reported that they, too, were given educational and emotional support by professionals, friends and relatives were more likely to have husbands who were at work and who had recovered from the condition than those who reported few such supports. It may be that one way to help a patient is to help his or her relatives.

Summary

The ways that people act are not determined solely by intrapsychic variables but are affected by the environment, both social and physical. There are some social situations in which people tend to react in undesirable ways, such as failing to help in emergencies, following unethical orders or conforming to others' views even when these are clearly mistaken. Certain factors affect these tendencies such as the number of people present and their reactions. Aspects of the physical environment have been implicated in institutionalization, and social activities in psychiatric hospitals have been shown to increase with improved ward conditions. In acute hospitals, too, the physical environment can affect patient care and the efficiency of working conditions for staff.

One specific social situation is considered in detail: people's decision to request medical assistance and their recovery from illness. Many symptoms go untreated and the decision to consult a doctor depends on a number of social and psychological factors as well as the severity of symptoms. These include the person's perception of his or her state of health and the extent to which ill-health interferes with everyday activities. Similarly, recovery from illness is related only indirectly to objective state of health. Here, too, measures of general ability to cope and self-image can be used to describe the process of achieving full recovery. Rehabilitation may be helped by supporting the patient's relatives.

Suggested reading

There are many books concerned with the sick role and medical sociology generally. One that extends the outline given in this chapter is Fitzpatrick, R. et al. (1984) *The Experience of Illness* London: Tavistock. For a more detailed look at the psychology of symptoms and illness, see Sanders, G.S. & Suls, J. (eds.) (1982) *Social Psychology of Health and Illness* London: Lawrence Erlbaum.

References

1. Stimson, G. & Webb, B. (1975) *Going to See the Doctor* London: Routledge and Kegan Paul.

2. Darley, J.M. & Latané, B. (1968) Bystander intervention in emergencies: diffusion of responsibility. *Journal of Personality and Social Psychology* **8**: 377–383.
3. Latané, B. & Darley, J.M. (1970) *The Unresponsive Bystander* New York: Appleton–Century–Crofts.
4. Milgram, S. (1974) *Obedience to Authority: an Experimental View* New York: Harper and Row.
5. Hofling, C.K., Brotzman, E., Dalrymple, S., Graves, N. & Pierce, C. (1966) An experimental study in nurse–physician relationships. *Journal of Nervous and Mental Disease* **143**: 171–180.
6. Asch, S.E. (1951) Effects of group pressure upon the modification and distortion of judgements. In: Guetzhow, H. (ed.) *Groups, Leadership and Men* Pittsburgh: Carnegie Press.
7. Sherif, M. & Sherif, C.W. (1953) *Groups in Harmony and Tension* New York: Harper.
8. Wing, J.K. & Brown, G.W. (1961) Social treatment of chronic schizophrenia: a comparative survey of three mental hospitals. *Journal of Mental Science* **107**: 847–861.
9. Wing, J.K. & Brown, G.W. (1970) *Institutionalism and Schizophrenia* Cambridge: Cambridge University Press.
10. Holahan, C. & Saegert, S. (1973) Behavioural and attitudinal effects of large-scale variation in the physical environment of psychiatric wards. *Journal of Abnormal Psychology* **82**: 454–462.
11. Lee, R. (1965) The advantage of carpets in mental hospitals. *Mental Hospitals* **16**: 324–325.
12. Sommer, R. (1969) *Personal Space* Englewood Cliffs, New Jersey: Prentice-Hall.
13. Trites, D.K., Galbraith, F.D., Sturdvant, M. & Leckwart, J.F. (1970) Influence of nursing-unit design on the activities and subjective feelings of nursing personnel. *Environment and Behaviour* **2**: 303–334.
14. Dalgleish, M. & Matthews, R. (1980) Living as others do. *Community Care* 26 June: 18–21.
15. McKeown, T. (1979) *The Role of Medicine* Oxford: Basil Blackwell.
16. Kelvin, P. (1971) *The Bases of Social Behaviour* London: Holt, Rinehart and Winston.
17. Parsons, T. (1951) *The Social System* New York: Free Press.
18. Robinson, D. (1972) The alcohologist's addiction. *Quarterly Journal of Studies on Alcohol* **3**: 1028–1042.
19. Epsom, J.D. (1978) The mobile health clinic: a report on a first year's work. In: Tuckett, D. & Kaufert, J. *Basic Readings in Medical Sociology* London: Tavistock.
20. Banks, M.H., Beresford, S., Morrell, D., Walker, J. & Watkins, C. (1975) Factors influencing the demand for primary medical care in women aged 20–24 years. *International Journal of Epidemiology* **4**: 189–195.
21. Goldberg, D. & Huxley, P. (1980) *Mental Illness in the Community* London: Tavistock.
22. Robinson, D. (1971) *The Process of Becoming Ill* London: Routledge and Kegan Paul.
23. Cowie, B. (1976) The cardiac patient's perception of his heart attack. *Social Science and Medicine* **10**: 87–96.
24. Radye-Yarrow, M., Schwartz, C., Murphy, H. & Deasy, L. (1955) The psychological meaning of mental illness in the family. *Journal of Social Issues* **2**: 12-24.
25. Suchman, E. & Phillips, B. (1958) An analysis of the validity of health questionnaires. *Social Forces* **36**: 223–232.
26. Cartwright, A. (1979) Minor illness in the surgery: a response to a trivial, ill-defined or inappropriate service? In: *Management of Minor Illnesses* London: King Edward's Hospital Fund.

27. Blackwell, B. (1973) Drug therapy: patient compliance. *New England Medical Journal* **289**: 249–252.
28. Adam, S.A., Horner, J. & Vessey, M. (1980) Delay in treatment for breast cancer. *Community Medicine* **2**: 195–201.
29. Koos, E.L. (1954) *The Health of Regionville* New York: Columbia University Press. Copyright, by permission.
30. Zola, I.K. (1973) Pathways to the doctor — from person to patient. *Social Science and Medicine* **7**: 677–689.
31. Sanders, G.S. (1982) Social comparisons and perceptions of health and illness. In: Sanders, G.S. & Suls, J. (eds) *Social Psychology of Health and Illness* London: Lawrence Erlbaum.
32. Horwitz, A. (1978) Family, kin and friendship networks in psychiatric help-seeking. *Social Science and Medicine* **12A**: 297–304.
33. Mechanic, D. (1964) Influence of mothers on their children's health attitudes and behaviour. *Pediatrics* **33**: 445–453.
34. Mechanic, D. & Volkart, E. (1961) Stress, illness behaviour and the sick role. *American Sociological Review* **26**: 51–58.
35. Alonzo, A.A. (1979) Everyday illness behaviour: a situational approach to health status deviations. *Social Science and Medicine* **13A**: 397–404.
36. Gallagher, E.B. (1976) Lines of reconstruction and extension in the Parsonian sociology of illness. *Social Science and Medicine* **10**: 207–218.
37. Scott, R. (1969) *The Making of Blind Men* New York: Russell Sage.
38. Doehrman, S.R. (1977) Psycho-social aspects of recovery from coronary heart disease: a review. *Social Science and Medicine* **11**: 199–218.
39. Mayou, R., Foster, A. & Williamson, B. (1978) Psycho-social adjustment in patients one year after myocardial infarction. *Journal of Psychosomatic Research* **22**: 447–483.
40. Garrity, T.F. (1973) Social involvement and activeness as predictors of morale six months after first myocardial infarction. *Social Science and Medicine* **7**: 199–207.
41. Querido, A. (1959) An investigation into the clinical, social and mental factors determining the results of hospital treatment. *British Journal of Preventative and Social Medicine* **13**: 33–49.
42. Grundle, M.J., Reeves, B., Tate, S., Raft, F. & McLaurin, L. (1980) Psycho-social outcome after coronary artery surgery. *American Journal of Psychiatry* **137**: 1591–1594.
43. Litman, T.J. (1966) The family and physical rehabilitation. *Journal of Chronic Diseases* **19**: 211–217.
44. Finlayson, A. (1976) Social networks as coping resources. *Social Science and Medicine* **10**: 97–108.

Part 2

Human Development

7

Early Social Relationships

Introduction

In this second part of the book, the emphasis is on social relationships, and this chapter is concerned with how such relationships develop. Research in this field provides information that can be practically applied in detecting interpersonal problems and suggesting ways in which they might be overcome. In the delivery room, for instance, medical staff witness the first social encounter between a baby and its parents, which can be related to future family difficulties. Some researchers believe that separation from the primary caregiver can markedly affect the development of a child, a belief that has clear implications for medical practice where such separations are imposed if children are admitted to hospital or if the mother goes to hospital for the birth of a sibling. Children in long-term care are typically involved in a greater number of social relationships than children brought up at home, and these tend to be less constant. The professional's understanding of the effects of such relationships on the development of children owes much to the systematic study of these situations.

Some variables, such as the influence of specific aspects of an adult's behaviour on an infant, lend themselves to experimental study: adults can be asked to alter their behaviour systematically while the effects on the infant are recorded. Another way to study these aspects is to observe naturally occurring situations and to monitor their outcome. This type of approach underlies much of the work with infants and children in areas such as separation and long-term care, where it would clearly be unethical to produce the required conditions experimentally. To assess long-term effects, the same children would, ideally, be studied for several years, but such 'longitudinal' studies are expensive and time-consuming, so that many researchers resort to a 'cross-sectional' design, comparing samples of children of different ages.

That the newborn child can develop into a socially aware and competent individual in just a few years is intriguing. The process appears to be remarkably complex and unlikely given the amount of information that a child must learn and the range of skills which a child must master. A child of five or six years of age would be expected to speak in a way that adults could understand without difficulty and to be learning about such abstractions as time, space and number. But some other abilities are not so obvious. For example, you could observe what happens next time you make a purchase. Typically, the customer's hand moves up with the money as the vendor's hand moves forward as well: the money is exchanged mid-way between them. After the exchange both customer and vendor withdraw their hands while change is counted. This dance of the hands is then repeated: the vendor offers the change and the customer's hand comes up to meet the vendor's half-way. If this series of moves is not respected, certain conclusions may be drawn. Initially, if the vendor's hand is waiting in position before the customer's arrives, the vendor may be seen as somewhat grasping; if the customer's arm does not fall to his or her side while waiting for change, he or she may be seen as impatient or rude. The rules and roles involved in even such a simple social encounter are remarkably complex. *Socialization* is the term given to the process whereby an individual becomes reasonably predictable to others and other people become predictable to him or her. To the extent that the customer and the vendor in the hand dance are mutually predictable, they can be said to be socialized.

The aim of this chapter is to explore the beginnings of socialization, particularly the importance of the relationship between parent and infant. The topics which are covered here can be grouped under two headings. The first concerns social behaviour, concentrating particularly on the patterning of early relationships. In the second part of the chapter, the possibility that the quality of early relationships has long-term effects on the child is explored.

There are many other aspects of social relationships that, although not covered here, are of much interest. Most of the research mentioned in this chapter concerns the mother–child relationship: recently there has been an increased interest in the father–child relationship as well.[1] Another aspect of early social relationships is the effect of the arrival of a sibling on the parents and their first born child. Presumably because of the increased demands on the mother due to the new infant, there is a marked decrease in positive interactions between the mother and the first child, with an increase in controlling or prohibitive statements.[2] The significance of play in social and cognitive development has also been studied. Amongst the primates, the time between birth and adolescence lengthens as we go up the phylogenetic scale. This has led to the suggestion that an opportunity to play has evolutionary advantage: the individual has a chance to learn about social relationships and about the use and construction of tools in a relatively pressure-free environment.[3]

The development of social behaviour

Pre-natal influences

The process of socialization is often considered to begin only after birth, but the kinds of experience that the child will encounter and influence begin at conception. The foetus itself is a socializing agent for its parents. They begin to adapt to the child by attending antenatal clinics, preparing a cot and clothes, and telling friends and relatives. Conversely, the mother's state of health and social position has considerable effect on the unborn infant. Activity in the womb increases during stressful periods in the mother's life, particularly when the stressful events continue over a long period of time.[4] Mothers who have experienced long periods of severe anxiety during late pregnancy are more likely to have children who are highly active and intolerant of delays of feeding. Crandon[5,6] gave mothers-to-be a questionnaire designed to measure anxiety and then reviewed their records for the incidence of obstetric complications. On several measures such as length of labour, use of forceps, distress and Apgar scores (which measure infants' muscle tone, heart rate, respiratory effort, etc.) those who scored highly on the questionnaire had more complications than those who had low scores.

Although it is not possible to establish cause and effect here, such results have led to an increasing interest in the usefulness of preparing parents for childbirth. The weight of evidence indicates that preparation is useful, but methodological problems are common in studies in this area. Participation in pre-natal classes is highly related to socioeconomic status (those of the higher social classes being much more likely to attend), making it difficult to specify the reasons for any differences between those who have attended and those who have not.[7,8]

The degree of stress that a pregnant woman experiences may affect the date of birth. Newton et al.[9,10] studied mothers who gave birth to full term (at least 37 weeks), moderately premature (33–36 weeks) and very premature (less than 33 weeks) infants. Although there were no significant differences between these groups in age, gravidity and parity, levels of psychological and social stress were higher in mothers of pre-term infants than full-term infants. Mothers of pre-terms were more likely to have undergone a major life event such as marital separation, unemployment of the husband, or the death of an immediate family member. Eighty-four per cent of the very premature group indicated that a major event had occurred during their pregnancy.

Many other social and psychological factors have been found to be related to the state of the unborn infant. The social support available to the mother is related to the likelihood of obstetric complications and such psychological factors may be better predictors of complications than biomedical ones.[11,12] It has been repeatedly shown that infant mortality is highest in the lower socioeconomic classes. The marital status of the mother is also significant. Weeks[13] found that infants whose mother had married between the time of conception and birth were less likely to survive than post-maritally conceived infants. Although this effect seems valid regardless of the age of the mother, Weeks reports that there is also substantially higher risk of infant death for mothers 15–17 years of age than those older. One difficulty with survey studies such as this is interpretation of the data. The higher mortality of infants conceived when the mother was unmarried may be due to several factors. There may be nutritional differences, for example, or poorer living conditions. Another possibility is the stress involved in 'shotgun' marriages. Perhaps it is society's attitude to pre-marital conceptions that affects the mother and thence the foetus.

Abilities of the neonate

If infants were in some way biologically primed for social interaction their chances of survival would be increased. Bowlby[14] has argued that infants are genetically programmed to cry when distressed or when out of contact from their caregivers. Three patterns of crying have been distinguished — a basic rhythmical cry, a pain cry and an angry cry — and mothers have been found to attend to these different patterns appropriately. At first sight, it appears that crying provides an example of an innate ability in the newborn that triggers off innate responses in adults, but there are indications that this view is too simplistic since other factors affect caregivers' responses to a cry. For example, Western mothers respond to crying much more slowly than those living in the foraging Zhun/twa tribe. Infants in this Botswanan society rarely cry (other signals are used by mothers to anticipate hunger), but the cry when it occurs is treated as an emergency signal. It then brings an immediate response. In the United States, by contrast, about 17 per cent of cries of first-borns were ignored and that response was delayed for from 10 to 30 minutes for one-third of the cries.[15] Further, experienced women are better than inexperienced women at discriminating between different kinds of cries. Thus, although it appears that crying is an important signalling mechanism for the infant, it is open to cultural and personal variation.[16]

Incidentally, there is no evidence that attending to infants when they cry leads to greater demands for attention. In fact, observations suggest the opposite. Ainsworth et al.[17] observed mothers and their children at home, noting particularly the frequency and speed with which mothers attended to their infants' cries over the first year of life. The results indicated that those mothers who intervened (by picking up, touching, playing with the children) were less likely to have infants who cried frequently or for long periods than mothers who ignored or responded slowly to the cries. At least until one year of age, maternal responsiveness did not reinforce the crying — rather, it reduced its probability.

Smiling and hearing are two other abilities of infants that have important social consequences. Since adults find smiles attractive, smiling may be an evolutionary advantage. It is an endogenous activity for the first weeks after birth, occurring at the rate of about 11 smiles per 100 minutes. It is present in blind infants and in all cultures, suggesting that it is innate. Neonates are able to locate sounds and attend to them visually. Further, they will not only attend preferentially to human voices over impersonal clicks, but also to a female voice rather than to a male one.[18] An ingenious method for exploring neonates' ability to hear was developed by giving three-day-old infants a nipple to suck. If they sucked in a particular way they could hear a tape-recording of their mother's voice. If they sucked in any other way the voice of another woman, who had given birth in the same hospital at about the same time, was heard instead. Recordings of the babies' activity showed that they could, indeed, learn to suck in this particular way, indicating that they could not only discriminate between their mother's voice and someone else's, but also that they were capable of repeating behaviour which was rewarding and eliminating that which was not.[19]

The infant's appearance, particularly the eyes, may also be important to survival and social interaction. Infants as young as three weeks look at human faces and objects resembling faces more than other stimuli. Roskies[20] describes mothers who were considering institutionalizing their children soon after birth when they found they had been affected by thalidomide. These mothers remembered the decision to keep their children within the context of an engagement of eyes. Klaus and Kennell[21] filmed mothers and their newborns shortly after birth. The mothers were given their naked babies in privacy, except for the presence of a camera and sound recording equipment. Besides touching the baby in a fairly predictable way (first tentatively with the fingertips and later with the palm of the hand), most mothers encouraged the infant to waken and open its eyes with comments like 'Let me see your eyes' and 'Open your eyes and then I'll know that you love me'. Several of the mothers reported that they felt closer to their children once they had achieved eye contact (see also Macfarlane).[22]

Thus, infants possess several attributes and abilities that increase the probability that adults will take an interest in and care for them. Neonates are able to learn quickly, are able to signal their needs and are visually attractive. When such abilities are lacking, as can be the case with handicapped children, frustration and lack of parental care may result. Robson and Moss[23] conducted retrospective interviews with mothers in their third post-natal month, and concluded that a mother's feelings of attachment with her children decreased if crying, fussing and other demands did not lessen. They describe one woman in particular who was enthusiastic about her pregnancy but later wanted little to do with the child. The child did not respond to holding, smiled infrequently and showed little eye-to-eye contact. This child was later found to have brain damage. When mutual predictability between caregiver and child is difficult to establish, their relationship may be unsatisfactory.

Parent–infant interaction

The age at which infants engage in interaction has been variously estimated — the more recent the estimation, the younger it is thought to occur. Brazelton and his colleagues report that they could predict, from filmed records of a baby's behaviour at four weeks of age, whether he was looking at his mother or an object.[24] Further, the behaviour of infants at four weeks of age towards strangers was similar to that towards inanimate objects.[25] This result may mean that infants of this age can discriminate between individuals or, alternatively, that strangers are not as skilled as family members at eliciting the familiar patterns of interaction.

Brazelton has also explored the effects of a non-responsive mother on the infant. In this study, the mothers were asked to present a still, mask-like face to their infants instead of their usual animation. Infants initially oriented and smiled, but then sobered, became quiet and looked away. Several cycles of looking, smiling and then looking away were reported. Eventually, when repeated attempts failed to achieve a response, the infant withdrew into 'an attitude of helplessness, face averted, body curled up and motionless' (Ref. 26, p.143). When the mothers returned to their more usual form of behaviour the infants, after an initial period of 'puzzlement', began to smile and return to their usual cycle of interaction.

Related to this experimental study is a case description of a naturally occurring distortion of a similar kind. It seems that in order to develop a full range of adult facial expressions, visual information from others is necessary. Without this information, a mask-like appearance is often present, as is sometimes found in adults who have been blind from birth. Some effects of congenital blindness in a mother on her infant's behaviour have been examined. At four weeks of age the (sighted) child was very alert but would glance only briefly at her mother's eyes and would avert her face when the mother leaned over to talk. With the researchers, on the other hand, she 'greedily watched our eyes and followed every move'.[26] By eight weeks the infant reacted normally with the researchers but not with her mother. The infant still searched her face and eyes and then averted her own face. Not until some weeks later did the pair adapt successfully. Apparently, they had learned to use other modes of communication, such as the auditory, in place of the visual one.

Differences between children (temperament)

Another approach to parent–infant interaction has concentrated on individual differences between infants, examining their temperament or 'behaviour style'. In an extended interview, Thomas et al.[27] asked mothers to describe their children in terms of their behaviour in several situations. They assumed that the parents could be used as an effective source of information about their children if they were asked about current situations and if the questions were specific. Answers were validated by observing the children in different situations, and the issue of consistency was explored by observing them over a period of time. Nine variables or dimensions were used, including activity level (how much the infant moves during bathing, eating, etc.), rhythmicity (how predictable the child's eating and sleeping patterns are), adaptability (how long the child takes to adjust to new situations), and approach–withdrawal (whether a child smiles and approaches new stimuli, such as toys, food or strangers; or whether the child cries and pulls away). Interviews can be replaced by questionnaires,[28] where parents are given alternatives to check off as in the following item measuring rhythmicity:

When does the child wake up in the morning?

(a) The time usually varies by more than one hour.
(b) Quite often at the same time, but sometimes more than half an hour earlier or later (than usual).
(c) At the same time (within half an hour of the usual time).

This system thus describes the child in terms of how he and she *acts*. Patterns can be discerned as early as three months and there appears to be a genetic influence at work, with the temperamental characteristics of monozygotic twins being more similar than those of dizygotic twins. There is also some evidence that there is a relationship between early assessments of this sort and later behavioural and psychiatric difficulties.[29] Perhaps most importantly, this research shows that there is no one 'correct' way to rear children, since each child has different requirements. A child who is unpredictable, adapts slowly and withdraws from novel situations (a 'difficult child') will require a different pattern of care from one who shows high rhythmicity, adaptability and approach (an 'easy child').

Predictability

Predictability may be particularly important because parents who are able to anticipate their child's needs will have enhanced feelings of competence and will be able to adapt their own routines to fit the child's. By contrast, an unpredictable child could be very disruptive for the parents who may become increasingly unsure about their abilities. This could put a strain on the relationship between parent and infant that might, in combination with further difficulties, lead to later problems.

Compared to full-term infants, predictability may be more difficult to achieve with premature infants, because they tend to be less responsive, look at their mothers less, and are more likely to break off interactions.[30] Mothers of premature infants are more likely to initiate communication and to poke, pinch and rock frequently than are mothers of full-terms, who tend to share the responsibility for interaction. Usually, as an infant matures, he or she becomes increasingly responsive and predictable, while a caregiver gains experience with a particular child and develops increased sensitivity to and skill in meeting needs. Unfortunately, this is not always the case. Parents of children who are severely mentally handicapped or who have sensory impairments may be faced with a continuing lack of predictability and responsiveness. The lack of response from children with cerebral palsy and the excess of cues from hyperactive children have been shown to affect the mother–child relationship.

Brazelton has instituted a programme in which mothers are able to view themselves and their children on videotape in an attempt to call their attention to inappropriate behaviour. He notes that many unsatisfactory relationships are due to inordinately high levels of maternal stimulation: many mothers, when able to view themselves on tape, recognize this tendency. In other cases, the mother is not stimulating enough, and Brazelton is able to show how the infant responds to imitation.

These studies on the development of social behaviour show that the child and parent affect each other before birth. Stressful episodes in the life of pregnant women seem particularly important, increasing movement in the womb and being associated with prematurity. True social interaction begins soon after birth, with the neonate being able to attend to its mother's voice. Because adults find newborns attractive, most children will be cared for and nurtured. However, interaction can be difficult when there are problems in predicting the child's behaviour, for example because of brain damage, prematurity or being a 'difficult child'. In addition, the disabilities of the caregiver (e.g. being blind) can adversely affect the relationship.

Long-term effects of early experience

The effect of early experience on later development has become one of the most intensively studied aspects of psychology, stimulated considerably by the work of John Bowlby. He reviewed the research on the intellectual and social development of children who had been separated from their mothers at an early age.[31] Many of these children had been brought up in residential institutions and were considered to be intellectually retarded (especially in language), to display excessive attention-seeking, and unable to make close and trusting relationships with others. He attributed these effects to a lack of a continuous, warm and intimate relationship with a single mother or mother-figure. Although he later pointed out that it could be beneficial if the child could be taken care of by other adults occasionally, he repeated his point that a single bond is crucial. He also believed there was a 'critical' period, such that if a child had not formed a bond by the age of 2½–3 years, the social and intellectual damage would be irreversible.

Central to his theory of *attachment* is the idea of a secure base. A mother may fulfil the needs of food and clothing, but it is equally important that she also provide a secure base from which the child can explore and develop self-reliance. For Bowlby, protection is seen as being fully as important as the more obvious biological needs. In many respects, his theory is consistent with the psychodynamic approach to personality development (Chapter 2): the infant's first relationship with a parent is seen to be critical for later development. If the parents — particularly the mother — do not provide a secure base, later development is said to be adversely affected. Trust and openness in later relationships will be much more difficult to achieve.

Ethology

Bowlby has used several *ethological* studies of mother–infant behaviour to support his case. Ethological methods emphasize observation of behaviour in natural surroundings, and the observations are given an evolutionary explanation. This method of research was first used in zoology, Lorenz's descriptions of infant ducks becoming imprinted on and following their mothers soon after birth being an example. He suggested that this response has evolutionary advantage, keeping the chicks near their mother and thus less likely to wander away. Once an observation has been made, the researcher often attempts to manipulate the situation, systematically altering features until the important stimuli are discovered. In the case of imprinting, it seems that it is the first moving object that the chicks encounter that is important. Lorenz was able to arrange conditions so that the chicks became imprinted on him. Later studies have indicated that they could become attached to almost any moving object (gloves, cubes) and that they will attempt to mate with these objects when mature. There seems to be a critical period involved: if the moving object is shown after several days, the response is much less likely to occur. Thus, imprinting is the result of both innate and environmental factors. The application of ethological methods to children is more complicated, since infants reared in technologically advanced societies develop in very different conditions from the 'natural' environment, making it difficult to apply evolutionary explanations to their behaviour. Nevertheless, the emphasis on *observation* of how children behave has made this approach attractive to many psychologists.

Bowlby's theory has generated much research, probably because of its practical implications for child care. One result is the easier access given to parents while their children are in hospital. Some of his other conclusions have been less well accepted, such as his belief that it was beneficial for the child under three years of age if the mother was not employed outside the home. Similarly, if his critical period hypothesis is correct, this raises important questions about the possibility of successfully adopting older children who have never had the opportunity of forming a single continuous bond.

In the remaining section of this chapter the effects of separating the parent and the child are considered: first, the disruption of the parent–infant bond that may occur due to separation soon after birth; second, the effects of parent–infant separation due to factors such as hospitalization or marital disruption. In the third section, the effects of 'multiple' caregiving as may occur in residential nurseries or if the mother works are examined. The chapter concludes with a discussion of whether any adverse effects of such experiences on the child's development can be remedied later in life.

Bonding

That the period immediately after birth is particularly important or 'sensitive' for parent–infant bonding is based on evidence from various experimental and observational studies. The research conducted by Kennell and his colleagues has been particularly helpful in understanding the usefulness of the concept of a sensitive period. In an important experiment one group of women was given routine contact with their newborns: a glance at the baby shortly after birth, a short visit at 6–12 hours, and then every four hours of 20–30 minutes each for feeding over the first three days. This was the normal procedure at the hospital, so that this group of women and their children formed the control group. A second group of women were given this routine contact plus additional contact with their infants. They were given their naked babies to hold for one hour within the first three hours after birth and five extra hours per day over the next three days. Although the mothers in each group were comparable with respect to age, socioeconomic status, colour, days spent in hospital and amount of premedication, Klaus and Kennell[21] found some striking differences in how the mothers in the two groups communicated with their children. After one month, the extended contact mothers were observed to establish more eye contact with their children during feeding and to initiate more active play with their infants than the routine contact mothers. Both groups were asked to keep diaries of their daily behaviour. Once again, the differences between the two groups suggested that the strength of the bond between the mother and the infant was related to the amount of contact shortly after birth. The extended contact mothers reported thinking about the baby more frequently and staying at home more often than the control group. They also picked up the child more frequently when it cried, soothed their children more, and were more likely to feed their children *en face* (turning the head so that it was on the same plane as the infant's).

Early contact may have some long-term effects as well. Kennell et al.[32] report that the differences between the groups still existed one year after the birth. Although about 50 per cent of the mothers in both groups had returned to work by this time, most of the control group mothers did not mention their baby when asked how they felt about this, whereas most of the extended group mothers volunteered the information that they missed their children. At two years, there appeared to be differences in the way the mothers spoke to their children, with the extended contact mothers asking more questions and issuing fewer commands,[33] and differences in IQ have been reported at 42 months.[34]

Another group of researchers has been interested in the effects of extended contact on child abuse and neglect. In their study, mothers were randomly assigned to either a control group, in which the mothers had 20 minutes of contact for feeding every four hours in the first two days post-partum or they were assigned to a 'rooming-in' group, in which the child and mother had an additional six hours together for each of these first two days. Although the children in these two groups did not differ in the frequency with which they visited the hospital for out-patient care or were ill, at least some were treated differently by their parents. Of the 277 children in the study, no rooming-in children were considered to have experienced abuse, neglect or non-organic failure to thrive, whereas nine control group children were considered to have suffered these conditions. Five of this group eventually died. These researchers concluded that mothers who were given close and extended physical contact with their newborn infants were less likely to abuse or neglect their children than women given more limited exposure.[35]

Although these results have not been consistently replicated, and no other team of researchers have found such long-term effects,[36] they have encouraged many obstetricians and paediatricians to make provision for early contact between the mother and her infant. Kempe and Kempe[37] have found that there is some predictive value in observing this first contact, their work indicating that the way a mother reacts to her child in the delivery room is related to the probability of later abuse and neglect (see Chapter 9). Other researchers have suggested that it may be possible to specify the optimal conditions for the establishment of the mother–infant bond. Kennell's work indicates that it is important that the mother hold her infant as soon as possible after birth. Fathers, too, seem to benefit from early contact with the newborn.

These findings on bonding also relate to the effects of pain-relieving drugs during labour. Several studies have indicated that these medications have some short-term effects, making the newborn drowsy and unresponsive.[38] By using short and simple tests on the child (such as Apgar scales) some idea of the general health and responsiveness of the infant can be gained directly after birth. Pain-relieving drugs are associated with low scores on such scales. Since these activities may be important for the bonding process, the use of these medications needs to be carefully considered.

Separation

A second aspect of Bowlby's theory of attachment concerns separation. Because of the need for protection, separation from the mother causes the baby distress — shown by the baby crying and attempting to locate her. Most babies show *separation anxiety* to some extent, usually between the ages of 8 and 24 months. It is most acute in novel situations. Many children also show anxiety in the presence of unfamiliar adults (*stranger anxiety*) around 8–12 months. Bowlby suggests that these are examples of attachment responses in humans that have an innate basis and serve to protect, keeping the infant close by the mother. The importance of the experience of separation has been studied in several ways, but most notably in those circumstances where the child enters hospital or where contact with a parent is lost due to divorce.

Children in hospital

When children are placed in hospital, they may pass through three stages during their attempts to cope with the new environment. At first, they may show distress and protest, then misery and apathy followed, in the long term, by detachment and loss of interest in their parents. Douglas[39] found that repeated hospital admissions in childhood were associated with a slight increase in enuresis, being most marked in children who underwent surgery. However, the interpretation of this finding must be cautious. Was the increase in bed-wetting due to the admissions or to the family background of these children? Children who are hospitalized frequently during the pre-school years are not altogether typical. For example, they are more likely to come from large families with parents who take little interest in their education. In addition, there appears to be considerable individual variation in how children react to hospitalization. Although 22 per cent of children in one study showed some deterioration in their behaviour after having been in hospital (as indicated by their mothers), 10 per cent showed some improvement. Nevertheless, even when social class and the reason for hospitalization is taken into account, *repeated* admissions do seem to be associated with later disturbance.[40]

This raises the possibility that some children may be more vulnerable to the experience than others. Can the minority of children who do show distress be predicted? Preliminary results reported by Brown[41] indicate that this might be possible. He conducted extended interviews with mothers, took observations of the patterns of mother–child interaction and observed the children (aged 3–6 years) on the hospital wards. Those children who, at home, were prone to spend much time with the family and stayed in close proximity to them were those who showed high distress in the hospital — they were upset, laughed little and were clinging when parents visited. Those children who were given more control over their own activities at home were likely to become involved with others on the ward and less likely to remain in bed. As in the case of other studies, the mothers' attitudes towards hospitalization were also relevant. Those who were anxious themselves about hospitals tended to have children who were withdrawn on the wards. Stacey et al.[42] report that those children who have poor relationships with adults and other children, who are socially inhibited or who are aggressive and uncommunicative before entering hospital, are more likely to be disturbed by the experience. They also suggest that certain kinds of pleasant separations, such as having a babysitter or staying overnight with relatives, may prepare them for the stressful effects of hospitalization. A child coming from a secure background is less likely to be disturbed by the experience.

Helping children cope

Although more than one interpretation of the results from these studies is possible, there is growing concern over the effects of hospitalization on young children, [43,44] particularly when repeated admissions are necessary. The studies on psychological preparation for hospitalization and surgery discussed in Chapter 1 indicated that the stress involved could be reduced for children if adequate preparatory information was provided for the parents. The use of modelling via short films is effective (Chapter 3). Distress can also be relieved by providing emotional support for the child more directly, through the nursing and medical staff. Fassler[45] assigned children who were to have minor surgery to one of three conditions. One group was given no information or

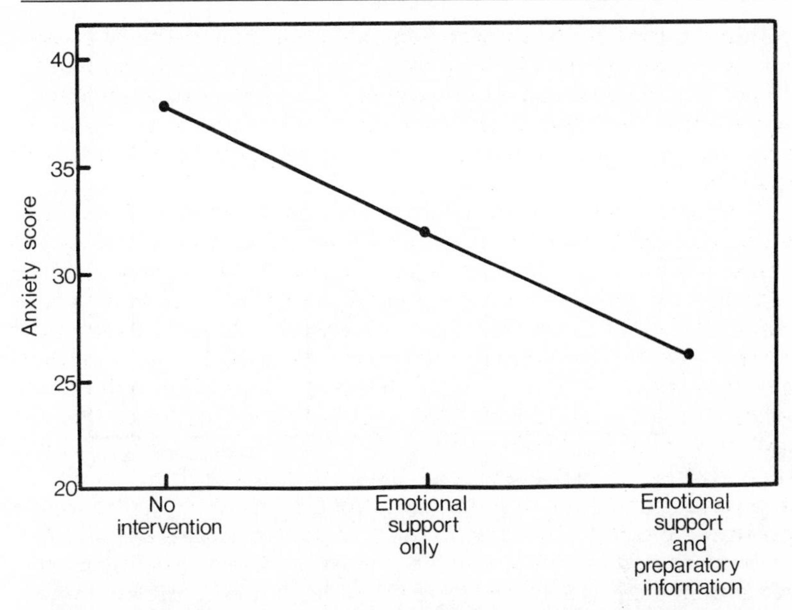

Fig. 12. Anxiety scores for hospitalized children who had received no intervention, received emotional support, or who received both emotional support and preparatory information. (Reproduced from Fassler, D. (1980) *Patient Counselling and Health Education* **2**: 130–134, by permission.)

emotional support during their stay. A second group was given emotional support alone, the experimenter reading a story to the children, giving them a set of toys to play with, and talking with them about their interests, school and family. Little mention of hospitalization was made, but the procedure of this condition ensured that the children were given some emotional support. The third group was given this support, but also information concerning hospitalization; the children were given a set of toys to play with which included an operating table (providing an opportunity of talking about the treatment), they were shown a film about a child entering hospital (similar to that discussed in Chapter 3) and their concerns and fears about their stay were discussed. Thus, this condition provided emotional support plus information. Afterwards, each child was tested for his or her degree of anxiety. As shown in Fig. 12, those who were given no interventions were most anxious, followed by those who were given emotional support. The most effective intervention for reducing the children's anxieties before the operation was the combination of both emotional support and preparatory information. (However, it is worth noting that these studies deal with

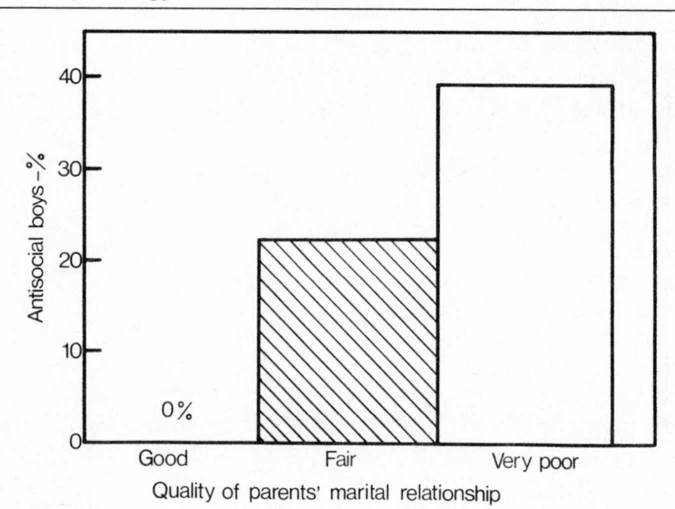

Fig. 13. Incidence of anti-social behaviour in boys as related to the quality of their parents' marital relationship (all boys living with both natural parents). Although no children whose parents had a 'good' marriage were in trouble with the law, almost 40% of those whose parents had a 'very poor' marriage were in trouble. (Reproduced from Rutter, M. (1971) *Journal of Child Psychology and Psychiatry* **12**: 233–260, by permission.)

planned admissions: there is little research on how to help the many children admitted as emergencies.)

Longer-term separations

A child can also be separated from parents because of divorce, marital separation or death. If separation *per se* is the important variable, then all these could be expected to have similar consequences. This is usually not the case. Gibson,[46] for example, found that only divorce and marital separation showed any association with delinquency (frequently used as an index of social adjustment), whereas death of a parent was not so related. Another study compared the rate of delinquency in families that had been disrupted due to divorce and separation with the rate in families where the parental relationship was quarrelsome and neglectful but divorce had not taken place. They found significantly less delinquency in the former type of family. Similarly, Rutter[47] examined the relationship between the quality of parental marriage and incidence of anti-social behaviour in the children. A linear relationship was found between these two variables, such that children showing anti-social behaviour were more likely to have parents with a very poor marriage (Fig. 13). Rutter also compared the incidence of delinquency in children who had been separated from their parents because of physical illness with those who had been separated because of family discord or psychiatric illness. The incidence of anti-social behaviour was some four times higher in the second group.[48]

Thus, it seems to be the meaning and circumstances of the separation which are important. Entering hospital is a frightening experience for most children because they are not only being separated from parents but also being placed in a threatening setting. Although there is little evidence that a single hospitalization has any long-term effects, the experience is very stressful for those who are vulnerable and repeated admissions are associated with later disturbances. An important aspect of helping children in hospital is to provide them with emotional support. The long-term effects of separation from parents due to divorce or death depends on the cause: when the parents' relationship is disturbed or quarrelsome the child may have difficulties. Perhaps early separations are best viewed as a sensitive index to the type of upbringing that might lead to later problems. Long-term discord between the child and parents or between the parents themselves is more significant than any single separation. It may be that repeated separations have a cumulative effect on development.

Multiple caregiving

Some questions do not lend themselves, either ethically or practically, to experimental methods. The problem of long-term parent–child separation is one such instance, hence the reliance on survey methods. The effects of caregiving by several adults is another example. Accordingly, attempts to answer this question have been made by examining naturally occurring situations in which infants have been given care by several adults. Of direct relevance to Bowlby's work are more recent efforts to extend and replicate his observations. In several reports, Barbara Tizard has explored the effects of residential nurseries on the cognitive and social development of children.

Cognitive development

Tizard began by examining 65 children with an average age of 24 months. All of these children were born full-term and none was considered to have any physical or mental handicap. The staff of these nurseries changed frequently and close emotional contact was discouraged. Her nurseries were, however, much more stimulating than those studied by Bowlby. Toys, mobiles and picture books were freely available and staff were encouraged to communicate with the children.

On most measures, these children were very similar to a comparison group of working-class London children, except that they were less likely to approach strangers and their language development was slightly retarded. In further studies, Tizard has found little evidence of cognitive retardation. Tizard and Rees[49] reported their findings on the same children at four years of age. Some of them had remained in the institution while others had been restored to their natural mothers. Both restored and institution groups had IQs similar to the working-class comparison group.

The children's cognitive development seemed to be related to the quality and frequency of staff contact. Tizard et al.[50] studied 85 children of 2–5 years of age who were being cared for in 13 residential nurseries. They found that the verbal abilities of the children were positively correlated with the frequency of informative staff talk, staff social activity and the frequency with which staff answered children's remarks. No evidence of developmental retardation was found in this sample.

Social development

These results suggest that although the quality of adult–child contact is important for cognitive and language development, it may not be necessary to have a single continuous relationship. However, some continuity of care may well be necessary for the development of trust in social relationships. In a follow-up to the earlier studies, Tizard[51] reports that at eight years of age the institution-reared children seemed overly affectionate and 'clinging'. It is possible that this clinging was an attempt to obtain some sort of continuity of caregiving: a response to the frequent changing of caregivers. Related to this finding is research on the effects of adoption on later development. Tizard, in keeping with many studies, reports few social and emotional difficulties in the adopted children from her sample.

Other naturally occurring situations can be used to study the importance of multiple caregiving. One situation is maternal employment, where mothers arrange for their children to be taken care of by another adult during their working day. Ethugh[52] concluded that employment itself was only weakly related to children's development and behaviour. If the home environment was disrupted due to marital difficulties or if adequate provision for supervision were not made, then problems may occur.

Evidence from other cultures also supports the idea that care could be given by more than one person without adverse effects.

In many societies, several members of a family share the responsibility for caretaking (indeed, this often happens in ours) and breast-feeding is not necessarily given by the mother alone. From an evolutionary point of view it would be advantageous for an infant to be somewhat selective in forming attachment bonds, but having an inability to form more than one bond could have severe negative consequences. A sociobiological viewpoint would also support the importance of the whole family, since grandparents, older siblings and aunts and uncles would all have a greater opportunity to pass on their genes if they invested energy in the child and the child was receptive to this.[53]

Conversely, there may well be a limit to the number of caregivers who could be helpful to the child. In so far as good caregiving implies a sensitivity to a child's needs, this would require time and considerable contact. Some personal commitment on the part of the caregiver would be necessary for this. For the child — who also has a need for predictability — the different styles of interaction shown by a large number of adults may be disturbing. If only because time is required to form a relationship, it is likely that there is an upper limit on the number of people who could give satisfactory care.[53] For cognitive development, adequate stimulation and interest is needed, and it seems likely that for good social and emotional development at least one stable relationship, with commitment on the part of the caregiver, is required.

Resilience

Another conclusion that John Bowlby drew from his review concerned the irreversibility of the effects of early deprivation. He argued that children would suffer a lasting inability to form close relationships if they had not been given the opportunity to do so before 2½ years of age. Many researchers have questioned the validity of Bowlby's conclusions in this respect. They suggest a child is not necessarily doomed to an unsatisfactory life because of an unsatisfactory childhood. Several naturally occurring situations can be used to examine the issues of the resilience of children in the face of early deprivation. It will be remembered that studies on mother–infant interaction indicated that premature infants can provide less interesting and fulfilling responses for the mother than do full-term infants. If this early experience is so significant, then differences could be expected later in life, yet few differences have been found. In one study, patterns of interaction between mothers and their premature infants proved to be poor predictors of cognitive or social ability at age three.[54] Similar results have been found concerning the effects of perinatal anoxia.[55]

Case studies

Perhaps the strongest evidence that early deficits can be overcome comes from several case studies. Koluchova[56] describes the recovery of twin boys who were totally isolated from others from 18 months to seven years of age. They were locked in a cupboard for most of this time. When they were eventually released, they could barely walk, suffered from rickets and their IQs were in the 40s. Although they were 18 months old at the time of their incarceration, this long period of isolation would be expected to have severe long-term effects on their intellectual and emotional development if early experience were crucial. However, after seven years of fostering in a supportive and emotionally caring home, they were found to have average IQs and average social development.

Kagan[57] describes a girl of 14½ years of age who spent most of the first 30 months of her life in a small bedroom with no toys and a sister one year older than herself. When she was removed at 2½ years, she was severely malnourished and retarded in height and weight. At the time Kagan conducted his interview, she had spent 12 years in a foster home. He reported that her IQ was 88 (within the normal range) and that she gave an average performance on several cognitive tests. He noted that her interpersonal behaviour compared favourably with other adolescents.

It may be that the presence of a sibling in these two case reports helped these children considerably. There is increasing interest in the significance of friends in the social development of young children. It has been argued that poor peer relationships are amongst the most powerful predictors of later social and emotional adjustment. One method of assisting troubled children with their difficulties has been to encourage play with peers, a method that has met with some success. Hartup and his colleagues describe a study in which children who were considered socially withdrawn or isolated were divided into three groups. One group acted as a control. The other two groups were encouraged to participate in special play sessions for 4–6 weeks: for half of these children the playmates were some 15 months younger, for the other half about the same age. Exposure to children younger than the withdrawn children was particularly effective in reducing isolation — perhaps the younger playmates were less threatening than the same age playmates. This study is particularly convincing because the ratings of isolation were made by people who did not know the purpose of the study (teachers) in a situation providing a good example of the children's behaviour (the classroom).[58]

It is possible, of course, that the general failure to find enduring effects of early experience may be due to the insensitivity of methods currently used. Early deprivation and neglect are likely to have some long-term consequences, just as years of isolation in adulthood could be expected to affect an individual, but it appears that these consequences may have been overestimated. Children seem more resilient and responsive to change than was thought a decade ago.

A more fruitful approach may be to consider early experience within the context of later circumstances. It could be concluded from the studies of early separation on later development that children who have difficulties in their first years are more likely to continue to experience difficulties as they grow, and that it is the cumulative effect that has significant consequences. This conclusion is not incompatible with the emphasis placed on mother–infant interaction earlier in the chapter. A mother and child may be able to cope with, say, a pre-term birth without undue difficulty, but further adverse experiences such as physical abnormality or unavoidable and unwanted separations, may increase the risk of adversely affecting the development of the child.

Summary

Even before birth, the child is influenced by and influences the parents. The newborn infant has various characteristics that elicit caring responses. By four weeks of age children engage in complex interactions with their parents. This relationship can be distorted by either parent or child: for instance if the mother is insensitive to her child's needs for stimulation or if the child is developmentally delayed.

The period shortly after birth may be particularly sensitive for the formation of emotional bonds between parent and child, which has implications for the management of childbirth. In older children, detrimental consequences of separation due to hospitalization appear to depend on the number of admissions and the family background. Distress is less if the parental relationship is good and if the child feels secure in the home environment. While cognitive development seems to be related to the quality and frequency of adult contact, adequate social development may require continuity of care as well. It is important that relationships are predictable and consistent. Children appear resilient to the effects of poor relationships early in their life; early deficits can be remedied. The bulk of the evidence suggests that isolated negative experiences have few long-term effects. Continuing adverse circumstances, on the other hand, may seriously affect later development. It seems that the continuing experience of adversity can have a cumulative effect on the child.

Suggested reading

Several of the edited books referenced above (e.g. Refs. 24, 41, 48) are helpful. J. Osofsky (1979) *Handbook of Human Development* Chichester: Wiley, also considers many of the topics covered in this chapter. Another possibility is M. Rutter (ed.) (1980) *Scientific Foundations of Developmental Psychiatry* London: Heinemann Medical Books, which gives extensive coverage of many aspects of child development. For readers who are interested in the effects of premature birth, Davis, J.A., Richards, M.P.M. & Robertson, N. (eds.) (1983) *Parent–Baby Attachment in Premature Infants* London: Croom Helm, can be recommended.

References

1. Beail, N. & McGuire, J. (eds) (1982) *Fathers: Psychological Perspectives* London: Junction Books.
2. Dunn, J. & Kendrick, C. (1980) The arrival of a sibling. *Journal of Child Psychology and Psychiatry* **21**: 119–132.
3. Tizard, B. & Harvey, D. (1977) *The Biology of Play* London: Heinemann.
4. Sontag, L.W. (1966) Implications of fetal behaviour and environment for adult personalities. *Annals of the New York Academy of Science* **134**: 782.
5. Crandon, A.J. (1979a) Maternal anxiety and obstetric complications. *Journal of Psychosomatic Research* **23**: 109–111.
6 Crandon, A.J. (1979b) Maternal anxiety and neonatal wellbeing. *Journal of Psychomatic Research* **23**: 113–115.
7. Beck, N.C. & Siegel, L.J. (1980) Preparation for childbirth and contemporary research on pain, anxiety and stress reduction: a review and critique. *Psychosomatic Medicine* **42**: 429–447.
8. Nelson, M.K. (1982) The effect of childbirth preparation on women of different social classes. *Journal of Health and Social Behaviour* **23**: 339–352.
9. Newton, R.W., Webster, P., Binu, P., Maskrey, N. & Phillips, A. (1979) Psychosocial stress in pregnancy and its relation to the onset of premature labour. *British Medical Journal* **2**: 411–413.
10. Newton, R.W. & Hunt, L.P. (1984) Psychosocial stress in pregnancy and its relation to low birthweight. *British Medical Journal* **288**: 1191–1194.
11. Norbeck, J.S. & Tilden, V. (1983) Life stress, social support, and emotional disequilibrium in complication of pregnancy: a prospective multivariate study. *Journal of Health and Social Behaviour* **24**: 30–46.
12. Smilkstein, G., Helsper-Lucas, A., Ashworth, C., Montano, D. & Pagel, M. (1984) Predictions of pregnancy complications: an application of the biopsychosocial model. *Social Science and Medicine* **18**: 315–321.
13. Weeks, J.R. (1976) Infant mortality and premarital pregnancies. *Social Science and Medicine* **10**: 165–169.
14. Bowlby, J. (1971) *Attachment and Loss: Vol. 1. Attachment* Harmondsworth, Middlesex: Penguin Books.
15. Bernal, J. (1972) Crying during the first ten days of life and maternal responses. *Developmental Medicine and Child Neurology* **14**: 362–372.

16. Murray, A.D. (1979) Infant crying as an elicitor of parental behaviour. *Psychological Bulletin* **86**: 191–215.
17. Ainsworth, M., Bell, S. & Stayton, D. (1972) Individual differences in the development of some attachment behaviours. *Merrill–Palmer Quarterly* **18**: 123–143.
18. Goldberg, S. (1977) Social competence in infancy. *Merrill–Palmer Quarterly* **23**: 163–177.
19. DeCasper, A.J. & Fifer, W.P. (1980) Of human bonding: newborns prefer their mother's voice. *Science* **208**: 1174–1176.
20. Roskies, E. (1972) *Abnormality and Normality: the Mothering of Thalidomide Children* Ithaca, New York: Cornell University Press.
21. Klaus, H.M. & Kennell, J.H. (1970) Human maternal behaviour at first contact with her young. *Pediatrics* **46**: 187–192.
22. Macfarlane, A. (1978) *The Psychology of Childbirth* Harmondsworth, Middlesex: Penguin Books.
23. Robson, K.S. & Moss, H.A. (1970) Patterns and determinants of maternal attachment. *Journal of Pediatrics* **77**: 976–985.
24. Brazelton, T.B., Koslowski, B. & Main, M. (1974) The origins of reciprocity. in: Lewis, M. & Rosenblum L.A. (eds.) *The Effect of the Infant on its Caregiver* London: Wiley.
25. Brazelton, T.B. (1976) Early parent–infant reciprocity. In: Vaughan, V.C. & Brazelton, T.B. (eds.) *The Family — Can it be Saved?* New York: Year Book Medical Publisher.
26. Brazelton, T.B., Tronick, E., Adamson, K., Als, H. & Wise, S. (1975) Early mother–infant reciprocity. In: CIBA Foundation Symposium *33, Parent–Infant Interaction.*
27. Thomas, A., Birch, H.G., Chess, S., Hertzig, M. & Korn, S. (1963) *Behavioural Individuality in Early Childhood* London: University of London Press.
28. Personn-Blennow, I. & McNeil, T. (1979) A questionnaire for measurement of temperament in six-month-old infants. *Journal of Child Psychology and Psychiatry* **20**: 1–13.
29. Dunn, J. (1980) Individual differences in temperament. In: Rutter, M. (ed.) *Scientific Foundations of Developmental Psychiatry* London: Heinemann.
30. Brown, J.V. & Bakeman, R. (1979) Relationships of mothers with their infants during the first year of life: effects of prematurity. In: Bell, R. W. & Smotherman, W. P. (eds.) *Maternal Influence and Early Behaviour* Holliswood: Spectrum.
31. Bowlby, J. (1951) *Maternal Care and Health Care* Geneva: World Health Organisation.
32. Kennell, J.H., Jerauld, R. & Wolfe, H. (1974) Maternal behaviour one year after early and extended post-partum contact. *Developmental Medicine and Child Neurology* **16**: 172–179.
33. Ringler, N.M., Kennell, J.H., Jarvella, R., Navojosky, B. & Klaus, M. (1975) Mother-to-child speech at two years — effects of early post-natal contact. *Behavioural Pediatrics* **86**: 141–144.
34. Trause, M.A., Kennell, J. & Klaus, M. (1977) Parental attachment behaviours. In: Money, J. & Musaph, H. (eds.) *Handbook of Sexology* London: Excerpta Medica.
35. O'Connor, S.M., Vietze, P.M., Hopkins, J.B. & Altemeir, W.A. (1977) Postpartum extended maternal infant contact. *Pediatric Research* **11**: 380.
36. Lamb, M.E. (1983) Early mother–neonate contact and the mother–child relationship. *Journal of Child Psychology and Psychiatry* **24**: 487–494.
37. Kempe, R.S. & Kempe, C.H. (1978) *Child Abuse* London: Fontana.
38. Aleksandrowicz, M. & Aleksandrowicz, D. (1974) Obstetrical pain-relieving

drugs as predictors of neonate behaviour variability. *Child Development* **45**: 935–945.

39. Douglas, J.W.B. (1975) Early hospital admissions and later disturbances of behaviour and learning. *Developmental Medicine and Child Neurology* **17**: 456–480.
40. Quinton, D. & Rutter, M. (1976) Early hospital admissions and later disturbances of behaviour. *Developmental Medicine and Child Neurology* **18**: 447–459.
41. Brown, B. (1979) Beyond separation: some new evidence on the impact of brief hospitalisation on young children. In: Hall, D. & Stacey, M. (eds.) *Beyond Separation* London: Routledge and Kegan Paul.
42. Stacey, M., Dearden, R., Pill, R. & Robinson, D. (1970) *Hospitals, Children and their Families* London: Routledge and Kegan Paul.
43. Nagera, H. (1978) Children's reactions to hospitalisation and illness. *Child Psychiatry and Human Development* **9**: 3–19.
44. Eiser, C. (1984) Communicating with sick and hospitalised children. *Journal of Child Psychology and Psychiatry* **25**: 181–189.
45. Fassler, D. (1980) Reducing preoperative anxiety in children. *Patient Counselling and Health Education* **2**: 130–134.
46. Gibson, H.B. (1969) Early delinquency in relation to broken homes. *Journal of Child Psychology and Psychiatry* **10**: 195–204.
47. Rutter, M. (1971) Parent–child separation: psychological effects on the children. *Journal of Child Psychology and Psychiatry* **12**: 233–260.
48. Rutter, M. (1979) Parent–child separation. In: Clarke, A. & Clarke, A. *Early Experience* London: Open Books.
49. Tizard, B. & Rees, J. (1974) A comparison of the effects of adoption, restoration to the natural mother and continued institutionalisation on the cognitive development of 4 year old children. *Child Development* **45**: 92–99.
50. Tizard, B., Cooperman, O., Joseph, A. & Tizard, J. (1972) Environmental effects on language development. *Child Development* **43**: 337–358.
51. Tizard, B. (1979) Early experience and later social development. In: Schaffer, D. & Dunn, J. *The First Year of Life* Chichester: Wiley.
52. Ethugh, C. (1974) Effects of maternal employment on children. *Merrill–Palmer Quarterly* **20**: 71–78.
53. Smith, P.K. (1980) Shared care of children. *Merrill–Palmer Quarterly* **26**: 371–389.
54. Bakeman, R. & Brown, R. (1980) Early interaction: consequences for social and mental development at three years. *Child Development* **51**: 437–447.
55. Corah, N.L., Anthony, E.J., Painter, P., Stern, J. & Thurston, D. (1965) The effect of perinatal anoxia after seven years. *Psychological Monographs* **79**: Whole number 596.
56. Koluchova, J. (1976) The further development of twins after severe and prolonged deprivation. *Journal of Child Psychology and Psychiatry* **17**: 181–188.
57. Kagan, J. (1979) Resilience and continuity in psychological development. In: Clarke, A. & Clarke, A. (eds.) *Early Experience* London: Open Books.
58. Furman, W., Rahe, D. & Hartup, W. (1979) Rehabilitation of socially withdrawn preschool children through mixed-age and same-age socialisation. *Child Development* **50**: 915–922.

8

Sexuality

Introduction

Sexuality is a topic that interests most people. When a child is born, the first question asked is often about gender, indicating that this is a very important consideration. Expectations about people are affected by their gender, resulting in different ways of treating even very young children. During adolescence, interest in sexuality can become intense, often being a prime motivator of changes in appearance, interests and choice of friends.

Although there are obvious genetic and hormonal components affecting gender and sexual behaviour, the development of sexual behaviour is open to considerable variation depending on cultural and familial influences. Sexual functioning is emotional as well as physical, so that past experiences and the expectations of the individual play an important part in behaviour. The advent of effective oral contraceptives has increased the opportunity for couples to enjoy their sexuality as fears of unwanted pregnancy recede. This chapter considers some of these social influences on sexuality.

There are several topics that are not covered in depth in this chapter although literature is generally available to the interested reader. Only brief mention is made of the physiological aspects of sexual response, although inadequate or inaccurate information about physiology and anatomy often contributes to sexual difficulties. Nor is there much discussion of sexual myths, however widespread they may be. In both these respects, the physician can have a crucial educational role. Additionally, the sexual problems faced by physically or mentally handicapped people are increasingly being recognized. Their sexual needs are often disregarded and it is sometimes the medical and nursing staff who may have to adjust their thinking on this. Finally, there is much research on the sexual 'deviations' such as incest and paedophilia. Both psychotherapeutic and behavioural methods have been used in treating these difficulties, and reviews can be found elsewhere.[1]

Gender identity

There is an important distinction between gender identity and sexual identity. The latter is a biological concept, relying on such characteristics as genitalia, hormone levels and chromosomes. Gender identity, on the other hand, refers to a person's feelings and perceptions about whether he or she is male or female. It is difficult to imagine a more basic attribute and if the reader were asked to provide a self-description, it is likely that this would be the first piece of information volunteered.

Hermaphroditism

It is tempting to conclude that gender identity is biologically determined, unaffected by socialization processes. However, such an assumption has been called into question by several studies — many by John Money — on hermaphrodites, people who at birth show the physical characteristics of both sexes. In most people, gonadal sex, chromosomal sex, hormonal sex and external genitalia are consistent with each other giving unambiguous cues about gender. In hermaphrodites they are not, in that both male and female characteristics are present. In the case of testicular feminization, for example, the foetus is insensitive to androgens. While the chromosomal sex is male, the external genitalia are female. In the androgenital syndrome (an excess of androgens) the internal structure of the chromosomally female foetus is unaffected, but the external genitalia sometimes resemble those of the male. The ambiguity of sex at birth means that, unlike most instances, a decision has to be made about gender. The choice is called the 'sex of assignment'. Several studies with different kinds of hermaphrodites have indicated that this decision is a more reliable predictor of later gender identity and behaviour than chromosomal, hormonal or gonadal indices of sex. In Money and Erhardt's series of studies only about 5 per cent of the cases showed indications of ambiguous gender identity or behaviour in later years.[2]

Money does not claim that gender identity is purely environmental in origin. Rather, he suggests that innate mechanisms interact with environmental influences. Usually, these factors are consonant, but when innate and external influences are inconsistent, the environment can have a strong effect on whether individuals see themselves as male or female.

Occasionally, children are assigned one gender but later investigation indicates that a change would be appropriate. Early studies suggested that if gender is reassigned after 2–3 years of age, problems arise for the children, but some later research indicates that this may not always be the case. In some circumstances, gender reassignment can occur even as late as puberty without undue difficulty being experienced.[3]

A case study

One problem with these studies on hermaphrodites is that they are based on a small and atypical population. For most people, gender attributes are consistent with sexual ones and Money's findings may not be applicable to this larger group of people. Before too much weight can be placed on the hermaphrodite studies, evidence is needed that genetically, hormonally and gondally typical males or females can be reassigned. There is one such case in the literature, again reported by Money.[4] One of a pair of monozygotic twin boys lost his penis in a surgical accident at seven months of age. At 17 months, his sex was reassigned on the opinion that a child without a penis could function more adequately as a female than as a male. Surgery and hormonal treatment were instituted (testes removed, a vaginal canal constructed and oestrogen administered). The parents also began to treat the children differently with respect to attitudes to sex, domestic activities, career expectations and toys. They began to dress the child in dresses, blouses and ribbons. At nine years of age, the child had a normal female gender identity and engaged in typical female behaviours. Although it is important not to place too much emphasis on a single case, this report seems to illustrate the malleability of gender identity in a child whose sexual identity was unambiguous before the accident.

Sex roles

As defined in Chapter 6, roles are those activities that fulfil others' expectations. When playing the role of a student, a person is expected to turn up at lectures, to take some notes and to write exams. Most behaviour is overlaid with what is perhaps the most important role of all: the sex role. If the topic of study is medicine, men are more likely to be doctors, women nurses. Men are expected to be assertive and logical, women expressive and warm. There is much evidence that men and women do differ along these lines, with female medical students, for example, being more concerned with the social and psychological aspects of medicine than their male counterparts.[5,6] A notion of what behaviour is appropriate for one's own sex is learned very early. By three years of age, children can discriminate between different classes of toys — boys tend to choose tools and vehicles whereas girls choose prams and dishes to play with. By the age of five years, children have learned that men dominate some professions whereas women dominate others. Generally the roles that boys wish to take are those involving logical thought and objectivity whereas the positions that girls expect to take are those requiring warmth and support. One of the more interesting debates in psychology is whether these differences are due to innate, biological influences or to learned, environmental ones.

The biological viewpoint

The human embryo is initially neuter. If a Y chromosome is present, the primordial gonad differentiates into the testes, secreting hormones which promote male genital development. If these hormones are not present, the gonads develop into the ovaries. Those who hold that sex differences are innate point to these differences suggesting that these will have effects on behaviour and cite several examples. First, women are more adept at tasks involving the left cerebral hemisphere (verbal ability) and men at those involving the right cerebral hemisphere (spatial abilities). Second, differences in aggression have been found cross-culturally, with men tending to be more active and aggressive than women in most (but not all) societies. Third, there are several physiological differences at birth, male babies being heavier, taller, having higher metabolic rates and larger muscle to fat ratios. Fourth, there are indications that pre-natal exposure to the male hormone progestin (sometimes used to inhibit miscarriage) can have an effect on later behaviour. Reinisch and Karlow[7] studied 16 boys and 10 girls whose mothers were given synthetic progestin during pregnancy. As compared with their siblings, they were more independent, more self-assured and more self-sufficient on a personality questionnaire measure.

More evidence for the importance of hormones comes from a study on male pseudo-hermaphrodites born with a 5 α-reductase deficiency. Eighteen children who had female-appearing genitalia at birth were reared unambiguously as girls. At puberty, however, their male hormone levels increased naturally, and this resulted in the development of secondary sexual characteristics (a deeper voice, more hair, etc.) When studied as adults, 17 had transferred to a male gender identity and 16 to a male sex role. Their functioning seemed to depend on hormonal levels and not on previous environment.[3]

A fifth argument concerns the difference in sexual behaviour of men and women. For example, women generally find it more difficult to experience orgasm than men. Some sociobiologists argue that this is not due to society's restrictions on female sexuality but rather to biological function. For Wilson,[8] orgasm serves two purposes: to tell the coital partners when to stop and to reward them for having begun intercourse. He argues that if women had orgasms as quickly as men coitus would be ended on 50 per cent of occasions before male ejaculation, thus reducing the chances of conception. He suggests this behavioural difference is due to evolutionary pressure. These and other differences are taken to indicate that biology plays an important part in sex-typed behaviour.

The environmental viewpoint

Those who argue that sex roles are learned reject many of these arguments, believing instead that the observed differences between men and women are mainly due to parental and societal reactions to boys and girls. They, too, use evidence from several sources. Some of the gender differences in cognitive functioning which have been well documented in the past are now beginning to fade in significance,[9] a result that cannot be easily accounted for using a purely biological explanation. Cross-culturally, behaviour that is associated with men in some cultures had been found to be associated with women in others. For example, the Mundugmor women disliked childbearing and were as fierce and angry as the men; in the Tschambuli society, the men were given to adornment and gossip while the women showed comradely solidarity, were prone to hearty laughter and were responsible for food-gathering. Both the men and the women in the Arapesh society were expected to be gentle, sympathetic and non-aggressive.[10] Sociobiology may provide an inadequate understanding of human sexual behaviour because, as suggested by Money's work on hermaphrodites, genetic and hormonal factors are open to environmental influence. The time women require to reach orgasm through masturbation is only slightly longer than men on average, suggesting more similarity in sexual response than some researchers have allowed.

Those who stress the effect of the environment have also pointed out an important aspect of statistical analysis: even when two populations are shown to differ significantly, there can be considerable overlap in scores between them. For example, one study found girls scored higher than boys on a test of creative thinking.[11] However, the scores were not dichotomous, as shown in Fig. 14: although the difference is significant statistically, the practical significance is debatable. It is not possible to predict the results on the basis of gender alone with great accuracy, since

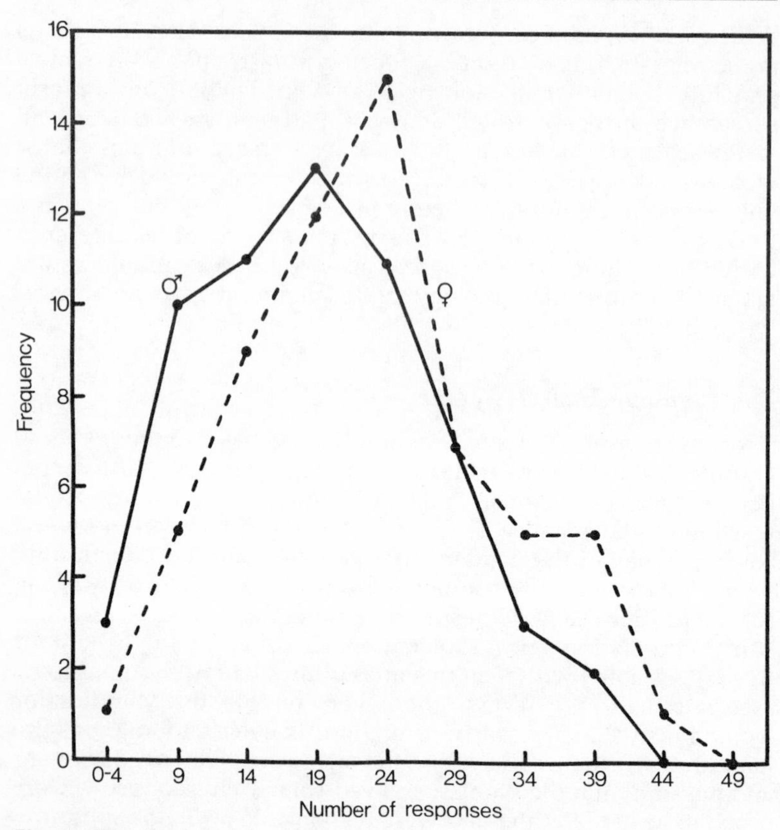

Fig. 14. Distribution of the scores for 60 boys and 60 girls on a test for creativity. Although the populations differ statistically, there is considerable overlap between their results. (Reproduced from Bhavnani, R. & Hutt, C. (1972) *Journal of Child Psychology and Psychiatry* **13**: 121–127, by permission.)

there is considerable overlap. Simply because two populations differ on average, does not preclude similarity between them.

Parental reactions

Much of the work in this area concerns the differences in parental reactions to young boys and girls. Block[12] asked parents to agree or disagree with some statements. Parents of boys endorsed items such as 'I think a child should do better than others', whereas parents of girls tended to agree with items like 'I express affection by holding, hugging and kissing my child'. It seemed that boys were socialized along Protestant ethic lines, with an emphasis on achievement, competition and control of feelings, whereas girls were encouraged to develop close personal ties, to talk about problems, and were given comfort and reassurance. Parents begin to describe the behaviour of their newborns along gender-stereotyped lines soon after birth. Girls are described as soft and fine-featured, whereas boys are seen as better co-ordinated, hardier and larger featured. It may be, of course, that these differences do indeed exist in infants, so that this study alone is not adequate to show socialization differences.

A better test of the hypothesis that adults react to and interpret infants' behaviour according to assigned gender would be to lead adults to believe that the same infant was a boy or girl and ask the adults to describe and play with the child. This research strategy has been followed in several studies. For example, in one experiment[13] 200 students were shown a videotape of a nine-month-old infant. Half of the students were told that the infant was a male, and half were told that the child was female. During the videotaped sequence, toys (a teddy bear and a jack-in-the box) were presented to the infant and a loud buzzer sounded. The students' task was to describe the infant's responses to these occurrences. As predicted, the ascribed gender of the child affected the descriptions. Crying was usually perceived as anger in the 'male' child but as fear in the 'female', and the 'male' was seen as more potent and active. Apparently the students' expectations affected their perceptions. Other studies have shown that the time taken to respond to infants' cries[14] and the toys adults choose to give to infants are similarly affected by ascribed sex.

The different toys and reading materials actually received by children as presents have been examined. It seems that boys are given more vehicles, sports equipment and military machines than girls, who are likely to be provided with dolls, dolls' houses and domestic toys.[15] In a study of early school reading books, boy characters were portrayed as displaying more aggression, physical exertion and problem-solving, whereas girl characters were more likely to engage in fantasy and to be obedient.[16]

Thus, while some psychologists have argued that the differences between men and women are due to innate, biological factors, there is much evidence implicating social influences as well. The expectations of parents and other adults during the socialization of the child are very different for boys and girls. The problem here, as in the case of intelligence, is that it is difficult to disentangle the effects of nature and nurture. By the time differences in male and female behaviours can be distinguished in children, parental and societal influences are operating. While girls as young as 12 weeks of age show greater attention to auditory stimuli than do boys, parents talk to girl infants of this age more than to boys. Is it the case that mothers talk more to their female infants because the girls are more interested and responsive? Or do girls become more responsive than boys because they are talked to more frequently?[17] Although adults describe and play with 'male' infants differently from 'female' ones, is this due only to societal expectations, or have they found such differential behaviours to be effective in the past? The studies quoted above have been very short-term: would the subjects' descriptions and behaviours change with more contact?

Valuation of sex roles

Whatever the basis for the acquisition of sex-typed behaviour, many researchers have pointed out that male roles are more highly valued in Western society than female ones. Evidence for this proposition comes from many sources. One research strategy is to ask children which sex they would prefer to be: typically, more girls wish they could be boys than vice versa, one study finding a five-fold difference. In artistic and academic work, that done by men seems to be more highly valued than that done by women. Pheterson et al.[18] showed paintings to their subjects, crediting them to either male or female artists. When asked to evaluate the paintings, the subjects (all of whom were female) rated the 'men's' paintings higher than the 'women's' on such scales as technical competence and creativity. Only when the paintings were said to have won a prize were they evaluated equally. Similar results have been found with written materials.[19]

Success or failure at tasks also appears to have different meanings depending on the gender of the individual concerned. When attributing causes for success or failure, people often make a distinction between ability, task difficulty, luck and effort. Ability and effort are internal attributions, having to do with personality characteristics, whereas task difficulty and luck are seen to be outside the individual's control and are called external determinants. Thus, a student might blame failure in an exam to internal reasons (e.g. 'I didn't work hard enough') or to external ones ('The exam was too difficult'). When this analysis is applied to achievement and sex, some differences emerge in how people account for performance in men and women. In one study, subjects read a description of a highly successful doctor who volunteered for charity work while still in training, who increased the size of the practice, and who was given an award as 'Doctor of the Year', the youngest person ever to have received it. Half the subjects were told that the physician was a man whereas the rest were told the physician was a woman, and all were asked to suggest why this doctor was so successful. Both male and female subjects considered that the woman physician worked harder than the man: to be equally successful, the woman would have to put more effort into her work. However, the reason why she would have to work harder was different for the male and female subjects. The males saw the woman as having less ability than the man, whereas the females perceived a greater task difficulty for her.[20] It seems that the subjects in these and similar experiments[21] had different expectations of the performance of men and women, attributing different reasons for identical performances.

Analysis of conversations

These studies rely on hypothetical situations rather than on actual observations of how men and women relate to one another. Perhaps a better test of the hypothesis that men and women have different status in Western society comes from analysis of conversations. A rather obvious, but important, feature of conversation is that only one person speaks at a time. A listener will usually wait until the speaker has finished before talking. There are some exceptions to this rule — interruptions — where the listener begins to talk before the speaker ends. Again, this is obvious, but it seems that interruptions are not randomly distributed between conversationalists, in that they are associated with status. Higher status individuals are more likely to interrupt those of lower status than vice versa. So it may be that some measure of relative status can be gained by recording how two people talk to each other and counting the interruptions.

In studies of this kind, men interrupt women more often than women interrupt men (96 per cent of the time in one investigation). This analysis has been applied to doctor–patient communication as well. Since in the consulting room doctors are generally considered to have more power and status than their patients, an asymmetry in interruptions could be expected and, indeed, this has been found to be the case. An important qualification to this finding, however, is that the sex of the doctor is significant. Whereas male physicians contributed some 70 per cent of the interruptions in their consultations with patients, female physicians initiated only 32 per cent, and even less when the patient was male.[22] If interruptions can be taken as a valid measure, then women doctors may either take on less status or be accorded less status by their patients than men.

Mental health

These studies, conducted in both laboratory and natural settings, suggest that the situation faced by women in society at present is quite different from that faced by men. It seems that their behaviour will be judged less positively than men's on a number of criteria and some writers have connected such differences in valuation with mental health. Women are more likely to request assistance for psychiatric difficulties. They are more likely to be depressed, to suffer from suicidal thoughts and to attempt suicide, for example. Although this difference may be due simply to a greater likelihood of women expressing their difficulties (i.e. men may have as many problems but keep them to themselves), there is evidence that this is not the case, and it has been argued that it is the way that women are valued which is responsible. In a society where tasks that require logical thinking and objectivity (the traditionally masculine qualities) are more highly valued than those requiring emotional support and warmth (traditionally feminine qualities), women may become depressed because their roles are undervalued. There is some evidence that levels of depression are determined by levels of self-esteem[23] and the cognitive psychologist Beck (Chapter 2) suggests that women have a culturally fostered tendency to see themselves as powerless and to undervalue their achievements.[24] This interpretation is supported by the research on the effects of employment on women: those who have a job are less likely to suffer depression, perhaps because employment heightens self-esteem.[25]

It is possible also that physicians expect to find differences in symptomatology depending on the sex of the patient. Some have argued that the image of men and women put across by pharmaceutical companies leads physicians to expect psychogenic symptoms to occur more frequently in women than in men. In an analysis of medical journals, advertisements for drugs aimed at psychogenic symptoms were predominantly illustrated with women, who were shown to be emotional, irrational and complaining. Advertisements for drugs for organic illness, on the other hand, predominantly depicted men, who tended to be non-emotional, stoic and rational.[26,27] There is some evidence that such images may influence physicians' expectations of patients. In one study, clinicians were given short case histories said to be descriptions of a man (or woman) suffering from low back pain or epigastric pain. Although there are no sex differences in the prevalence of these conditions in the general population, 'female' patients were said to be excessively demanding of doctors' time, to be more likely to suffer from psychosomatic illnesses, and to have complaints in which emotional factors are important.[28]

Psychological androgyny

There is an assumption in many people's minds that masculinity and femininity represent the ends of a single continuum. The

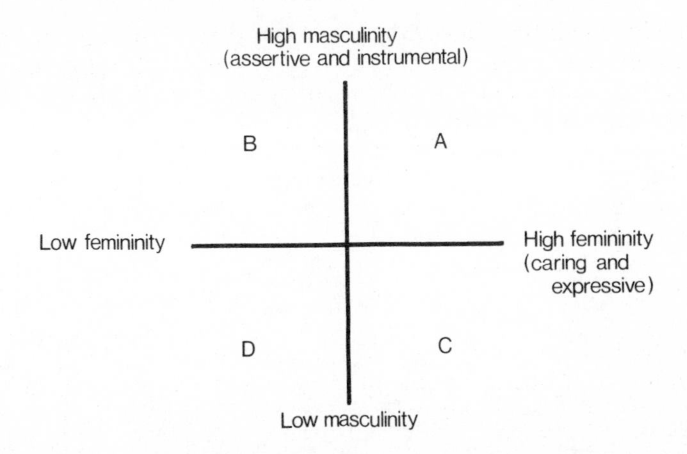

Fig. 15. In this model of masculinity and femininity, members of either gender can possess both masculine and feminine characteristics. The quadrants A, B, C and D are explained in the text.

ideal man might be considered assertive and instrumental, whereas women would be unassertive and passive. Women might be idealized as compassionate and expressive, while men would be low on these qualities. Women may be thought to be more dependent than men and less concerned with achievements. This model would place men and women on a single dimension: men would tend to fall at one end, women at the other.

Recently, psychologists have questioned the traditional assumption of a single dimension, exploring the possibility that masculinity and femininity are separate dimensions, each present in varying degrees in both men and women. In this model, the two dimensions are independent, so that an individual could score highly on both masculine and feminine characteristics, being both compassionate and assertive for example. Such a person would be called 'psychologically androgynous' and would fall in quadrant A in Fig. 15. Someone who was high in masculine characteristics but low in feminine ones would be termed masculine (quadrant B), and someone high in femininity and low in masculinity, termed feminine (quadrant C). Those who lie in the fourth quadrant (D) would be termed 'undifferentiated'.

There are now several self-report questionnaires designed to measure psychological androgyny. The Bem Sex Role Inventory (BSRI), for example, contains 20 items on each of the masculinity and femininity scales. The subject is asked to describe how well each item describes him or herself, placing an X where appropriate. An item on the masculine scale is:

Act as a leader

Never true -------------------------- Always true

and one on the femininity scale is:

Affectionate

Never true -------------------------- Always true

An individual might answer near the 'Always true' end of both scales, and if many such items are endorsed, he or she would be considered androgynous. There is evidence that these individuals are more adaptable than those who are sex-typed, showing masculine or feminine behaviours depending on their appropriateness in different situations. An androgynous man is more likely to be nurturant (e.g to smile, talk with and touch a baby or to show sympathy and understanding to a lonely person) than a masculine one, and an androgynous woman is more likely to resist social pressures to conform than a feminine one.[29,30] Although there have been many criticisms of the concept of androgyny in general and the BSRI in particular,[31] the notion that individuals can be both masculine and feminine in behaviour and that this flexibility has advantages for adjustment has gained a firm foothold in psychology.

Recently there have been attempts to relate androgyny to the psychological health and orientation of medical students. Zeldow et al.[32] first gave a questionnaire designed to measure androgyny to the students during their first week at university. Eight months later, a second series of tests were given which measured the students' ability to cope with the course and their orientation to patient care. Those who originally scored high on the masculinity scale were less depressed, more confident, and more emotionally stable than low scorers, whereas those who scored high on femininity were more likely to be satisfied with their interpersonal relationships, to consume less alcohol and to set a higher value on the interpersonal aspects of medical practice than those who scored low on femininity. In other words, those who scored high on both scales were able to both cope with the course and maintain caring attitudes, two attributes which are particularly important in medicine.

Sexual behaviour

Clearly, there is a taboo in Western cultures about discussing sexuality and admitting to sexual problems. Although 60–70 per cent of women and over 90 per cent of men masturbate at some time (as reported in anonymous questionnaires and in-depth interviews), feelings of guilt abound. Similarly, although significant proportions of both men and women have homosexual experiences during their lives, being 'gay' continues to carry a social stigma. It has been argued that such behaviours are aberrant and a reflection of either immaturity or an abnormal upbringing. These views have been brought into question by the work of cultural anthropologists — researchers who live with a tribe or society for several months or years and attempt to describe and explain their cultural patterns of behaviour. A cultural anthropologist might examine the beliefs of a people concerning the causes of a disease (Chapter 6), the patterns of marriage and kinship (Chapter 9) or, relevant to the present chapter, sexuality. Such studies illustrate the wide variety of sexual experiences that *homo sapiens* finds acceptable. Although homosexuality is abhorred in some cultures, it is accepted or even encouraged in others,[33] for example. Meggot[34] describes the contrast between two cultures who have very different views about sexuality. In the Mae Enga tribe, men and women sleep apart, the men believe intercourse is debilitating and purify themselves afterwards, while bachelors swear sexual abstinence. The Mae Enga believe that contact with menstrual blood can cause sickness and death. In contrast, the Kuma have a much less restrictive sexual code. Men and women share their sleeping quarters and girls select their sexual partners from both married and unmarried men. There are no taboos about intercourse during menstruation. Anthropologists often invoke economic reasons to explain their observations. For example, it has been suggested that the high population pressure experienced by the Mae Enga makes it necessary for there to be a mechanism that reduces the frequency of intercourse and thus limits fertility, whereas the Kuma have a relatively low population density.[35] The patterns of sexuality found in a culture may depend on the scarcity of resources to support the population.

Perhaps because of the taboos surrounding sexuality in the West, only recently have there been systematic attempts to describe and analyse sexual behaviour. Alfred Kinsey[36] is considered an important researcher because he sought to document the incidence of sexual behaviour in a large sample of people. By conducting some 18,000 interviews, he was able to show the mythological basis of many views of sexuality. For example, his results indicated that, to the apparent surprise of many, women can become sexually aroused quickly and enjoy and actively seek out sexual gratification. Many were also surprised at the prevalence of homosexuality in males: Kinsey found that 37 per cent of his sample had at least one homosexual experience to the point of orgasm between adolescence and old age. Two other important researchers are Masters and Johnson,[37] who took detailed physiological measurements of male and female sexual arousal: they concluded that there are many similarities in the sexual responsiveness of men and women.

Contraception

At first sight, the use of contraceptives appears to be a relatively simple procedure, but in fact it requires a series of complex and difficult decisions. There must first be some prior awareness that sexual intercourse may soon occur. If it is not expected, it is unlikely that contraceptive precautions will be taken, perhaps accounting for the 50 per cent of women who report they did not take any precautions at their first intercourse. Second, there must be some public behaviour by one of the partners in order to acquire a contraceptive, which appears to be difficult for some. This difficulty has led to a debate about whether parents should be informed by physicians about their young daughters' requests for contraceptives, an issue involving questions of confidentiality. In this context it is important to note that there is little evidence that women become indiscriminate in their sexual behaviour after beginning to use the pill. There may, of course, be a reluctance to report more sexual partners, but Reichelt[38] found that the young women in one clinic claimed to have exactly the same number of partners one year after the initial prescription as before. A third important decision about contraceptives is that they must be used consistently in order to be effective. For many methods a fresh choice must be made on every occasion. Because there are so many steps involved, contraceptive use may break down at any one of several points. Using this analysis, it may be possible to determine the reason for contraceptive failure more accurately and make intervention more effective.[39,40]

Locus of control

Another research approach has explored the personality characteristics of contraceptive users and non-users. A personality questionnaire that has gained great popularity is the Locus of Control questionnaire. Earlier in the chapter the idea that people give different reasons for events was mentioned: the causes of an event could be external (luck and task difficulty) or internal (ability and effort) or a mix of the two. The Locus of Control questionnaire was designed to measure the extent to which an individual used internal or external attributions to explain events. A person with an internal locus of control has an expectation that he or she will be able to control the environment, either through ability or effort. Someone with an external locus of control expectation would tend to believe that outcomes are not contingent on personal qualities but rather on outside influences, such as luck. In this questionnaire, subjects are given a series of choices to make, for example between:

a 'I have often found that what is going to happen will happen', and

b 'Trusting to fate has never turned out as well for me as making a decision to take a definite course of action.'

People who tend to make choices like **b** which suggest that ability or effort are important would be termed 'internals', and others who show the opposite tendency would be 'externals'.

This personality questionnaire has been shown to distinguish between contraceptive users and non-users.[41] One study compared couples who began to use contraceptives before their first pregnancy (early users) with couples who began to use them after the first pregnancy (late users). After controlling for socioeconomic status (which is an important variable — it seems that lower-income individuals have less confidence in any method), the early users reported greater emphasis on education and long-term goals. They had more faith in the future being predictable and were more willing to sacrifice short-term goals than the later users.[42] Incidentally, locus of control has been implicated in a wide range of health-related behaviours, with internals more likely to take a variety of preventative measures than externals.[43]

Abortion

Studies on the psychological effects of abortion are plagued with methodological problems. This is due to lack of control groups on the one hand and poor measurement on the other. In order to assess the effects of abortion, it is important to take into account, first, whether or not the pregnancy was wanted — not all women who have an abortion have unwanted pregnancies (e.g. those whose pregnancies are terminated for genetic reasons), and not all women with unwanted pregnancies seek an abortion; and second, whether a request for abortion is refused — in answering questions about the effects of abortion, women (and their children) whose requests had been turned down as well as those whose requests had been granted need to be studied. Measurement is also poor in most abortion studies: estimates of disturbance are usually taken by one individual who knows the history of the women involved, so that judgements may be coloured by prior expectations.

Early reports on abortion often employed no control groups, relying mainly on psychiatrists' observations.[44] Prospective studies are rare, but they suggest that early termination of pregnancy has little long-term adverse effect on most women.[45] Nevertheless, it may have great emotional significance at the time and few women find the decision an easy one.[46] Women who have terminations due to diagnosis of genetic abnormality seem to be particularly 'at risk'. Donnai et al.[47] interviewed 12 women who had an abortion for this reason. Although all showed strain at the time of the interview, emotional recovery was considered to be good for seven of the women, fair for three of the women and poor for the remaining two women at 7 and 10 months after termination. The findings led the authors to change their clinical practice in similar cases, ensuring that a health visitor contacts the women while in hospital and offers future support.

In a long-term study (over 15 years), 90 children of women whose applications for abortion were refused were compared with 90 children of the same sex born in the ward at about the same time. The mothers were matched for age, parity and social class. The initially unwanted children were more likely to have an unmarried mother, to be born into a family where divorce occurred, and to do less well at school than the wanted children. There was also evidence that they were more likely to have psychosomatic symptoms (headaches, stomach-aches, etc.) and to be referred to a school psychiatrist.[48] Although these differences between groups were statistically significant, it should be noted that there were several other measures on which no differences were found: many of the unwanted children had satisfactory intellectual achievement and social adjustment, for example.

Several factors seem to affect the decision whether or not to grant an abortion. Religious and moral beliefs, rape, the possibility of a handicapped child and danger to the mother's physical or mental health are all relevant. It is possible that an abortion is sometimes granted as a reward for conscientious contraceptive use or refused on the basis of irresponsibility. These possibilities were tested by giving subjects short case histories of women who had become pregnant and wanted an abortion. In order to give the experiment some real-life validity, the subjects were asked to imagine that they were members of a board which considered abortion applications. They were asked to read the case histories and to indicate whether they were in favour of or against granting the request. The histories were systematically varied in content: some women were said to have a casual relationship with the father while others had a steady and involved one: some women were said to have become pregnant because of personal failure (i.e. not preparing for intercourse by forgetting to take contraceptives on a camping trip) while others had become pregnant because the method had failed. The subjects were more strongly in favour of granting an abortion when the conception was due to a failure in the method than when it was due to a failure of the person to use the method consistently, and when the relationship was steady than when it was casual. These results are interesting, because they show the subjects were more likely to confer motherhood on those women who were less able to plan their pregnancy and less likely to have the emotional support of the father. It was as if requests were withheld in order to punish inconsistent use of contraceptives and the less socially acceptable behaviour of having several sexual partners.[49]

Sexual dysfunction

Despite the increased openness in society about sexual matters, there is much difficulty in performing research in this area. The high refusal rates that investigators encounter attests to the embarrassment that people feel. This applies particularly to the issue of sexual dysfunction, where people are very reticent about disclosing their problems. Simply asking people is unlikely to give an accurate picture: it would be surprising, for example, if a man were as willing to volunteer the information that he ejaculates prematurely or a woman that she never reaches an orgasm as to volunteer that they have a medical condition such as diabetes. One way of overcoming the problem of embarrassment is to give people anonymous questionnaires, as Frank et al.[50] did to 100 couples. Most were middle class and well educated, yet the incidence of sexual problems was quite high — 40 per cent of the men reported erection or ejaculatory dysfunction, and 63 per cent of the women reported arousal or orgasmic difficulties.

Another way of finding out about the incidence of dysfunction might be to canvas physicians for estimates on the basis of their experience. However, when this was done in one study, there was a great range in the percentage of patients who presented with a sexual problem. As expected, physicians in some specialities (such as general practice and obstetrics) reported a higher incidence than others. But even within specialities there was a wide range of reported rates, from 1–60 per cent in general practice, depending on the doctor canvassed. When the investigators attempted to understand this range, they found that characteristics of the doctors themselves were significant. Those physicians who routinely asked about sexual problems reported twice as many patients with sexual difficulties as those who did not, while doctors who were observed to be embarrassed while talking about sexual histories (as shown by blushing and fidgeting) had rates some five times lower than those who did not show such embarrassment. It seems that the willingness of patients to disclose and of physicians to inquire was associated with the doctors' own feelings about sexuality.[51]

The sexual problems faced by the chronically ill and the handicapped are often significant in their lives. Those who have had a severe illness, such as myocardial infarction, are often unsure about the risks of sexual intercourse, even though the physiological 'cost' of coitus is comparatively modest. The consequences of some operations such as colostomy and mastectomy have also received greater attention recently. It would be surprising if such operations did not have a significant effect on sexual anxieties. In one study, almost a third of mastectomy patients who had had satisfactory sexual relations before the operation lost interest or ceased to enjoy them afterwards[52] and there is a general decline in both the frequency of sexual contact and level of sexual arousal.[53] In another study, all of the 41 women approached showed an interest in psychological assistance. Once the immediate prospect of death had passed, practically without exception sexual concerns dominated their thinking. Sexual attractiveness was of central importance to their emotional functioning and a major fear was that their partners would leave them. Counselling was found to be appropriate and useful.[54]

People may have sexual problems arising from less obvious causes. Masters and Johnson outlined a learning theory approach to sexual difficulties. Their book, *Human Sexual Inadequacy*,[55] has provided an important contribution to sexual therapy. They suggest that through cultural prohibitions or familial admonitions, the naturally occurring growth of sexual skills can be inhibited. These past experiences are said to thwart sexual expression and increase fears of performance. Once the fear of failure has been aroused, the dysfunction operates in a vicious circle. For the man who is unable to attain an erection, his anxieties serve to interfere with the natural cycle of sexual arousal and are thus confirmed. The relationship with the sexual partner is also affected; as her concern is increased, she too is unable to enjoy her own sexuality.

Masters and Johnson's therapy is essentially an attempt to break this pattern. They seek to remove the goal-oriented basis of many of their patients' sexual encounters. Fear of performance is important, they reason, only if the partners are attempting to reach a goal of some kind, usually orgasm. If this goal is no longer required, they would then have the opportunity to respond spontaneously to the emotions and pleasures of physical sensation. Their technique for accomplishing this is termed 'sensate focus'.

The therapists place a ban on intercourse on the first few days of therapy so that neither partner need fear failure. Each is instructed to give and receive sessions of gentle, non-sexually stimulating touch, for as long as both partners find it pleasurable. Sensate focus serves two purposes. First, as the name implies, it focuses the partners' attention on the physical sensations of their encounter, rather than on the fears that physical contact often engendered in the past. The second purpose of sensate focus exercises is to emphasize the importance of accurate communication between the partners. While indicating to each other which kinds of touch are pleasurable, the channels of sensory communication are being opened. Indeed, Masters and Johnson see their role primarily as catalysts to communication. For them, sexual dysfunction indicates that the most important channel of communication is disrupted, and sensate focus is designed to encourage the partners to share and understand each other's needs.

The couple is the patient

Accordingly, Masters and Johnson stress the importance of involving both partners. They do not consider it useful to treat one partner in isolation, since they see any form of sexual inadequacy as essentially a problem of mutual involvement. Because communication between partners is so significant, it would not be appropriate to treat only the person with the presenting difficulty. Indeed, the diagnosis of sexual dysfunction cannot be made on the basis of any objective criteria: a condition that presents a problem for one couple may not be a problem for another. In the study mentioned earlier where 40 per cent of the men and 63 per cent of the women said that they had difficulties, 80 per cent of the couples said that they were satisfied with their sexual lives. In fact, 'the marital relationship is considered as the patient . . . sexual dysfunction is indeed a marital-unit problem, certainly never only a wife's or a husband's personal concern' (Ref. 55, p.3).

The focus on the relationship is aided by the use of co-therapists — one man and one woman. Masters and Johnson stress the necessity for the therapists to have resolved their own feelings about sexuality before attempting work of this kind. Those who have conflicts about sexuality may well make it more difficult for the patients to come to terms with their own problems. This emphasis on self-examination applies to psychotherapeutic work in general as discussed in Chapter 2. Success rates are very high compared to many forms of psychological therapy with only 20 per cent failing to improve.

A notable contributer to recent developments in sex therapy is

Helen Kaplan[56] who has attempted to integrate the psychotherapeutic approach with the behavioural one. Whereas for Masters and Johnson the presenting sexual difficulty is seen to be the real problem, Kaplan considers the possibility that it could be an indication of another underlying problem, such as marital discord or depression. Seen in this way, sexual dysfunction would be treated within the larger context of the marital relationship.

Summary

One of our basic attributes is our sense of gender identity. Although this may appear to be entirely genetically determined, studies have shown that environmental factors can have a strong effect on whether individuals see themselves as male or female. Sex roles refer to the activities which are expected of a person on the basis of their sex, with men expected to be assertive and logical, women expressive and warm, for instance. Like gender identity, there is some controversy over the extent to which sex roles are innately determined or created by environmental influences: certainly, there is considerable variation in sex-linked behaviours cross-culturally, and people treat even small babies differently on the basis of their sex. In Western society, male roles are generally more highly valued, and attempts have been made to link this with women's greater susceptibility to psychological problems. While masculinity and femininity have traditionally been seen as opposite ends of the same dimension, the view that they are independent factors, such that it is possible to have some characteristics of both (psychological androgyny), is gaining popularity.

Sexual practices vary widely both between and within cultures. Recent studies have attempted to dispel myths and misconceptions about sexual activities. Analysis of contraceptive use has shown a number of decision points at which effectiveness can break down and has isolated certain personality characteristics (internal locus of control) associated with contraceptive users. Attempts to study the effects of abortion indicate that, although early termination generally has little adverse psychological effect on most women, it can still be useful to isolate factors which identify those women who experience difficulties.

The incidence of sexual dysfunction is difficult to establish through the reticence of both patients to tell and their doctors to ask. Some illnesses and operations can lead to sexual difficulties and psychological assistance may be valuable. Sexual dysfunction can be successfully treated through therapy which views the problem as a learned difficulty.

Suggested reading

Unger, R. (1979) *Female and Male*, London: Harper and Row, reviews much of the research on sex roles, taking mainly an environmental position. As an introduction to sexual medicine, Bancroft, J. (1983) *Human Sexuality and its Problems* Edinburgh: Churchill Livingstone, is recommended.

References

1. Leiblum, S.R. & Pervin, L.A. (eds.) (1980) *Principles and Practice of Sex Therapy* London: Tavistock.
2. Money, J. & Erhardt, A.A. (1972) *Man and Woman: Boy and Girl* Baltimore: Johns Hopkins University Press.
3. Imperato-McGinley, J., Peterson, R.E., Gautier, T. & Sturla, E. (1979) Androgens and the evolution of male gender identity among male pseudohermaphrodites with a 5 α-reductase deficiency. *New England Journal of Medicine* **300**: 1233–1237.
4. Money, J. (1975) Ablatio penis: a normal male infant sex-reassigned as a girl. *Archives of Sexual Behaviour* **4**: 65–71.
5. Bean, G. & Kidder, L. (1982) Helping and achieving. *Social Science and Medicine* **16**: 1377–1381.
6. Leserman, J. (1980) Sex differences in the professional orientation of first-year medical students. *Sex Roles* **6**: 645–660.
7. Reinisch, J.M. & Karlow W.G. (1977) Prenatal exposure to synthetic progestins and estrogens. *Archives of Sexual Behaviour* **6**: 257–288.
8. Wilson, G. (1979) The sociobiology of sex differences. *Bulletin of the British Psychological Society* **32**: 350–353.
9. Maccoby, E.E. & Jacklin, C. (1974) *The Psychology of Sex Differences* Stanford, Calif.: Stanford University Press.
10. Mead, M. (1950) *Sex and Temperament in Three Societies* New York: Mentor.
11. Bhavnani, R. & Hutt, C. (1972) Divergent thinking in boys and girls. *Journal of Child Psychology and Psychiatry* **13**: 121–127.
12. Block, J.H. (1973) Conceptions of sex role. *American Psychologist* **28**: 512–526.
13. Rubin, J.Z., Provenzano, F.J. & Luria, Z. (1974) The eye of the beholder. *American Journal of Orthopsychiatry* **44**: 512–519.
14. Condry, S.M., Condry, J. & Pogatshnik, L. (1983) Sex differences: a study of the ear of the beholder. *Sex Roles* **6**: 697–704.
15. Rheingold, H.L. & Cook, K.V. (1975) The content of boys' and girls' rooms as an index of parents' behaviour. *Child Development* **46**: 459–463.
16. Saario, T.N., Jacklin, C. & Tittle, C. (1973) Sex role stereotyping in the public schools. *Harvard Educational Review* **43**: 386–416.
17. Lewis, M. & Weinraub, M. (1979) Origins of sex role development. *Sex Roles* **5**: 135–153.
18. Pheterson, G.I., Kiesler, S. & Goldberg, P. (1971) Evaluation of the performance of women as a function of their sex, achievement and personal history. *Journal of Personality and Social Psychology* **19**: 114–118.
19. Paludi, M.A. & Bauer, W. (1983) Goldberg revisited; what's in an author's name? *Sex Roles* **9**: 387–390.
20. Feldman-Summers, S. & Kiesler, S. (1974) Those who are number two try harder. *Journal of Personality and Social Psychology* **30**: 846–855.
21. Feather, N.T. & Simon, J. (1975) Reactions to male and female success and

failure in sex-linked occupations. *Journal of Personality and Social Psychology* **31**: 20-31.
22. West, C. (1980) When the doctor is a 'lady'. In: Stromberg, A. (ed.) *Women, Health and Medicine* Palo Alto, Calif: Mayfield.
23. Wilson, A.R. & Krane, R. (1980) Change in self-esteem and its effects on symptoms of depression. *Cognitive Therapy and Research* **4**: 419–421.
24. Beck, A.T. & Greenberg, R. (1974) Cognitive therapy with depressed women. In: Franks, V. & Burtle, V. (eds.) *Women in Therapy* New York: Bruner/Mazel.
25. Nathanson, C.A. (1977) Sex, illness and medical care. *Social Science and Medicine* **11**: 13–25.
26. Prather, J. & Findell, L. (1975) Sex differences in the content and style of medical advertisements. *Social Science and Medicine* **9**: 23–27.
27. Thompson, E.L. (1979) Sexual bias in drug advertisements. *Social Science and Medicine* **13A**: 187–191.
28. Bernstein, B. & Kane, R. (1981) Physicians' attitudes towards female patients. *Medical Care* **19**: 600–608.
29. Bem, S.L. (1974) The measurement of psychological androgyny. *Journal of Consulting and Clinical Psychology* **42**: 155–162.
30. Bem, S.L., Martyna, W. & Watson, C. (1976) Sex-typing and androgyny. *Journal of Personality and Social Psychology* **34**: 1016–1023.
31. Kelly, J.A., Furman, W. & Young, V. (1978) Problems associated with the typological measurement of sex roles and androgyny. *Journal of Consulting and Clinical Psychology* **46**: 1574–1576.
32. Zeldow, P.B., Clark, D., Daugherty, S. & Eckenfels, E. (1985) Personality indicators of psychosocial adjustment in first-year medical students. *Social Science and Medicine* **20**: 95–100.
33. Evans-Pritchard, E.E. (1970) Sexual inversion among the Azande. *American Anthropologist* **72**: 1428–1433.
34. Meggot, M. (1964) Male–female relationships in the Highlands of Australian New Guinea. *American Anthropologist* **66**: 204–224.
35. Sexton, L. (1973) Sexual interaction and population pressure in Highland New Guinea. Paper presented to the *22nd Annual Meeting of the American Psychological Association* New Orleans.
36. Kinsey, A., Pomeroy, W. & Martin, C. (1948) *Sexual Behaviour in the Human Male* Philadelphia: W. B. Saunders.
37. Masters, W.H. (1966) *Human Sexual Response* London: Churchill Livingstone.
38. Reichelt, P.A. (1978) Changes in sexual behaviour among unmarried teenage women utilizing oral contraceptives. *Journal of Population* **1**: 57–68.
39. Byrne, D., Jazwinski, C., DeNinno, J. & Fisher, W. (1977) Negative sexual attitudes and contraception. In: Byrne, D. & Byrne, L. (eds.) *Explaining Human Sexuality* New York: Harper and Row.
40. Andres, D., Gold, D., Berger, C., Kinch, R. & Gillett, P. (1983) Selected psychosocial characteristics of males: their relationship to contraceptive use and abortion. *Personality and Social Psychology Bulletin* **9**: 387–396.
41. Lundy, J.R. (1972) Some personality correlates of contraceptive use among unmarried female college students. *Journal of Psychology* **80**: 9–14.
42. Kar, S.B. (1971) Individual aspirations as related to early and late acceptance of contraception. *Journal of Social Psychology* **83**: 235–245.
43. Strickland, B.R. (1978) Internal–external expectancies and health-related behaviours. *Journal of Consulting and Clinical Psychology* **46**: 1192–1212.
44. Ekblad, M. (1955) Induced abortion on psychiatric grounds. *Acta Psychiatrica and Neurologica Scandinavia* **Supplement 99**: 1–238.
45. Gillis, A. (1975) A follow-up of 72 cases referred for abortion. *Mental Health in Society* **2**: 212–218.
46. Hardy, J.A. (1982) Psychological and social aspects of induced abortion. *British Journal of Clinical Psychology* **21**: 29–41.

47. Donnai, P., Charles, N. & Harris, R. (1981) Attitudes of patients after 'genetic' terminations of pregnancy. *British Medical Journal* **282**: 621–622.
48. Blomberg, S. (1980) Influence of maternal distress during pregnancy on postnatal outcome. *Acta Psychiatrica Scandinavia* **62**: 405–417.
49. Allgeier, E.R., Allgeier, A. & Rywick, T. (1979) Abortion: reward for conscientious contraceptive use? *Journal of Sex Research* **15**: 64–75.
50. Frank, E., Anderson, C. & Rubinstein, D. (1978) Frequency of sexual dysfunction in 'normal' couples. *New England Journal of Medicine* **299**: 111–115.
51. Burnap, D.W. & Golden, J. (1967) Sexual problems in medical practice. *Journal of Medical Education* **42**: 673–680.
52. Maguire, G.P., Lee, E., Bevington, D., Kucheman, C., Crabtree, R. & Cornell, C. (1978) Psychiatric problems in the first year after mastectomy. *British Medical Journal* **1**: 963–965.
53. Andersen, B.L. & Jochiasen, V. (1985) Sexual functioning among breast cancer, gynecologic cancer and healthy women. *Journal of Consulting and Clinical Psychology* **53**: 25–32.
54. Witkin, M.H. (1978) Psychosocial counselling of the mastectomy patient. *Journal of Sexual and Marital Therapy* **4**: 20–28.
55. Masters, W. & Johnson, V. (1970) *Human Sexual Inadequacy* Boston: Little, Brown.
56. Kaplan, H.S. (1978) *The New Sex Therapy* Harmondsworth, Middlesex: Penguin Books.

9

Family Dynamics

Introduction

Although the family group is usually responsible for biological reproduction, it also plays a significant role in what can be termed 'social reproduction'. It is through relationships with parents or caregivers that a child acquires much knowledge about him or herself and about the customs and expectations of society. Research in this area forms the basis for discussion in the first part of this chapter. Within each family group, there will be several rules that are shared with the larger culture, but also many which are not. Each individual family can be seen as a kind of subculture with its own set of idiosyncratic ways of coping with such difficulties as illness. Some place more emphasis on prevention than others: the importance of good nutrition or views about the necessity of regular visits to the dentist are but two examples. The decision to consult the doctor is often taken within the family context. It seems that some families are more likely to consult than others, so in this sense the family can be involved in the recovery from illness (Chapter 6).

There may also be taboos about discussing certain topics or certain accepted ways of dealing with conflicts. Since children learn much through instruction by and observation of their parents, there is the possibility that children may grow up to use methods of coping with difficulties that are similar to their parents'. They may come to treat their children in the way that they themselves were treated when young, or may create a marital relationship similar to that of their parents'. Some of the variables associated with family discord are examined in the second half of this chapter, and ways of dealing with them, through family therapy, are also considered.

Family systems

The contributions made by cultural anthropologists have been mentioned in earlier chapters. One notable aspect of their work

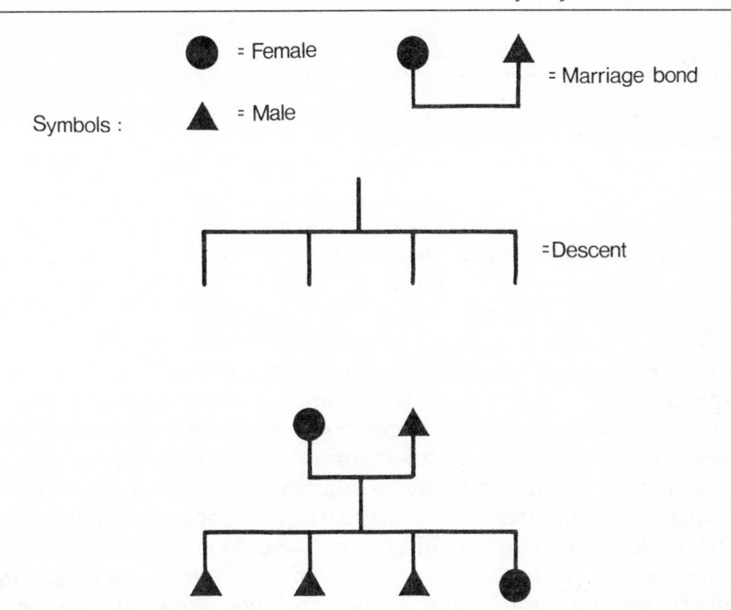

Fig. 16. The nuclear family. A man and a woman are linked by a marriage bond and have four descendants.

is the observation of family systems in various cultures. Some anthropologists have placed emphasis on inheritance rights: is the parents' wealth equally distributed between all the children, amongst the sons only, or, as in some agricultural societies, is the farm passed on to the youngest son? When a son or daughter marries, do the couple live near the man's parents, the woman's, or are there no set rules about this? In East London, at least, there seems to be a tendency for couples, when just married, to live near the woman's family.[1] By describing societies in these ways, anthropologists have pointed out the wide range of customs open to and used by mankind.

There is a standard way of portraying family systems, as shown in Fig. 16. This illustrates a nuclear family comprising two parents and four children. The parents are represented by the circle (woman) and triangle (man) joined by a 'marriage' bond. The degree of ritual involved in forming this bond differs both between and within cultures. Sometimes it is accompanied by an important ceremony, at other times by simple agreement. So, too, does the strength of the bond vary. Divorce can involve complicated legal procedures or a simple statement on one partner's side that he or she wishes to end the obligation. When anthropologists use the term marriage they do not necessarily mean it in the way it is used in Western cultures. Rather, it is simply a socially recognized bond with obligations. It is likely that marriage, as a universal custom, has to do with the legitimization of parenthood (so the society knows to whom which children belong) rather than the legitimization of sexual relationships. Figure 16 also portrays the descent of three boys and one girl from these parents. Generally, the children live in the same household as the parents. There are some exceptions to this rule (such as the Israeli kibbutzim)[2] but these are very rare. Even in kibbutzim there is an increasing trend for the children to live with their biological parents.

This virtually universal family system forms the basis of much anthropological research. Using the nuclear family as a basis, a wide variety of cultural customs can be described. One way is in terms of the number of generations living together. In the independent nuclear family — common in the West — only two generations live together, the parents and their children. In this system, marriage ties are seen to be more important than blood ties, i.e. the couple's first obligation is to each other rather than to their parents. In the extended family system, more than one nuclear family live together in the same household. This type of family can become very large, often including several generations, and be long-lived. Found predominantly in agricultural societies, it emphasizes blood-ties: the first obligations are to blood relatives and the marital obligations are relatively weak. A variation of the extended family is the joint family, found in India. Here, the men and their wives stay in the family home until younger siblings are educated and married, at which time the wealth is divided up and the nuclear families become independent. In this system, the tie between brothers is particularly strong.

Another way of describing family systems is in terms of the number of spouses that are socially acceptable. In the West the rule is monogamy, but only a minority of societies have a definite restriction on this. In most, polygamy is acceptable, in that there are no sanctions against having more than one spouse. There are two types of polygamy: polygyny (more than one wife for one man) is much more common than polyandry (more than one husband for one woman). The single husband or wife has definite financial and sexual obligations towards each spouse, and it is usually seen as a sign of economic status rather than of sexual attractiveness. In the more usual polygyny, the woman is often just as involved as the man in selecting a new wife and may exert pressure on him to do so. If both families live in the same household, her duties would be reduced by half (or more, since she would be the senior wife) and the enhanced status would reflect on her as well as her husband. Although polygyny is usually associated with wealth, polyandry is found in conditions of extreme poverty. In the very few societies where it is practised, it apparently serves to keep the birth-rate down, thus reducing the strain on resources.

One other way in which anthropologists describe family systems is in terms of the rules of descent: descent through the father's line is called patrilineal, that through the mother's matrilineal. This is interesting because it sometimes affects the definition of incest. Although there is an almost universal taboo against sexual relations within families, who counts as 'family' depends on rules of descent. A purely genetic description is not adequate to predict this.

Amongst the Trobrianders, for example, lineage is considered

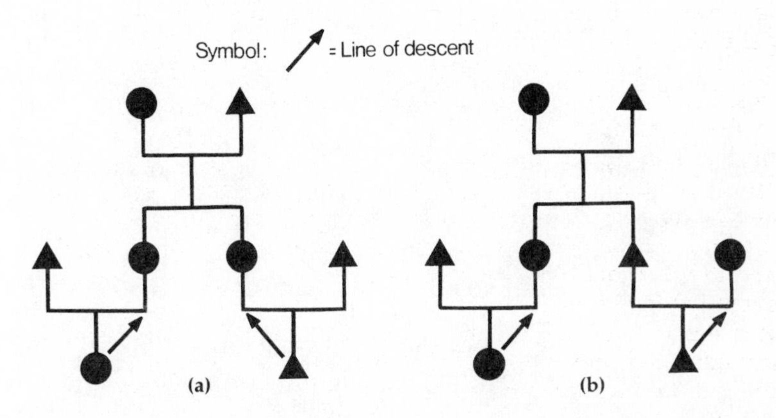

Fig. 17. Rules of descent. The cultural definition of descent can affect rules about incest. In (a), the male and female grandchildren are considered to share the same mother because of the matrilineal line of descent: sexual relationships between them are taboo. This is not the case for those in (b); they have different lines of descent and are considered potential marriage partners.

to operate through the mother. In Fig. 17 there are two examples of family trees. In Western society, no difference would be seen in the relationships of the two pairs of grandchildren, both being cousins, but the Trobrianders make an important distinction between them. Since the line of descent is matrilineal, the children in Fig. 17a are considered to have the same mother (the circle at the top), making them brother and sister. Sexual relations between them are taboo. Those in Fig. 17b, however, are considered to have different mothers, making sexual relations between them acceptable. In fact, this is a preferred marital bond in that culture.

Medical anthropology

Awareness of the great diversity of kinship patterns and cultural rules can help dispel *ethnocentrism*, the view that one's own culture provides the 'right' way of doing things and other systems are somewhat inferior. This has particular relevance to medical care. Medical anthropology is the area of study concerned with describing how people of different cultures interpret and treat their illnesses. Many people who have emigrated from Asia hold the view that some medical conditions (such as pregnancy) are 'hot', while others are 'cold'. Appropriate care for such conditions involves diet, with wheat, potatoes, fish and chicken being 'hot' foods appropriate for 'cold' diseases, whereas rice, peas and beans are 'cold' foods used in the treatment of 'hot' diseases.[3] The Muslim community might consult a *hakim* as well as their Western doctor, whereas the people of Java consult a *dukun* when ill, a person with great healing powers.[4] The illness may be cured through the use of herbal medicines, spells, or the intrinsic healing strength of the *dukun*. A person seeking assistance might be advised to rebury their child's umbilical cord or to sleep the other way round in bed. The Javanese recognize that a particular recommendation may not work, but this does not destroy their faith in the medical system: 'Sometimes they cure you and sometimes they do not. The only difference is that you have to pay a Western doctor even if you die in his hands, while a good *dukun* expects payment only if he succeeds.'

Although we might find the practice of eating 'hot' food for 'cold' conditions or reburying the umbilical cord both quaint and baffling, it should be pointed out that some standard medical procedures used in Western countries, such as the use of episiotomy (an incision in the perineum during childbirth), have little basis in experimental evidence.[5] It has been faith in the benefits of technology and intervention that has determined the widespread use of this procedure, not controlled studies. This is perhaps not so different from the faith the Javanese have in their *dukun*. It is likely that patients' belief in the Javanese system is significant, but this also applies to Western medicine.

Since many treatments involve a placebo effect (see Chapter 11), it seems important that both doctor and patient have confidence in the efficacy of a medication. Many herbal remedies do have properties that can be explained in Western terms, such as the presence of pain-killing substances in coca leaves. Others are less obvious. The reluctance to explore the effectiveness of acupuncture may be due to the (to us) nonsensical way it is explained in oriental cultures. In this case, ethnocentrism in medicine may have inhibited research into a potentially useful technique.[6]

Many anthropologists consider a culture's medical system not only to be based on faith and belief but also as part of an overall pattern of adaptation to the environment. It cannot, therefore, be understood without reference to the economic and social conditions of the people. The same might be said of preventative measures. Some cultures have taboos on post-partum sexual relations, for example. These taboos tend to occur in societies where the diet is restricted: by ensuring that pregnancy does not occur, the mother's milk is kept high in nutrients thus increasing the infant's chances of survival. Although the explanation given might be different (offending the spirits is sometimes evoked as a reason for such customs) the practice has effective results. Similarly, the extended family may not be a suitable system for people raised in the West who have been reared to believe in the independent nuclear family, but there are indications that it affords some protection against post-partum depression. This condition is largely confined to Western cultures and is very uncommon where there is much support available from relatives for the new mother.[7]

When people emigrate from one culture to another, a clash in belief systems about illness, treatment and diet may cause problems. Within the Asian community, for example, there are cultural norms that women should be confined indoors and wear clothes which cover most of the skin. This is not such a problem for families living on the Indian subcontinent, but these norms can result in vitamin D deficiency for those living in Britain, with its fewer hours of sunshine. In pregnancy, a 'hot' condition, this can be compounded by their avoidance of 'hot' foods high in vitamin D and iron. Not only can the foetus be at risk: rickets in infancy has been attributed to the Asian practice of weaning babies directly on to cow's milk without any vitamin drops or vitamin D-enriched baby foods. Older children, too, may suffer because Asian families often live in depressed inner city areas where opportunities for outdoor play are limited.

Thus, the family setting, where many of the decisions regarding health care are taken, is strongly influenced by cultural factors. This applies not only to the more obvious differences in marriage customs and the kinds of support available to an ill person, but also to his or her views about disease and appropriate treatment.

Family discord

Divorce

The ever-increasing divorce rate has made conflict within the family an area of concern. It is not clear if this increase is due to more marriages breaking down, to more broken marriages ending in divorce (due to the relaxation in divorce laws and the lessening social stigma) or to a combination of these factors. Divorce is more likely for couples who marry after a short courtship, who marry because of pregnancy or who come from different social and economic backgrounds. It is difficult not to make value-judgements, but it has been pointed out that divorce can have positive effects. Since most people marry again afterwards, the act of divorce can be seen as an indication that the people involved are looking for a fuller and more satisfying relationship than they were experiencing previously.

There has been particular concern about the effects of divorce or separation on children. As discussed in Chapter 7, it seems that it is not the divorce itself but the discord and disturbance that accompanies it that is most important. When comparisons are made between children whose parents are divorced and children whose parents remain unhappily married, few differences are found.[8] In a comparison between single-parent and intact families, only in those instances where there was parental conflict was the children's self-esteem adversely affected.[9] In another study of 3000 women who were having their first child, those who had been illegitimate themselves or whose parents were divorced or separated were twice as likely to conceive or give birth before marriage, but if their parents' marriage was broken by death, no effects were found.[10]

Perhaps a more useful way of considering marital conflict is not in terms of whether it results in divorce but rather how the conflicts are managed. It has been argued that all relationships involve a degree of conflict and that this should be accepted as an inevitable part of every marriage. According to this view, it is the ways in which couples cope with their disagreements that is important, not whether these disagreements exist. This approach underlies much marital therapy, examined later in the chapter.

Violence in the family

The incidence of violence in the family is difficult to ascertain. One difficulty concerns visibility. It is likely that only a small proportion of violent incidents are recorded by the police or by doctors. After a major newspaper ran a series of articles on child abuse, the incidence of reports increased 2–3 times in one city. Another problem is definition: does violence mean purely physical abuse, or does it also include nutritional and emotional neglect?

More important than incidence, perhaps, are the attempts to

understand — rather than simply condemn — violence in the home. Until comparatively recently, parents were considered to have every right to treat their children as they saw fit and there seems to be continuing ambivalence about violence towards wives. In one study, subjects were given a fictitious description of a man and a woman fighting. The fight ended in unconsciousness for the woman. Half the subjects were told that the couple were husband and wife, the other half that they were not married. As a measure of how acceptable violence was between these couples, the subjects were then asked how severely the man should be punished. Significantly, less severe punishments were recommended for the married man, indicating a greater acceptance of violence within the marital relationship than outside it.[11]

Child abuse

Studies on the characteristics of people who use violence as a means of resolving family conflict have produced inconsistent results. Some researchers (but not all) have found child abuse to be most prevalent in the lowest social classes. For example, Gil[12] provides evidence that child abuse is associated with such social conditions as low income, poor housing and unemployment. According to this viewpoint, the environment places stress on the individual, violence being one possible result. The suggestion is that anyone could become an abusive parent given such circumstances. But here again there is the problem of visibility: abuse may indeed by more prevalent in the lowest social classes or it may simply be more likely to be detected. Social and community workers visit families whose economic plight is apparent to welfare authorities more frequently, making evidence of abuse visible and more likely to be reported to the police. Others have argued that violence is due to personality disturbances — there is a higher rate of divorce, separation and minor criminal offences in abusive families, and depression in the mother is commonly found. She is also likely to have had her first child when very young. Another suggestion is that abuse is triggered by difficult children. Although only 7–8 per cent of live births are premature, approximately 25 per cent of abused children are born prematurely. Perhaps these infants are more difficult to rear because they fuss and cry more than full-term infants and give fewer rewards to their parents. Prematurity is also associated with young mothers who are under stress. Perhaps these women, because of their relative social immaturity, have greater difficulty in coping with their infants' demands.

Another possible reason for this link between prematurity and abuse is failure of early bonding (see Chapter 7). Since the parents have only limited access to the child for the first weeks, the attachment between them may be weaker than usual. Relevant to this, Lynch[13] studied the relationship between ill-health and child abuse. She used the siblings of abused children as the comparison group, reasoning that they were similar in many ways and that the personalities and social circumstances of the parents would be relatively stable. She found several differences, including a higher incidence of abnormal pregnancies and deliveries and, important for the attachment hypothesis, a greater likelihood of separation between mother and child for the first 48 hours after birth and over the next six months. A later study indicated that abused children were twice as likely to have been in a special care nursery after birth than a comparison group.

Early experiences

Receiving or witnessing violence as a child could also be relevant: it may serve as a model for a method of resolving conflicts in later life. Gelles[14] interviewed 43 women who had suffered violence from their husbands. Forty of the 43 reported that they had been the victims of violence as children; and 25 reported that they had witnessed their parents being violent to one another. In a larger study, over 80 per cent reported that their husbands' parents had used violence, either towards their children or between themselves.[15]

In the absence of control groups in these studies, it is not possible to say how high these figures are in comparison to the rest of the population. In fact, the incidence of the use of force in the population as a whole seems considerable. Many parents use some form of physical punishment towards their children, often at a very early age. One quarter of the mothers (out-patients at a medical clinic) had begun to use 'spanking' as a punishment before their children were six months of age.[16] In another study of university students, more than half reported actual or threatened use of violence from parents.[17] Gelles[18] conducted in-depth interviews with husbands and wives: about 60 per cent had used physical aggression during a marital conflict. With such a high incidence of violence in the population, it is difficult to conclude that childhood experience with violence is closely associated with the use of violence in adulthood.

Nevertheless, it seems possible that as children grow they learn ways of coping with conflict from their parents. Several investigations have attempted to correlate ways of coping experienced as a child with favoured methods as adults. Owens and Straus[19] found such associations. Those who observed and received violence as children were more likely to have committed violence themselves as children and were more likely to approve of violent behaviour as adults (such as a husband slapping his wife).

An important qualification is needed here, however. In many studies, an individual's own reports of past events are relied upon to give a picture of upbringing. There are two main reasons why this might be inadequate. First, there is the problem of *memory*. People may be more likely to remember their parents engaging in violence if violence has recently occurred in their own homes. Second, there is the question of *social desirability*. People might be more willing to admit parental violence to investigators if they have committed violence themselves.

Prediction

The lesson from these studies is that there does not seem to be any one factor that is unique to violent families. While, as a group, abusive parents have been found to differ from the non-abusive, there is much overlap between the two populations, so that there is no one factor that can be pinpointed as being solely responsible. Many parents who use violence come from deprived backgrounds, but not all with such childhood experiences become abusive. Similarly, many battered children are premature, but only a minority of premature children are battered. This has two implications. First, abuse might be more appropriately considered as lying along a continuum that includes nutritional and emotional neglect as well as physical abuse, so that it is a question of degree rather than of kind. When some 95 per cent of parents report that they smack their children, 7 per cent daily,[20] it does not seem sensible to say that physical punishment itself is a sign of serious abuse. Second, it may be more fruitful to consider violence as a result of many factors, several of which in concert can make it more probable. The cumulative effects of prematurity in the child, youthfulness in the parents, social and economic stresses, personality and past experience with violence, may all contribute. This notion of accumulating experience and stress is similar to that mentioned in Chapter 7, where it was suggested that no single negative experience is likely to have long-lasting effects on personality development, but that continued deprivation will. Possibly, consideration of all of these factors will contribute to predictive power.

Accurate prediction is valuable because the resources open to doctors and the social services generally are limited. Services would be used inefficiently if too many *false-positives* were identified — instances where violence is predicted to occur but where, in fact, it is unlikely. Conversely, *false-negatives* — instances where unpredicted violence occurs — could have serious consequences.

Thus, the problem in this kind of research is to minimize the number of these types of error. In many research studies on prediction, the primary concern has been to minimize false-negatives (often resulting in many false-positives), based on the judgement that this is the less serious error to make.

A method of predicting potential abuse which has had some success and is stimulating interest is based on observations in the delivery room and post-partum ward. In the delivery room, the concern is with the mother's reactions to her infant — is she ambivalent, disappointed, angry? — and the support she is given by her spouse. In the post-partum period, continuing critical or disparaging remarks would be noted. Some 75 per cent of 'high-risk' families can be identified through these observations.[21]

Prevention

Several attempts have been made to prevent child abuse. There is a statistical problem in evaluating the effectiveness of intervention programmes because of the low number of children who are actually physically harmed, but there are some encouraging results. In Chapter 7, a study concerned with the effects of extended contact at birth between mother and child was discussed: the incidence of injuries requiring hospitalization was lower in the extended contact families than in the routine contact ones. In some hospitals all parents who may have difficulty in forming attachment bonds because of the baby's need for special care are seen by a social worker and given the opportunity to discuss practical and social problems. In another study, three groups of mothers were followed up after the birth of their child. One group consisted of mothers not considered at risk on the basis of labour room and post-partum observations. A second group of 'at risk' mothers was given comprehensive paediatric follow-up by a physician and a health visitor, and a third group, similar to the second, was given no such assistance. In this latter group of 50 families, five children were later hospitalized for treatment of serious injuries whereas, by contrast, none of the high-risk intervention group nor of the low-risk group required such hospitalization.[22]

The behavioural approach may also have much to offer. It will be remembered from Chapter 3 that some psychologists consider behaviour to be the result of rewards and punishments. By analysing the patterns of stimulus and response, the contingencies that lead to abuse and neglect may be discovered. Perhaps parents who abuse their children see punishment as the main means of control. They might be briefed in the basics of the operant model and encouraged to achieve control with rewards instead of punishments.[23]

Prediction and prevention of violence between adults may be more difficult to achieve, partly because of the greater reticence to interfere with marital relationships and partly because of practical considerations — it may be very difficult to elicit the co-operation of both partners. Recent attempts to prevent the re-occurrence of marital violence include the establishment of battered women's refuges. They provide a much needed service for women: several studies have indicated that many women return to a violent home because they have 'nowhere else to go'.

Family therapy

Helping people with their psychological difficulties can take many forms. Some of these were discussed in Chapters 2 and 3: there, the emphasis was on treating the individual independently from his or her family group. Although the patient's relationships within the family might be discussed, parents or spouses would not usually be invited into the consulting room. A somewhat different approach is used by Masters and Johnson in their sex therapy (Chapter 8). They consider a sexual difficulty to reside not within one individual, but within the couple. For them, the couple's relationship is the patient and in order to treat the problem both partners are seen together.

A basic tenet of family therapy is that an individual's difficulties cannot be considered or treated adequately unless the nuclear family (and sometimes a larger network of relatives) is seen in therapy. There are several advantages to such a treatment strategy. First, it provides an opportunity to observe how members of a family actually relate to one another. Rather than relying on one individual's view of what happens in the family, the therapist is able to see the patterns of interaction. The therapist's perceptions may be less clouded by personal needs. Second, the therapist is able to act as a kind of referee, encouraging the family members to consider how they are relating to each other and pointing out their conflicts. By acting in this way, the therapist may be able to help one member explain himself more clearly. Having someone present who is not punitive and who will provide support if necessary may make it easier to a child to articulate his point of view, for example. Third, the therapist might choose to role play occasionally, indicating possible ways of reacting to comments other than those used by the family. In conjoint therapy, where there are two therapists, their relationship can act as a model for open and honest interaction between adults. A fourth advantage over individual therapy concerns the problem of generalization. Many therapists consider psychological difficulties to be evidence of trouble in relationships. In the therapeutic relationship, the patient is given the opportunity to discover the problems inherent in his or her usual ways of relating to people. However, if this person is then required to return to a family in which difficulties remain, it may be harder to put into practice what has been learnt. By considering the whole family, this problem is lessened. Of course, family therapy may not always be possible. One member may refuse or be unavailable for some other reason.

Although there are some circumstances where family therapy is inappropriate,[24] there is considerable evidence about the importance of the family in the re-emergence of psychiatric difficulties.[25] Brown et al.[26] were interested in factors associated with relapse in schizophrenic patients after they left hospital. They took several measures including prior behavioural disturbance, impairment at work and the support the patients could be expected to receive once they were discharged from hospital. As a measure of support, they interviewed a key relative soon after the patient entered hospital, being especially interested in the number of critical and hostile comments made by this relative about the patient and the illness. When the relapse rates were later considered, this variable turned out to be the best single predictor: 58 per cent of patients whose relative expressed several negative comments relapsed, but only 16 per cent with relatives who expressed few negative comments. Indicators of previous behavioural disturbance had little predictive power. Similar results have been found for depressed patients.[27]

Leff et al.[28] tested the possibility that if members of a patient's family were included in therapy, the probability of relapse would be reduced. In all of the families chosen, there was much expressed hostility, so that a high relapse rate would be expected. One half of the families were assigned to the routine care group, which consisted of the typical out-patient care for the patients themselves. The other half were given a treatment package, which included information about schizophrenia, a group where the relatives could get together to discuss their difficulties, and family therapy. As expected, 50 per cent of the routine care patients later relapsed, but only 9 per cent of those whose families were involved in their treatment. This difference was maintained at a follow-up conducted two years later.[29]

Marital therapy

A particular example of family therapy concerns the relationship between spouses. Earlier in the chapter, the idea that all relationships — including the marital one — involve some kind of conflict was mentioned. This viewpoint is based on the premise that it is most unlikely that two people will always have the same goals and requirements, thus making disagreement inevitable at times. The aim of marital therapy is not to end conflict between partners but rather to provide ways of resolving disagreements that would not rely on coercion or result in hostility.

Several approaches have been taken in this area. Some therapists consider marital distress in operant terms — that couples who are having difficulty are more punishing and less rewarding than is conducive to a satisfying relationship.[30] The partners would be discouraged from threatening punishment to achieve goals and to use rewards instead.[31] In another approach, the therapist would aim to encourage sensitivity to the partner's needs and expression of feelings.[32,33] Many comments which pass between people can be interpreted on several levels and sensitivity involves looking for the emotional content behind what is said. For example, the comment 'I never see you in the evenings. You're always out' could be interpreted and reacted to simply as a complaint, with a response like: 'Complain, complain. If you were more pleasant, maybe I would stay home more often.' But on another level the comment can often be seen to reflect an underlying need, so that a reply like: 'Are you saying you're feeling lonely and you would like to see me more?' might result, a much more sensitive response.

Thus, family and marital therapy concentrate upon the relationships between family members. Instead of considering an individual's problems in isolation, difficulties are seen to be a family problem: even if one person has been diagnosed as ill in some way (for example, suffering from schizophrenia), the illness will affect the whole family and the way the family reacts will affect recovery. In marital therapy, much attention is given to the ways that the partners interpret and respond to each other's behaviour.

Summary

The family plays an important role in transmitting the cultural beliefs and values which order our everyday lives. Because we are so steeped in these influences, it can be difficult to understand other cultural systems, yet awareness of the beliefs and values of other peoples can contribute to a fuller understanding of their behaviour. This is particularly important when providing medical care for someone from a different cultural background. While a patient who lives in an extended family may be less likely to have some difficulties (such as post-partum depression, for instance), there may be other problems due to cultural differences. For example, the dietary habits and restrictions of Asian families result in low vitamin D intake leading to high incidence of rickets in Britain.

Studies on family discord have attempted to pinpoint factors associated with divorce or violence, the aim being to develop predictive or preventive measures. Differences in marital communication patterns and pre-marital circumstances have been found between distressed and happy couples. Family discord can result in violence, though the incidence of family violence is difficult to ascertain. Some workers believe that child abuse is associated with poor social conditions and environmental stresses; others suggest that abuse is triggered by difficult children. Premature babies are more likely to be abused, perhaps because they are harder to rear, because their mothers tend to be younger, or through failure of bonding after birth. No single factor discriminates between families where violence occurs and those where it does not. Since the re-occurrence of psychiatric difficulties in an individual is associated with the attitudes of the person's family, therapy which involves all the members of a household may be an appropriate way of resolving a variety of psychological problems.

Suggested reading

The idea that children learn ways of behaving from their parents and carry these on to adulthood is considered in some detail by M. Rutter & N. Madge (1976), *Cycles of Disadvantage* London: Heinemann. T.M. Field (ed.) (1980) *High-Risk Infants and Children* London: Academic Press, includes papers on many aspects of parent–child relationships, including child abuse. For those who are interested in medical anthropology, Helman's book (Ref. 3) is recommended; and an introduction to the problem of violence against women is given by E. Pizzey (1983) *Scream Quietly or the Neighbours will Hear* Harmondsworth, Middlesex: Penguin Books.

References

1. Young, M. & Willmott, P. (1957) *Family and Kinship in East London* Harmondsworth, Middlesex: Penguin Books.
2. Gerson, M. (1974) The family in the kibbutz. *Journal of Child Psychology and Psychiatry* **15**: 47–57.

3. Helman, C. (1985) *Culture, Health and Illness* Bristol: Wright and Sons.
4. Geertz, C. (1960) *The Religion of Java* New York: Free Press.
5. Harrison, R.F., Brennan, M., North, P., Reed, J. & Wickham, E. (1984) Is routine episiotomy necessary? *British Medical Journal* **288**: 1971–1975.
6. Anon. (1981) How does acupuncture work? *British Medical Journal* **283**: 746–747.
7. Stern, G. & Kruckman, L. (1983) Multidisciplinary perspectives on post-partum depression: an anthropological critique. *Social Science and Medicine* **17**: 1027–1041.
8. Bane, M.J. (1976) Marital disruption and the lives of children. *Journal of Social Issues* **32**: 103–117.
9. Raschke, H.J. & Raschke, V. (1979) Family conflict and children's self-concepts: a comparison of intact and single-parent families. *Journal of Marriage and the Family* **41**: 367–374.
10. Illeley, R. & Thompson, B. (1961) Women from broken homes. *Sociological Review* **9**: 27–54.
11. Straus, M.A. (1976) Sexual inequality, cultural norms and wife-beating. *Victimology* **1**: 54–70.
12. Gil, D.G. (1970) *Violence against Children* Cambridge, Mass.: Harvard University Press.
13. Lynch, M.A. (1975) Ill health and child abuse. *Lancet* **2**: 317–319.
14. Gelles, R.J. (1976) Abused wives: who do they stay? *Journal of Marriage and the Family* **38**: 659–668.
15. Roy, M. (1977) *Battered Women* New York: Van Nostrand.
16. Korsch, B.M., Christian, J., Gozzi, E. & Carlson, P. (1965) Infant care and punishment. *American Journal of Public Health* **55**: 1880–1888.
17. Straus, M.A. (1971) The social antecedents of physical punishment. *Journal of Marriage and the Family* **33**: 658–663.
18. Gelles, R.J. (1974) *The Violent Home* Beverly Hills: Russell Sage.
19. Owens, D.J. & Straus, M. (1975) The social structure of violence in childhood and approval of violence as an adult. *Aggressive Behaviour* **1**: 193–211.
20. Newson, J. & Newson, E. (1968) *Four Years Old in the Urban Community* Harmondsworth, Middlesex: Penguin Books.
21. Gray, J., Cutler, C., Dean, J. & Kempe, C. (1976) Perinatal assessment of mother–baby interaction. In: Helfer, R.E. & Kempe, C.H. *Child Abuse and Neglect* Cambridge, Mass.: Ballinger.
22. Lynch, M.A., Roberts, J. & Gordon, M. (1976) Child abuse: early warning in the maternity hospital. *Developmental Medicine and Child Neurology* **18**: 759–766.
23. Hutchings, J. (1980) The behavioural approach to child abuse: a review of the literature. In: Frude, N. *The Understanding and Prevention of Child Abuse: Psychological Approaches* London: Batsford.
24. Waldron-Skinner, S. (1978) Indications and contra-indications for the use of family therapy. *Journal of Child Psychology and Psychiatry* **19**: 57–62.
25. Hirsch, S.R. (1983) Psychosocial factors in the cause and prevention of relapse in schizophrenia. *British Medical Journal* **286**: 1600–1601.
26. Brown, G.W., Birley, J. & Wing, J. (1972) Influence of family life on the course of schizophrenic disorders. *British Journal of Psychiatry* **121**: 241–258.
27. Vaughan, C.E. & Leff, J. (1976) The influence of family and social factors on the course of psychiatric illness. *British Journal of Psychiatry* **129**: 125–134.
28. Leff, J., Kuipers, L., Berkowitz, R., Eberlein-Vries, R. & Sturgeon, D. (1982) A controlled trial of social intervention in the families of schizophrenic patients. *British Journal of Psychiatry* **141**: 121–134.
29. Leff, J., Kuipers, L., Berkowitz, R. & Sturgeon, D. (1985) A controlled trial of social intervention in the families of schizophrenic patients: two-year follow-up. *British Journal of Psychiatry* **146**: 594–600.

30. Birchler, G.R., Weiss, R. & Vincent, J. (1975) A multimethod analysis of social reinforcement exchange between maritally distressed and non-distressed and stranger dyads. *Journal of Personality and Social Psychology* **31**: 349–360.
31. Jacobson, R. (1977) Problem-solving and contingency contracting in the treatment of marital discord. *Journal of Consulting and Clinical Psychology* **45**: 92–100.
32. Bissonette, R. & Tapp, J. (1978) Premarital and marital counselling. In: Taylor, R. B. (ed.) *Family Medicine* New York: Springer-Verlag.
33. Clements, W.M. & Wilson, J. (1978) Marriage and family counselling within the context of family practice. In: Rakel, R.E. & Conn, H. (eds.) *Family Practice*, 2nd edn. London: W.B. Saunders.

10

Adjustment to Life Changes

Introduction

This second part of the book is concerned with the ways that people develop throughout their lives. An important aspect of this process is predictability: as an individual develops, he or she learns how to predict the daily events of life. When circumstances change, however, a person must make adjustments in order to understand this novel situation and learn new ways of behaving within it. Adjustments are particularly evident when important events occur, such as marriage or the birth of a child but even minor, everyday events ensure that life is a constant process of adaptation.

The adjustments required by the changes can be said to place the person under *stress*, a concept that has been used in several different ways. Selye[1] has concentrated on the way the organism adapts to events. His viewpoint is primarily physiological, arguing that it is the person's autonomic response to events that is the source of stress rather than the events themselves. This stress response is believed to be a non-specific and automatic response to all stressors. According to his model, the organism is weakened by prolonged or recurrent stresses since, over time, there is a decreasing ability to adapt. As the person is constantly knocked out of a homeostatic balance, the adjustments become progressively more difficult to make.

Although this 'response' model skirts the problem of what a stressor is, another approach to stress has concentrated on the events themselves, the stimuli, rather than the organism's responses to them. Some events are considered to be intrinsically more stressful than others, so that an understanding of adjustment could be gained through the consideration of these alone. This approach also has some inherent plausibility. The rate of psychological and somatic distress following natural disasters and severe accidents is very high and it would seldom make sense to equate the loss of a spouse with, say, a change in residence. Support for this environmental view comes from a number of experimental

studies, such as those on noise levels,[2] where exposure to high decibel levels has been shown to affect performance on a wide range of tasks. The problem with this approach is that the same stressors may produce quite different reactions in different people.

Although both approaches provide insights into the process of adjustment, neither, on its own, can provide a full account. Additionally, both fail to take the *meaning* of events into consideration. It is difficult to see, for example, how either approach could adequately account for the results of the experiments on preparing patients for hospitalization and surgery discussed in Chapter 1. The events are the same for both prepared and unprepared patients, yet the responses differ. A more attractive approach to stress would not only take environmental and response factors into account but also provide an indication of how cognitive variables affect stress.

A transactional model of stress

Cox[3] agrees that both the organism's responses and environmental demands are important in understanding stress, but, he argues, these are mediated by cognitive factors. These three aspects — demands, perceptions and response — are considered in some detail by Cox, along with a fourth influence, evaluating the consequences of the chosen response.

Demands

First, the demands an individual might experience are examined. These might be due to external environmental events or internal events due to psychological or physiological needs. A person may find that their environment has changed (e.g. losing a job) or that their physiological needs have not been met (e.g. being hungry), and both kinds of demands require adjustment of some kind. It seems that too few demands can be just as stressful as too many, as has been shown experimentally. In one study, subjects were assigned to one of three conditions. In the understimulating condition, they were asked to perform a monotonous and unstimulating task (judging the intensity of a light in a sound-proof room for three hours). In the overstimulating condition, they were required to monitor several lights and sounds for three hours. Both of these tasks placed considerable demands on the subjects. As compared to a control condition group (who read magazines), the understimulated group showed increased noradrenaline

secretion and the overstimulated group higher adrenaline and noradrenaline secretion.[4]

Perceptions

The second aspect of Cox's analysis involves cognition: the person's perception of the demand is crucial for the understanding of stress. There may, for example, be the external demand of an exam in psychology, but if the student does not perceive the demand as being important, or feels well prepared, there will be little stress. Hunger may become stressful if there is no food about and it seems difficult to obtain, but not if a simple trip to the refrigerator will relieve it. Stress is said to occur when there is an *imbalance* between perceived demand and the perception of capability to cope with it. It follows from this that if the way people perceive events or the way they perceive their resources can be changed, then their reactions to the events should also change. A study in support of this view[5] involved showing an explicit film of circumcision procedures performed as part of the initiation rites of an Australian aboriginal tribe. The subjects' appraisal of the operation was manipulated through the use of three soundtracks. One emphasized the pain, the mutilation and the danger of disease; the second soundtrack emphasized the positive aspects of the procedure, indicating that the boys looked forward to it happily as a ritual which gave them manhood in the eyes of the tribe. Pain, danger and disease were denied. The third soundtrack provided the viewers with an opportunity to be detached from the operation, a scientific and objective view being taken. The researchers took several measures of the stress response, and found that the subjects showed significantly greater reactions to the first condition than to either of the latter.

Similarly, Leif and Fox[6] describe how the setting for medical autopsies is made clinical, encouraging detachment in students who witness them for the first time. The autopsy room is brightly lit, certain parts of the body such as the face and genitals are covered and once the vital organs are removed the body is taken from the room, thus bringing the autopsy to the level of tissue alone. Similar efforts are sometimes made for students about to learn dissection: at first the bodies are face downwards, and the aspects of the person most related to life (the face and the hands) are left until the last.

Responses

The third aspect of Cox's model involves the psychological, behavioural and physiological responses to the stressful events.

Responses can be described as involving direct action or as being palliative. *Direct action* can take many forms. If the stressful event can be anticipated, the person may take steps to reduce harm. Studying for a psychology exam or asking about the effects of an operation would be examples of such preparation. Another response would be to attempt to avoid or escape from the source of the problem, which may be possible in physically stressful situations but more difficult in psychologically disturbing ones.

Although direct action strategies involve attempts at mastery over stressful demands, *palliative* strategies involve moderating the distress evoked by the events. These measures could be intrapsychic — some of the defence mechanisms suggested by Freud such as denial and rationalization might be used — or symptom-directed — alcohol and tranquillizers could be used to control the somatic response. In some instances, it may be that the person does not consciously perceive the nature of either the demands or his somatic response, as might be the case for Type A personalities (Chapter 2). Psychologists disagree about the appropriateness of these palliative measures. Although those who believe that the cause of the distress and the individual's reaction to it may need to be altered question the appropriateness of strategies such as denial or tranquillizers, others have argued that their use is effective, at least in the short run. They may be more appropriate for short-term difficulties (such as surgical operations)[7,8] than longer-term stresses.

Linked with these psychological responses to stressors are physiological changes. Central and peripheral neurochemical activity, hormonal secretion and immunological functioning are all affected. The extent of these changes are influenced by how easily the stressors can be controlled and their chronicity.[9] Henry[10] reviews much research supporting the idea that different systems in the brain respond to different kinds of stressful experiences. The pituitary adrenal-cortex system is activated by conditions where the organism is helpless, being linked with loss of control and depression. The sympathetic adrenal–medullary system is mobilized when the organism retains control over a challenge and is associated with the release of catecholamines and sympathetic nervous system reactions. A third system, the hypothalamic-pituitary sex steroid axis, is related to the degree of persistence in attempting to control stressors.

Consequences

Cox's final considerations involve consequences and feedback. A response may occur and be found to be adequate. If so, the individual may use the same response again at a later time. A student may find that studying for a psychology exam results in a pass mark — the demand has been met successfully. The next time an exam is set, the same response may be tried. If the action is found to be inadequate, however, the student may try another approach. The nature of psychology exams may be reappraised — perhaps they aren't so easy to pass after all, so that more study seems to be necessary. In other words, the consequences of a response feed back and influence the appraisal of demands. Similarly, a patient's initial response to a poor prognosis might be denial but if increasing pain makes this response untenable (i.e. if it provides inadequate adjustment), the patient may come to use another coping strategy — a not uncommon one is for patients in such circumstances to become angry and disappointed with medical and nursing staff. Cox's model also accounts for the circularity of some stress reactions. A response may itself serve as a further source of stress. For example, a common response to widowhood is difficulty with sleeping; the lack of sleep may be felt to compound the problem so that a further response might be to consult a physician in order to request a sedative.

Of much interest is the eventual effect of stressors on health. The neuroendocrine changes outlined by Henry[10] can induce physiological abnormalities which eventually lead to pathology if neuroendocrine feedback controls are overridden. For example, heightened steroid release may be associated with susceptibility to infections (perhaps through changes in the immunological system) and depression, while the stimulation of catecholamines may be linked with high blood pressure and sudden cardiac death.[11]

In this model of stress, then, the effect of environmental demands are altered by the individual's perceptions. A response can involve direct actions or palliative measures which are used to restore the imbalance between demand and perceived capability. There are also physiological responses associated with different systems in the brain. These psychological and physiological responses have consequences: if behaviour does not reduce the stress, another strategy might be tried. Over time there may be pathologic changes leading to illness. Much of the research which follows in this chapter can be characterized as *psychosomatic* research, which involves the exploration of this relationship between psychological and physiological mechanisms in the onset of illness. Although there is much research on the physiological changes mediating this link, our interest here is mainly with its psychological aspects.

Life events

One way of studying life events that has gained considerable popularity is based on the idea that adjustment is proportional to both the number and severity of experienced changes. Originally, Holmes and Rahe[12] chose 43 events which they considered to be relatively common, shown in Table 5. They asked a sample of people to rate each event for the degree of adjustment that would be required, so that their relative importance could be ascertained. Some events, such as the death of a spouse or divorce were rated highly, while others such as a vacation or minor violations of the law were given low values. The ratings, which are also shown in Table 5, are called Life Change Units (LCUs). The death of a spouse was considered to be twice as stressful as marriage, which in turn was seen to be twice as stressful as a change in living conditions. This has been termed the Social Readjustment Rating Scale (SRRS). Organized into a questionnaire format — the Schedule of Recent Experiences (SRE) — the list provided a means whereby subjects could check off events they had experienced over the previous six months or year.

Physical illness

The SRE has been used in several studies on physical illness. For example, the incidence of such events in physicians' lives has been examined. The doctors were asked to fill out the questionnaire for the previous 18 months and were divided into three groups according to the number of LCUs they reported: high, moderate or low. Nine months later, the physicians were contacted again and asked about their illnesses since they filled out the questionnaire. LCU and significant health problems were, indeed, related to each other, in that 49 per cent of the high LCU group reported illnesses, 25 per cent of the moderate group, but only 9 per cent of the low LCU group. One might also expect that not only the incidence of illness, but also its seriousness would be related to the number and severity of life events. In order to test this hypothesis, Wyler et al.[13] asked 232 surgical, psychiatric and gynaecological patients to check off life events which had occurred during the previous year. Each patient's diagnosis was coded for seriousness, so that the researchers could test the strength of the relationship between seriousness and LCUs experienced. They did in fact find a correlation between these variables for chronic diseases such as diabetes and hypertension, but not for acute illnesses.

Although there are many studies which have found similar results, caution is required in several respects. First, many of

Table 5. The Social Readjustment Rating Scale.

Rank	*Life event*	*Mean value*
1	Death of spouse	100
2	Divorce	73
3	Marital separation	65
4	Jail term	63
5	Death of a close family member	63
6	Personal injury or illness	53
7	Marriage	50
8	Fired at work	47
9	Marital reconciliation	45
10	Retirement	45
11	Change in health of family member	44
12	Pregnancy	40
13	Sex difficulties	39
14	Gain of new family member	39
15	Business readjustment	39
16	Change in financial state	38
17	Death of a close friend	37
18	Change to different line of work	36
19	Change in number of arguments with spouse	35
20	Mortgage over £10,000	31
21	Foreclosure of mortgage or loan	30
22	Change in responsibilities at work	29
23	Son or daughter leaving home	29
24	Trouble with in-laws	29
25	Outstanding personal achievement	28
26	Wife begins or stops work	26
27	Begin or end school	26
28	Change in living conditions	25
29	Revision of personal habits	24
30	Trouble with boss	23
31	Change in work hours or conditions	20
32	Change in residence	20
33	Change in schools	20
34	Change in recreation	19
35	Change in church activities	19
36	Change in social activities	18
37	Mortgage or loan less than £10,000	17
38	Change in sleeping habits	16
39	Change in number of family get-togethers	15
40	Change in eating habits	15
41	Vacation	13
42	Christmas	12
43	Minor violations of the law	11

Reproduced from Holmes, T. H. & Rahe, R. H. (1967) *Journal of Psychosomatic Research* **11**: 213–218, by permission.

the studies have been retrospective, relying on memory for the incidence of events and sometimes for the incidence of illness. As shown in the chapter on memory, retrospective data are not reliable and the possibility that patients look for reasons for their illness in life events cannot be overlooked. Perhaps people who are likely to remember life events are also those who remember illnesses so that the correlations may simply reflect differences in recall. This problem could be overcome to a large extent if prospective studies were undertaken and if medical records could be consulted. Perhaps the investigator could give the questionnaire to a group of people and then return later to collect evidence of physical illness.

This research method was used by Rahe[14] in a study of enlisted navy men. They were asked to indicate their recent life events before six months' deployment on a ship. On board, nearly identical environmental conditions existed for all the men and medical records were kept by the ship's doctor. At the completion of the trip, those who had high LCU scores before the cruise had a higher incidence of illness during it.

Even so, there are still problems with the interpretation of this kind of result, particularly in attributing causality. Many of the life events sampled (losing a job, divorce) could be the result of unrecognized illness, which only became apparent later. Inspection of Table 5 indicates that some of the events actually concern physical illness, thus confounding the picture. A further point is that the rating scale does not distinguish between positive and negative life events. The idea is that stress results whether events are welcome or unwelcome, since all require adjustment. According to the transactional model of stress, however, the person's appraisal of environmental demands is seen as being crucial, so one might expect that negative experiences would have more severe effects than positive ones. This viewpoint has been receiving greater support in recent years as the evidence mounts that only experience of negative life events is associated with subsequent illness.[15,16] Another reason why attributing causality is problematic has to do with the distinction between disease and illness behaviour. In Chapter 6 it was pointed out that the incidence of symptoms in the general population is actually very high, with most people having some sign of disease much of the time. There is some evidence that life events make people more aware of their health status and more likely to consult their doctors.[17] Many of the events could be expected to have a demoralizing effect on people, making them less able to cope with their symptoms and more prone to seek medical help. In seeking this assistance, undiagnosed conditions may become more visible.

Effects on the immunological system

Although these difficulties with life events research in general and the SRE in particular have led some to argue that a causal link with disease has yet to be substantiated,[18] the evidence is accumulating. Some of the more recent ideas have involved the immunological system, with the suggestion that stress has an immunosuppressant effect.[19] In one recent study,[20] blood samples were taken from first-year medical students on two occasions, the first time a month before their exams (to provide a baseline) and a second time during the exam week. The Holmes and Rahe SRE and a scale to measure the students' loneliness was administered at baseline and the blood samples were assayed for natural killer cell (NK) activity (one indicator of the cellular immune response) on both occasions. There was a significant decrease in NK activity from the first to the second blood sample, suggesting that the students were more vulnerable to disease during the examination week than a month before. The students who reported that they felt lonely had lower NK activity than students who did not report loneliness and, most importantly for the validity of the SRE, students who had experienced many life events had lower NK activity than those who had experienced only a few. These results suggest that there is a causal link between the experience of stressful life events (including the examinations) and vulnerability to disease. Unfortunately, no measures of changes in the use of drugs or alcohol, amount of sleep or diet were taken, so it is not possible to say if changes in NK activity were mediated by these factors.

Psychiatric illness

Some of the more important studies in this area have been conducted by Brown and his colleagues. Rather than giving questionnaires, they conducted extended personal interviews with each person, being careful to date events and verifying the events through relatives. In their research, the degree of adjustment that an event entailed depended on both the particular circumstances and the interviewers' judgements of the threat such an event would pose for the average person. Objective data (e.g. police records) were consulted whenever possible. Some of the difficulties associated with memory can be reduced in these ways. Following other researchers, Brown has compared samples of 'healthy', 'normal' subjects who were randomly chosen from the population (to serve as control groups) with groups of psychiatric patients. His noteworthy contributions have involved studies of depressed women and people with schizophrenia.

In the study of depressed women,[21] 73 in-patients and 41 out-patients were interviewed, and their reports of life events were compared with a community sample of 250 women. The researchers inquired about a wide range of life experiences, but they found that most of the women had experienced some kind of event recently. It was only those experiences which implied a long-term threat of some kind, such as the loss of a trusted friend or spouse, learning that a husband was seriously ill, or the necessity of making an important decision, which distinguished between the two groups of women. Some 59 per cent of the patients had experienced such a severe life event within the nine months preceding the onset of depression, while only 26 per cent of the community sample (some of whom were considered to be clinically depressed although they had not sought assistance) gave comparable reports. This indicated that severe events were associated with depression. Brown argued that these events were causally related to depression, in that they often preceded the time when patients were beginning to feel a need for psychiatric help.

Vulnerability

But this is only one aspect of his contribution. Unlike investigators who have been content to find variables which distinguish between two populations, Brown wanted to provide an explanation of why some of the women who underwent stressful life events did not become depressed. By analysing his data again, Brown was able to find several variables that were relevant. Loss of the mother before the age of 11, lack of intimacy with a husband or boyfriend, having three children at home under the age of 14 or lack of paid employment were found to make the women vulnerable to the provoking effects of life events. In one or more of these circumstances, the individual may be less likely to believe that she will be able to cope with life's problems or to be able to resolve the present difficulties.

Thus, the argument is that experiencing severe life events is not in itself sufficient to bring on depression. Nor is vulnerability by itself enough: a person may not have a close confidant but this would not result in depression if no severe life event was experienced. Rather, it is the combination of provoking events and vulnerability factors that is significant. Table 6 illustrates some of this data, giving in percentages the proportion of women who were depressed in the presence or absence of life events. For example, 32 per cent of the women who experienced a severe event without an intimate relationship became depressed, but only 10 per cent of those who had such a tie.

Table 6. Percentage of women who were depressed and who had a severe life event and either lack of intimacy or three children at home under the age of 14.

Severe event or major difficulty	*Lack of intimacy with husband/boyfriend*		*At least 3 children aged under 14 years*	
	Yes	*No*	*Yes*	*No*
Yes	32%	10%	43%	17%
No	3%	1%	0%	2%

Reproduced from Brown, G. W. & Harris, T. (1978) Social origins of depression. *Psychological Medicine* **8**: 577–588, by permission of Cambridge University Press.

In his studies of acute schizophrenia, a slightly different causal mechanism was suggested. Here, Brown argued that life events trigger the onset of symptoms in those people already likely to suffer, rather than being responsible for the formation of the condition. The illness is said to be 'brought forward' in time due to these events (which could be quite minor). Interviews with schizophrenic patients and their relatives indicated a higher incidence of events in the three weeks before onset than in a sample of people chosen from the general population. Although the schizophrenic episodes seem to have been triggered by the events, the events themselves were not considered to be sufficient cause: long-term tension in the home appeared to be associated with the probability that people would become disturbed after such changes.

Further support for Brown's conclusions on psychiatric illness has been provided by other workers using somewhat different research designs. But stressful life events occur fairly commonly and only a small proportion of people become clinically depressed, so it appears that other factors are also important in the aetiology of psychiatric illness. Brown seems to have identified some of these, the vulnerability factors. Additionally, genetic influences are likely to be relevant. Prospective studies will provide a better estimate of the significance of the link between life events and psychiatric illness than is currently available.

Stressful effects of illness

The interaction between life events and illness is well illustrated by the research examining the effects of disease and hospitalization described in Chapter 6. It became clear during the discussion of the sick role that the effects of disease are not purely biological — when someone becomes ill, the whole person is affected, including his or her social and psychological aspects.

In coping with some illnesses, depression is a common response. Devlin et al.[22] found that 25 per cent of patients who underwent surgery for anorectal cancer had psychiatric difficulties with depression. This was associated with loss of sexual relationships (due to embarrassment and fear of spillage). A hysterectomy in a young woman is often followed by depression, and the loss of a limb through amputation has been compared to the loss of a friend or spouse through death.[23] Both involve a process of grieving.

In many illnesses, both depression (through loss of normal functioning) and severe anxiety (through perceptions of danger) are common. Breast cancer is a particularly stressful disease that has implications for women's sexual identity and self-confidence as well as their physical health. Although most women do appear to adjust to the operation, it is associated with increased use of alcohol and tranquillizers.[24,25] Renal dialysis, although often considered to be a life-saving development, also poses many problems for patients and disabling levels of anxiety and depression have been found in many dialysands. Nichols and Springford[26] found that patients have many difficulties that go unrecognized by medical staff. Although staff expect patients to feel physically well between sessions, this was not the case for 44 per cent of the sample. Additionally, 60 per cent of the patients said that they 'felt no good as a parent' and 50 per cent that they were 'spoiling' their spouses' lives. Nineteen per cent reported suicidal wishes. Indeed, survival by dialysis has been likened to a terminal illness, with a slow, progressive multi-system failure and growing weakness and discomfort. These studies illustrate the circularity of stress and disease: the illness may be due in part to stress and the illness, in turn, results in the need for further adjustment.

Hospitalization

Part of the stress involved in illness can be related to factors of uncertainty and unpredictability in medical care. The research on preparation for surgery discussed in Chapter 1 is relevant, but there are other events occurring in hospital besides the operation and the associated pain. A scale similar to the Holmes and Rahe SRRS has been developed to assess the degree of adjustment involved in being in hospital.[27] This was developed by asking patients to rank events they had experienced when in hospital from most stressful to least stressful. These events fell into several categories, such as unfamiliarity of surroundings and loss of independence. Interestingly, many of the most highly ranked events were concerned with the incidental aspects of being in hospital — having strangers sleep in the same room and having to eat at different times than usual. It seems that the greatest adjustment has to do with the experience of hospitalization rather than the reason for going into hospital. This scale has been given some validation by a later study: those patients who reported that they had experienced many of the events on the scale were observed to show the largest changes on cardiovascular measures.[28] Observing the illnesses and deaths of other patients has an adverse effect on some individuals. Bruyn et al.[29] examined patients' reactions to death and emergencies in a coronary care unit. Of the 29 patients studied, 17 witnessed such an event, and their blood pressure and anxiety levels were compared with those of the remaining 12 patients who did not. Thirteen of the 17 patients showed abnormal physiological responses, and over half became more anxious, compared to only one of the 12-patient comparison group. These studies reflect the problem of iatrogenic illness (illness caused by the process of medical care itself) which is a topic considered in the final chapter.

Occupational stress

Stress at work has been implicated in both mental and physical health. One way of isolating the effects of a specific variable, such as occupation, is by taking groups who differ on the variable and looking for differences between them. Groups studied in this way have included the employed and unemployed, and those in different types of occupation.

Unemployment

Employment has several functions besides the purely financial, including social contact, a means of structuring time, and providing a sense of identity and personal status. There is no doubt that the psychological health of unemployed people is poorer than that of people with jobs, and that this is due to the job loss rather than a reflection of previous poor health.[30] One measure of mental health is the General Health Questionnaire (GHQ), which is designed for the detection of non-psychotic psychiatric disorders: the unemployed show higher scores than the employed. Further, GHQ scores have been shown to vary with employment status, with those who gain a job showing improvement in mental health and those who lose one showing some deterioration.[31]

There are also physiological changes associated with job loss. Kasl and Cobb[32] approached the management and unions of two companies who had just heard that the companies were to close. They took blood pressure measures at this initial point, then at termination of the jobs and again at 6, 12 and 24 months afterwards. Compared to a control group (who showed no changes over the two-year period), the blood pressure of the redundant workers was highest just before and just after their jobs were lost, and fell when a new position was found.[33]

Doctoring

Although doctoring can be seen as a 'good' job, there is evidence that it is a particularly stressful occupation, with physicians having a higher incidence of drug abuse, alcoholism and divorce than the general population.[34] The stress begins early in medical students' careers, with competition for a place in medical schools being intense. The volume of material to be learned, together with frequent assessments, make the course difficult. Even after qualification, there is continuing competition for jobs and, recently, the threat of unemployment. The deprivation of sleep, particularly during the qualifying year, is associated with decrements in reasoning ability and an increase in irritability.[35] When newly qualified doctors were asked, 'Do you think your hours of duty are so long as to impair your ability to work with adequate efficiency?', 37 per cent reported that this was 'often' or 'always' the case.[36]

The longer-term stresses of being a doctor have been explored by Vaillant et al.[37] who, in the late 1930s, selected a large group of male university students for intensive study. Forty-seven who attended medical school were compared with 79 fellow students who followed other occupations. There were no differences between the groups in socioeconomic status or intellectual aptitude at the time of their entrance to university. All were followed by questionnaire and occasional interview over the next 30 years, and contact was lost with less than 5 per cent of the sample. Information on three areas was collected: each individual's marital history was examined, not only through their own reports but also through their wives' reports; they were asked about their drinking and drug use histories in an attempt to gain some idea of the incidence of abuse; they were asked if they had consulted a psychiatrist for personal help, particularly if ten or more visits had been made. Difficulties in these areas were considered to be symptoms of stress. On all of these measures, the group of students who became physicians showed greater indications of stress, as shown in Table 7.

Other studies have shown that, within medicine, some specialities are more stressful than others. A comparison was made of the incidence of coronary heart disease in highly stressful medical specialities (general practice and anaesthetics) with that in low

Table 7. Relative incidence of difficulties in physicians and control group. All comparisons were statistically significant.

Difficulty	*Physicians (%)*	*Controls (%)*
Poor marriage or divorce	47	32
High drug use	36	22
10 or more visits to a psychiatrist	34	19
2 or more of the above difficulties	36	18

Reproduced from Vaillant, G. E., Sobowale, N. C. & McArthur, C. (1972) *New England Journal of Medicine* **287**: 372–375, by permission.

stress ones (pathology and dermatology). Questionnaires were sent to 1000 physicians in each group, and a respectable response rate of 65 per cent was achieved. Coronary disease was some three times more prevalent in general practitioners and anaesthetists than in dermatologists and pathologists.[38]

Attributing these results to occupational stress alone ignores the possibility of self-selection. Perhaps certain kinds of people are likely to choose medicine rather than another profession, or general practice rather than dermatology. Here, Vaillant's longitudinal study is helpful. When the students arrived at university, their childhood was evaluated by a psychiatrist over several interviews and by home visits with the parents. These included a discussion of the students' early development, so that an indication of their life adjustment before they entered university could be gathered. When the medical and other students' results were pooled, childhood experiences provided a good predictor of how well they were coping in later years. Amongst those with good adjustment, only 15 per cent experienced two or three of the difficulties shown in Table 7, whereas almost half of those with a relatively poor childhood experienced two or more symptoms. Other analyses of the data indicated that it was primarily those physicians whose early adjustment was poor who were most prone to symptoms in adulthood. These doctors were more likely to take up specialities that required primary responsibility for patient care, such as psychiatry, obstetrics and paediatrics. It appeared that self-selection into a speciality could account for the higher incidence of divorce, drug abuse and visits to a psychiatrist, rather than the stress of the profession itself. Vaillant speculated that some physicians may elect to assume direct care of patients in order to give others the care they did not receive in their own childhood, an idea that has gained some currency in other caring professions.

Whether such problems are due to the job, self-selection into the profession or the relative ease with which doctors can obtain drugs, they have consequences for the care of patients. The idea that doctors should be encouraged to request assistance is becoming more acceptable. This is in line with thinking in other professions such as social work and nursing, where care for the caregivers is seen as an important aspect of practice.

In summary, research on the effects of stressful life events leads to the tentative conclusion that negative experiences are causally related to the onset of illness, both physical and psychiatric. Although there is controversy about this, with some psychologists arguing that the evidence is weak, this is proving to be a fruitful area of research with many findings which support a link. Several types of life events have been implicated, from the severe kind identified by Brown (e.g. loss of employment) to some of the more trivial ones identified by the Holmes and Rahe SRE (e.g. a vacation). Stressors can also be chronic (as in the occupational stressors of doctoring) or more acute (as in entering hospital for an operation). It seems that an individual's ability to cope with these demands is also very important. Vulnerability to depression, for instance, is related to the absence of a close confidant, while doctors whose childhood adjustment was poor appear to be more vulnerable to later symptoms of stress such as excessive drinking.

Old age

While life events research concentrates upon particular incidents, which might or might not happen to any one individual, there are many adjustments which must be made by everyone. A five-year-old entering school, a young person leaving home for the first time to get married, take a job or go to university, parenthood — all of these changes are stressful because they involve coping with new demands.

The process of adjusting to old age is a particularly important one. Coupled with an increased vulnerability to disease, there is a loss of power and control. For example, retirement has more than financial implications, it can also result in a decrease in self-esteem, social support and satisfaction with life. This section of the chapter discusses some of the research on the problems that elderly people have in making such adjustments.

Defining old age

Although chronological age is usually the way we decide whether a person is elderly, many of the important features of old age are masked by this measure. The range of the physical and social capabilities of elderly people is wide, so that chronological age does not provide a good criterion for predicting how a person will behave. Although many cognitive and physical differences have been found between the old and the young, these differences are due in part to other factors besides age itself. Different generations have had very different life experiences: younger people have more practice and experience in many of the tasks used by psychologists, such as IQ tests, thus overall lower scores of older people could be attributed to less experience with the type of test rather than to lowered intelligence. The young are more likely to engage in tasks, such as driving a car, which gives them practice in reaction times, and when the elderly are given practice in such tasks they approach the young in speed. Similarly, age-related differences have been found between healthy men 68–86 years of age and athletic males of 19–22, but not between the older subjects and non-athletic young men. Correlations between chronological age and various psychological, social and physiological measures have generally been low.[39]

These results are important because views of the ageing process can have significant effects on how the elderly are treated. A doctor or nurse who considers ageing to be due primarily to physiological deterioration may be less likely to recommend training programmes for the elderly. Yet such problems as incontinence respond well to techniques of behaviour therapy.[40] Those who take such a physiological view might also be less likely to allow elderly patients to take responsibility for their decisions or to encourage independence. Barton et al.[41] observed residents and staff in a nursing home, paying particular attention to how the staff reacted to indications of independence in the residents. Residents who attempted to look after themselves were likely to receive responses which discouraged self-reliance, whereas praise was given if the residents accepted assistance.

Such practices may have important consequences for the welfare of patients, dissuading them from relying on and practising their own skills and abilities.[42] In another study, nursing home residents were divided into two groups. Some were told that many of the features of their living conditions were their own responsibility. They were each given a plant to care for, they were encouraged to review how the home was run, and to comment upon the complaints procedure, for example. The other residents were not encouraged to look after themselves to any degree, being told that the staff were responsible for their care. They, too, were each given a plant but were informed that the staff would water it, and so on. After three weeks, self-report questionnaires indicated that the first group were more active and were happier than the second group, and these reports were supported by nurses' observations. At an interview, the self-reliant group seemed more alert. Strikingly, 71 per cent of the group who were told that they would be given almost complete care showed some deterioration over the period of the study, whereas 93 per cent of the self-reliant group showed improvement.[43]

Eighteen months later, the researchers returned to the nursing home and found that 15 per cent of the self-reliant group had died, but 30 per cent of the staff-reliant group had died.[44] Although the numbers were small, the results could not be accounted for by such variables as their overall health status when the study began. The conclusion reached was that the debilitated condition of elderly people living in institutions is due in part to the environment in which they live. Without the opportunity and encouragement to make decisions about their lives, deterioration may result.

Problems faced by elderly people

Bearing in mind the wide variation in these processes of ageing, it is nevertheless worthwhile to consider many of the difficulties that older people encounter as a group. In modern Western society, youth is associated with promise and worth, whereas the elderly are considered less positively. (This is in contrast to some other cultures, where old age represents wisdom and leadership). The old are often considered to be less competent than the young, so that failure may be attributed to lack of ability in the elderly but lack of effort on the part of the young.[45]

As a group, the elderly show a diminished ability to adjust to change. Particular care is therefore needed when adjustments are required, such as a change of residence. Several studies have indicated that the mortality rate is excessively high when the elderly are rehoused or transferred from one hospital ward to another. In one study, elderly patients who were moved from one hospital to another were compared with those who remained. The patients were matched on several relevant variables, including age, sex, length of hospitalization and organic and functional illness. When their mortality rates were compared for the first four months after transfer, the group of patients who had been moved showed an incidence of death four times higher than those who had stayed.[46]

Part of the difficulty with relocation seems to be due to the relative lack of control the elderly have over events. Old age is a period of diminished power, both financial and social. As suggested by the study mentioned above on encouraging nursing home residents to take responsibility for their care, a lack of control may have adverse effects on health. An experimental study has been performed to test the importance of relocation, friendship patterns and personal control on mortality rates in the elderly. People living in the community were randomly assigned to one of three conditions — minimal, moderate or maximum care. Minimal care involved giving information about existing services and encouraging the elderly and their families to use them if they chose. By contrast, maximum care involved direct intensive aid, often resulting in a change from home to institution. After six months, the maximum care group showed the highest mortality rate, whereas those in the minimum care group showed the lowest. Those who were uprooted were deprived of the greater degree of family support they had enjoyed and placed in an unfamiliar environment, taxing their capacity to adjust.[47] The increasing emphasis on community (rather than hospital) care is, in part, a response to findings such as these.

In many respects, then, elderly people can have a great deal of trouble adjusting to changes in themselves and their environment. Because there is a reduced capacity to adapt, it is important to be aware of their difficulties in being relocated from home to institution or from one institution to another. Such difficulties can be compounded if medical and nursing staff assume full responsibility for their care because this can result in a further deterioration of their abilities.

Dying

Much has been written about the ways that people cope with their own death. Most of this work has come from doctors and nurses who are intimately involved with the dying, relying on their own feelings and observations of patients and their relatives. Kubler-Ross[48] has had a considerable impact with her contention that the dying work through five stages. The first reaction is often *denial*, a refusal to believe that death is imminent. This stage is characterized by statements such as 'No, not me, it can't be true' and may be coupled with isolation from others. Denial often recurs throughout the coping process. The second stage is characterized by *anger*, envy and resentment. Anger is often directed towards both staff and relatives, which may make it difficult for them to cope if it is taken personally. When anger does not prove effective, the third stage is entered. *Bargaining* is seen as an attempt to postpone death by looking for a reward for good behaviour. In the hope that doctors will take better care, offers to leave the body to science may be given. Fourth, and when death seems inevitable, *depression* is commonly experienced. Death involves more than the loss of one's own life, it also involves the loss of family, friends and plans for the future. This period is characterized by sadness and crying, and Kubler-Ross stresses the importance of allowing patients to work through this stage, rather than giving encouragement and reassurance that they will recover. Patients may need assistance in talking over their feelings. Finally, she believes that, given time and help, people come to the stage of *acceptance* when they realize that the struggle is over and that it is time to die. This stage is characterized by silence and an increasing wish to be detached from others.

Other writers have taken issue with Kubler-Ross, contending that the terminally ill do not go through stages in any set order but may show all at any time. Some have found that few patients reach the stage of acceptance at the end of their lives. It seems from their observations that denial, anger, bargaining, depression and acceptance are not stages but reactions that occur and re-occur throughout the illness.

There is agreement, however, on the importance of considering not only the patient but also his or her family. On the one hand, their reactions are important for the patient. The spouse's ability to cope with financial and personal affairs may make it easier or more difficult for the patient to accept death. Kubler-Ross also points out that the reactions of friends and family may not be compatible with those of the patient: if they continue to deny death, it would be difficult for the patient to talk with them. On the other hand, the patient's family have needs in their own right and they, too, often cope in similar ways to the ill themselves. It is not uncommon for them to have feelings of anger and resentment towards the patient because of 'desertion' and feelings of guilt for not noticing the illness sooner. The family is sometimes angry at medical staff since they can be seen as somehow responsible, coupled with envy because they are able to care for the patient. It seems that the family often withdraws from the patient, leaving him or her isolated.

It may be difficult for nursing and medical staff to cope with the complexity of emotions shown by patients and their families, and it has been argued that the difficulties are sometimes compounded by the staff's own feelings about death. Some writers contend that an important reason for entering the medical profession is to cure people, and that an inability to do so is a sign of failure for many, failures for which there is 'nothing else which can be done'. There is some evidence that, indeed, the terminally ill receive poorer care than those who are recovering. Leshan[49] measured the delay between the time that nurses received a bedside call from their patients to their reply. They took longer to answer the calls from the terminally ill than from those less seriously ill. The nurses were unaware of this difference in their responses. Another study indicated that those patients who had declined the most were moved the greatest distance from the nursing station.[50]

A terminal prognosis

There has been much discussion about whether patients and their relatives should be told of a terminal prognosis. Practising physicians disagree about this but, generally, the more recent the study the greater the proportion who favour informing. In the early 1960s, 60–90 per cent of doctors were found to be against it, whereas more recent studies have indicated that most are now in favour of giving this information. The decision seems to be influenced by several factors. One possibility is a general reluctance to transmit bad news: there is a reticence in people to give this kind of information, particularly if the news is to be given personally.[51] Another factor involves the patient's personality. 'Calm' patients are more likely to be told than 'emotional' ones although there is actually little evidence that personality patterns can be used to predict the individual's response to terminal illness with any consistency.[52] A third factor concerns the patient's family circumstances. Although 67 per cent of the physicians in one study said that the patient should be told, 37 per cent reported that when their wishes were in conflict with the family's, the spouse's wish should be honoured. The patient's age and the way questions are asked also seem important. Cartwright[53] asked a sample of doctors what they would do in different situations: 65 per cent reported that they would tell a 55-year-old businessman who asks, but only 2 per cent a young mother who seemed unaware.

In the caring professions it seems most vital to minimize the number of instances where a problem is missed. When examining X-rays, for example, physicians make many more false-positive errors than false-negatives. When this tendency is applied to informing patients of a terminal prognosis, it is easy to see one reason for the reluctance. Since some patients may lose all hope after being given the information and since it is difficult to know which patients really want to be told, the safe course of action is to inform very few. Just as it may seem better to judge a well person sick than a sick person well, perhaps physicians find it preferable not to tell a patient who does want to know than to tell a patient who doesn't.[54,55]

Another approach to research in this area has been to ask patients themselves whether they would wish to be informed of a terminal prognosis. Several studies have indicated that among patients who are not terminally ill, most would wish to be told.

The problem with research of this kind is that the decision is largely hypothetical, with patients being asked to imagine how they would react under the circumstances. Since people are not particularly adept at predicting how they would respond in unfamiliar situations, as the research in Chapter 6 has suggested, these studies form a poor basis for indicating whether or not dying patients want to be told. One study has examined this point in more detail. Capon[56] interviewed a range of people, some who were healthy, others who were ill, and yet others who were terminally ill. To the question 'If you were very sick, would you want to know you were going to die?', there was a gradation of responses with, for example, 91 per cent of the healthy wishing to know but only 67 per cent of the dying. Although it seems that most terminally ill patients want to have this information, this is not always the case.

Although the results of survey studies are confusing and there are ethical problems with experimental designs, action cannot be avoided. Skirting mention of the terminal illness has consequences as much as open discussion, although the consequences will be different. Some have argued that keeping the information from patients can mean that staff have to guard against disclosure (distancing them from their patients) and that this can result in suspicion and mutual pretence. Behind the decision not to inform lies the assumption that patients will not be able to discern the deception, an assumption which may not be warranted: patients seem very sensitive to the non-verbal cues given by staff.[57] Open awareness, on the other hand, can be seen to facilitate communication, giving the patient an opportunity to die as he or she would like, to reconcile long-standing misunderstandings with friends and family, and to help make plans for the bereaved.[58] It may be that the question is not 'What do you tell your patients?' but rather 'What do you allow your patients to tell you?'.[59] Listening to the terminally ill and observing the extent to which each individual attempts to gain information may provide the surest clues as to appropriate action. The attitudes that the care-giving staff have towards death are therefore critical, in that patients may not be able to discuss the possibility of death with those who are uncomfortable and avoid the topic.

If the decision to inform is taken, there are additional problems to be considered. One is that patients may not remember much of what they have been told. Perhaps because of repression (Chapter 2) or perhaps because of the shock involved (Chapter 4), some patients may not be able to recall their prognosis or related information. Simply because the patient has been informed does not necessarily mean that this will be remembered.

The care of the dying has changed in recent years. An increasing awareness of their difficulties has helped define the responsibilities of the caregivers. The idea of 'safe conduct' has been suggested as the caregivers' role, requiring commitment not only to control pain, but also to approach the patient with acceptance, candour, compassion and mutual accessibility. An important development is the hospice, an environment in which openness about death is encouraged. Children and pets are welcome, and drugs such as heroin and alcohol are available. The needs of the whole family are considered and not just those of the patient.[60]

Bereavement

The adjustment required of the bereaved is considerable. The number of consultations with general practitioners increases sharply with bereavement, one study showing a seven-fold increase in prescriptions for sedatives.[61] Many of the widowed report that their children show behaviour problems, and these difficulties have been found to be associated with poor adjustment in the parent.[62] Suicide among the widowed is high in the first few years after bereavement.[63] An increase in physical symptomatology has also been found by several researchers, with something like a 40 per cent increase in mortality rates in the first six months following a spouse's death.[64]

Several explanations for these findings could be suggested. The higher incidence of mortality could be due to a tendency for people of similar health status to marry, mutual infection, a joint unfavourable environment or the loss of care that one spouse gives to the other.[65] Although these factors are probably of importance, many researchers have argued that the most important is the 'broken heart' suffered by the survivor.[66] That loneliness is associated with low NK cell activity was mentioned earlier, and Bartrop et al.[67] found that people who were bereaved six weeks previously had decreased thymus-derived (T) lymphocyte response to mitogen stimulation as compared to a group of non-bereaved people.

The bereaved frequently show periods of somatic distress (loss of appetite and initiative) and preoccupation with images of the deceased. These reactions are considered to be part of normal grief and to be signs of deeper difficulties only when they are not resolved. Organizations for the bereaved are of considerable assistance. In an attempt to determine factors that are associated with poor outcome after bereavement, Parkes[62] interviewed the surviving spouse 3 weeks, 6 weeks and 13 months after the death. The following factors were identified: low economic status, multiple life crises, severe distress, yearning, anger and self-reproach, and short terminal illness with little warning of the death. The significance of this last factor has been given further support in another study that indicated that the risk of mortality in the bereaved was twice as high if the death occurred suddenly without the opportunity to prepare for it.[68] This result suggests that grieving begins before the death of a relative and that the shock may be lessened if the bereaved are given an opportunity to begin to adjust beforehand. Perhaps adjustment is easier when there has been the opportunity to say 'good-bye'.

The distressing effects of sudden death are perhaps nowhere better illustrated than in the case of stillbirth or neonatal death. Although about 1 in 70 babies dies at or around the time of birth, it is only recently that the extent of the family's grief has been recognized.[69,70] There is a lack of facilities in maternity hospitals for the women and, as a result, they are often sent home soon afterwards.[71] Several approaches have been taken to help families with their grief. Many hospitals now encourage parents to hold their child and arrange to have a photograph taken, while others provide counselling.[72] It does not seem useful to recommend that the parents try for another child immediately since this can inhibit mourning.

To summarize this section, when someone is dying, he or she may go through a series of stages, some of which may be difficult for the family and staff to cope with. The decision about whether or not to tell a patient of a terminal prognosis should not be made on principle, but should depend on the individual patient: many argue that it is crucial to listen carefully to what the patient says, following his or her lead. Bereaved people are vulnerable to psychological and organic illnesses and may require much support in the months following the death. It seems that they face particular problems when the death is sudden and unexpected, as after a stillbirth or traffic accident.

Stress buffering

The theme of this chapter is adjustment to change — the learning of ways of coping with new situations. It is important to remember that adjustment is continuous, in that novel events occur throughout life. If the stresses involved in such changes as the birth of a child, redundancy and bereavement can be moderated or buffered in some way, then the negative psychological and physiological responses involved in adjustment may be reduced to some extent. Drugs are often used by the medical profession to help their patients and by the general population itself to cope with their anxieties. There are some 20 million prescriptions issued each year in the United Kingdom for benzodiazepines (tranquillizers) and 10 per cent of the women and 5 per cent of the men in this country can be considered to be dependent upon them. Three areas of research that point to alternative psychological approaches to stress buffering are considered in this part of the chapter.

Cognitive restructuring

The model of stress outlined earlier in the chapter indicated that stress involves not only demands from the environment but also individuals' appraisal of those demands. The way people react depends in part on their beliefs, values and attitudes about the event. Although it is true to say that some events are inherently stressful for humans (e.g. prolonged lack of sleep), many researchers have argued that in most everyday situations the 'cause' of the stressful response lies within the perceptions of the individual. This is not to say that these perceptions are wrong, but that they reflect belief systems. The implication is that if these beliefs can be altered the events will result in less stress.

Some researchers have noted that defence mechanisms can be effective. The study that examined subjects' responses to a film on circumcision procedures described earlier in the chapter provides a typical example of an experiment on cognitive defences. Denial is a common initial response to the possibility of one's own or a relative's death and may assist people in eventually coming to terms with the fact. Evidence that denial can be effective in reducing stress responses is given by a study of people whose children were dying of leukaemia. Parents who denied the fatal significance of the disease showed lower levels of cortical stress hormones than those parents who recognized the implications.[73] It will be remembered from Chapter 1 that although it was generally beneficial to inform patients explicitly of the procedures and consequences of surgery, certain patients showed somewhat worse outcomes. It seemed that these patients were using denial or distraction in order to cope and that these mechanisms were overridden by the information.

Stress inoculation training

A procedure for providing alternative ways of coping with stress is called 'stress inoculation'. This approach is based on the notion that people have difficulty in coping with change because they do not have adequate strategies available. Rather than encouraging denial of stressful events, attempts are made to provide new skills. The importance of self-instruction in dealing with novel situations was discussed in Chapter 3. Briefly, the suggestion is that in learning new skills — whether the skill is riding a bicycle or taking an exam — people often give themselves silent instructions about how to act. Stress inoculation training involves attempts to encourage adaptive rather than maladaptive self-instructions through three phases: education, rehearsal and application. The educational phase is designed to give the individual a framework for understanding the nature of responses to stressful events. The ways that interpretations of a situation can serve to increase physiological arousal and exacerbate the situation are discussed. To take an example of this approach, Novaco[74] described a programme with patients who commonly reacted with anger to frustrating events. When provoked, these patients would say to themselves things like: 'Who the hell does he think he is: he can't do that to me' or 'He wants to play it that way, okay, I'll show him'. By discussing these self-instructions, the patients were led to see the possibility that their emotional reactions to the situations were influenced by their cognitive appraisals.

The second phase — rehearsal — involves the exploration of alternative self-statements. Instead of maladaptive ones, adaptive responses are encouraged. In Novaco's study, the patients were asked to analyse the situations in which they found themselves uncontrollably angry, looking for the events that triggered the anger and reflecting on alternative self-instructions they could have used. Instead of 'He thinks I'm a pushover; I'll get even', the patients were encouraged to instruct themselves to 'Stay calm. Just continue to relax', 'Don't assume the worst or jump to conclusions', and 'Time to take a deep breath'. In both imagination and role play, the patients were asked to congratulate themselves when they successfully coped with their anger. An important point about this programme was not that it sought to inhibit anger itself but to give the patients a greater repertoire in their coping reactions and to encourage more socially acceptable ways of expressing themselves.

The third phase involves application of these new self-instructions. By asking the patients to keep diaries of their experiences outside the training sessions, Novaco was able to show that the programme was successful in real life. Encouraging an awareness of the importance of interpretations and providing alternative strategies for coping with situations enabled the patients to adjust to events more effectively. Similar programmes have been used with cardiac catheterization patients (Chapter 3) and in the control of pain (Chapter 11).

Predictability and control

A recurring theme throughout this book is that people have a strong need to be able to predict what will happen to them. The frequency with which patients complain that they are not given enough information about their care (Chapter 1), the problems that parents may encounter if their child behaves in an unpredictable way (Chapter 7) and the extra difficulties faced by the bereaved if a relative's death is sudden and unexpected are all examples of the importance of this need. In Chapter 1 it was shown that giving people information about their impending operation reduced their anxiety. Positive benefits were also achieved by preparing patients for a change in their care while they were in hospital. In this experiment, 14 patients who were transferred from coronary care units to ordinary wards were randomly assigned to one of two groups. Seven were given a routine transfer, while the other seven were given preparation (when the transfer would occur, what the new ward would be like) and a member of the coronary care unit staff visited the patients in the new setting. The researchers measured the incidence of complications in these two groups: five of the first group but only one of the second group had complications in the novel setting.[75]

One reason why predictability is important is that it allows the patient to exert some control, if not over the situation at least over his or her responses to it. Several studies in psychological laboratories have indicated this. A typical study could involve giving electric shocks to subjects and taking psychological and physiological measures of distress. The experimental manipulation would involve giving one group of subjects a degree of control over the timing of the shocks whereas another group are not given any control. For example, Hokanson et al.[76] gave the subjects in one condition the opportunity to call for a rest from shocks whereas those in the second condition were dependent on others for their rests. In this particular study the measure was of systolic blood pressure: the pressure in the second group was higher than that of the first.

Amongst the experimental studies with clinical populations on the importance of control is the one mentioned earlier in this chapter: elderly people assigned to minimal care within the community had a lower rate of mortality than those assigned to either moderate or maximum care, over whom considerable control was exercised. Another study which nicely illustrates the importance of control, and predictability, has been conducted with dental patients. Some patients were given only the routine care usually found during a dental appointment, with the dentist simply performing the work with few comments. Another group of patients were given more control over the dentist's behaviour: they were told that if they wanted the dentist to stop or simply wanted a rest, they were to raise an arm. A third condition was designed to increase the predictability of the work. Here, the dentists gave a running commentary of their work as they performed it — what they were doing, when some discomfort might occur, and when there would definitely be no pain. When the patients were interviewed after the appointment, 50 per cent of those in the routine care condition reported that they had felt some pain, but only 15 per cent of those given a stop signal (which was rarely used) and only 22 per cent of those given the commentary felt any pain. Being able to predict or control the situation significantly reduced discomfort.[77]

Social support

The notion that fulfilling and intimate relationships with others assist in coping with changes has a long history. In this century, Durkheim — often considered the father of modern sociology — noted that suicide rates among the married were much lower than those among the divorced and never-married. He attributed this difference to a protective effect engendered by close relationships: life may not seem so stressful if there is at least one close relationship. Brown's findings (mentioned earlier in this chapter) concerning the low incidence of depression in women with a confidant is also relevant. To take another example, Nuckalls et al.[78] reviewed the records of mothers for the incidence of complications during pregnancy and delivery (e.g. high blood pressure, prolonged labour), the extent to which they experienced life changes, and the degree of psychosocial support felt by the women (as measured by their marital happiness, friendships and confidence in the support they would be given by their families). For mothers who had high life-change scores both before and during pregnancy, those with low social support were some three times more likely to have one or more complications than those with high social support (91 vs. 33 per cent). In the absence of stressful events, no relationship between support and complications was found.

The problem with studies of this kind concerns causality again: being unmarried, divorced or unsupported implies more than just lack of social contact; there may be associated financial difficulties for example. Much of the evidence for the moderating effect of social support is correlational and based on retrospective studies. However, this does not mean that the idea is misplaced and there is considerable descriptive and clinical evidence testifying to its importance. There is some research that at least meets the criticisms about retrospective analyses. In one longitudinal study, over 4700 adults were interviewed in 1965. They were asked about several aspects of their lives, including socioeconomic status, social contacts and the number of preventative measures they took to safeguard their health. Nine years later, the investigators managed to follow up 96 per cent of the sample. Those adults who reported close contact with others in 1965 were much less likely to have died by 1974 by a factor of 2.3 in the case of men, 2.8 for women.[79] This association held even when such variables as socioeconomic status, smoking habits, obesity, alcohol intake and physical activity nine years earlier were taken into account. Preliminary results of a similar study concerning psychiatric illness have also been reported. Henderson[80] examined a cross-section of the population in Canberra. Residents were interviewed a total of four times over a one-year period. All were considered to be psychologically healthy at the time of the first interview. At each interview, measures of social support, life events and psychiatric disorder were taken. In keeping with the increasing evidence that only adverse life changes (rather than change *per se*) provide the important predictors of illness, the subjects were asked to indicate their negative experiences for the four months prior to the interviews. Henderson found support for his hypothesis that lack of adequate social relationships was associated with the onset of neurosis, but only in the presence of adverse life changes. As Brown's work indicated, it is the combination which is significant, and not one or the other independently.

These methods for buffering the effects of stress are effective because they modify the individual's perceptions of his or her ability to cope. Stress inoculation training involves both a reappraisal of situations and provides new strategies for reacting to them. Giving patients a measure of predictability and control over their care may give them time to prepare for what is to come, and social support is important for the maintenance of self-esteem and hope for the future in the face of adversity.

Summary

To cope with events such as the birth of a child, bereavement or an illness, a person must make adjustments. These can impose stress. The term stress has been used to refer to both the physiological reactions to the event and to the event itself, but a more adequate definition also takes the person's perception of the event into account.

Many studies have shown that the amount of change recently experienced by an individual — particularly adverse change — is related to the incidence of physical illness. This may simply be due to a lowered ability to cope with an already present illness or, more likely, to actual changes in health mediated by the immunological system. The experience of severely threatening life events is also associated with the onset of psychiatric illnesses in certain individuals who are vulnerable. Illness itself causes stress, compounding the problem. The effects of stress may be lessened by the presence of social support, by providing alternative strategies, and by giving people more control over events.

Both redundancy and retirement have been shown to have stressful effects. Elderly people as a group show a diminished ability to adjust to changes, such as a change in residence or a move between hospital wards. Whether or not patients are informed of a terminal prognosis, the process of dying requires considerable adjustment on the part of both patient and family. Specific stages in this adjustment process have been identified, and caregivers can assist in helping the family through the array of emotions expressed.

Suggested reading

Howells, J.G. (ed.) (1976), *Modern Perspectives in the Psychiatric Aspects of Surgery* London: Macmillan; Moos, R.H. (1977), *Coping with Physical Illness* London: Plenum; and Nichols, K.A. (1984), *Psychological Care in Physical Illness* London: Croom Helm, consider the difficulties in coping with many conditions. The book edited by Steptoe and Mathews (Ref. 9) provides several chapters that review many of the topics covered in this chapter.

References

1. Selye, H. (1956) *The Stress of Life* New York: McGraw-Hill.
2. Glass, D. & Singer, J. (1972) *Urban Stress Experiments in Noise and Social Stressors* New York: Academic Press.
3. Cox, T. (1978) *Stress* London: Macmillan.
4. Frankenhauser, M., Nordheden, B., Myrsten, A. & Post, B. (1971) Psychophysiological reactions to understimulation and overstimulation. *Acta Psychologica* **35**: 298–308.
5. Speisman, J.C., Lazarus, R., Mordkoff, A. & Davidson, L. (1964) The experimental reduction of stress based on ego-defense theory. *Journal of Abnormal and Social Psychology* **68**: 367–380.
6. Leif, H.I. & Fox, R. (1963) Training for 'detached concern' in medical students. In: Leif, H.I., Liet, V. & Leif, N. (eds.) *The Psychological Bases of Medical Practice* New York: Harper and Row.
7. Cohen, F. & Lazarus, R. (1979) Coping with the stresses of illness. In: Stone, G.C., Cohen, F. & Adler, N. (eds.) *Health Psychology* London: Jossey-Bass.

8. Cohen, F. & Lazarus, R. (1973) Active coping processes, coping dispositions and recovery from surgery. *Psychosomatic Medicine* **35**: 375–389.
9. Anisman, H. & Sklar, L. (1984) Psychological insults and pathology. In: Steptoe, A. & Mathews, A. (eds.) *Health Care and Human Behaviour* London: Academic Press.
10. Henry, J.P. (1982) The relation of social to biological processes in disease. *Social Science and Medicine* **16**: 369–380.
11. Steptoe, A. (1984) Psychophysiological processes in disease. In: Steptoe, A. & Mathews, A. (eds.) *Health Care and Human Behaviour* London: Academic Press.
12. Holmes, T.H. & Rahe, R. (1967) The social readjustment rating scale. *Journal of Psychosomatic Research* **11**: 213–218.
13. Wyler, A.R., Masuda, M. & Holmes, T. (1971) Magnitude of life events and seriousness of illness. *Psychosomatic Medicine* **33**: 115–122.
14. Rahe, R.H. (1974) Life change and subsequent illness reports. In: Gunderson, K.E. & Rahe, R. (eds.) *Life and Stress and Illness* Springfield, Illinois: Thomas.
15. Dohrenwend, B.S. & Dohrenwend, B. (1978) Some issues in research in stressful life events. *Journal of Nervous and Mental Disease* **166**: 7–15.
16. McFarlane, A.H., Normàn, G. & Streiner, D. (1980) A longitudinal study of the psychosocial environment on health status. *Journal of Health and Social Behaviour* **21**: 124–133.
17. Rundall, T.G. (1978) Life change and recovery from surgery. *Journal of Health and Social Behaviour* **19**: 418–427.
18. Andrews, G. & Tennant, C. (1978) Being upset and becoming ill: an appraisal of the relation between life events and physical illness. *Medical Journal of Australia* **1**: 324–327.
19. Rogers, M.P., Dubey, D. & Reich, P. (1979) The influence of the psyche and the brain on immunity and disease susceptibility. *Psychosomatic Medicine* **41**: 147–164.
20. Kiecolt-Glaser, J.K., Garner, W., Speicher, C., Penn, G., Holliday, J. & Glaser, R. (1984) Psychosocial modifiers of immunocompetence in medical students. *Psychosomatic Medicine* **46**: 7–14.
21. Brown, G.W. & Harris, T. (1978) *Social Origins of Depression* London: Tavistock.
22. Devlin, B.H., Plant, J.A. & Griffin, M. (1971) Aftermath of surgery for anorectal cancer. *British Medical Journal* **3**: 413–418.
23. Parkes, C.M. (1975) Psychosocial transitions: comparison between reactions to loss of a limb and loss of a spouse. *British Journal of Psychiatry* **127**: 204–210.
24. Jamison, K.R., Wellisch, D. & Pasnau, R. (1978) Psychosocial aspects of mastectomy: 1. The woman's perspective. *American Journal of Psychiatry* **135**: 432–436.
25. Lewis, F.M. & Bloom, J. (1979) Psychosocial adjustment to breast cancer: a review of selected literature. *International Journal of Psychiatry in Medicine* **9**: 1–17.
26. Nichols, K.A. & Springford, V. (1984) The psycho-social stressors associated with survival by dialysis. *Behaviour Research and Therapy* **22**: 563–574.
27. Volicer, B.J., Isenberg, M. & Burns, M. (1977) Medical–surgical differences in hospital stress factors. *Journal of Human Stress* **3**: 3–17.
28. Volicer, B.J. & Volicer, L. (1978) Cardiovascular changes associated with stress during hospitalisation. *Journal of Psychosomatic Research* **22**: 159–168.
29. Bruyn, J.G., Thurman, A., Chandler, B. & Bruce, T. (1970) Patients' reactions to death in a coronary care unit. *Journal of Psychosomatic Research* **14**: 65–70.
30. Warr, P. (1983) Work, jobs and unemployment. *Bulletin of the British Psychological Society* **36**: 305–311.
31. Jackson, P.R. & Stafford, E. (1980) Work involvement and employment status

as influences on mental health. Paper presented to the B.P.S. Social Psychology Section Conference.

32. Kasl, S.V. & Cobb, S. (1970) Blood pressure changes in men undergoing job loss. *Psychosomatic Medicine* **32**: 19–38.
33. Cobb, S. (1974) Physiologic changes in men whose jobs were abolished. *Journal of Psychosomatic Research* **18**: 245–258.
34. Cartwright, L.K. (1979) Sources of stress and effects of stress in health careers. In: Stone, G.C., Cohen, F. & Adler, N. *Health Psychology* London: Jossey-Bass.
35. Asken, M.J. & Rahan, D.C. (1983) Resident performance and sleep deprivation. *Journal of Medical Education* **58**: 382–388.
36. Wilkinson, R., Tyler, P. & Varey, C. (1975) Duty hours of young hospital doctors: effects on the quality of their work. *Journal of Occupational Psychology* **48**: 219–229.
37. Vaillant, G.E., Sobovale, N.C. & McArthur, C. (1972) Some psychologic vulnerabilities of physicians. *New England Journal of Medicine* **287**: 372–375.
38. Russek, I. (1962) Emotional stress and coronary heart disease in American physicians, dentists and lawyers. *American Journal of Medical Science* **243**: 716–725.
39. Fozard, J.L. & Thomas, J. (1975) Psychology of ageing. In: Howells, J. G. (ed.) *Modern Perspectives in the Psychiatry of Old Age* New York: Brunner/Mazel.
40. Mandelstam, D. (1980) *Incontinence and its Management* London: Croom Helm.
41. Barton, E.M., Baltes, M. & Orzech, M. (1980) Etiology of dependence in older nursing home residents during morning care: the role of staff behaviour. *Journal of Personality and Social Psychology* **38**: 423–431.
42. Baltes, M.M. (1982) Environmental factors in dependency among nursing home residents. In: Wills, T.A. (ed.) *Basic Processes in Helping Relationships* London: Academic Press.
43. Langer, E.J. & Rodin, J. (1976) The effects of choice and enhanced personal responsibility for the aged. *Journal of Personality and Social Psychology* **34**: 191–198.
44. Rodin, J. & Langer, E. (1977) Long-term effects of control-relevant intervention in the institutionalised aged. *Journal of Personality and Social Psychology* **35**: 897–902.
45. Reno, R. (1979) Attribution for success and failure as a function of perceived age. *Journal of Gerontology* **34**: 709–715.
46. Killian, E.C. (1970) Effects of geriatric transfers on mortality rates. *Social Work* **15**: 19–26.
47. Blenkner, M. (1967) Environmental change and the ageing individual. *Gerontologist* **7**: 101–105.
48. Kubler-Ross, E. (1970) *On Death and Dying* London: Tavistock.
49. Leshan, L. (1964) In: Bowers, M., Jackson, E., Knoght, J. & Leshan, L. (eds.) *Counselling the Dying* New York: Thomas Nelson.
50. Watson, W.H. (1976) The ageing sick and the near dead; a study of some distinguishing characteristics and social effects. *Omega* **7**: 115–123.
51. Tesser, A. & Rosen, S. (1975) The reluctance to transmit bad news. In: Berkowitz, L. (ed.) *Advances in Experimental Social Psychology* London: Academic Press.
52. Hinton, J. (1975) The influence of previous personality on reactions to having terminal cancer. *Omega* **6**: 95–111.
53. Cartwright, A., Hockey, L. & Anderson, J. (1973) *Life before Death* London: Routledge and Kegan Paul.
54. Scheff, T.J. (1963) Decision rules, types of errors and their consequences in medical diagnosis. *Behavioural Science* **8**: 97–107.
55. McIntosh, J. (1978) The routine management of uncertainty in communication with cancer patients. In: Davis, A. (ed.) *Relationships between Doctors and Patients* Westmead: Teakfield.

56. Capon, D. (1962) Attitudes of and towards the dying. *Canadian Medical Association Journal* **87**: 693–700.
57. Shands, H.C. (1951) Psychosocial mechanisms in patients with cancer. *Cancer* **4**: 1159–1170.
58. Glaser, B.G. & Strauss, A. (1966) *Awareness of Dying* London: Weidenfeld and Nicolson.
59. Saunders, C. (1969) The moment of truth: care of the dying person. In: Pearson, L. (ed.) *Death and Dying* Cleveland: Case Western Reserve University Press.
60. Saunders, C. (1972) A therapeutic community, St Christopher's hospice. In: Schoenberg, B. Carr, A., Peretz, D. & Kutscher, A. (eds.) *Psychological Aspects of Terminal Care* New York: Columbia University Press.
61. Parkes, C.M. (1967) Bereavement. *British Medical Journal* **3**: 232–233.
62. Parkes, C.M. (1975) Determinants of outcome following bereavement. *Omega* **6**: 303–324.
63. MacMahon, B. & Pugh, T. (1965) Suicide in the widowed. *American Journal of Epidemiology* **81**: 23–31.
64. Parkes, C.M., Benjamin, B. & Fitzgerald, R. (1969) Broken heart: a statistical study of increased mortality among widowers. *British Medical Journal* **1**: 740–743.
65. Stroebe, W., Stroebe, M., Gergen, K. & Gergen, M. (1982) The effects of bereavement on mortality: a social psychological analysis. In: Eiser, J. R. (ed.) *Social Psychology and Behavioural Medicine* Chichester: Wiley.
66. Lynch, J.J. (1977) *The Broken Heart* New York: Basic Books.
67. Bartrop, R.W., Luckhurst, E., Lazarus, L., Kicoh, L. & Penny, R. (1977) Depressed lymphocyte function after bereavement. *Lancet* **1**: 834–836.
68. Rees, W.D. & Lutkins, S. (1967) Mortality of bereavement. *British Medical Journal* **4**: 13–16.
69. Oglethorpe, R. (1983) Stillbirth: a personal experience. *British Medical Journal* **287**: 1197–1198.
70. Forrest, G.C. (1983) Mourning perinatal death. In: Davis, J.A., Richards, M. & Robertson, N. (eds.) *Parent–Baby Attachment in Premature Infants* London: Croom Helm.
71. Lovell, A. (1983) Some questions of identity: late miscarriage, stillbirth and perinatal loss. *Social Science and Medicine* **17**: 755–761.
72. Forrest, G.C., Standish, E. & Baum, J. (1982) Support after perinatal death: a study of support and counselling after perinatal bereavement. *British Medical Journal* **285**: 1475–1479.
73. Wolff, C.T., Hofer, M. & Mason, J. (1964) Relationship between psychological defenses and mean urinary 17-hydroxy corticosteroid excretion rates. *Psychosomatic Medicine* **26**: 576–591.
74. Novaco, R. (1975) *Anger Control: The Development and Evaluation of an Experimental Treatment* Lexington: Heath.
75. Klein, R.F., Kliner, V., Zipes, D., Troyer, W. & Wallace, A. (1968) Transfer from a coronary care unit: some adverse responses. *Archives of Internal Medicine* **122**: 104–108.
76. Hokanson, J.E., DeGood, D., Forrest, M. & Brittain, T. (1971) Availability of avoidance behaviours in modulating vascular stress response. *Journal of Personality and Social Psychology* **19**: 60-68.
77. Wardle, J. (1983) Psychological management of anxiety and pain during dental treatment. *Journal of Psychosomatic Research* **27**: 399–402.
78. Nuckalls, C.B., Cassel, J. & Kaplan, B.H. (1972) Psychosocial assets, life crises and the prognosis of pregnancy. *American Journal of Epidemiology* **95**: 431–444.
79. Berkmal, L.F. & Syme, S. (1979) Social networks, host resistance and mortality. *American Journal of Epidemiology* **109**: 186–204.
80. Henderson, S. (1981) Social relationships, adversity and neurosis. *British Journal of Psychiatry* **138**: 391–398.

Part 3

Doctor–Patient Communication

11

Pain

Introduction

This third section of the book considers fields of study that are of direct relevance to medicine, including pain, the doctor–patient consultation and the influence of the doctor's attitudes, beliefs and training on medical care. Many of the topics covered in the first two sections of the text assist in the understanding of these areas. In this chapter, research on pain and the placebo effect is covered. Like the discussion of stress given in the previous chapter, these are areas where the distinction between psychological and physiological processes is far from clear.

Another similar area which should be given at least brief mention is drug dependence (or addiction). Although agents can be ranked according to their addictive properties (opiates more than barbiturates and alcohol), these properties are not sufficient to explain why some people come to be dependent and others do not. Theories of dependence have been shaken by observations of American servicemen who returned from Vietnam after the war. From urine analyses, about 40 per cent of the enlisted men were considered to have used heroin regularly, raising fears of widespread use on their return home. But very few continued to use heroin after discharge. Only 7 per cent of those detected as users were addicted 9–12 months after their return.[1] This result, found with a drug which is considered to be highly addictive, has forced a fundamental reconsideration of the social and psychological factors in addiction.

There is increasing emphasis on the addict's environment. Once drug administration is established it becomes more than simply reinforcing, it becomes part of the person's lifestyle. Smokers given cigarettes with no nicotine will continue to puff at them for days.[2] Those using heroin often become addicted to the ceremony of inserting the needle. Dependence fills time, structures life, provides a reassuring ritual and offers an identity.[3] In fact, it is this aspect of dependence, rather than the pharmacological properties of drugs, which makes it so difficult to treat. It is popularly assumed that physical dependence is more dangerous than psychological dependence, but from the viewpoint of relapse and rehabilitation, psychological dependence is the more important. Even if abuse originally had a personality or genetic component and was reinforced by the pharmacological action of the drugs involved, addiction becomes part of the individual's lifestyle and identity. This suggestion is supported by the observation that cravings for drugs are not marked in institutions after the first weeks (and it seems that the trauma of 'cold turkey' has been over-emphasized), but become significant to the individual after discharge and return to the old way of life. This has led Winkler,[4] a leading proponent of the learning theory approach, to stress the importance of stimulus control. He suggests that the 'street' environment provides the conditions usually associated with drug-taking, withdrawal symptoms and the need for a fix. Some programmes for smokers include asking the person not to smoke in his or her usual location, but in an unfamiliar and unconducive location, such as the garage.

The puzzle of pain

Experiencing pain

The topic of pain is often considered in terms of pain receptors and neural pathways. Consideration of only the sensory pathways involved in the experience of pain suggests that a good, perhaps even a one-to-one, relationship between the magnitude of tissue damage and the person's experiences could be found. There is strong evidence that this is not always so and these exceptions to the rule need to be taken into account when understanding pain.[5] For instance, studies show that the amount of pain experienced by patients (as measured by the amount of analgesia required) can be modified by giving information about what to expect during their stay in hospital and the sensations that could be expected after surgery (Chapter 1).

Much of the impetus for research into the experience of pain has been provided by Beecher, an anaesthetist. While treating soldiers in the Second World War, he was struck by the lack of correspondence between their reports of pain from injuries sustained on the battlefield and reports from civilians having less traumatic injuries and operations during peacetime. The surprising observation was that only 25 per cent of the soldiers requested pain relief for severe wounds, with about 60 per cent reporting either slight pain or no pain at all. By contrast, 90 per cent of civilians requested analgesics for similar injuries due to operations. Beecher at first considered the possibility that there were some inhibitions about reporting pain even if they felt it, but this was not an adequate explanation because the soldiers were willing to voice their complaints about the relatively slight pain involved in injections. He concluded that it was not necessarily the magnitude of an injury that was significant in the experience of pain but, rather, the circumstances in which it occurred.[6] Childbirth provides another example. Although there are large individual differences during childbirth, it would be expected from the magnitude rule that there would be some correlation between obstetric measures and women's self-reports about how painful labour had been. However, neither amount of bleeding, labour time nor the weight, head circumference and presentation of the foetus have been found to be associated with how women describe their delivery.[7]

The puzzle of pain is complicated further by observations about when it occurs. From a biological view, no pain would be expected when there is no injury, and every injury should result in pain. However, there are some reports of quite severe injuries being suffered with little pain, as in some religious ceremonies in India where large steel hooks are inserted into the back muscles. At the height of the ceremony, the participants are suspended by these hooks, but they seem to tolerate these injuries with little discomfort.[8] Conversely, there are occasions when people experience pain without recent injury, as in phantom limb pain. Patients sometimes complain of pain which is located in the leg or arm which has been amputated, pain that is persistent, long-term and difficult to relieve.[9] In a large proportion of patients who complain of abdominal and gastrointestinal pain, no organic basis for their discomfort can be found, yet it is clear that they are in considerable pain.

Reacting to pain

One fundamental problem with most of these studies is that pain is a private experience, one that cannot be seen or felt by anyone other than the individual involved. People vary in their willingness to *express* pain as well as in their *sensitivity* to it. For example, patients who score high on the extraversion scale of the Eysenck Personality Inventory (see Chapter 2) are more likely to express discomfort, while high scores on the neuroticism scale are associated with heightened sensitivity. There are also cultural differences in how inhibited people are in expressing their pain, suggesting that as children grow up they learn how much (or how little) they should complain about discomfort.[10] There is experimental evidence which supports this possibility. In one study,[11] subjects were persuaded to undergo several electric shocks. They were asked to rate the intensity of the shocks on a scale of 1 to 100, which served as a measure of discomfort. Half the subjects were given the shocks with a confederate who was instructed to give ratings about 25 per cent below theirs. The confederates thus acted as a model whose apparent discomfort was less than the subjects'. The other half of the subjects were given the shocks with the confederate acting only as an observer, so they were not exposed to a person who gave low ratings. When the shock intensity ratings for the two groups were compared, the subjects exposed to the tolerant model gave lower ratings than those not so exposed.

Reactions to painful stimuli seem to 'run in families' and a similar learning process may be occurring here as in the laboratory. Apley[12] compared children for whom no organic cause for complaints of abdominal pain could be discovered with a control group who did not make such complaints. The incidence of similar pains was some six times higher in the families of the complaint group. He argued that this difference between the groups was due to a combination of heredity and environment: children coming from families in which one or both parents continually suffer from recurrent pains are likely to grow up learning that pain is one way of coping with anxiety.

Apley also noted that the children's complaints were often associated with stressful events, such as beginning school or the birth of a sibling. In fact, there appears to be a particularly important relationship between the experience of stressful events (especially those which imply a long-term and severe threat, such as the death of a relative or loss of employment) and the onset of abdominal pain. For example, Creed[13] interviewed appendicectomy patients after their operation. Some 59 per cent had experienced such an event in the 38 weeks prior to the onset of pain. This compared with only 31 per cent of a non-patient community sample, so the finding is consistent with the work discussed in the previous chapter which related stressful events and illness. However, in some appendicectomy patients the appendix is found not to be acutely inflamed, even though the symptoms mimic those of appendicitis. Only 25 per cent of the acutely inflamed patients in this study had experienced such an event, compared to 59 per cent of the rest. In most cases the event had occurred within nine weeks of the operation. Similarly, Craig and Brown[14] compared patients who were found to have an organic cause for gastrointestinal pain with those whose pain was diagnosed as psychogenic or functional (i.e. without an organic basis): 23 per cent of the former group but 67 per cent of the latter had experienced a major event or difficulty recently.

Thus, there are several reasons to believe that a straightforward anatomical model of pain is inadequate. Pain can occur when there has been no recent injury (as in phantom limb pain) and some patients report little pain after severe injuries (as in Beecher's Second World War wounded soldiers). These observations could be due in part to differences in how willing people are to express their pain, but this does not appear to be the whole story. We learn to express or inhibit complaints in keeping with cultural and family norms, and the experience of stressful life events can be associated with the onset of abdominal pain.

Gate theory

Several theories have been put forward to account for such observations. Perhaps the best known is Melzack and Wall's 'gate theory'.[15] Briefly, they suggest that pain involves not only physical sensations but also emotional and evaluative reactions to these sensations. They argue that signals from an injured site run to the dorsal horn of the spinal cord which acts like a gate between peripheral fibres and the brain. The gate is opened (i.e. the dorsal horn cells are excited) by small fibres running from the site of stimulation and is closed by other larger fibres from the same site. But the gate is affected by fibres from the reticular system of the brain, which can serve to inhibit or excite the dorsal horn cells. The reticular formation is also affected by cortical activity, so that past experiences, anxiety, attention and the meaning of the situation influence the opening and closing of the gate.

Melzack and Wall make a distinction between three components which contribute to the experience of pain. The first component is the *sensory–discriminative*, which determines the sensory information received by the individual. Such information includes the location, magnitude and timing of the injury. The second is the *affective–motivational* component, which provides the motivation to act as a result of this information. The third, *cognitive–evaluative* component is affected by past experiences and expectations. Taken together, these components interact to determine how much distress a person feels and how he or she will react to the distress.

Melzack and Wall use this model to account for many of the above observations. They argue, for example, that the sudden loss of a limb through amputation removes not only the excitatory fibres running from the site of the injury but also the inhibitory ones, so that the gate may remain permanently open. This could explain why people who have phantom limb pain may feel the discomfort involved in the injury which led to the amputation rather than the amputation itself. For the World War II soldiers seen by Beecher, being injured on the battlefield had positive connotations, in that it meant that they would be rested away from the fighting and unlikely to be killed. For the civilian patients, a similar operation was life-threatening and a disruption to their normal routine.

The important point about their model is that the emotional and evaluative reactions to an injury affect the perception of pain. This raises the possibility that a wide range of treatment programmes could be used when dealing with patients who are troubled by pain. For example, discomfort could be alleviated by supporting patients emotionally or by helping them reinterpret their sensations. Gate theory also makes it clear that there is no strict distinction between organic and functional pain, since every pain has both somatogenic and psychogenic components, although one or the other may predominate for any individual in a particular situation.

Problems of pain research

Two important considerations in pain control research must be mentioned before methods of relieving suffering are outlined. The first problem concerns measurement, the second concerns the context in which research is performed. Of these, the more intractable is measurement.

Measurement

Physiological measures, such as the level of corticosteroids in the blood, heart rate or respiration rate are useful, but there is often little relationship between measures, in that corticosteroid level is not always related to heart rate, for example.[16] *Self-report* measures, although they suffer from the fundamental problem that the expression of pain may not correspond particularly well to feelings of pain, are widely used. Perhaps the most popular is the simple Visual Analogue Scale (VAS). The patient is asked to place an 'X' on a 10–cm line, between the extremes of 'I have no pain at all' and 'My pain is as bad as it possibly could be'. Then it is a simple procedure to measure the distance from one end to give a numerical score.[17] Rosen[18] asked women in the first stage of labour to indicate on the VAS the amount of pain they felt as their contractions grew stronger: their pain scores paralleled cervical dilation.

The VAS provides a single score of severity, being intended to

Table 8. Some of the lists of adjectives from the Melzack Pain Questionnaire. Patients are asked to choose those words which best describe their pain. Adjectives marked by * indicate words often chosen by women to describe labour, those by ** words chosen by patients to describe toothache. (Table originally published in Kent, G. (1984) *The Psychology of Dental Care* Bristol: John Wright.)

Sensory	*Affective*		*Evaluative*
Flickering	Sickening**	Tiring	Annoying**
Quivering	Suffocating	Exhausting*	Troublesome
Pulsing			Miserable
Throbbing**			Intense*
Beating			Unbearable
Pounding*			

include the sensory, emotional and evaluative components of pain. A method which is designed to measure each of these components separately is the McGill Pain Questionnaire (MPQ).[19] The patient is asked to choose adjectives from a total of 20 lists which best describe the pain. Some lists refer to sensory aspects, others to the emotional and evaluative ones, as shown in Table 8. Within each list the adjectives are rank ordered, so that a choice of, say, 'pounding' would be given a higher score than 'flickering' or 'quivering'. Patients with some kinds of pain (e.g. the acute pain after an episiotomy) tend to score high on the sensory lists, while others (e.g. with chronic pain) score high on the affective lists.[20,21] Table 8 indicates the adjectives often chosen by two very different groups of patients, those who have just given birth[22] and those with toothache.[23] Thus, this approach is much more subtle than the VAS and could assist the doctor in tailoring treatment to the individual's needs.

Another method involves asking patients to match their discomfort with some sort of artificially induced pain. In tourniquet-induced ischaemic pain[24] (where the circulation of the arm is blocked), the time before the ischaemic pain reaches the intensity of the patient's clinical pain is taken as a measure of the clinical pain level, whereas the length of time the patient could endure the tourniquet is taken as a measure of maximum pain tolerance.

Although these self-report measures have validity (they do show a decrease in pain after analgesic administration), one problem is that they may increase the pain experienced by calling patients' attention to discomfort: those who are coping with pain by distraction, for example, may feel more pain when they are asked to think about it.[25] A third way of measuring pain would be to monitor the patient's behaviour. *Behavioural measures* are

Table 9. Pattern of administration of analgesic drugs to men and women in radiotherapy wards. Drugs requested and given during one week.

	Men	*Women*
Number of patients	15	12
Number of occasions drugs given at patient's request	23	28
Number of occasions drugs given on initiative of nurses	1	22
Number of occasions on which nurses refused patient's requests for drugs	18	0

Reproduced from Bond, M. R. (1979) *Pain*, by permission of Churchill Livingstone.

less intrusive than self-reports or physiological indices. Non-verbal signs such as grimacing or tightening of the muscles could indicate pain.[26] Darwin suggested that facial expressions are largely genetically determined and people from different cultures throughout the world show similar expressions for anger, fear, pain, and so on. However, it has been shown that when people in our culture believe themselves to be watched they show fewer indications of pain,[27] so that unobtrusive observation may be necessary. An alternative behavioural measure would be to monitor the amount of analgesics people request but, as outlined above, people vary in the amount of discomfort they are willing to tolerate before complaining. A third possibility would be to note the amount of analgesic given by staff. Nurses, for example, could be expected to be very able at recognizing the signs of pain due to their wide experience. Bond and Pilowski[28] took self-report measures of pain using the VAS, and then monitored patients' requests for analgesics and the responses of the nursing staff. They found that the perception of pain did not always result in a request for medication, requests when made did not always lead to administration by staff and the strength of the medication administered was not proportional to pain levels. The sex of the patient seemed particularly relevant, as shown in Table 9. Nursing staff were much more likely to take the initiative with female patients in administering analgesics and more likely to refuse requests from male patients. Perhaps cultural expectations were operating here: the nurses may have believed that men should be able to tolerate more pain than women.

These difficulties with the measurement of pain illustrate the complexity of the phenomenon. Since pain itself is open to so many influences it is not surprising that measuring techniques are similarly affected. Physiological, self-report and behavioural measures do not always correlate particularly well and this presents problems for pain control research.[29]

Clinical versus laboratory pain

A second problem with research in this area concerns the use of laboratory versus 'real-life' situations. Whereas experimentally induced pain is short-lived and can be controlled by the subject, clinical pain is often persistent, beyond the patient's control, and accompanied by high levels of anxiety. Although morphine is often ineffective in reducing the former, it is usually effective in controlling the latter. In the laboratory, pain is induced by stimuli that are novel to the subject (e.g. electric shock, the application of a tourniquet or immersion of a hand into ice-cold water for long periods) whereas patients often have prior experience with clinical pain, either personally or through observation of others. Given that the meaning of painful stimuli could be expected to be very different in the two situations, results found in the laboratory may not always be relevant for clinical populations. Certainly, laboratory tests do not predict post-operative need for analgesia with any reliability.[30]

In summary, then, there are several problems in conducting research on pain. Physiological, self-report and behavioural measures can all be used, but each has its drawbacks. They do not always correspond with each other (a patient may score high on a self-report index but low on a behavioural one, for example) and they are open to cultural and contextual influences.

The alleviation of pain

In order to understand the pain-control techniques discussed below, it is important to remember two points. The first is that pain involves sensory, emotional and cognitive components. Although these interact, there is the suggestion that the emotional and cognitive components are learned. If these can be changed, then the experience of pain can be modified. This has been shown experimentally. In one study, subjects were asked to report the amount of distress they experienced while their hand was immersed in very cold water (2 °C), being told about the sensations the immersion would give (i.e. coldness, tightness of the skin, numbness). One group of subjects was told that the experience would be painful whereas the other group did not receive the pain warning. Thus, the subjects' emotional and evaluative interpretations of the ice water were manipulated. The results indicated that the subjects given no pain warning were less distressed and actually showed higher hand temperatures, differences showing up during the latter half of the six-minute experiment. Although both groups had similar expectations about sensations, the way this information was processed was different, having both physiological and psychological effects on their ability to tolerate the experience.[31]

These observations should not be taken to mean that there is reason for making light of distress once it is experienced or is likely to be experienced. It may be that this experiment showed differences because the subjects had little prior experience with the particular situation — placing their hand in ice-cold water for six minutes. In this sense the experiment is artificial and makes only a theoretical point. There may appear to be some inconsistency with the research discussed in Chapter 1, where giving patients realistic information about hospital procedures and the sensations they would experience reduced anxiety and the need for analgesics. However, those researchers concentrated on providing information about purely sensory aspects of operations, without interpreting them as painful or otherwise. Although some psychologists have advocated clear and authoritative warnings about the likely pain, there are some situations in which this would appear to be inappropriate. The word 'pain' serves as a label for sensory information, so that a patient may come to interpret (and feel) sensations as painful. Beales[32] describes how children attending a hospital casualty department would rarely present with pain. When a bandage covering a skin lesion was removed, however, the unpleasantness of the lesion was emphasized by the staff through such remarks as 'Oh dear, you have got a mess there, haven't you', and when treatment was about to commence the children were told to anticipate pain by such comments as 'I'll try not to hurt too much'. When such remarks were made, the children's distress typically increased.

Functions of pain

The second point concerns the functions of pain. When pain is experienced, the feelings serve as a signal that attention is required. Since pain is a subjective symptom, some way of convincing others of the experience is necessary. If the individual can display tissue damage, assistance can usually be obtained. But if no organic problem can be found, the person may well have difficulty in gaining help. The doctor has several options. On the one hand, he or she might consider the possibility that the examining procedures and technology available to the medical profession are not adequate to discover the source of the discomfort. On the other hand, the doctor could speculate on the possible reasons why this complaint is being presented. Malingering is a possibility: the dismissal of a report of pain might be appropriate if the patient is faking, although it could be argued that faking is an indication of some psychological need. Alternatively, the doctor could conclude that the patient is hypochondriacal and then dismiss the complaint. However, the question arises as to whether the use of pain complaints for attention-seeking is unreasonable. Pain can serve as a 'ticket' for entry into the consulting room: by presenting a complaint the patient may be hoping for the opportunity to discuss personal affairs, an opportunity which might otherwise not be available. The concern would be to discover the underlying reasons behind the request for assistance. In such circumstances the patient may not be aware of how complaints are being used and may feel pain just as real as any other, as in the case of patients given an appendicectomy mentioned above.

Five techniques for alleviating pain and helping people to cope with the pain they feel are discussed here. Surgical techniques are beyond the scope of this book, but it is likely that they, too, involve a degree of reinterpretation of sensory information. Nor is acupuncture considered, although this technique is receiving increasing attention and acceptance, and may be effective because it involves the release of endorphins.[33]

Pharmacological techniques

Perhaps the most obvious method of pain relief involves the blocking of neural transmission. Novocaine, for example, is an effective analgesic because it blocks nerve conduction from the injured site. The operation of the opiates, such as morphine, is much harder to specify. It is difficult to state precisely what sites are responsible for its analgesic properties, although sites appear to exist in the midbrain and spinal cord.[34] The distinction between the physical sensation an injury causes and the reaction to that sensation is usually used to explain the effects of morphine, i.e. that it operates on the systems responsible for emotional and evaluative reactions.

It seems that morphine acts not by blocking sensations but by changing the patient's consciousness of the sensory input. For instance, the percentage of cancer patients who reported at least 50 per cent pain relief from morphine or saline solution is shown in Fig. 18.[35] All patients had chronic pain due to their disease, the majority from bone metastases. The evaluations of effectiveness were conducted 'double blind' (i.e. neither the person who administered the drug nor the person who evaluated its effectiveness knew which patients were receiving morphine or saline solution) and measures were taken at hourly intervals. There was a substantial response to the saline solution and the

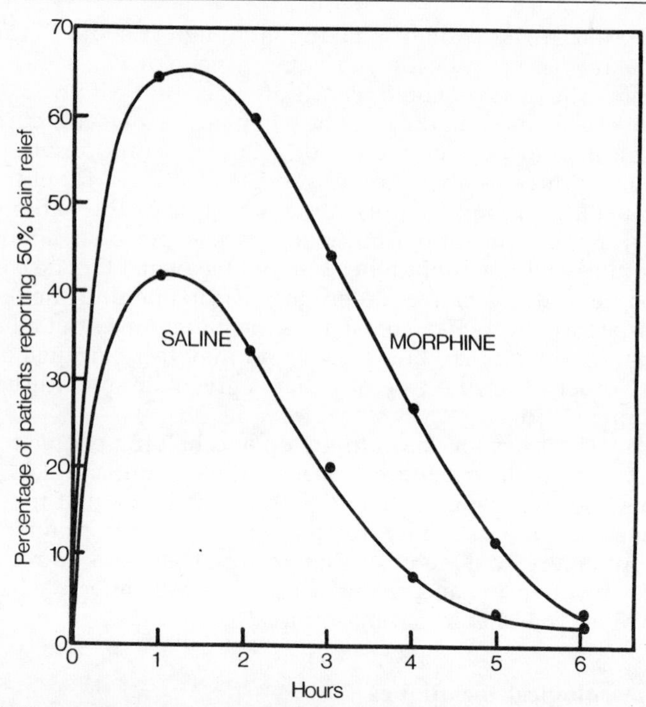

Fig. 18. Percentage of patients reporting 50 per cent pain relief over a six-hour period from 10 mg morphine sulphate or sterile saline. (Reproduced from Houde, R. W., Wallerstein, S. L. & Rogers, A. (1960) *Clinical Pharmacology and Therapeutics* **1**: 163–174, by permission.)

time-effect curve mimicked that of morphine, suggesting that some of the effect of morphine may be due to placebo effects as discussed in more detail later in this chapter.

Personality traits are related to patients' reports of the alleviation of pain. Typically, patients report relief from pain shortly after administration of an analgesic. The pain then slowly increases until the next administration. However, such a picture does not take personality differences into account, as shown by Fig. 19, where the pain scores of patients given pentazocine for lumbar disc disease are illustrated. Those who scored high on the neuroticism and extraversion scales of the EPI gave consistently higher reports of pain and were strongly affected by the analgesic, whereas medication seemed to have less effect on those patients who scored low on both scales.[36]

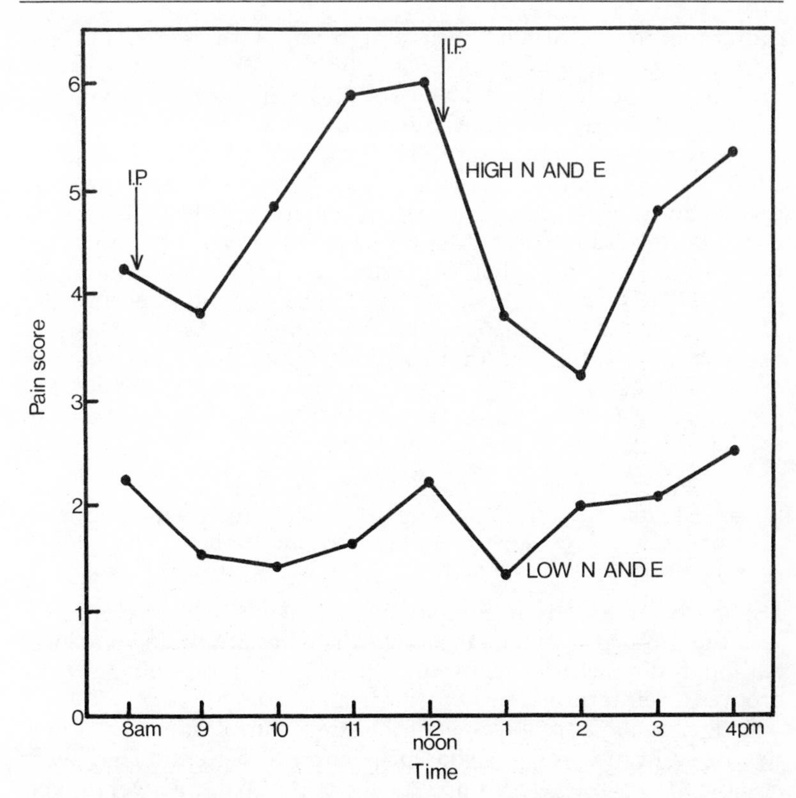

Fig. 19. Pain relief following injection of pentazocine in patients with high neuroticism and extraversion (N and E) scores (upper curve) and those with low scores (lower curve). (Reproduced from Bond, M. R., Glynn, J. P. & Thomas, D. G. (1976) *Journal of Psychosomatic Research* **20**: 369–381, by permission.)

Cognitive techniques

Cognitive techniques for alleviating pain encourage the individual to modify his or her evaluations of the sensory information. One way of doing this is through distraction, where the patient is encouraged to shift attention away from the wound or procedure. This approach is particularly helpful when there is only a brief period of stimulation, such as in drilling during a dental restoration, and in casualty departments, as when a wound is sutured. In the study of children attending a casualty department mentioned earlier, Beales[32] describes how nurses would successfully hide sutures from the children's sight and engage them in conversation. The children often gave no indication of pain until the doctor commented after a first suture 'There, you didn't feel that, did you?', thus interfering with attempts at distraction, focusing the child's attention on the lesion and the procedure, and labelling it as painful. In all cases, the children indicated pain as each subsequent suture was made.

Whereas distraction aims to shift the patient's attention away from any discomfort, a second method aims to encourage the patient to interpret and evaluate information in less distressing ways. In one study,[37] subjects were asked to place a hand in iced water and to report when they first felt pain. One group was requested to use a rationalization procedure, the experimenter asking them to say to themselves that they were in the study because they had to be. Another group of subjects were asked to imagine something distracting (being in a lecture), and a third group was asked to reinterpret the stimulation. Instructions to the latter group included the following:

> . . . I'd like you to try and imagine that you are in a desert. It is a very hot day. You are feeling uncomfortably hot and tired. Concentrate on the cool aspects of the water and try to interpret this as pleasant and refreshing.

As has been found in comparable studies, this last condition was the most effective of the three in increasing pain tolerance. Although distraction was useful (group 2 was more tolerant than group 1), reinterpretation was even more so.

Langer et al.[38] applied some of the stress inoculation techniques described in the previous chapter to surgical patients. They were assigned to one of two groups: one group of patients were given examples of how attention to, and perceptions about, a noxious event has an influence on how that event is experienced. They were taught to use selective attention, being encouraged to focus on the positive aspects (e.g. the improvement in health) that the treatment would bring. Compared to patients who were not given such instructions, the experimental group had fewer requests for sedatives, spent less time in hospital (an average 5.6 days compared to 7.6 days in the comparison group patients) and showed less anxiety and greater ability to cope as evaluated by nurses. No physiological differences between the groups were found. It seems that cognitive techniques are effective in real-life situations as well as in the laboratory.

Hypnosis

Hypnosis has only recently gained a measure of acceptance among psychologists, partly because of the difficulty in ascertaining what a hypnotic state might be. Although it can be characterized as a 'trance state' — a unique form of consciousness — it is difficult to distinguish hypnotized subjects from those who have been coached in how to behave. Experienced hypnotists cannot always tell the difference. Psychologists interested in hypnosis debate whether it is a unique state or an example of other, more established forms of behaviour such as role playing.

A profitable line of research has investigated susceptibility, defined as the degree to which a person is 'able to enter into hypnosis and become involved in its characteristic behaviour' (Ref. 39, p. 175). Several scales have been developed to test for susceptibility, such as the Stanford Hypnotic Susceptibility Scale.[40] Several short tests are used, such as the willingness of the subject to fall backwards into the hypnotist's arms. Hypnosis can only be used confidently for highly susceptible subjects.[41] There is evidence that the hypnotized subject actually registers the sensation, but there seems to be some barrier to its becoming painful.

The method has been used in helping cancer patients[42] and in childbirth, for example, not only in cases of normal births but also for caesarean sections, as the following case illustrates:

> Hypnosis has also been used in connection with caesarean sections, either planned in advance or in emergencies. A patient who presented an obstetrical emergency illustrates the advantages of having available someone familiar with hypnotic procedures. A woman expecting a baby had been poorly handled on the ward of the hospital. She had been there for hours with an impacted breach before . . . the ward consultant became aware of her. At that time she had a high fever, a systolic blood pressure of over 200, and a heart rate of more than 150 beats per minute. She evidently needed a caesarean operation, but the anesthetist refused to give any general chemoanesthesia, and the operation under local anesthesia was not judged feasible. Hence (the consultant) who was to do the surgery, determined to use hypnosis. Although he had not seen her before and she was completely naive to hypnosis, he hypnotized her during the ten to fifteen minutes in which he was scrubbing and preparing her abdomen. The record obtained by the anesthetist during the course of the operation showed that the vital signs steadily returned to normal despite the progress of surgery. A normal infant was delivered and the mother's recovery was uneventful. The record was later reviewed by a senior obstetrician who described it as remarkable. (Ref. 43, p.22)

Although hypnosis can certainly be effective, it should be noted that it is more effective for some problems than others. While patients with pain and anxiety respond well, other difficulties such as smoking, eating disorders and alcoholism are less successfully treated by hypnosis.[44]

Behavioural approaches

Thus far in this chapter, the emphasis has been on acute pain, such as that resulting from an injury or an operation. The psychological effects of acute pain are quite different from those of chronic pain, with anxiety being a common reaction to the former, depression in the latter. Chronic pain may begin with a specific episode, but prescribed treatments do not always provide relief and the patient may suffer for years without comfort, losing sleep and curtailing activities. For such people, chronic pain can become the most important feature of their lives, so that complaints, inactivity and requests for analgesics become increasingly frequent. It has been argued that such 'pain behaviours', like other kinds of behaviour, are shaped and maintained by rewards such as attention and sympathy, so that an operant approach (see Chapter 3) would be a method of reducing them. Bonica and Fordyce[45] have reported a study in which 36 patients who had difficulty with chronic pain were no longer given reinforcements for their 'pain behaviour'. Instead of receiving analgesics on request, the patients were given medication at fixed time-intervals. Rewards were given for increases in activity and exercise. Over a period of some months, activity levels increased while medication intake and subjective reports of pain decreased. When asked, the patients rated their pain as being less intense and as causing less interference with daily activities. Further, these results were maintained some 22 months later. Although there was no control group in this study and there was considerable screening of patients, the lack of previous success with more traditional treatments makes the results encouraging. More recently an additional behavioural intervention, relaxation training, has been tried with such patients, further increasing activity and reducing analgesic use.[46] This applicability of behavioural treatments to pain relief illustrates the multifactorial nature of pain and the interdependence of behavioural and physiological variables.

Psychotherapeutic approaches

This perspective concentrates on the way that pain and illness are used to deal with unpleasant situations. Taking on the sick role and complaining of pains are ways of coping and seeking attention and help. It is often the case that individuals are unaware of how they are using pain and even if careful investigation does not show evidence of physical abnormality, the pain is real to the patient.

It is likely that the behavioural treatment outlined above was effective because the patients were given rewards not for their 'pain behaviour' but rather for indications that they were learning to cope with their difficulties. The psychotherapeutic approach also holds that pain and illness are sometimes used by the patient in order to gain care and sympathy and agrees that attention-seeking behaviour requires examination. The difference is that pain complaints are seen as an indication of an underlying conflict, suggesting that this conflict should be explored. An extract from a case report illustrates this point of view. The woman involved had a history of cancer:

> The present hospitalization was prompted when the woman came into the surgery outpatient clinic complaining of a severe and constant pain in her left side. No apparent cause for this pain could be ascertained by physical examination in the clinic, but a coincident finding was the presence of another enlarged submandibular lymph node. She was admitted for an excision biopsy of this node.
>
> When interviewed, she appeared to be in considerable discomfort and was preoccupied with what she described as a severe and sharp pain in her left side. Signs of depression were immediately noted, including psychomotor retardation, poor eye contact, low-pitched and monotonous voice and expressions of fatigue and despair. Early in the interview it was learned that she was well aware of her diagnosis of reticulum cell sarcoma and the eventual possibility of death as a consequence of that disease.
>
> However, she talked almost exclusively about the pain in her side, which had been the only reason for her seeking help at this time. She stated that the pain had been constant and severe over the last three months and prevented her from being more active around the house and socially. The pain concerned her much more than did the enlarged node in her neck, which she dismissed by stating that the surgeons would simply 'cut it out' in the same fashion as they had two years earlier, and there would be no further consequences. The pain in her side was a different story altogether, for it had never occurred before and she was afraid that it represented a new direction of spread or growth of her tumour. Further exploration of this notion revealed concern that this meant death was imminent. The woman confessed that in recent months she had been spending more and more of her time preoccupied with thoughts about her death.
>
> She was encouraged to elaborate some of her thoughts concerning death, and the balance of the interview was focused on this topic. Among her greatest fears was leaving behind her 11-year-old son in the care of his untrustworthy father. She also expressed fear that death would be painful and that in the end her doctors would abandon her. The patient received support from the interviewer for her fears and concerns. She cried spontaneously throughout this part of the discussion.
>
> As the interview ended, all observers noted that the woman's

affective state had improved dramatically: she had become more animated, and her eye contact with the interviewer had increased.

One day later, during routine rounds, the woman was seen again. She enthusiastically summoned the interviewer to her bedside and somewhat sheepishly reported that the pain in her side had disappeared immediately following the interview on the previous day and had not returned. It was the first time in three months that she had been without pain in that area. Owing to complications in the subsequent biopsy procedure, she remained in the hospital a total of six weeks, with no recurrence of pain. (Ref. 47, pp. 494–495).

For this patient, simply listening to her concerns and taking them seriously resulted in disappearance of the symptom of pain. Apley,[12] in his work with children with abdominal pains, reported similar findings. Many of the children, once they had been reassured that their abdomens were normal and had been given some attention, had no recurrence of pain. In these cases only minimal psychotherapy was required in order to alleviate the pain.

All of these approaches to pain relief are effective for particular patients. The choice of method will depend on the individual and his or her problems. For a patient who has suffered chronic pain for several months or years, a behavioural approach could be the most useful for encouraging activity. Many pain clinics now incorporate this method. A psychotherapeutic approach should be considered for patients if no organic cause can be found and they are suffering stress in their lives. For those who are susceptible, hypnosis has found support, but much training is required before it can be used safely. Certainly, the cognitive techniques are helpful on an everyday basis. It should be remembered that the efficacy of pharmacological methods, too, varies between patients and many chemical agents have a placebo component, a topic which is considered next.

Placebo effects

Placebo effects are generally defined as those effects of a treatment that are not attributable to the mechanics of the treatment itself, but rather to the circumstances surrounding it. For example, in Fig. 18 just over 40 per cent of the patients who received a saline solution reported substantial pain relief one hour after its administration, compared to just over 60 per cent who received morphine. When a new drug is tested it is therefore necessary to compare it with placebos, lest any demonstrated effect is due to non-specific factors. Similar precautions are taken in psychological experiments. One of the purposes of control groups is to guard against the possibility that the real reason for a change is some aspect of the situation that the experimenter is not intending to manipulate. In this sense, placebo effects are something of a nuisance because they make evaluations of treatments more difficult than they might otherwise be.

In another sense, they are a fascinating subject of study in their own right. That saline solutions can affect patients' reports of their pain is very surprising and this phenomenon provides much information about the psychology of medical care. Placebo effects have been shown in dentistry and in surgery. Placebos can be addictive, mimic the effects of active drugs, reverse the effects of potent drugs and have an effect on bodily organs. The placebo effect is considered in some detail here because unwarranted conclusions are often drawn from data such as those shown in Fig. 18 and it is important to examine the methods of many of the studies that have been frequently cited.

One of the better known of the placebo studies was conducted by Park and Covi in 1965.[48] Placebo effects are particularly strong in psychiatric populations and they set out to test the hypothesis that placebos work because patients have a belief in the active potency of the drugs that their doctors prescribe. If this is the case, they reasoned, then when patients are told that the medication is inert the effect should be lost. Park and Covi did this with 15 newly admitted patients believed to have neurotic disorders. They told their patients: 'Many people with your kind of condition have been helped by what are sometimes called "sugar pills", and we feel that a so-called sugar pill may help you, too . . . A sugar pill is a pill with no medicine in it at all. I think this pill will help you as it has helped so many others . . .' (p.37), and one week later interviewed them again. Of the 14 patients who agreed to the course of treatment, 13 showed improvement, often substantial improvement.

This result has been termed remarkable and in many ways it is, but a closer look at the researchers' behaviour makes the findings much more understandable. Psychiatric patients — particularly those with a neurosis — often improve after an initial interview. Perhaps some of the factors discussed in Chapter 3 are operative, in that the patient is given hope, sympathy and warmth during the interview. This is relevant because Park and Covi did conduct such an interview with all their patients: an hour in the first instance and then a further 15–30 minutes when the placebo was offered. This adds up to a considerable amount of time with each person. It is possible that a large proportion of the improvement was due to these interpersonal factors.

Additionally, Park and Covi's original message showed some confidence in the pill. That the enthusiasm of the practitioner for the placebo can influence its effectiveness is shown by a study on dental patients who were due to have a pain-killing injection before a filling.[49] Before the injection, patients were given a placebo pill, but for some of the patients the dentist was very enthusiastic about it, saying, 'This is a recently developed pill that I've found to be very effective in reducing tension, anxiety and sensitivity to pain. It cannot harm you in any way. The pill becomes effective almost immediately.' Other patients received a message in which the dentist expressed some doubt about the pill's effectiveness. Those patients who were given the enthusiastic message subsequently reported less pain from the injection than those given the more ambivalent message. In the same study, the manner of the dentist was also varied. For some patients the dentist was very warm and friendly, engaging them in open and reassuring conversation, while for others the dentist was more neutral, being polite but with limited verbal exchanges. This difference in manner also had an effect, with the patients treated by the 'warm' dentist reporting less pain from the injection than patients treated by the 'neutral' dentist.

How do placebos work?

Although the results portrayed in Fig. 18 are not unusual for placebo-controlled studies, they are often misinterpreted, apparently suggesting to some that placebos will be effective for most patients. This is not the case. On average, about 35 per cent of patients obtain relief, but the range is probably from 0 to 100 per cent depending on the treatment in question, the condition, and the situational factors such as the patients' and physicians' belief in the efficacy of treatment. Personality traits (such as suggestibility or IQ) and demographic characteristics (such as age and sex) are not consistently related to whether an individual responds to a placebo. Figure 18 can also be taken to suggest that no patients are harmed by placebos, but this too is incorrect. A small proportion can show *reverse* placebo effects, where they report a worsening of symptoms.

Classical conditioning

When placebos are effective, though, what processes are involved? One theory relies on classical conditioning. In some studies, dogs were given morphine and, as in the case of food and salivation with Pavlov's dogs, some of the animals came to show a response to morphine before they were given the injection. The suggestion is that, in humans, the placebo effect works similarly: patients feel better because this is a conditioned response to taking medication.[50] The classical conditioning position would predict that as the number of occasions on which placebos are administered increases, the percentage of patients reporting relief would decrease. This is, in fact, what occurs.

Cognitions

A second possibility is based on the notion of cognitive consistency. People seek consistency in their interpretations of the environment, in order to make it predictable and meaningful (Chapter 1). When consistency is difficult to discover, special efforts are made to fit events into an individual's theories about the way the world works. This notion can be applied to placebo effects with some success. Patients who take a (placebo) medication have several perceptions. These include trust in the physician who has recommended the medication and interpretations of their bodily state. According to the cognitive approach, these two perceptions should be consistent and this could be achieved by re-evaluating views of either the doctor or the illness. It seems that some people rely on self-produced cues to provide information about how they feel more than others, who tend to rely more heavily on external, situational cues. For example, in deciding whether one is hungry, a person could rely primarily on the time of day or on the internal physiological state. Perhaps those patients who respond positively to a placebo are people who rely on the external perception — a belief in the doctor. For them, the situation suggests an effect from the placebo, and they react accordingly. Those who rely on internal cues, on the other hand, place more emphasis on their physiological state. After feeling no better after a placebo, they could change their beliefs about the doctor (coming to doubt his or her competence) or about the illness (now believing that it must be worse than they originally thought). This last group of patients could show reverse placebo effects, now feeling worse than before.[51]

A related possibility has to do with selective attention. In most illnesses, the amount of discomfort varies, so a patient will feel better at some times than others. Placebo effects could occur if patients became more aware of the times when they did feel better and paid less attention to the times when they felt unwell. Yet another possibility is that patients may come to interpret their sensations as less unpleasant following the doctor's advice. Gate theory postulates that the experience of pain is enhanced by anxiety, such that the gate in the dorsal horn is opened by fear. When the doctor says that a pill will make them better — implying that the condition is treatable and not too serious — their anxiety could decrease and the gate close.

These explanations assume that placebos affect the experience of discomfort, but this is not necessarily the case. It could be that placebos are given the credit for spontaneous recovery from the illness.[52] A more disturbing possibility is that they only bias patients' responses, so that they report they feel better when just as much discomfort is felt. It may be that some patients feel obliged to say the treatment has worked when a doctor has taken time to treat them.

Endorphines

However, response bias does not provide a full explanation for the placebo effect and there are some clues to its physiological action. In the case of both placebos and narcotics, there is a tendency to increase the dosage over time. With repeated dosages over long periods both become less effective and there are withdrawal difficulties. These similarities have led to the suggestion that placebos work by releasing endorphines (endogenous morphine-like substances) into the body. This suggestion could be tested through the injection of naloxone, an opiate antagonist that blocks the opiate receptor sites. If, when naloxone is given the placebo effect is no longer found, this would provide evidence for a link between placebos and endorphines.

Levine et al.[53] studied patients whose impacted wisdom teeth were to be removed. Two hours after surgery, all patients were given a placebo and then, after a further hour, either placebo or naloxone. The first prediction the researchers made concerned the effect of naxolone versus placebo. As expected, those patients who were given naloxone reported greater pain one hour after administration than did those given placebos, indicating that the naloxone enhanced the pain relative to placebos. In addition, the difference in pain reports given by reactors and non-reactors diminished after naloxone administration, providing evidence that placebo effects are naloxone-reversible. Finally, the researchers observed that naloxone had no obvious effect on placebo non-reactors.

Thus, this study suggests that the analgesic effect of placebos is real (i.e. not simply due to response biases) and is based on the action of endorphines. Placebos cannot be used to distinguish functional from organic illnesses. Like morphine, placebos seem to operate on the emotional and evaluative components of pain and not the sensory components.[54] This study does not indicate, however, how the message 'Take this, it will be good for you' from a trusted physician is translated into the release of endorphines.

Side-effects of placebos

Part of the 'magic' of placebos is their apparent ability to induce side-effects. Often, the type of side-effect is related to the type of medication under study, such as nausea with antispasmodic placebos or drowsiness with tranquillizer placebos. This seems very odd indeed and is sometimes used as an indicator of the strength of placebo reactions. However, the emphasis on placebo side-effects may be due to the lack of adequate control groups. Studies reporting side-effects have only a small proportion of their patients presenting complaints. While some of the complaints are dramatic (e.g. visible skin rashes) these are in the minority.

The most likely explanation for the reporting of side-effects is a greater awareness of bodily reactions during illness and clinical trials than usual. If clinical trials included a control group of healthy subjects, a better estimate of the incidence of minor illness could be uncovered. In a survey of healthy subjects not taking medication, 25 per cent reported an inability to concentrate in the three days before the survey, 23 per cent reported excessive sleepiness and 40 per cent fatigue. Had these subjects been taking medication or placebos, these difficulties might have been attributed to the drugs, and called side-effects.[54] The inclusion of control groups in this area of research is vital, but often neglected.

Summary

An understanding of the topics covered in this chapter — pain and placebos — relies on an appreciation of the interdependence of psychological and physiological factors (mind and body).

The magnitude of an injury does not always predict the amount of pain experienced and, indeed, pain may be experienced when no injury is apparent. Pain involves not only physical sensations from the injured site, but also emotional and evaluative reactions to these sensations. Responses are affected by many factors including personality, cultural variables and family background. Measurement is difficult. Objective physiological measures show little correlation with one other, while the amount of analgesic requested by a sufferer or provided by a caregiver is open to social and psychological influences. Subjective measures, such as rating scales, provide other possible techniques of measurement.

Five different methods of pain relief are considered. First, relief of pain through pharmacological techniques appears to work in different ways with different drugs. For example, cocaine seems to block nerve conduction from the injured site, unlike morphine which does not stop input but rather changes the patient's consciousness of this sensation. Second, cognitive techniques are effective in relieving pain. Instructions to re-interpret the painful stimulation are more effective than simple distraction from the sensation, although this has benefit. Third, hypnosis can provide relief for 'susceptible' individuals, although the mechanism is not clear. Fourth, behavioural analysis and suitable alteration of the rewards which shape and maintain an individual's reactions to pain reduces the need for analgesics. Fifth, psychotherapeutic techniques consider how to meet the needs underlying pain expression.

In certain cases, individuals can show improvement after a treatment, even when given a non-active drug — placebo effects. Around a third of people react to placebos and reactivity seems highest in psychiatric populations, although few predictive personality variables have been identified. Placebos may work because, after taking medication, 'feeling better' is a conditioned response; alternatively people may re-interpret their bodily sensations. Another possibility is that reactors may simply *say* they feel better when in fact they are experiencing the same sensations. There is some evidence that placebos operate by releasing endorphines in the body.

Suggested reading

Melzack, R. & Wall, P. (Ref. 15) gives a good introduction to pain research. Many of the issues in addiction research are discussed in Miller, W.R. (ed.) (1980) *The Addictive Behaviours* Oxford: Pergamon.

References

1. Lufoff, I.F. & Kleinman, P. (1977) The addict life-cycle and problems in treatment evaluation. In: Schecter, A. & Mulre, S. (eds.) *Rehabilitation Aspects of Drug Dependence* Cleveland: CRC Press.
2. Goldfarb, T.L., Jarvik, M. & Glick, S. (1970) Cigarette nicotine content as a determinant of human smoking behaviour. *Psychopharmacologica* **17**: 89–93.
3. Hafen, B.Q. & Peterson, B. (1978) *Medicine and Drugs*, 2nd edn. Philadelphia: Lea and Febiger.
4. Winkler, A. (1973) Dynamics of drug dependence. *Archives of General Psychiatry* **28**: 611–616.
5. Leventhal, H. & Everhart, D. (1979) Emotion, pain and physical illness. In: Izard, C.E. (ed.) *Emotion and Psychopathology* New York: Plenum.
6. Beecher, H.K. (1956) Relationship of significance of wound to the pain experienced. *Journal of the American Medical Association* **161**: 1609–1613.

7. Uddenberg, N. (1979) Childbirth pain. In: Oborne, D.J., Gruneberg, M. & Eiser, J. (eds.) *Research in Psychology and Medicine 1* London: Academic Press.
8. Kosambi, D.D. (1967) Living prehistory in India. *Scientific American* **216**: 105–114.
9. Simmel, M.L. (1962) The reality of phantom sensations. *Social Research* **29**: 337–356.
10. Koopman, C., Eisenthal, S. & Stoeckle, J. (1984) Ethnicity in the reported pain, emotional distress and requests of medical outpatients. *Social Science and Medicine* **18**: 487–490.
11. Craig, K.D. & Prkachin, K. (1978) Social modelling influences on sensory decision theory and psychophysiological indexes of pain. *Journal of Personality and Social Psychology* **36**: 805–815.
12. Apley, J. (1975) *The Child with Abdominal Pains* London: Basil Blackwell.
13. Creed, F. (1981) Life events and appendicectomy. *Lancet* **1**: 1381–1385.
14. Craig, T.K. J. & Brown, G.W. (1984) Goal frustration and life events in the aetiology of painful gastrointestinal disorders. *Journal of Psychosomatic Research* **28**: 411–421.
15. Melzack, R. & Wall, P. (1982) *The Challenge of Pain* Harmondsworth, Middlesex: Penguin Books.
16. Leiderman, P.H. & Shapiro, D. (1965) *Psychobiological Approaches to Social Behaviour* London: Tavistock.
17. Huskisson, E.C. (1983) Visual Analogue Scales. In: Melzack, R. (ed.) *Pain Measurement and Assessment* New York: Raven Press.
18. Rosen, M. (1977) The measurement of pain. In: Harcus, A.W., Smith, R.B. & Whittle, B. (eds.) *Pain — New Perspectives in Measurement and Assessment* Edinburgh: Churchill Livingstone.
19. Melzack, R. (1983) The McGill Pain Questionnaire. In: Melzack, R. (ed.) *Pain Measurement and Assessment* New York: Raven Press.
20. Reading, A.E. (1982) A comparison of the McGill Pain Questionnaire in chronic and acute pain. *Pain* **13**: 185–192.
21. Melzack, R., Wall, P. & Ty, T. (1982) Acute pain in an emergency clinic: latency of onset and descriptor patterns related to different injuries. *Pain* **14**: 33–43.
22. Melzack, R., Taenzer, P., Feldman, P. & Kinch, R. (1981) Labour is still painful after prepared childbirth training. *Canadian Medical Association Journal* **125**: 357–363.
23. Dubuisson, D. & Melzack, R. (1976) Classification of clinical pain description by multiple group discrimination analysis. *Experimental Neurology* **51**: 480–487.
24. Sternbach, R.A. (1983) The tourniquet pain test. In: Melzack, R. (ed.) *Pain Measurement and Assessment* New York: Raven Press.
25. Levine, J.D., Gordon, N.C., Smith, R. & Fields, H.L. (1982) Post-operative pain: effect of extent of injury and attention. *Brain Research* **234**: 500–504.
26. Craig, K.D. & Prkachin, K. (1983) Nonverbal measures of pain. In: Melzack, R. (ed.) *Pain Measurement and Assessment* New York: Raven Press.
27. Kleck, R.E., Vaughan, R.C., Cartwright-Smith, J., Vaughan, K.B., Colby, C. & Lanzetta, J. (1976) Effects of being observed on expressive, subjective and physiological responses to painful stimuli. *Journal of Personality and Social Psychology* **34**: 1211–1218.
28. Bond, M.R. & Pilowski, I. (1966) Subjective assessment of pain and its relationship to the administration of analgesics in patients with advanced cancer. *Journal of Psychosomatic Research* **10**: 203–208.
29. Reading, A.E. (1980) A comparison of pain rating scales. *Journal of Psychosomatic Research* **24**: 119–124.
30. Parbrook, G.D., Steel, D.F. & Dalrymple, D. (1973) Factors predisposing to

post-operative pain and pulmonary complications. *British Journal of Anaesthesia* **45**: 21–33.
31. Leventhal, H., Brown, D., Schacham, S. & Engquist, G. (1979) Effects of preparatory information about sensations, threats of pain and attention on cold pressor distress. *Journal of Personality and Social Psychology* **37**: 689–714.
32. Beales, J.C. (1979) The effect of attention and distraction on pain among children attending a hospital casualty department. In: Oborne, D.J., Gruneberg, M.M. & Eiser, J.R. (eds.) *Research in Psychology and Medicine 1* London: Academic Press.
33. Anon. (1981) How does acupuncture work? *British Medical Journal* **283**: 746–748.
34. Goldstein, A. (1976) Opioid peptides (endorphins) in pituitary and brain. *Science* **193**: 1081–1086.
35. Houde, R.W., Wallerstein, S. & Rogers, M. (1960) Clinical pharmacology of analgesics. *Clinical Pharmacology and Therapeutics* **1**: 163–174.
36. Bond, M.R., Glynn, J. & Thomas, D. (1976) The relation between pain and personality in patients receiving pentazocine (Fortral) after surgery. *Journal of Psychosomatic Research* **20**: 369–381.
37. Jaremko, M.E. (1978) Cognitive strategies in the control of pain tolerance. *Journal of Behaviour Therapy and Experimental Psychiatry* **9**: 239–244.
38. Langer, E., Janis, I. & Wolper, J. (1975) Reduction of psychological stress in surgical patients. *Journal of Experimental Social Psychology* **11**: 155–165.
39. Engstrom, D.R. (1976) Hypnotic susceptibility, EEG-alpha and self-regulation. In: Schwartz, G.E. & Shapiro, D. (eds.) *Consciousness and Self-Regulation* London: Plenum.
40. Weitzenhofer, A.M. & Hilgard, E.R. (1959) *Stanford Hypnotic Susceptibility Scale* Palo Alto, Calif.: Consulting Psychologists Press.
41. Hilgard, E.R. (1975) The alleviation of pain by hypnosis. *Pain* **1**: 213–231.
42. Finer, B. (1979) Hypnotherapy in pain of advanced cancer. In: Bonica, J.J. & Ventafridda, V. *Advances in Pain Research and Therapy 2* New York: Raven Press.
43. Hilgard, E.R. (1978) Hypnosis and pain. In: Sternbach, R.A. (ed.) *The Psychology of Pain* New York: Raven Press.
44. Wadden, T.A. & Anderton, C.H. (1982) The clinical use of hypnosis. *Psychological Bulletin* **91**: 215–243.
45. Bonica, J.J. & Fordyce, W.E. (1974) Operant conditioning for chronic pain. In: Bonica, J.J., Procacci, P. & Pagni, C. (eds.) *Recent Advances in Pain* Springfield, Ill.: C.C. Thomas.
46. Linton, S.J. & Gotestam, K.G. (1984) A controlled study of the effects of applied relaxation and applied relaxation plus operant procedures in the regulation of chronic pain. *British Journal of Clinical Psychology* **23**: 291–299.
47. Kuhn, C.C. & Bradnan, W.A. (1979) Pain as a substitute for the fear of death. *Psychosomatics* **20**: 494–495.
48. Park, L.C. & Covi, L. (1965) Non-blind placebo trial. *Archives of General Psychiatry* **12**: 336–345.
49. Gryll, S.L. & Katahn, H. (1978) Situational factors contributing to the placebo effect. *Psychopharmacologica* **57**: 253–261.
50. Voudouris, N.J., Peck, C.L. & Coleman, G. (1985) Conditioned placebo responses. *Journal of Personality and Social Psychology* **48**: 47–53.
51. Duncan, J.W. & Laird, J.D. (1980) Positive and reverse placebo effects as a function of differences in cues used in self-perception. *Journal of Personality and Social Psychology* **39**: 1026–1036.
52. Ross, M. & Olson, J. (1982) Placebo effects in medical research and practice. In: Eiser, J. R. (ed.) *Social Psychology and Behavioural Medicine* Chichester: Wiley.

53. Levine, J.D., Gordon, J.C. & Fields, H.L. (1978) The mechanism of placebo analgesia. *Lancet* **2**: 654–657.
54. Feather, B.W., Chapman, C.R. & Fisher, S. (1972) The effect of a placebo on the perception of painful radiant heat stimuli. *Psychosomatic Medicine* **34**: 290–294.

12

The Consultation

Introduction

The way a doctor interviews a patient determines to a large extent the kinds of information that will be discussed. A physician who concentrates solely on organic difficulties is unlikely to become aware of how health problems are influenced by other people or how the condition will affect the other aspects of a patient's life. The doctor may not discover, for example, that a recommendation of bed rest could not be followed because the patient is responsible for the care of an elderly relative. In the first part of this chapter, some of the problems that doctors encounter when interviewing patients and some ways of overcoming them are discussed.

The majority of this book has been concerned with patients — the ways they see their illnesses and the psychological components of their care. However, there have been several indications that a physician's viewpoint can affect care. For instance, the personal feelings of doctors towards sexual matters are related to patients' willingness to discuss them (and thus to gain help), and the childhood background of physicians is related to personal use of drugs and alcohol (and thus affects the doctor's ability to give help). These results indicate that the type of care given depends not only on the patient and the condition but also on the attitudes and perceptions of the doctor. The latter part of the chapter covers some of the research on these factors.

Interviewing

There are several reasons why skill in interviewing is important for the practising doctor. As mentioned above, consideration of the patient's obligations and perceptions of the illness are significant. In so far as these are related to outcome, an understanding of these factors is an important aspect of medical care.

There is a more general reason for competent interviewing, however, having to do with the satisfaction that a patient feels about the consultation. Roughly speaking, satisfaction with care has cognitive and emotional components, although they are often related to each other. Cognitive satisfaction appears to be associated with the doctor's verbal behaviour. In general practice consultations, the opportunity to ask questions and to gain information about illness and treatment is predictive of patients' satisfaction with interviews. On average, one-third of patients feel they have not received sufficient information about their illness when asked after consultations.[1] Emotional satisfaction, on the other hand, seems to be related more closely to the doctor's non-verbal behaviour. The ability to show care and concern by tone of voice, body movements and body posture is significant in this respect.[2] Both verbal and non-verbal aspects of interviewing are discussed below.

Deficiencies in interviewing

That there is room for improvement in doctors' interviewing skills has been shown by Peter Maguire. As discussed in Chapter 1, it seems that physicians often have the expectation that patients have *either* a social/psychological difficulty *or* an organic complaint. Physical illness is often missed in psychiatric patients and surgeons and general practitioners often do not inquire about personal difficulties associated with physical disease. For example, Maguire[3] found that most of the women who were clearly upset after a mastectomy received little assistance. For only 5 per cent of the women was distress heeded, while in 20 per cent the doctors appreciated their needs but dealt with them by such comments as 'Don't worry, there's nothing to be bothered about' or 'We'll sort it all out for you'. In the remaining cases, there was no evidence that the emotions were noted by the doctors. Consequently, many of the women who were distressed before the consultation were distressed afterwards.

Although much of the work on interviewing skills has involved medical students (rather than practising physicians) there is little evidence that length of training or experience are in themselves related to interviewing ability. For example, Helfer[4] compared the interviewing skills of senior medical students with those of students just entering the medical course. He found that senior students fared worse at eliciting important problems besides those presented by the patients themselves. They obtained less information about personal difficulties than did the new students, suggesting that medical training actually had a detrimental effect on some interviewing skills. Further, the senior students often inhibited the patient's communication by the use of medical jargon.

Initially, students encounter many problems when interviewing patients. When asked to indicate the kinds of difficulties they find, beginning the conversation, coping with emotions and keeping an open mind about possible diagnoses were cited by many.[5] This is consistent with research by Maguire and Rutter,[6] who asked students who were close to their final examinations to conduct a 15-minute interview with a psychiatric patient. They were asked to concentrate on current problems and to write up the history afterwards. The emphasis here was on history taking, a situation which is 'doctor-centred' in the sense that the doctor directs the interview in order to collect specific information. The same emphasis would be less appropriate to interviews where the doctor and patient have met several times before: the consultation could be more 'patient-centred'. Seven of the common deficiencies were:

1 *Insufficient information obtained*

The students obtained only one-quarter of the information an independent judge considered important and easily obtainable. One-third of the students failed to elicit the patients' main illnesses or problems, and relevant psychological and social aspects were most commonly neglected. The students were unaware of the paucity of information they obtained, seriously overestimating the amount of useful information they had recorded. In another study,[7] 80 per cent of the students avoided personal aspects of the patients' problems, particularly sexual or marital problems. When these topics were raised by the patients, the students avoided any further inquiry, perhaps because they were concerned not to appear intrusive or perhaps because these topics were personally embarrassing.

2 *Failure to control the interview*

The students often allowed the patients to talk at length about matters apparently unconnected to the problem at hand. Realizing that the patients' communications seemed inappropriate, the students felt unable either to redirect the interview or to examine the reasons why they were being given this information. Although Maguire suggests that the patient should be encouraged to be relevant, it can also be argued that redirection of the interview is not always suitable when the purpose is not primarily history-taking. Patients' emotional satisfaction with general practice consultations is associated with the opportunity to tell their own story in their own words.[2]

3 Lack of systematic procedure

The interviews were conducted in a rather haphazard way, with little obvious connection between consecutive topics. This lack of procedure often resulted in important gaps in the history and patients were sometimes left confused about the purpose of the interview.

4 Premature focus on problems

The students often assumed that the problem first presented was the only relevant one and focused the interview prematurely. Usually, this focus took either a social or organic direction. In Maguire's study, the students tended to assume that the patients would only have one problem and concentrated on this to the exclusion of related problems or unconnected but equally important difficulties.

5 Lack of clarification

Students were reluctant to ask for clarification on vague or contradictory information. In a similar study,[7] only 22 per cent of the students attempted to clarify what patients meant by such vague phrases as 'feeling run-down' or 'tense'. Since most people are unable to specify the position of many of their internal organs or to understand the meaning of many common medical terms such as constipation or palpitation, the need to clarify what each patient means by such statements is important. Students were also unlikely to establish the medications currently used by the patients or to encourage accurate dating of symptoms, even though the patients often possessed the necessary information.

6 Deficiencies in style

Two main deficiencies in the way students asked questions were found. One concerned the use of leading questions (questions which make an assumption about the patient). On the one hand, they are helpful in inquiring about topics that the patient may find too embarrassing to volunteer. For example, renal dialysis often has considerable effect on patients' sexual relations. In such an instance it may be more appropriate to ask, 'In what ways has dialysis affected your sexual relationship?' (which assumes that it has) than 'Has dialysis affected your sexual relationship?' (which may be too embarrassing to acknowledge). On the other hand, leading questions can restrict the information gathered: the above question may provide information on sexual matters, but perhaps not on feelings of dependency on the dialysis machine, another common anxiety. Asking too many leading questions can easily bias the interview towards what the doctor feels is important and not what the patient wants to say.

A related deficiency involved the use of several questions at once, without waiting for an answer to each one. For example, one student inquiring about feelings of depression asked, 'You were losing weight? . . . and what about sleeping? . . . waking early? . . . I mean, how did all this affect you?'. The patient responded to one question but the student did not follow up on other aspects.

7 *Failure to prepare the patient*

After the interviews, patients often reported that they wished the students had made some effort to explain the kinds of information they required and the time they had available. Most of the students began immediately by asking questions about the patients' main complaints. Maguire et al.[7] reported that only 8 per cent of the students explained the purpose of the interview and only 4 per cent mentioned the time available. Only 10 per cent of the students ended the interview within the time specified: perhaps more co-operation between the participants could have been gained if patients understood the restrictions and the intentions of the interviewer.

An interviewing model

These findings suggest that doctor–patient communication could be improved by providing students with a model for conducting an interview. This protocol could point out many of the deficiencies listed above and suggest remedies. Maguire has shown that students are able to increase the amount of information they acquire by seeing and hearing themselves interview a patient and by following a systematic procedure during the interview. In one typical study, students were divided into two groups. Those in the experimental group were first videotaped while interviewing a patient. They were then presented with a handout explaining the model and the course tutor asked the student to consider the problems the consultation presented while referring to the model and to the videotaped interview. Students in the control group also interviewed a patient, but were not given a handout or any other feedback.

When the students in both groups interviewed a second patient a week later, those in the experimental group obtained three times as much relevant and accurate information as those in the control group. Further, the patients of the experimental group rated their student interviewers somewhat more favourably than did patients of the control group, suggesting that the patients benefited as well.

In his model, Maguire makes a distinction between content (what information should be collected) and technique (how it might be gathered). Students hearing themselves on audiotape learn the skills related to content adequately, but in order to develop a good interviewing technique, videotape seems to be particularly helpful. (A synopsis of his model is presented below, and a fuller description can be found in Ref. 6). Similar training programmes have been found to be helpful in improving the interviewing skills of practising physicians.[8]

Content

(i) Details of the main problems. The interviewer should be particularly aware that a patient may have several problems and that these may be physical, social and psychological in nature. After establishing the primary difficulty, the interviewer should ask whether there are any problems the patient would like to mention: in fact, the interviewer should assume they exist. For the problems that there is time to explore, the date of onset, the subsequent development of the problem, precipitating or relieving factors, the help given to date and the availability of support should be discussed.

(ii) Impact of the problem on patient and family. It is unlikely that physical complaints have no social and psychological consequences. Patients' abilities to do their jobs, to pursue leisure activities and the quality of their relationship with their families are all relevant here.

(iii) Patients' view of their problems. As was shown in Chapter 6, the patients' beliefs about their illnesses and treatment are often better predictors of their behaviour than medical views. By obtaining a clear understanding of these beliefs the physician is in a better position to provide effective reassurance and to correct misconceptions. Maguire provides an example of a patient who had been admitted to hospital after a myocardial infarction. Having been led to believe by a staff member that it was of a minor nature, he was unwilling to follow his doctor's advice to restrict his activities. The doctor failed to realize the reason for the lack of compliance because he did not understand the patient's view of the illness.

(iv) Predisposition to develop similar problems. The patient's background is significant here, both psychologically and organically. Details of the family of origin, occupation, the patient's early development and childhood, sexual development, interpersonal relationships and previous health may be noted.

(v) Screening questions. Finally, the content of the interview should include an exploration of areas not yet covered. If the consultation has been primarily concerned with physical complaints, then it is appropriate to inquire about social and psychological difficulties; if the interview has been biased towards personal problems, then the physical well-being of the patient should be considered.

Technique

(i) Beginning the interview. The interviewer should take particular care to greet the patient both verbally, using the correct name and title, and non-verbally (e.g. by shaking hands). The interviewer should also indicate clearly where the patient is to sit and to introduce him or herself if they have not met before.

(ii) Discussing the procedure of the interview. As aids to understanding and remembering, a short explanation of the time available and the procedure to be used is in order. For example, if the interviewer plans to take notes, this should be mentioned and the patient's feelings about it should be elicited. Although note-taking may improve the accuracy of the doctor's memory, it may also inhibit the patient. If the interview is to be conducted in public (e.g. a hospital ward), the patient should be given the opportunity to voice hesitations about talking of personal matters and to move somewhere with more privacy. The theme of this aspect of the consultation is that doctors should make every attempt to put the patient at ease.

(iii) Obtaining the relevant information. After the opening of the interview, the patient should be encouraged to outline the important difficulties. Perhaps an open-ended question such as 'Can you begin by telling me what problems brought you here today?' could be used. The doctor could encourage the patient to continue by saying 'Go on' or 'Can you tell me more about that?'.

Most commonly, questions will be used to gain information. As mentioned above, asking several questions at once is not conducive to good communication. Nor are questions that restrict the range of possible answers always appropriate. To ask 'Was it because you walked too quickly or ate too much?' forces the patient to choose between two alternatives: perhaps both or neither seems correct. Open questions (e.g. 'How do you feel about your mother coming to stay?') allow the patient considerable latitude for reply, while closed questions (e.g. 'Will there be enough room?') narrow the possibilities considerably. Frequent use of closed questions will elicit answers to the questions asked, but suffers from the problem that the doctor may not ask the most appropriate questions. This is particularly likely when social and psychological information is being sought.

Listening is another important skill in interviewing. Rather than determining the direction of the interview entirely, it is often important to allow patients to say what they want in their own way. Silence is often needed by patients (and doctors) to consider what has gone on before, or to formulate questions.

(iv) Terminating the interview. Students report that ending an interview is often difficult. Two or three minutes should be left at the end to review the information given, to ask if any important information has not been transmitted and to provide the patient with an opportunity to ask questions.

This research on interviewing has helped students and doctors to relate to their patients in a more satisfactory way. Through first discovering the kinds of difficulties encountered by students — such as premature focus on problems, lack of clarification and the use of inappropriate questioning styles — a model was developed. Emphasis is placed on the procedure of the interview (e.g by greeting the patient warmly and by ensuring privacy) as well as on content (where, for example, the impact of the illness on the patient and family is noted).

Non-verbal behaviour

Although verbal behaviour is important in the consultation, the understanding of the relationship between doctor and patient requires consideration of non-verbal behaviour as well — 'While we speak with our vocal organs, we converse with our whole body' (Ref. 9, p.55). The gestures and bodily movements that surround a verbal statement modify its meaning. For instance, the comment 'Come in, Mr Smith' can give very different impressions depending on the speaker's non-verbal behaviour. If the speaker looks at the visitor, rises in greeting and perhaps shakes hands, friendliness is indicated, but if the speaker continues to look down at the desk and issues the invitation in a routine manner, indifference is the likely impression. Non-verbal aspects of conversation are mainly responsible for the emotional quality of the relationship between two people whereas verbal communication is more relevant to their shared cognitive tasks and problems. For example, non-verbal signals have a greater impact than verbal ones on assertiveness and friendship.[10] The aim of this section of the chapter is to explore the importance of non-verbal behaviour in doctor–patient communication.

Broadly speaking, researchers in this area have taken one of two positions. One group of workers has maintained that every expression or bodily movement is part of a larger context that will influence its meaning to a large extent. For example, eye gaze can have two distinct and incompatible meanings, depending on the circumstances. When two people know each other well and the circumstances are friendly, long periods of looking at each other suggests intimacy, but when issues of status are at hand, gaze may indicate aggression. Similarly, touching may indicate caring or dominance.[11] In adopting this position, the behaviour of both participants must be taken into account, since they both contribute to the context.

A second group of researchers has suggested that many expressions bear a close relationship to emotional state. They are concerned with the relationship between behaviour and emotional feelings — that looking downwards is a sign of embarrassment, for example. This approach is often associated with either psychoanalytic or evolutionary traditions. One of the lines of evidence that Freud gave for his contention that emotions are often repressed and find expression in ways that the ego does not monitor (Chapter 2) comes from his observations of patients in analysis:

> When I set myself the task of bringing to light what human beings keep hidden within them, not by the compelling power of hypnosis, but by observing what they say and what they show, I thought the task was a harder one than it really is. He that has eyes to see and ears to hear may convince himself that no mortal can keep a secret. If the lips are silent, he chatters with his finger tips . . . (Ref. 12, p.77)

It may be inappropriate to ask which of these approaches is the correct one. As in many areas of psychology, one model does not account for all observations, and in this case both provide insights into the reasons why people behave as they do. In the outline of research given in this section, both approaches are used and their implications for doctor–patient communication considered.

Vision

One way to explore the importance of different non-verbal cues is by experimenting with various combinations and testing for general principles. For example, the amount of time two people look at each other and the distance between them appear to be inversely related. Argyle and Ingram[13] reported that people look at their fellow conversationalists more frequently when they are separated by a large distance than when they are close together. They suggest that eye gaze and distance can substitute for each other as signs of intimacy, so that in order to keep a constant level of intimacy people will look at each other less often and for shorter periods of time as they come closer together. An example of a similar situation to this experiment can be found in crowded buses — everyone is standing close together and studiously looking out of the window or at the advertisements.

Eye gaze is not necessary for person-to-person interaction (talking over the telephone is possible, for instance), but it does play an important role. When a person is speaking, he will tend to look at his partner infrequently and for short periods of time, presumably because he is concerned with formulating what he is going to say. Attention is mainly focused on thinking. However, speakers do look at their partners occasionally, apparently to gain information as to whether they are being understood. Observation of conversations indicates that it is during these times that listeners provide feedback, nodding their heads and murmuring agreement. When listening, a person will spend most of the time looking at the speaker, showing attention to what is being said. Listeners who do not look and who do not nod their heads are often judged to be unfriendly or uninterested. Whether speaking or listening, the amount of gaze a person gives appears to affect others' perceptions of friendliness and warmth.[14]

Patients who are not looked at by their doctors may well feel that the physician is not especially warm or caring. Several examples of the practical importance of these considerations are given by Byrne and Heath.[15] They videotaped consultations and related the physicians' behaviour to the patients' reactions. In several cases, patients hesitated or fell silent when their doctors began to read or write on the medical records. In the following example, the patient stopped talking about her problem at line 3, just when the doctor began writing. Only at line 4, when the doctor looked up, did the patient begin again:

1. Patient: No, well, even the training centres for the unemployment ... unemployed ... they don't like them after a certain

age to return there 'cos they say it's . . . they're too old . . . you see.

2. Doctor: I see.
3. Patient: So . . .
(3.5 seconds)
4. Patient: So I don't think there's . . . (Ref. 15, p. 30)

It seemed that the shift of eye gaze and attention away from the patient and towards the records effectively suspended the consultation.

It is also important that both interactants have an equal opportunity to see the other's face and eyes during conversation. Argyle et al.[16] compared conversations in which both participants could see (or not see) each other equally well with those in which one participant could see the other better but not be seen. This latter condition, where visibility was asymmetrical, resulted in more feelings of discomfort and difficulty in the person who was seen but who could not see the other. The person with more visual information tended to dominate the encounter and felt more comfortable.

This result provides another pointer for doctor–patient communication. It is usual for a doctor to place the desk near a window, because of the light it throws. Yet a disadvantage of this position is that the doctor often sits between the window and the patient, with the light behind. This seating arrangement can result in the doctor's face being cast in shadow while the patient's face is well-lit, a situation similar to that of the experiment described above. In such circumstances, the patient may be unable to see the doctor's face clearly, and therefore may be unsure of facial expressions and the direction of gaze.

Posture and gestures

The posture assumed by interactors is important for conversation. A slight forward lean has been shown to be associated with perceptions of warmth.[17] Although closed arm positions appear to indicate coldness, rejection and inaccessibility, moderately open arm positions convey warmth and acceptance.[18] Movement is used to emphasize a point or to demonstrate an idea. The representation of size with hands is a common occurrence: people often hold them far apart when describing a large object, close together when describing something small. Changes in posture can convey a wealth of information. They often accompany a change in topic and can be used to signal the end of a conversation. If people are seated while talking, for instance, when one participant stands up the aim is often to finish the exchange.

Conversationalists may serve notice that they want to say something important by changing position or becoming restless. It is important that physicians recognize the significance of movements not only in their patients but also in themselves. Doctors who find themselves changing position constantly and keeping their arms closed around their bodies might reflect on their feelings towards their patients.

Facial movements comprise perhaps the most expressive non-verbal signals. Many appear to be common to all cultures, since people of very different upbringings smile, laugh and cry in similar ways. That the congenitally blind show these expressions to some extent suggests there is an innate basis. Paul Ekman is an important researcher in this field, taking as his starting point Darwin's observations about the cross-cultural nature of many facial expressions. Ekman[19] presented photographs of models portraying various expressions to people from very different cultures. There was considerable agreement in identifying the nature of emotions shown (happiness, surprise, anger, and so forth).

This is not to say that everyone uses these expressions to the same extent, even within cultures. Women are generally more expressive than men, and part of the reason why some people seem to be warmer than others is due to their expressiveness. Counsellors who often smile and who show interest by nodding their heads frequently are rated as being more facilitative than counsellors who show little emotional involvement.[20]

Proximity

One way of describing the distance between people is in terms of 'personal space' — a kind of bubble of territory that surrounds people. In order to find out the size of this space, several strategies can be used. One method is simply to observe conversationalists and measure the distance between them. When standing or talking casually, interactants usually keep about 2–2½ feet between them. A way of testing the validity of this observation is, simply, to walk closer to someone and measure the distance at which he or she begins to move backwards. The point at which this occurs is the edge of the bubble. It seems, from experiments of this type, that the bubble is not round: people will tolerate more proximity at their sides than at the front or back.

The boundaries of personal space vary according to several situational factors as well. Intimacy of topic is one variable, as is the relationship between the participants (e.g. friends or strangers) and cultural background (e.g. Mediterranean peoples generally stand closer together than Anglo-Saxons). Hall[21] categorized proximity into four zones: intimate (0–18 inches), personal (18in –

4ft), social (4ft – 12ft) and public (greater than 12ft). The topic of conversation and the relationship between the participants using these different zones varies. For example, two people standing or sitting 4 to 12 feet apart are more likely to be speaking socially than personally or intimately.

Status is also related to proximity. Those with high status are observed to have more territory than those with low status.[22] A director of a company will not only have a larger office than junior staff but also a larger desk that serves to maintain a large personal space. The way in which a person enters another's office is a good example of how non-verbal behaviour can indicate relative status. Burns[23] reports a study in which subjects were asked to fill out questionnaires indicating which of the people in various situations was superior to the other in status. Three of these situations are represented in Fig. 20.

To some extent, patients entering a doctor's office are entering territory that 'belongs' to the physician. The way in which they act may provide a good indication of how comfortable or uncomfortable they feel in a doctor's presence. Conversely, the way patients are greeted may give them an indication of the doctor's concern with status. If the doctor stays seated and waits for patients to come to the desk, they may consider the doctor to be asserting higher status. Ley and Spelman[24] suggest that one reason why patients do not follow doctors' advice is because when they do not understand it, they are diffident about asking questions. It may be that any feature of the consultation that emphasizes a difference in status may not be conducive to good communication.

Associated with proximity are studies on touching. Just as the distance between interactors depends on their cultural background, touching is associated with culture. Jourard observed the frequency of touching between couples in restaurants in various countries. In France, it was 110 contacts per hour, in the United States 2, and in England none. The nature of the relationship between two people is also relevant to touching. Jourard[25] asked his subjects to indicate who touched them (e.g. mother, father, same-sexed friend) and how frequently they were touched on various parts of their bodies. As would be expected, only the hands were touched by everyone and the trunk of the body and the genitals were touched infrequently. The relevance of this study to doctor–patient communication is that touching and intimacy seem to be closely related to each other, such that if touch occurs the relationship is interpreted as a close one. Johnson[26] reported that nurses often find their patients begin disclosing very personal information during intimate forms of touching. Conversely, patients may feel violated when being physically

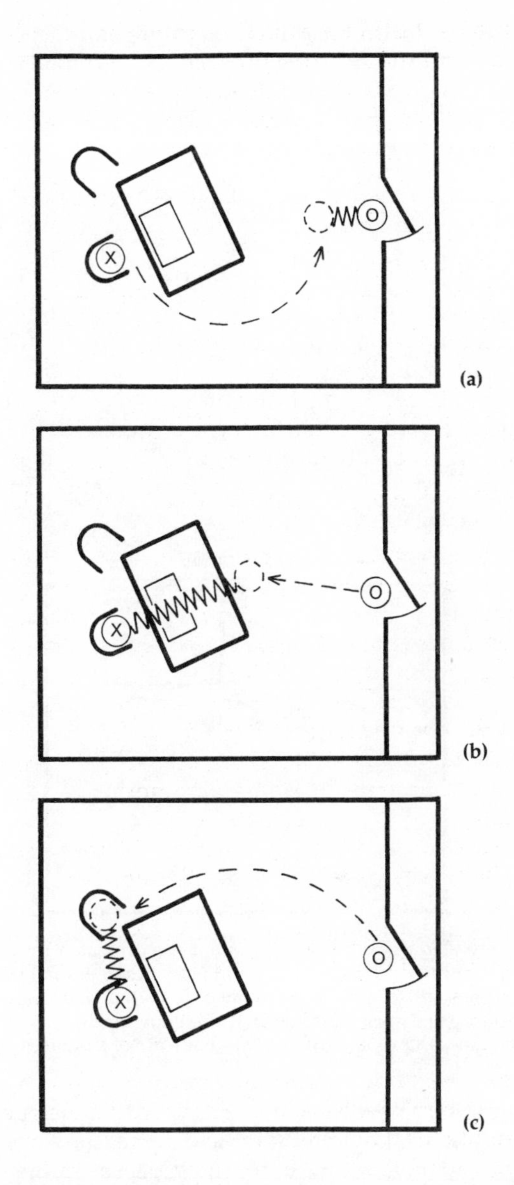

Fig. 20. Three examples of the way one person could enter another's office. In (a), person O steps into the office while person X rises and greets him: O was considered to have higher status than X. In (b), O moves towards X, who remains seated: O was seen as being of lower status than X. (c) illustrates one situation in which both were considered to be of equal status: O moves towards X and sits beside him without hesitation. (Reproduced from Burns, T. (1964) *Discovery* **25**:30–37.)

examined by a doctor who has not taken time to establish some rapport.

Arrangement of furniture in the surgery

The research discussed above indicates that the non-verbal behaviour of conversationalists has a considerable effect on their relationship. Eye gaze is important for showing interest in the patient, the doctor's posture and gestures can show interest and concern or indifference, and the distance between doctor and patient says much about their degree of intimacy and the doctor's concern with status. Besides these non-verbal signals, the physical environment has a strong influence on the encounter. Although there is little research specifically concerned with the arrangement of furniture in the consulting room, it is possible to suggest a setting that is conducive to good communication and not at odds

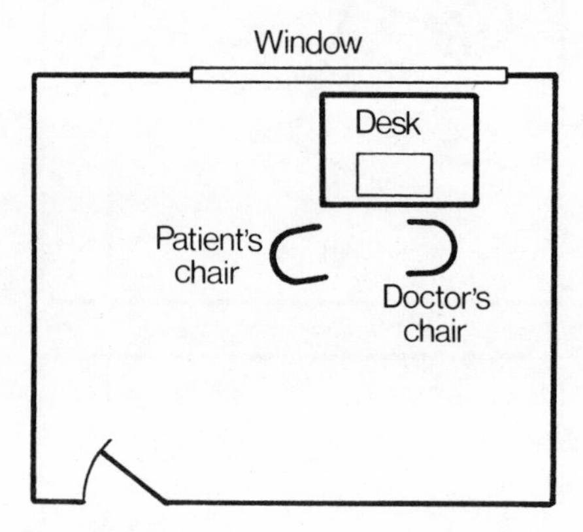

Fig. 21. A suggested office design consistent with research in social psychology. The window is at the side of the doctor and patient, rather than behind the doctor. Both participants are seated on the same side of the desk, so that the distance between them can be varied and so that the situation is likely to be considered co-operative rather than competitive. The chairs are of similar height and comfort.

with it. Figure 21 illustrates one possibility. Since people become uncomfortable if they are unable to see the face of a fellow conversationalist yet can themselves be seen, the desk in this room is sited beside the light source, so that the doctor's face is not lost in the window's glare. Both doctor and patient are seated on the same side of the desk for two reasons. First, the distance between them can be varied to suit the requirements of the situation. It may be that the common practice of placing a desk between the doctor and the patient restricts the degree of intimacy between them, keeping them always about 4 feet apart and outside the personal zone. Typically, conversationalists move between zones as their relationship and topics of conversation change: greater proximity may be needed in times of distress than the intervening desk may easily allow. Secondly, there is some evidence that the positions people take up around a desk reflect the nature of their encounter. Sommer[27] reported that individuals who are asked to interact casually prefer corner seating, co-operating individuals prefer to sit on the same side of the desk, and competing individuals choose to sit opposite one another. It may be that people are more likely to regard the situation as competitive if they are asked to sit opposite one another — an expectation inappropriate to the consultation. Finally, in order to minimize differences in status — perhaps encouraging patients to be less diffident and ask more questions when they do not understand a doctor's recommendations — chairs are similar in height and comfort.[28]

Sensitivity

Perhaps the most important psychological aspect of the consultation is the physician's sensitivity to the behaviour and feelings of the patient. Part of this sensitivity involves an awareness of patients' non-verbal behaviour, such as hesitations, restlessness and signs of embarrassment. It is not possible to specify the 'best' way to communicate with all patients. Psychology has been able to provide some guidelines — for example, it is important not to assume that once information has been given to a patient it has been understood or that further information is unnecessary — but studies in this area do not indicate that all patients should be treated in the same way. What might be appropriate for one person may be hurtful or shocking for another. In many of the studies on preparing patients for hospitalization and surgery mentioned elsewhere in the book, providing information about procedures and sensations they are likely to experience has been useful for most patients, but not all. Perhaps because people under the care of doctors are given the same label — patients — there is a tendency to consider the people in this heterogeneous group as being very similar to each other.

An example of a difficult communication is telling parents that their child is handicapped. Parents of Down's syndrome children have complained that they were not told together (one spouse being left to inform the other), that they were not told soon enough, that they were told in front of a large group of people rather than in private, and that they were not given enough information.[29] Svarstad and Lipton[30] reported a significant relationship between parental acceptance of mental handicap in their child and the nature of professional communication to them about the condition. Parents who received specific, clear and frank communication were more likely to accept the diagnosis than those who received vague and hurried information. Coming to terms with the disability was not related to any measured characteristics of the child (age, sex and IQ), the parents (social class) or the professional who informed them (age, sex and level of experience).

These findings do not, however, indicate that all parents should be informed in the same way. While 60–80 per cent of parents would have liked to have been told together, there remains the 20–40 per cent who would not have wished this. While some were glad that they had been told about the mental handicap straight away, others report that they would 'prefer to wait until the diagnosis is confirmed' or 'glad they waited a week — we might have rejected him'.[31]

Another aspect of sensitivity is a recognition that the physician's own behaviour will be studied and interpreted by patients particularly when they are unsure about diagnosis and treatment. To take Down's syndrome as an example again, Cunningham[29] describes how it was the changes in hospital routine and reactions of the staff that had made some parents concerned about their children:

> I knew something was wrong as soon as he was . . . born. They all looked at each other and went very quiet. Some other people then came in . . . but when I asked was he all right, they said he was fine and not to worry . . . but I knew they knew all the time, so why didn't they say something instead of keeping me wondering and worrying all that time?

and

> I guessed she wasn't all right. She was always the last baby brought up from the nursery after feeding and people — doctors, students and nurses and all that — kept popping in to see us but never seemed to want anything. (Ref. 29, p.314)

There has been considerable emphasis on the concept of 'accurate empathy', particularly in the literature on psychotherapy. Empathy requires an ability not only to understand feelings but to *express* this understanding as well. There is evidence of its importance in doctor–patient communication. DiMatteo and Taranta[32] focused on patients' perceptions of the rapport they had with their doctors and on the characteristics of physicians that contributed to this rapport. They found that the ability of physicians to understand the emotions of others and the ability to communicate this understanding was associated with patient satisfaction. There is also evidence that medical training does little to encourage empathy, in that final-year students have no greater skill than first-year students, and the level of empathy remains low throughout.[33] However, some studies have shown that sensitivity can be improved through teaching programmes.[33] These often include an opportunity for trainees to role-play a consultation and then the patients (who are sometimes actors and actresses, and sometimes patients living nearby) provide information on how they felt about the interview.[32,34]

Deciding on treatment

In Chapter 6 the notion that patients do not consult their doctor on the basis of symptoms alone was discussed. It became apparent that going to see the doctor was influenced by social and personal factors as well as physiological ones. It seems that people often consult their physician only when their difficulties become physically or socially disabling. Similarly, there has been research conducted into the factors that influence treatment decisions. These include the views of the individual physician, prevailing medical norms, the resources available and patients' wishes.

Prescribing

The most important decision is whether to provide medical treatment at all. Perhaps 3 in 10 patients who consult a general practitioner require only reassurance and support.[35] This has led Bain,[36] for example, not to intervene for about 20 per cent of the patients who consult him and there is some evidence to suggest that more stringent prescribing would not work to the detriment of patients. Marsh, a general practitioner, reports that he avoids prescribing when social, psychological or interpersonal needs seem more relevant than pharmacological ones. He has also attempted to reduce the number of drugs he uses, claiming that by using a limited range of medications he understands their effects well and can monitor their side-effects. When asked, only 1 per cent of his patients felt that they were not given a prescription often enough.[37] Indeed, since up to 20 per cent of patients do not cash their prescriptions,[38] it can be argued that the doctor and patient fail to agree about appropriate action in about 1 in 5 of consultations where a prescription is given.

There is a wide variation amongst doctors in their tendency to intervene, some giving up to six times as many prescriptions than others. Part of this variation might be due to patient selection: in group practices patients can choose one doctor when they have a complaint which requires medication and another doctor when they prefer a sympathetic ear. However, it seems unlikely that all the variation could be due to this kind of selection and several other factors have been found to be associated with prescribing patterns. The doctor's training, use of advice from colleagues and the advertising of pharmaceutical companies all seem important.[39] General attitudes towards prescribing are also relevant, with physicians who have favourable attitudes towards tranquillizing drugs, for example, prescribing them for a higher proportion of patients than those with less favourable attitudes.[40]

The quality of prescribing

Besides the number of prescriptions written, the quality of prescribing is also important. In one study, an indication of physicians' dissatisfaction with their job was related to incautious prescribing. A group of doctors were asked to indicate their degree of agreement or disagreement with a number of statements, such as: 'Assuming that pay and conditions were similar, I would just as soon do non-medical work'; 'My work still interests me as much as it ever did.' Those doctors who disagreed with items like the first one and who agreed with items like the second were said to have high job satisfaction. Prescribing records were then reviewed, particularly those prescriptions for drugs which current pharmacological research has suggested were contra-indicated in some way. The results showed that the more satisfied doctors were less likely to prescribe these medications than the less satisfied ones. They were also less likely to sign prescriptions without first seeing the patient and so were perhaps in a better position to observe signs which could lead to adverse reactions.[41]

In another similar project, physicians' attitudes towards emotional disturbance in their patients was found to be related to prescribing patterns. Those who agreed with such statements as: 'The distress shown by many neurotic patients is due more to a lack of control than real suffering'; and 'Until the advent of more effective methods of treatment there is little to be done for psychiatric patients', were more likely to issue repeat prescriptions for tranquillizers and to ask ancillary workers to fill out the forms. Agreement with such statements was also related to low job satisfaction and low general morale.[42]

The enthusiasm of the physician for a particular drug may actually alter its effectiveness. Although much of the evidence for this notion is correlational (so that other factors may be relevant as well: perhaps enthusiastic doctors prescribe more appropriate drugs or dosages), there is some experimental evidence which provides further support. Haefner et al.[43] first divided their sample of physicians into two groups: those whose attitudes were favourable towards the use of medication and those whose attitudes were less positive. Then 111 newly admitted patients (diagnosed as schizophrenic) were randomly assigned to the physicians. For the first four weeks of the patients' stay, all doctors were asked to give the same dosage of medication. Measures of patient improvement were based on interviews (where the assessors did not know which doctor the patient had seen) and on observation of behaviour on the wards. Patients who were under the care of doctors with more favourable attitudes towards chemotherapy showed greater improvement than did patients under doctors with less favourable attitudes, despite the fact that they were given the same dosages of the same medication. Such studies support the suggestion that the doctor is one of the most potent drugs available to his or her patients.

Personal characteristics of the physician are also relevant to patient care in hospitals. One study[44] examined the effects of the sensitivity of junior doctors on patients with chronic asthma. The doctors' supervisors rated their sensitivity according to the following instructions:

> Please rate each physician according to the degree to which each treated his patients as real, whole persons with feelings rather than a representative case of pulmonary pathology.

In making their ratings, the supervisors felt that concerns about the general welfare of the patient and willingness to respond to the patients' demands were two important features of a sensitive physician. The researchers then took several measures of how the doctors cared for their patients, particularly their prescribing patterns. Those doctors who were rated high in sensitivity were less likely to give medications which had adverse side-effects. They were more likely to treat different kinds of patients in different ways, adjusting their prescribing practice to suit each patient. There was also evidence that they took the patients' general welfare into account in their prescribing, giving aid to difficulties other than asthma more frequently.

It seems, then, that prescribing patterns are not altogether rational and scientific or based solely on the appropriateness of a particular drug. Some doctors prescribe drugs much more frequently than others, with those who are pessimistic about the treatment of psychiatric patients being more likely to use tranquillizing drugs. Doctors who have favourable attitudes towards medication seem to achieve better results, whereas incautious prescribing is related to low job satisfaction.

Surgery

Similar points can be made about surgical procedures. Like prescribing, there is evidence that the decision to operate depends on the physician's expectations and the resources available. The classic study on surgical procedures was conducted in the 1930s. At that time, most children had their tonsils removed, a procedure that is currently practised much less frequently. At first, 1000 children, 11 years of age, were examined. Some 61 per cent of these had had their tonsils removed previously. The remaining 39 per cent were then examined by a group of physicians who selected 45 per cent of these for tonsillectomy and passed the rest as fit. Those said to be healthy by this group of doctors were then re-examined by a second group of physicians, who recommended that 46 per cent of these be given a tonsillectomy. When the remaining 116 children were seen again by a third group of doctors, 51 more were advised to have the operation. After three examinations, only 65 children remained. These were not examined further because the supply of doctors ran out. There seemed to be no correlation between the recommendation of one physician and that of another regarding the advisability of the operation, so that the probability of a child being given a tonsillectomy depended principally on the physician rather than on the child's health.[45]

Even today there is a wide variation in the use of surgical interventions. Here again, it is unlikely that this is due only to medical factors. Part of the variation seems to be related to the supply of surgeons: it has been estimated that a 10 per cent increase in the surgeon:population ratio results in about a 3 per cent increase in the per capita utilization of their services. An increase in the number of surgeons living in an area does not appear to be the result of increased demand; rather, demand seems to follow supply to some extent.[46] In one study, the surgical rates in Ontario, Canada, were examined. Considerable variation in the proportion of patients who underwent operations was found for different areas of the province: 7-fold differences for colectomies, 5-fold for appendicectomies. The factors which could explain most of the variation in these rates were the availability of hospital beds and the number of physicians living in the area. The more resources available, the larger the number of operations that were performed.[47]

Even within one hospital there is variation in the number of operations performed, with some surgeons taking a more 'radical' approach than others. Howie[48] studied five surgical units that worked in strict rotation on emergency admissions. Three of the units took a cautious or conservative approach to appendicectomies, preferring not to operate if the patient seemed to have a reasonable chance of recovery. The surgeons in the other units were more radical, believing that it would be proper to operate in most instances and only refraining if there were good reason not to intervene. Over a period of nine months, the radical surgeons removed an average of 72 acutely inflamed appendices per unit, while the conservative surgeons removed only 46 per unit.

Thus, it seems that the decision on how to treat a patient is not determined solely by the condition. Such variation in treatment rates have been found with several other types of intervention, including use of endoscopy services[49] and admissions to neonatal care units. In East Anglia, some units admitted 30 per cent of newborn babies, others only 6 per cent.[50] However, such differences did not correlate with clinical need (such as the percentage of low birthweight children). Again, this variation could be explained by the size of the hospital and the number of cots available. Further, physicians who felt sympathetic about the problem of separating the mother and her infant were less likely to admit neonates to units. Each physician has his or her own personal experience and beliefs that will influence treatment decisions.

The patient's view

There is relatively little research on how patients view treatment decisions. Perhaps this is because the responsibility has, traditionally, been the doctor's alone. However, this view has been questioned in recent years,[51] with more recognition being given to the rights of patients. There are two questions of interest here. One concerns the choice of treatment, the other its effect on the quality of life.

An example of how doctors and patients can use different criteria for deciding between courses of treatment is provided by some work in oncology. As a measure of clinical effectiveness, a five-year survival rate is generally used: using this criterion, surgical procedures are preferable to radiotherapy. The operation provides a better chance of prolonged life at the risk of an early death, whereas radiotherapy provides a smaller chance of prolonged survival but with little risk of an early death. However, this criterion may not be the most suitable from the patient's point of view. McNeil[52] found that for elderly patients at least, the longer-term gain offered by surgery was not as important as its short-term threat. Many patients preferred radiotherapy. Here, the five-year survival rate criterion was not the optimum one from the patients' standpoint.

Not only might a patient have preferences because of possible risks, but he or she might also be involved in the negotiation about the choice of treatment because of its effects on the quality of life. Attempts to define the efficacy of treatment come up against the difficulty of knowing what a 'cure' might be. As in the case of psychiatric illness (Chapter 2), it is not always possible to say that a patient has completely recovered from a physical illness. No one measure is adequate to give a complete picture of recovery.[53] Patients self-reports of health do not necessarily correspond to the medical view, so that a physician might consider an individual well but this might not be that person's perception. A patient may recover from a myocardial infarction from a physiological point of view, but never return to work. Renal dialysis may prolong a life but create feelings of dependency. The word 'cure' is certainly a relative term when it is applied to cancer, where there may be much suffering due to the treatment.[54,55]

In other words, the measures used to assess outcome may not give results that are consistent with each other. The weighting given to one kind of measure (e.g. organic) over another kind (e.g. psychological) is largely a value judgement, rather than a scientific one. There is the need to choose treatments and assess their outcomes on the basis of several criteria, including the beliefs and attitudes of patients themselves.

Summary

Studies indicate that medical students do not learn interviewing skills adequately through observation and experience alone. They tend, for example, to gather too little information, to focus prematurely on problems and to accept patients' ambiguous statements without seeking clarification. The interviewing model outlined in this chapter provides several pointers, including a summary of how information could be gathered (e.g. the kinds of questions which might be used, how an interview could be ended) as well as what information might be relevant (e.g. the social and psychological consequences of the illness, the support a patient's family might be able to provide). The amount of information obtained can be increased after training in the use of this model.

The non-verbal behaviour of both doctor and patient is also important for the consultation. The interest an interviewer shows by the use of eye contact and facial expression determines the impression given more effectively than does verbal behaviour, indicating that physicians should be aware of the way they present themselves to patients. A busy hospital ward may not be the most conducive environment for talking of personal matters and the organization of furniture in the consulting room may have consequences for the self-assurance and comfort of the patient.

There is a wide variation in the kinds of prescribing patterns and rates of surgical interventions which patients encounter. This seems to result from differences in physicians' beliefs and expectations rather than differences in patients' conditions. Recently, there has been an increasing interest in patients' views: they may use different criteria than doctors in making decisions about the choice of treatment.

Suggested reading

A short guide to doctor–patient communication, with many useful references, is *Talking with Patients* (1980) London: Nuffield Provincial Hospital's Trust. For a more comprehensive review, see Pendleton, D. & Hasler, J. (eds.) (1983) *Doctor–Patient Communication* London: Academic Press.

References

1. Ley, P. & Morris, L.A. (1984) Psychological aspects of written information for patients. In: Rachman, S. *Contributions to Medical Psychology 3* Oxford: Pergamon.
2. Stiles, W.B., Putnam, S., Wolf, M. & James, S. (1979) Interaction exchange structure and patient satisfaction with medical interviews. *Medical Care* **17**: 667–681.
3. Maguire, G.P. (1976) The psychological and social sequelae of mastectomy. In: Howells, J. (ed.) *Modern Perspectives in Psychiatric Aspects of Surgery* New York: Brunner/Mazel.
4. Helfer, R.E. (1970) An objective comparison of the paediatric interviewing skills of freshmen and senior medical students. *Paediatrics* **45**: 623–627.
5. Batenburg, V. & Gerritsma, J. (1983) Medical interviewing: initial student problems. *Medical Education* **17**: 235–239.
6. Maguire, P. & Rutter, D. (1976) Training medical students to communicate. In: Bennett, A.E. (ed.) *Communication between Doctors and Patients* Oxford: Oxford University Press.
7. Maguire, P., Roe, P., Goldberg, D., Jones, S., Hyde, C. & O'Dowd, T. (1978) The value of feedback in teaching interviewing skills to medical students. *Psychological Medicine* **8**: 695–704.
8. Verby, J.E. (1979) Peer review of consultations in primary care. *British Medical Journal* **1**: 1686–1688.
9. Abercrombie, K. (1968) Paralanguage. *British Journal of Disorders of Communication* **3**: 55–59.
10. Argyle, M., Alkema, F. & Gilmour, R. (1972) The communication of friendly

and hostile attitudes by verbal and non-verbal signals. *European Journal of Social Psychology* **1**: 385–402.
11. Whitcher, S.J. & Fisher, J. (1979) Multidimensional reactions to therapeutic touch in a hospital setting. *Journal of Personality and Social Psychology* **37**: 87–96.
12. Freud, S. (1973) Fragments of an analysis of a case of hysteria. *The Standard Edition of the Complete Works of Sigmund Freud,* Vol. 7 London: Hogarth Press; also in *The Collected Papers of Sigmund Freud,* Vol. 3, ed. Ernest Jones, MD, authorized translation by Alix and James Strachey. Basic Books, Inc., by arrangement with the Hogarth Press and the Institute of Psychoanalysis, London. By permission of Basic Books Inc., Publishers, New York.
13. Argyle, M. & Ingram, R. (1972) Gaze, mutual gaze and proximity. *Semiotica* **6**: 32–49.
14. Exline, R.V. & Winters, L.C. (1965) Affective relations and mutual gaze in dyads. In: Tomkins, S. & Izard, C. (eds.) *Affect, Cognition and Personality* New York: Springer.
15. Byrne, P.S. & Heath, C. (1980) Practitioners' use of non-verbal behaviour in real consultations. *Journal of the Royal College of General Practitioners* **30**: 327–331.
16. Argyle, M., Lalljee, M. & Cook, M. (1968) The effects of visibility on interaction in a dyad. *Human Relations* **21**: 3–17.
17. LaCrosse, M.B. (1975) Nonverbal behaviour and perceived counsellor attractiveness and persuasiveness. *Journal of Counselling Psychology* **22**: 563–566.
18. Smith-Hanen, S. (1977) Effects of nonverbal behaviour on judged levels of counsellor warmth and empathy. *Journal of Counselling Psychology* **24**: 87–91.
19. Ekman, P. (1973) *Darwin and Facial Expression* London: Academic Press.
20. Tepper, D.T. & Haase, R. (1978) Verbal and non-verbal communication of facilitative conditions. *Journal of Counselling Psychology* **25**: 35–44.
21. Hall, E.T. (1969) *The Hidden Dimension* London: Bodley Head.
22. Argyle, M. (1969) *Social Interaction* London: Methuen.
23. Burns, T. (1964) Non-verbal communication. *Discovery* **25**: 30–37.
24. Ley, P. & Spelman, S. (1967) *Communicating with the Patient* London: Staples Press.
25. Jourard, S.M. (1966) An exploratory study of body accessibility. *British Journal of Social and Clinical Psychology* **5**: 221–231.
26. Johnson, B.S. (1965) The meaning of touch in nursing. *Nursing Outlook* **13**: 59–60.
27. Sommer, R. (1965) Further studies of small group ecology. *Sociometry* **28**: 337–348.
28. Editorial (1980) Non-verbal communication in general practice. *Journal of the Royal College of General Practitioners* **30**: 323–324.
29. Cunningham, C. (1979) Parent counselling. In: Craft, M. *Tregold's Mental Retardation,* 12th edn. London: Baillière Tindall.
30. Svarstad, B.L. & Lipton, H. (1977) Informing parents about mental retardation. *Social Science and Medicine* **11**: 645–651.
31. Armstrong, G., Jones, G., Race, D. & Ruddock, J. (1980) *Mentally Handicapped Under Five* University of Sheffield: Evaluation Research Group Report 8.
32. DiMatteo, M.R. & Taranta, A. (1979) Non-verbal communication and physician–patient rapport. *Professional Psychology* **17**: 540–547.
33. Poole, A.D. & Sanson-Fisher, R. (1979) Understanding the patient. *Social Science and Medicine* **13A**: 37–43.
34. Kent, G., Clarke, P., & Dalrymple-Smith, D. (1981) The patient is the expert. *Medical Education* **15**: 38–42.
35. Thomas, K.B. (1974) Temporarily dependent patients in general practice. *British Medical Journal* **1**: 625–626.

36. Bain, D.J.G. (1983) Diagnostic behaviour and prescribing. *British Medical Journal* **287**: 1269–1270.
37. Marsh, G.N. (1981) Stringent prescribing in general practice. *British Medical Journal* **283**: 1159–1160.
38. Rashid, A. (1982) Do patients cash prescriptions? *British Medical Journal* **284**: 24–25.
39. Hemminki, E. (1975) Review of literature on factors affecting drug prescribing. *Social Science and Medicine* **9**: 111–115.
40. Mason, A.S. & Sacks, J. (1959) Measurement of attitudes towards the tranquillizing drugs. *Diseases of the Nervous System* **20**: 457–459.
41. Melville, A. (1980) Job satisfaction in general practice: implications for prescribing. *Social Science and Medicine* **14A**: 495–499.
42. Melville, A. (1980) Reducing whose anxiety? In: Mapes, R. (ed.) *Prescribing Practice and Drug Use* London: Croom Helm.
43. Haefner, D.P., Sacks, J. & Mason, A. (1960) Physicians' attitudes towards chemotherapy as a factor in psychiatric patients' responses to medication. *Journal of Nervous and Mental Diseases* **131**: 64–69.
44. Staudemayer, H. & Lefkowitz, M.S. (1981) Physician–patient psychosocial characteristics influencing medical decision-making. *Social Science and Medicine* **15E**: 77–81.
45. Bakin, H. (1945) Pseudocia pediatrica. *New England Journal of Medicine* **232**: 691–697.
46. Fuch, V.R. (1978) The supply of surgeons and the demand for operations. *Journal of Human Resources* **13**: 36–56.
47. Stockwell, H. & Vayda, E. (1979) Variations in surgery in Ontario. *Medical Care* **17**: 390–396.
48. Howie, J.G.R. (1964) Too few appendicectomies? *Lancet* **1**: 1240–1242.
49. Holdstock, G., Wiseman, M. & Loehry, C. (1979) Open access endoscopy service for general practitioners. *British Medical Journal* **1**: 457–459.
50. Campbell, D.M. (1984) Why do physicians in neonatal care units differ in their admission thresholds? *Social Science and Medicine* **18**: 365–374.
51. Duncan, W. (1985) Caring or curing: conflicts of choice. *Journal of the Royal Society of Medicine* **78**: 526–535.
52. McNeil, B. (1978) Fallacy of the five-year survival in lung cancer. *New England Journal of Medicine* **299**: 1397–1404.
53. Sechrest, L. & Cohen, R. (1979) Evaluating outcomes in health care. In: Stone, G.C. & Cohen, F. (eds.) *Health Psychology* London: Jossey-Bass.
54. Rosser, J.E. & Maguire, G.P. (1982) Dilemmas in general practice: the care of the cancer patient. *Social Science and Medicine* **16**: 315–322.
55. Greer, S. (1984) The psychological dimension in cancer treatment. *Social Science and Medicine* **18**: 345–349.

13

Compliance

Introduction

The emphasis of this chapter is on compliance — the extent to which patients do or do not follow their doctors' advice and the factors which affect this. Some of the work in this area has been concerned with doctors' beliefs about patients' adherence to their recommendations. Davis[1] reported that most of the physicians in his sample believed that when they prescribed a drug, most or all of their patients complied promptly, but empirical investigations of adherence suggest that this expectation is an unrealistic overestimation. Further, doctors do not seem able to distinguish between patients who comply and those who do not.[2]

Non-compliance can be said to occur if a patient makes an error in dosage or timing or takes other medications that interact dangerously. Studies on this problem have given various indications of the degree of non-compliance, ranging from about 4 to 92 per cent, with a median of about 45 per cent. To take one example, children on a 10-day course of penicillin prescribed for streptococcal infection were studied. Parents were responsible for the medication and although most of them correctly identified the child's diagnosis, knew the name of the medication and how to obtain it, few of them ensured the completion of the programme. Although the medication was free, their physicians were aware of the study and the families were given advance notification that they would be visited, by the third day 59 per cent of the children were not receiving penicillin and by the sixth day only 29 per cent were continuing treatment.

The wide range of reported findings may be due to various factors such as design and measurement. Some researchers have taken 90 per cent compliance as satisfactory while others have insisted on 100 per cent. If patients are simply asked about their adherence, the rate often appears reassuring but if objective tests are taken (e.g. urine or stool analysis) the rate of adherence is often much lower. Thus simply asking a patient if he or she has followed advice does not seem to be a valid way of measuring compliance.[3]

The emphasis placed here on compliance is not intended to suggest that it is necessarily important that patients always follow advice. It has been noted[4] that there is an implicit assumption that patients should obey their doctors' instructions and failure to do so indicates some kind of deficiency within the patient. The terms used (by some researchers) — obedience, refusal, failure to co-operate, indeed the words 'patient' and 'compliance' themselves — suggest that some blame lies with a person who does not take prescribed medication or does not follow advice. Such a view can be justified only if the doctor–patient relationship is seen as an authoritarian one, with the physician being the expert who knows what is best. However, this view has been strongly challenged in recent years, with many preferring to consider the relationship as one in which both parties *negotiate* a course of action. Seen in this way, it may not be appropriate for patients always to adhere to their doctor's advice. Indeed, it has been argued that this is unimportant for many conditions[5] and that in some circumstances non-compliance can be the only rational course of action open to a patient. As considered here, compliance is used as an example of how doctor–patient communication can succeed or fail, depending on the care physicians take in understanding the needs and circumstances of their patients. It is more appropriately seen as a dependent measure of communicative success, rather than an end in itself. The first section of the chapter does, however, include many suggestions about how adherence to doctors' advice can be improved (and see Chapter 4).

In another respect, compliance can be detrimental to health. The second section gives a brief outline of some of the research on iatrogenic illnesses — those that result from medical care. In part, such conditions are a result of a medical system that includes large hospitals, where the risk of infection is high, and a reliance on drugs that may have unexpected side-effects. Further, medical staff themselves can also detract from good health, as in the case of incautious prescribing patterns. Because of such risks, people may come to believe that the disadvantages of medical care outweigh the advantages.

Factors affecting compliance

Several suggestions have been put forward to account for the low rates of compliance mentioned above. The eventual aim is to identify factors which reduce compliance and then take steps to minimize their influence. There is evidence that this approach is effective. Inui et al.[6] randomly assigned hospital doctors responsible for hypertensive patients to one of two groups. One group received a 1–2-hour tutorial on compliance, and the other group served as a control. The experimental group was encouraged to be sceptical about compliance and many of the factors outlined below were discussed. A 40 per cent increase in the number of patients taking most of their pills was reported and at the end of the study hypertension was considered to be adequately controlled in 67 per cent of the patients of this tutored group but only in 36 per cent of the patients of the untutored group. The patients of the tutored doctors were also found to be more knowledgeable about their drug regime and dietary requirements and had more accurate views of the seriousness of the disease, the efficacy of the drugs, and the consequences of not taking them. These results indicate that, with greater awareness on the part of physicians, non-compliance can be reduced. Although Davis[1] reported that two-thirds of the doctors in his sample attributed non-compliance to patients' unco-operative personalities, few associations between compliance and this aspect of personality have been found. Other aspects of the problem have been investigated as described below.

Situational factors

An individual's unique circumstances influence the decision to comply or not comply with medical advice. Many of the factors explored in relation to the sick role (Chapter 6) are relevant here. As in the case of acceptance of the sick role, family support is important. For example, mothers who report that they have difficulty in caring for their children tend to be non-compliant.[7] The example set by others in the family is also significant. Osterweis et al.[8] looked at the strength of the association between use of medication in individuals and their families. They found that use by other family members was a good predictor, a better one than severity of the illness.

Often, the patient is not the person responsible for compliance — children, for example, depend on parental advice. The presence of family members living with the patient seems to be related to compliance in adults too. In one study[9] patients living with a spouse or relatives were found to be twice as likely to take their medication as those living in isolation. There is also evidence that the degree of medical supervision is relevant. Hare and Wilcox[10] reported that non-compliance was found in only 19 per cent of in-patients, 37 per cent of day patients and 49 per cent of outpatients. Results such as these have led to the suggestion that teaching self-medication while in hospital may increase outpatient compliance.

It should also be pointed out that compliance with medical advice is often considered in broader terms than simply pill-taking. Francis et al.[11] asked mothers why they missed appointments made for their children. Some of the most frequent replies were lack of transport and the presence of other family problems. It seems that the decision to make and keep appointments is not as closely related to the severity of the illness as to its relative urgency. Gabrielson et al.[12] examined factors that affected parents' decisions to make an appointment with a doctor when a school nurse indicated one was needed. Over 90 per cent of the parents who saw the condition as more urgent than other family problems complied, whereas 50 per cent of the parents who felt it was not as urgent ignored the advice. As in accepting the sick role, compliance appears to be related to the costs and benefits to the individual and these will be determined to some extent by his or her unique circumstances.

The treatment regime

The treatment regime influences the degree of compliance in several ways. One reason for the variation in reported compliance rates may be due to the possibility that patients are likely to adopt the portion of the prescribed regime that requires least adjustment in habits or disruption of family routines. For example, more compliance in weight-reduction programmes could be expected when oral medication designed to suppress appetite is recommended rather than changes in diet.[13] (This is not to say that pill-taking should be the treatment of choice in such a situation.) The complexity of the regime has also been shown to be important, in that as the number of drugs or their frequency is increased, the likelihood of compliance is decreased. Hulka et al.,[14] who examined the compliance rates of patients with diabetes or congestive heart failure, found fewer than 15 per cent errors when only one drug was prescribed, 25 per cent when there were two or three, and 35 per cent errors when more than five drugs were used to control these conditions. Similarly, the frequency with which pills should be taken is associated with compliance. One report[15] indicated a doubling in the number of patients not complying when the frequency was increased from one to four tablets per day.

A third way in which a treatment regime may affect compliance concerns unpleasant side-effects. Adherence could be expected to decrease if the treatment feels more painful than the illness.

However, the relative contribution of this aspect of treatment may be smaller than imagined: only 17 per cent of patients treated for hypertension mentioned this as a reason for stopping treatment. Possibly the degree to which side-effects lower compliance is related to patients' preparation for them. Nor would side-effects necessarily have to be actually experienced. Elling et al.[16] reported that one reason why inadequate dosages of penicillin were given by mothers to their children with rheumatic fever was their concern over the long-term effects of such a medication. One mother gave her child only some of the medication because she believed strong drugs should be given sparingly.

Patients' beliefs

This last point is related to another factor: patients' beliefs about the efficacy of a particular treatment. On the one hand, there is the question of diagnosis. A patient could not be expected to follow a physician's advice if he or she did not believe that the doctor had the condition correctly identified. Becker et al.[7] measured both the degree to which mothers agreed with the physician's diagnosis and mothers' opinions of how sure the doctor was of the diagnosis for their children. They combined these measures to give a 'degree of certainty' score and found that this measure was predictive of compliance. The higher the certainty score the more closely were the doctor's recommendations followed.

Even if both doctor and patient agree on the diagnosis, however, there is agreement about the treatment to be considered. This, too, must make sense to the patient. Doubts about the recommended procedure have been identified as a reason for not following advice. It may also be necessary for the patient's beliefs about the causes of the illness to be similar to the doctor's. For example, many people believe that the 'cause' of ulcers is emotional (e.g. anger), while few see the stomach's acidity as relevant.[17] If a patient believes that emotions alone are responsible, then the necessity for acid neutralization would not be apparent and the point of small meals and drugs less sensible. Two further examples illustrate this point. In attempting to reduce the incidence of cervical cancer, screening procedures have been advised and efforts have been made to discover why some women attend these clinics whereas others do not. Compared with non-attenders, women who followed the advice for screening were more likely to believe that (i) the test could detect the cancer, (ii) the test could detect the cancer before the women themselves could notice it, and (iii) that early detection leads to a more favourable prognosis.[18] The non-attenders apparently saw little

reason to come since they did not believe in the efficacy of the screening. Similarly, Gabrielson et al.[12] found a relationship between parents' faith in the effectiveness of professional care and their decision to take up the school nurse's advice to seek further help. Thus, the patient's beliefs about the illness and treatment are of clear relevance to compliance.

Nature of the illness

The severity of the illness could be expected to affect the degree of compliance. However, this is not strictly the case, since it seems that it is the patient's perceptions of severity that are significant. There is little relationship between doctors' views of seriousness of condition and compliance,[19] but the way in which a patient views the illness does have some predictive value. In the research mentioned above by Gabrielson et al.,[12] parental belief that the child's condition was sufficiently serious to affect his school work was associated with seeking help.

Related to perceived seriousness is perceived susceptibility. Continued use of penicillin prophylaxis in patients with a history of rheumatic fever was related to their subjective estimate of the likelihood of having another attack as well as their view of the seriousness of the attack.[20] Similarly, mothers who felt that their children contracted illness easily and often and who perceived illness as a serious threat to children in general, were more likely to give medication and to keep follow-up appointments than mothers who did not hold these views.[21] The findings are similar to those concerning young adolescents' use of contraceptives: girls who feel more susceptible to pregnancy are more likely to use contraceptives conscientiously.

Other indications that perceived seriousness is important for compliance come from work concerning patients' decisions to end treatment. If how the person feels is a significant factor, then it would be expected that as symptoms are reduced, compliance would decrease. This view is supported by several studies. For example, Caldwell et al.[22] asked patients why they had discontinued therapy: the most frequent reason, mentioned by 39 per cent, was that they now felt well. Again, compliance seems to be related to the sick role: if someone no longer feels ill, then some of the expectations surrounding the sick role — which include co-operation with the doctor — no longer appear to be relevant.

A third feature of illness is its duration. A good example of an illness that requires long-term control is diabetes. Charrey[23] examined the adherence rates in diabetics who had been diagnosed either 1–5 years or more than 20 years before the study.

Although non-compliance was 30 per cent in the new group, longer-term patients showed an 80 per cent non-compliance rate. Other studies have indicated that as illness passes the acute stage patients seem less likely to adhere to the treatment regime.

Understanding

Even if patients felt able to cope with situational factors, had confidence in their treatment and believed that non-compliance could have serious consequences, they would nevertheless be unable to adhere to their physician's recommendations if they did not understand them. The extent of misunderstanding can be surprising. For example, Boyd et al.[24] found that about 60 per cent of patients misunderstood their doctors' verbal directions about the method for taking medication. This is not an unusual result. The lack of understanding may be due to factors such as doctors' belief that patients are not concerned with understanding their treatment (and therefore do not take care to explain it) or because patients do not ask questions when they are unclear about recommendations. Doctors may also overestimate the knowledge that patients possess. Boyle[25] found a high proportion of people had incorrect beliefs about the location of their internal organs: 80 per cent wrongly located their stomachs and 58 per cent their hearts. Another possibility is that material given to patients is too difficult for many to understand. There are ways of estimating the percentage of the population who could be expected to understand a given piece of writing. In one study these techniques were applied to leaflets explaining X-rays: for some of these leaflets, only 40 per cent of the target population could be expected to understand them.[26]

Studies concerning the interpretation of labels on medicine bottles indicate that here, too, lack of understanding is prevalent. Often, this is due to ambiguity in the instructions. In one project, the researchers asked their subjects to specify when they would take the medication given the instructions on the bottles. Some of the results from this study are shown in Table 10. Taking thioridazine first, only 13.4 per cent of the subjects interpreted the instructions correctly — three dosages spread throughout the 24 hours. Apparently, many considered the day to mean only the waking day, some 18 hours. In the case of penicillin G, 89.5 per cent would take the drug after meals, whereas it ought to be taken on an empty stomach. Conversely, Nitrofurantoin should be taken on a full stomach, but 53.7 per cent said they would take it before eating. These results can be compared with interpretations when the instructions are more specific and less ambiguous, as shown

Table 10. Interpretations given to some labels on medicine bottles.

Medication and instructions	*Interpretation*	*% Subjects giving interpretation*
1 Thioridazine		
'3 times a day'	With meals	80.5
	Every 8 hours	13.4
	10 a.m., 2 p.m., 6 p.m.	4.4
2 Penicillin G		
'3 times a day and at bedtime'	After meals and at bedtime	89.5
	10 a.m., 2 p.m., 6 p.m., 10 p.m.	4.5
	Other	5.0
3 Nitrofurantoin		
'with meals'	Before	53.7
	With	32.8
	After	13.4

Reproduced from Mazzulo, J. M., Lasagna, L. & Griner, P. F. (1974) *Journal of the American Medical Association* **227**: 929–931, by permission of American Medical Association.

Table 11. Percentages of subjects who gave correct and incorrect interpretations to instructions on medicine bottles when the instructions were made less ambiguous.

Medication and instructions	*Interpretation*	*Percentage*
1. Penicillin G		
'30 minutes before meals and at bedtime'	Correct	91.0
	Incorrect	9.0
2. Nitrofurantoin		
'To be taken immediately after meals, 4 times a day'	Correct	85.1
	Incorrect	14.9

Reproduced from Mazzulo, J. M., Lasagna, L. & Griner, P. F. (1974) *Journal of the American Medical Association* **227**: 929–931, by permission of American Medical Association.

in Table 11. Here a much smaller proportion of the subjects made mistakes.[27]

Remembering

Yet another factor to be considered is memory. Patients would need to remember the recommendations if they are to take medication without error. Svarstad[28] reported that more than 50 per cent of the patients he interviewed made at least one error in describing their doctors' recommendations one week after the consultation. As might be expected, those patients who remembered more accurately adhered more completely. Other evidence indicates that many of the doctor's statements are forgotten much more quickly than within one week. Different studies have found that patients had forgotten about 40 per cent within 80 minutes, 50 per cent within 5 minutes and over 50 per cent immediately after the consultation. It also seems that the number of statements forgotten increases with the number given, such that a patient could be expected to remember three out of four statements, but only four out of eight.[29] Perhaps the high rate of forgetting found in these studies is due to a tendency by doctors to give too many directions at one time.

Some solutions to the difficulties that memory poses to doctor–patient communication have been suggested. One possibility is to reduce the number of instructions to a minimum. Another suggestion comes from experimental work in the psychology of memory — the 'primacy effect'. People remember the first item they hear better than subsequent items. That is, people recall best what they hear first. Ley[30] reports that when advice in a consultation was given first, as compared to when it was usually given, recall increased from 44 per cent to 75 per cent. In the same study, he also asked physicians to stress the significance of advice that they considered crucial: in this condition recall increased from 44 per cent to 64 per cent. A third possibility concerns the specificity with which advice is given. Bradshaw et al.[31] provide evidence that recall of instructions about dieting increases if the advice is specific (i.e. 'You must lose 7lb in weight') rather than general (e.g. 'You must lose weight'). Patients who were given specific instructions recalled 49 per cent of the advice, whereas patients given general recommendations remembered only 19 per cent. It was shown above that precise instructions are understood more readily than vague ones: it also appears that precise advice can be recalled more readily.

Another way to assist memory is to give patients written information as well.[32] In one study, patients leaving hospital were given detailed information concerning their diagnosis, the name, dosage and purpose of the drugs prescribed, and some general advice of diet, etc. All were given this material verbally but, in addition, about half were also provided with the information in written form, which they could take away with them. When they returned for follow-up, both groups were asked about their recollections of the information: significantly more material was remembered by those patients who had been given both verbal and written material.[33]

Ley[29] reports the results of an attempt to improve the communication between doctors and patients based on some of the findings considered above. Patients' recall of information was monitored before and after the doctors in the study read a manual outlining the importance of such factors as stressing important advice, making recommendations specific rather than general, and giving instructions before other information. The proportion of statements recalled by patients increased for all four doctors in the study after they had put the manual's recommendations into practice.

The doctor–patient relationship

The quality of this relationship (often measured by patients' satisfaction with their care) is also relevant to compliance. Ben-Sira[34,35] points out that patients often have little knowledge of the principles of diagnosis and treatment, being unable to judge the technical competence of their doctor accurately. Also, since medical treatment usually does not give immediate relief from physical disturbance, the quality of the relationship is the main source of information available to the patient about the doctor's skill. Ben-Sira found that patients' satisfaction was closely related to their doctors' show of concern and interest. Satisfaction was highest when the doctor related to the patient as a person and not as a 'case'. Patients were more likely to turn elsewhere when they felt dissatisfied with the personal aspects of their care than with the technical aspects, a result replicated in several other studies.[36] In other words, the way the doctor cared for the patients seemed more important to them than the treatments given.

This raises an interesting question about physician style. Should doctors be informal and friendly, or should they be distant and authoritarian? Szasz and Hollander[37] distinguish three approaches. The first is where the doctor is active and the patient passive. This approach is very 'doctor-centred', with the physician being completely in charge, deciding on treatment without taking the patients' wishes and views into account. Such a relationship would be appropriate to emergency settings, where the treatment takes place with little psychological involvement from the patient. The second approach is termed guidance-co-operation where, like a teacher guiding a student, the doctor would tailor treatment to the individual but nevertheless knows 'what is best'. In such a relationship the power resides with the doctor who can ask many questions while the patient simply replies. In the third approach, mutual participation, the consultation becomes a negotiation where both participants are aware of each other's individuality. The doctor has knowledge and skills that the patient does not possess, but these are put at the patient's disposal. The patient has the right to accept or refuse them. Most studies[38] have found that the authoritarian approach is not conducive to compliance and satisfaction. It is likely that the 'correct' approach depends on the individual patient (some may prefer and expect the guidance-co-operation approach, for example) and the condition (for long-term compliance, as for diabetes mellitus and chronic heart disease, mutual participation seems best).

In any case, intimacy seems important. Patients who did not keep appointments in one study tended to be those who felt they could not talk easily and intimately with their doctor.[39] Similarly, patients who described their physicians as 'personal' adhered to instructions better than those who described them as 'business-like'.[40] Some continuity of care may be significant: seeing the same doctor on subsequent visits increases the probability of compliance and appointment-keeping.[41]

Satisfaction with care

Some of these aspects of doctor–patient communication are often out of an individual doctor's control or awareness, but many of the factors discussed above (taking care that patients are able to remember recommendations, using time to understand the patient's beliefs about his or her illness, and taking the patient's unique circumstances into account when giving advice) can all be expected to improve the quality of the relationship. Other research has shown that ensuring adequate understanding of information given to patients in hospital increases their satisfaction with care. Certainly, inability to find out what they want to know about their condition, their treatment and the hospital routine have been found to be among the most frequently expressed complaints by hospitalized patients.[41]

One difficulty with some of these studies is that the researchers simply asked patients about their understanding, compliance and satisfaction. The relationship discovered between these variables could therefore simply be due to patient characteristics: i.e. that the same people who report they were satisfied would also report that they understood and would adhere to their physician's advice. Other patients may report that they are unhappy with their care regardless of the behaviour of the physician. An alternative method could be to measure what a patient knows about the treatment and compare this with what the doctor said the patient was told. If these two measures correspond, the communication could be said to be successful. This procedure, used with patients with diabetes mellitus, has indicated that there is an association between these two measures: patients who receive the message which the doctor intends to give tend to be satisfied with their care.[42]

An alternative strategy would be to observe examples of doctor–patient communication, measure behaviour which could be important, and then see if these measures relate to feelings of satisfaction and evidence of compliance. Using this method, failure to follow advice has been related to certain kinds of doctors' behaviour: these include collecting information but ignoring patients' requests for feedback, and concentrating on their patients' medical situation but ignoring their psychological and social circumstances.[43] Some important work has been conducted on communications between paediatricians and mothers who had brought their children to emergency casualty clinics. Medical interviews were tape recorded, the patients' charts reviewed and follow-up interviews were conducted. In this research, mothers' satisfaction with their care was related to the friendliness of the doctors and their show of understanding and concern for the children. The use of medical jargon was inversely related to satisfaction and mothers often complained about the lack of introduction to the doctors on duty.[44] In another study using the same research methods, a significant positive correlation was found between doctors' warmth and patients' compliance.[45] Interestingly, there was little association between the duration of the consultation and mothers' satisfaction or mothers' knowledge of the diagnosis,[46] a result also found in studies of general practice. Patients report that they are satisfied with the length of the consultation if they are given the opportunity to say what they want to say. These findings indicate that the way in which the time is used is more important than the actual length of the consultation.[36] The type of verbal behaviour that made the largest single contribution to patient satisfaction was found to be the giving of objective information about the illness and treatment.[47] Many of the verbal and non-verbal aspects of interviewing discussed in the previous chapter are important for the quality of the doctor–patient relationship. Table 12 presents a summary of the variables found to be important for compliance and satisfaction with care.

Iatrogenic illness

Behind the research on compliance lies the assumption that it is always in patients' best interests to follow their physicians' advice. Not all writers agree with this. Some have contended that the way medicine is organized in Western societies sometimes

Table 12. A summary of the findings related to patient compliance. These variables are important for successful doctor–patient communication.

Factor	*Consideration*
Situational factors	The support given by the patient's family and the difficulties the family faces are relevant. Complying with a physician's advice involves costs as well as benefits.
Treatment regime	The frequency and number of drugs prescribed have an effect, as do the patient's views of the side-effects and efficacy of treatment.
Nature of the illness	The patient's perception of the severity of the illness and of the consequences of non-compliance (rather than medical views) are significant. Compliance decreases with length of illness and with improvement in health.
Understanding	Patients cannot be expected to adhere to a doctor's recommendations if they do not understand them. The difficulty and ambiguity of material given to patients is often underestimated.
Remembering	Many patients do not comply simply because they cannot remember the doctor's instructions. Some solutions to this problem include giving important instructions first, reducing the number of instructions to a minimum and making recommendations specific.
The doctor–patient relationship	The quality of the relationship is associated with compliance, in that patients who are satisfied with the interpersonal aspects of their care are more likely to follow advice.

works to the detriment of patients. A leading proponent of this position is Illich,[48] who discusses iatrogenic illness (*iatros*, Greek for physician; *genesis*, meaning origin).

Clinical iatrogenic illness refers to the ways in which medications, physicians and hospitals can be pathogens or 'sickening agents'. As an example of how medications can produce ill-health, the side-effects of drugs could be mentioned. The use of barbiturates in the 1960s as appetite suppressants to aid slimming resulted in some people becoming addicted. The prescribing of thalidomide to help women during pregnancy is another instance that is often cited. Barraclough et al.[49] argue that many suicides could be prevented if barbiturate prescribing was more careful: in 1975 about half of those who died by overdose had received a prescription for the drug used within the previous week.[50] In Chapter 10 some of the stressful effects of hospitalization were noted, and this experience may have severe consequences for some patients. In one project, all the patients who entered a hospital over a one-year period were studied. One in 12 had some major adverse reaction to their care, particularly to the drugs they were given. About one-quarter of the deaths in the hospital during that time were considered to be due to adverse drug reaction.[51,52] In a survey of British hospitals, 19 per cent of the patients were diagnosed as having an infection — about half of these were acquired while in hospital.[53] Even in many cases of severe and acute illness, hospital care may not be necessary. Some studies of the effectiveness of coronary units have suggested that their popularity is not commensurate with their clinical effectiveness. Mather[54] randomly assigned coronary patients to home care with the support of family doctors or to intensive care in hospitals: they found no difference in mortality. Medical treatment has psychological effects as well. Attempts to balance the positive and negative effects of care are very difficult in the treatment of various forms of cancer, for example. Although surgery, chemotherapy and radiotherapy can be effective for some kinds of cancer, this is bought at the expense of much distress.[55]

Childbirth

Perhaps the strongest criticism of medical care has come from those concerned with childbirth. They argue that women who are giving birth are not 'patients' but people performing a natural act. They cite evidence that women who have babies at home run a lesser risk for themselves or their children than those who enter hospital,[56] a result which does not seem to be due to more 'at-risk' women being hospitalized.[57] It may be that part of the problem is the way women are confined to bed soon after they arrive. Flinn et al.[58] asked mothers-to-be if they would be willing to walk about during the first stage of labour (when the cervix is dilating) rather than be kept in bed. Of those women who expressed an interest, half were nursed in bed with traditional procedures. The other half were allowed to walk about, visiting the television room to be with friends and relatives or making a drink in the kitchen. So that the foetal heart beat could be recorded, they wore a compact monitoring device. All women were nursed in bed during the second and third stages of labour. When the birth records of these two groups of women were compared, the ambulant mothers had shorter first stages (on average two hours shorter), were more likely to have a normal delivery, and required less analgesia. Their foetal heart rate pattern was also more satisfactory during the birth. The researchers took Apgar scores of the infants, which gave an indication of their general health and responsiveness at birth: the scores of the ambulant group were significantly better.

Results such as these argue against routine medical interference at birth. A decade ago induction of labour received the strongest criticism. Richards[59] argued that its implications had not been adequately assessed and that its widespread use was not based on clinical advantage but rather on the belief that birth should be under the control of obstetricians. More recently, the value of episiotomy during birth has been questioned: cutting the perineum causes much discomfort for months afterwards, and there seems to be little justification for its routine use.[60] There is also disagreement about the currently routine practice of delaying discharge of low-birthweight babies until they have reached some criterion weight. Such enforced separations may have negative consequences for the parents' relationship with the baby and are certainly distressing for the parents.[61] When the policy at one maternity hospital was changed so that the timing of discharge was determined not so much by weight as by feeding patterns and satisfactory conditions at home, no complications were found.[62]

Responsibility for health

This relates to another of Illich's criticisms of the medical system — the social aspect. He argues that individuals have lost control over their health to the medical profession. Increasingly, when someone has a problem the doctor is called upon to relieve it. Although this has many advantages, there are also some distinct disadvantages. The proportion of the national wealth devoted to curative medicine has been increasing more quickly than virtually any other sector of the economy. Since many diseases could be prevented at a much lower cost, perhaps a greater proportion of resources should be aimed at providing a better diet and improved housing. It has been estimated that all the medical improvements made since the Second World War have been cancelled out by the increase in smoking. The emphasis on cures in the profession may lead people to believe that their health problems can be solved when the time comes, making them less likely to take preventive measures in the short term. When the medical system takes responsibility for health, it is argued, individuals are not encouraged to look after themselves.

As an example of this latter point, the prescribing of psychotropic drugs can be used. They are prescribed more often than any other group of medications. In one study, 87 per cent of doctors agreed that 15 mg Librium daily would be a reasonable recommendation for a middle-aged housewife who was having marital problems.[63] The argument against such a recommendation is two-fold. First, it treats only the symptom and not the cause of the difficulty. Although a tranquillizer may give palliative relief, the individual may become dependent on continuing dosages. Second, when a doctor prescribes a drug for the control of a personal or interpersonal problem, he or she may also be providing the patient with a model for dealing with it. By using a biochemical solution, the physician may imply that the problem is biochemical in origin and the patient's responsibility to examine and seek to alter relationships is reduced. The doctor may be prescribing a way of life as well as a drug.[64]

This brief discussion of iatrogenic illness should not be taken to mean that physicians or the medical system generally are solely responsible for these difficulties. Medical care in any culture reflects that society's values and beliefs, so that the emphasis on intervention, high technology and curative rather than preventive medicine is consistent with prevailing cultural views. There is also, of course, the problem in balancing the illnesses caused by medical care with the illnesses relieved. A medical procedure such as vaccination may prove detrimental to some people but this must be considered in relation to the lowered incidence of disease in the general population.

Summary

Some understanding of why so many patients do not adhere to their doctor's recommendations can be given by examining how they perceive their treatment. Several factors have been shown to be important in this respect, many similar to those involved in the decision to consult the doctor in the first place. These include situational factors such as family support and the patient's own views about the illness. Two often neglected factors concern the difficulties patients can have in remembering and understanding advice. All these aspects affect the general quality of the doctor–patient relationship.

Medical care involves risks as well as benefits: these include the side-effects of medical care, such as adverse reactions to drugs or hospitalization. These risks could affect patients' faith in medicine and hence their compliance. The medical system may also influence how people view illness, relieving them of the responsibility for their own health. This has implications for the treatment of personal problems and the adoption of preventive measures.

Suggested reading

More detail about research on compliance can be found in DiMatteo, M.R. & DiNicola, D.D. (1982) *Achieving Patient Compliance* Oxford: Pergamon. A reply to

Illich's (Ref. 48) contention that the medical system is causing more harm than good is provided by Horrobin, D.F. (1978) *Medical Hubris* London: Churchill Livingstone.

References

1. Davis, M.S. (1966) Variations in patients' compliance with doctors' orders. *Journal of Medical Education* **41**: 1037–1048.
2. Kasl, S.V. (1975) Issues in patient adherence to health care regimes. *Journal of Human Stress* **1**: 5–18.
3. Norell, S.E. (1981) Accuracy of patient interviews and estimates by clinical staff in determining medication compliance. *Social Science and Medicine* **15E**: 57–61.
4. Stimson, G.V. (1974) Obeying doctors' orders: a view from the other side. *Social Science and Medicine* **8**: 97–104.
5. Leading article (1979) Non-compliance: does it really matter? *British Medical Journal* **2**: 1168.
6. Inui, J.F., Yourtee, E. & Williamson, J. (1976) Improved outcomes in hypertension after physician tutorials. *Annals of Internal Medicine* **84**: 646–651.
7. Becker, M.H., Drachman, R. & Kirscht, K. (1972) Predicting mothers' compliance with pediatric medical regimes. *Journal of Pediatrics* **81**: 843–854.
8. Osterweis, M., Bush, P. & Zuckerman, A. (1979) Family context as a predictor of individual medicine use. *Social Science and Medicine* **13A**: 287–291.
9. Parkes, C.H., Brown, G. & Monck, E. (1962) The general practitioner and the schizophrenic patient. *British Medical Journal* **1**: 972–976.
10. Hare, E.H. & Wilcox, D. (1967) Do psychiatric in-patients take their pills? *British Journal of Psychiatry* **113**: 1435–1439.
11. Francis, V., Korsch, B. & Norris, R. (1969) Gaps in doctor–patient communication. *New England Medical Journal* **280**: 535–540.
12. Gabrielson, I.W., Levin, L. & Ellison, M. (1967) Factors affecting school health follow-up. *American Journal of Public Health* **57**: 48–59.
13. Davis, M.S. & Eichhorn, R. (1963) Compliance with medical regimes. *Journal of Health and Human Behaviour* **4**: 240–249.
14. Hulka, B.S., Cassel, J., Kupper, L. & Burdette, J. (1976) Communication, compliance and concordance between physicians and patients with prescribed medications. *American Journal of Public Health* **66**: 847–853.
15. Gatley, M.S. (1968) To be taken as directed. *Journal of the Royal College of General Practitioners* **16**: 39–44.
16. Elling, R., Whittemore, R. & Green, M. (1960) Patient participation in a pediatric program. *Journal of Health and Human Behaviour* **1**: 183–191.
17. Roth, H.P. (1962) Patients' beliefs about peptic ulcer and its treatment. *Annals of Internal Medicine* **56**: 72–80.
18. Kegeles, S.S. (1969) A field experiment attempt to change beliefs and behaviour of women in an urban ghetto. *Journal of Health and Social Behaviour* **10**: 115.
19. Bonnar, J., Goldberg, A. & Smith, J. (1969) Do pregnant women take their iron? *Lancet* **1**: 457–458.
20. Heinzelmann, F. (1962) Factors in prophylaxis behaviour in treating rheumatic fever. *Journal of Health and Human Behaviour* **3**: 73.
21. Becker, M.H., Drachman, R. & Kirscht, J. (1974) A new approach to explaining sick role behaviour in low-income populations. *American Journal of Public Health* **64**: 205–218.
22. Caldwell, J.R., Cobb, S., Dowling, M. & deJongh, D. (1970) The dropout problem in hypertension therapy. *Journal of Chronic Diseases* **22**: 579–592.

23. Charrey, E. (1972) Patient–doctor communication: implications for the clinician. *Pediatric Clinics of North America* **19**: 263–279.
24. Boyd, J.R., Covington, T., Stanaszek, W. & Coussons, R. (1974) Drug defaulting. *American Journal of Hospital Pharmacy* **31**: 485–491.
25. Boyle, C.M. (1970) Differences between patients' and doctors' interpretation of some common medical terms. *British Medical Journal* **2**: 286–289.
26. Ley, P. (1973) The measurement of comprehensibility. *Journal of the Institute of Health Education* **11**: 17–20.
27. Mazzulo, J.M., Lasagna, L. & Griner, P. (1974) Variation in interpretation of prescription instructions. *Journal of the American Medical Association* **227**: 929–931.
28. Svarstad, B. (1976) Physician–patient communication and patient conformity with medical advice. In: Mechanic, D. (ed.) *The Growth of Bureaucratic Medicine* New York: Wiley.
29. Ley, P. (1979) Memory for medical information. *British Journal of Social and Clinical Psychology* **18**: 245–255.
30. Ley, P. (1976) Towards better doctor–patient communications. In: Bennett, A. E. (ed.) *Communication between Doctors and Patients* Oxford: Oxford University Press.
31. Bradshaw, P.W., Ley, P., Kincey, J. & Bradshaw, J. (1975) Recall of medical advice. *British Journal of Social and Clinical Psychology* **14**: 55–62.
32. Ley, P. & Morris, L. (1984) Psychological aspects of written information for patients. In: Rachman, S. *Contributions to Medical Psychology 3* Oxford: Pergamon.
33. Ellis, D.A., Hopkin, J., Leitch, A. & Crofton, J. (1979) Doctors' orders: controlled trial of supplementary written information for patients. *British Medical Journal* **1**: 456.
34. Ben-Sira, Z. (1976) The function of the professional's affective behaviour in client satisfaction. *Journal of Health and Social Behaviour* **17**: 3–11.
35. Ben-Sira, Z. (1983) The structure of a hospital's image. *Medical Care* **21**: 943–954.
36. DiMatteo, M.R., Prince, L.M. & Taranta, A. (1979) Patients' perceptions of physicians' behaviour: determinants of patients' commitment to the therapeutic relationship. *Journal of Community Health* **4**: 280–290.
37. Szasz, T.S. & Hollander, M. (1956) A contribution to the philosophy of medicine — the basic models of the doctor–patient relationship. *Archives of Internal Medicine* **97**: 585–592.
38. DiMatteo, M.R. (1979) Non-verbal skill and the physician–patient relationship. In: Rosenthal, R. (ed.) *Skill in Non-verbal Communication* Cambridge, Mass: Oelgeschlanger, Gunn and Hain.
39. Alpert, J.J. (1964) Broken appointments. *Pediatrics* **34**: 127–132.
40. Geersten, H.R., Gray, R. & Ward, J. (1973) Patient non-compliance within the context of seeking medical care for arthritis. *Journal of Chronic Diseases* **26**: 689–698.
41. Cartwright, A. (1964) *Human Relations and Hospital Care* London: Routledge and Kegan Paul.
42. Romm, F.J. & Hulka, B. (1979) Care process and patient outcome in diabetes. *Medical Care* **17**: 748–757.
43. Davis, M.S. (1968) Variations in patients' compliance with doctors' advice. *American Journal of Public Health* **58**: 274–288.
44. Korsch, B.M., Gozzi, E. & Francis, V. (1968) Gaps in doctor–patient communication. *Pediatrics* **42**: 855–870.
45. Freemon, B., Negrete, V., Davis, M. & Korsch, B. (1971) Gaps in doctor–patient communication. *Pediatric Research* **5**: 298–311.
46. Korsch, B.M. & Negrete, V. (1972) Doctor–patient communication. *Scientific American* **227**: 66–74.

47. Stiles, W.B., Putnam, S., Wolf, M. & James, S. (1979) Interaction exchange structure and patient satisfaction with medical interviews. *Medical Care* **17**: 667–681.
48. Illich, I. (1977) *Limits to Medicine* Harmondsworth, Middlesex: Pelican.
49. Barraclough, B.M., Nelson, B., Bunch, J. and Sainsbury, P. (1971) Suicide and barbiturate prescribing. *Journal of the Royal College of General Practitioners* **21**: 645–653.
50. Murphy, G.E. (1975) The physician's responsibility for suicide. *Annals of Internal Medicine* **82**: 301–304.
51. Ogilvie, R.I. & Ruedy, J. (1967a) Adverse reactions during hospitalisation. *Canadian Medical Association Journal* **97**: 1445–1450.
52. Ogilvie, R.I. & Ruedy, J. (1967b) Adverse drug reactions during hospitalisation. *Canadian Medical Association Journal* **97**: 1450–1457.
53. Meers, P.D. (1981) Infection in hospitals. *British Medical Journal* **1**: 1246.
54. Mather, H.G. (1971) Acute myocardial infarction: home and hospital treatment. *British Medical Journal* **3**: 334–338.
55. Rosser, J.E. & Maguire, P. (1982) Dilemmas in general practice: the care of the cancer patient. *Social Science and Medicine* **16**: 315–322.
56. Barry, C.N. (1980) Home versus hospital confinement. *Journal of the Royal College of General Practitioners* **30**: 102–107.
57. Tew, M. (1979) The safest place of birth. *Lancet* **1**: 1388–1390.
58. Flinn, A.M. Kelly, J., Hollins, G. & Lynch, P. (1978) Ambulation in labour. *British Medical Journal* **2**: 591–593.
59. Richards, M.P.M. (1975) Innovation in medical practice: obstetrics and the induction of labour in Britain. *Social Science and Medicine* **9**: 595–602.
60. Harrison, R.F., Brennan, M., North, P., Reed, J. & Wickham, E. (1984) Is routine episiotomy necessary? *British Medical Journal* **288**: 1971–1975.
61. Jacques, N., Amick, J. & Richards, M. (1983) Parents and support they need. In: Davis, J.A., Richards, M. & Robertson, N. (eds.) *Parent–Baby Attachment in Premature Infants* London: Croom Helm.
62. Derbyshire, F., Davies, D. & Bacco, A. (1982) Discharge of preterm babies from neonatal units. *British Medical Journal* **284**: 233–234.
63. Linn, L.S. (1971) Physician characteristics and attitudes towards legitimate use of psychotropic drugs. *Journal of Health and Social Behaviour* **12**: 132–140.
64. Lader, M. (1978) Benzodiazepines – the opium of the nurses? *Neuroscience* **3**: 159–165.

Appendix

Using the Library

The contents of this book are, necessarily, selective. Many topics have not been covered, such as sleep and dreaming, and certain others have not been covered in great depth. Perhaps the biggest problem facing someone who wishes to study topics falling outside this book or who wishes to follow up areas in greater detail, is in knowing where to start. The purpose of this Appendix is to give a brief guide to some library resources.

In order to gain a general overview of an area, books and review articles are often useful. Research papers may be concerned with a small problem, which might be too specific for your interests.

The library catalogue of books is the key to finding a book on the shelf on the subject in which you are interested. The author catalogue will enable you to find a book by a given author, editor or institution. The subject catalogue can take two forms. There is the subject catalogue arranged alphabetically by the names of subjects. A book should be found under the most specific term used in the catalogue that describes the subject of the book. Cross-references guide you to related headings under which you may find books of interest. The second type of subject catalogue is the classified catalogue. In this catalogue the arrangement corresponds to the arrangement of books on the shelves, that is, the entries are grouped by the classification symbols. This should mean that all aspects of a subject are brought together by the classification system that the library is using.

While books will usually give a wide view, they are sometimes rather out-of-date. Journal articles provide up-to-date information — but how do you find an article on your subject out of the thousands printed in the hundreds of different scientific journals? To help with this, there are indexes, which are publications which list articles found in other journals: that is, they give the minimum information necessary to look up the original article. Abstracts are similar publications but they also give a brief summary of the original article.

The most important medical index is *Index Medicus*. Each month articles are listed in a subject section and also in an author section. Every year the entries in all twelve monthly issues are cumulated so that you only need to look up under one heading to find articles on that subject published during the year. A most important third section in each monthly issue and in each *Cumulated Index Medicus* is the *Bibliography of Medical Reviews.* This small section lists recently published review articles and thus provides articles giving a more up-to-date account of a subject than that found in books and yet still provides a wider view of a subject than the narrow special aspects dealt with in other articles. The review article also provides a good starting-point to locate relevant articles elsewhere through its normally extensive bibliography given at the end of the article.

The subject headings used in *Index Medicus* are listed in *Medical Subject Headings* which is published annually and should be consulted to obtain alternative terms and broader or more specific headings under which relevant material will be found.

All entries in *Index Medicus* give full details to enable you to look up the article elsewhere. For example under the heading SLEEP DEPRIVATION in the monthly issue of *Index Medicus* for August 1981 there are several references one of which is

> Cumulative effects of sleep restrictions on daytime sleepiness.
> Carskadon MA et al. Psychophysiology 1981 Mar;
> 18(2) 107–13.

which means that on pages 107–113 in the March 1981 issue of the journal *Psychophysiology* there is an article by Carskadon on sleep restriction. 18(2) means that this issue is part 2 of volume 18 of the journal, which is another way of identifying the journal issue.

All references in the scientific literature more or less follow the above style of citation, so you should be able to work out from the above what any reference you have means. A point to bear in mind is that the library will not take all the journals referred to in *Index Medicus* but the article should be available from the Inter Library Loans section. A further point is that *Index Medicus* gives the English translation of all articles cited even when the original article is in another language. In these cases the whole reference is given in brackets with an indication of the language of the original.

Another most useful index is *Science Citation Index.* There are thousands of scientific journals but only a fraction publish the bulk of the really significant literature and it is this literature which the *Science Citation Index* aims to cover. This index appears bi-monthly and has an annual cumulation.

The essential idea of the index is this. All scientific papers refer to other articles as support for what the author has written and therefore these other articles must be related to the subject of the article in which they are cited. The *Science Citation Index* allows you to start with an author who you know has written on a subject and to find out who has cited their work. The *Science Citation Index* also allows a direct subject approach. Using the *Permuterm Subject Index* section we can find names of authors who have used the subject in which we are interested, and the titles of their articles. If you then go to the Citation or Source Index you can proceed to discover further relevant articles using the author name once again as the key.

Two other publications of direct interest are *Psychological Abstracts* and *Sociological Abstracts*, which not only give the necessary details to enable you to look up original articles on psychological and sociological topics respectively, but also give a synopsis of the articles in question.

In addition to these printed sources another guide to the literature is the librarian who should be able to explain the catalogue, indexes and abstracts, locate relevant material on the shelf and obtain documents required from other libraries if they are not available in your own library.

Index

References in **bold** type are to principal sections